AGING

IN TODAY'S SOCIETY

PRENTICE-HALL SOCIOLOGY SERIES

Herbert Blumer, *Editor*

AGING
IN TODAY'S SOCIETY

edited by

CLARK TIBBITTS AND **WILMA DONAHUE**

with the assistance of

JOHN WALKER POWELL

PRENTICE-HALL, INC.

Englewood Cliffs, N. J.

1960

Acknowledgments

Acknowledgment is made to the following publishers and individuals who have granted permission to reprint selections from copyrighted publications.

Fortune Magazine for a selection adapted from "The Fabulous Future" by David Sarnoff, *Fortune*, January 1955.

The Viking Press for the selection from *Time for Living* by George Soule, copyright 1955 by the author.

The University of Michigan Press for "The Personal Challenge of Aging: Biological Changes and Maintenance of Health" by Edward J. Stieglitz, M.D.; "Mental Hygiene of Old Age" by Moses M. Frohlich, M.D.; "Biological Aspects of the Aging Process" by Carl V. Weller; and "Religion and Religious Observance in Old Age" by Leroy Waterman; from *Living Through the Older Years*, edited by Clark Tibbitts, copyright 1949.

Harcourt, Brace, and Company, Inc. for "On Freedom" by Albert Einstein from *Freedom, Its Meaning*, edited by Ruth N. Anshen, copyright 1940.

Random House, Inc. for "On Old Age" from *The Basic Works of Cicero*, Modern Library, copyright 1951.

W. Heineman & Co. (London) for the selections from *Aristotle's Rhetoric and Poetics*, translated by W. Rhys Roberts, copyright 1927.

McGraw-Hill Book Co. for the selection from *The Stress of Life* by Hans Selye, copyright 1956 by the author.

Pantheon Books, Inc. for the two selections from *Gift from the Sea* by Anne Morrow Lindbergh, copyright 1955 by the author.

The National Council of the Episcopal Church for the paragraphs from *Cycles and Turning Points* by Everett C. Hughes.

Parade Magazine for the article "What Is Middle Age?" by Sid Ross and Ernest La France, from *Parade* July 17, 1955.

The American Journal of Psychiatry for the reading from "The Human Life Cycle and Its Interruptions" by Maurice E. Linden, M.D. and Douglas Courtney, copyright 1953.

The Association Press for the reading from *Learning Comes of Age,* by John Walker Powell, copyright 1956.

E. P. Dutton & Co., Inc. for the paragraphs from *The Book of My Life* by Girolamo Cardano, translated by Jean Stoner, copyright 1930.

Doubleday & Company, Inc. and Mrs. George Bambridge for "My Rival" from *Departmental Ditties and Ballads and Barrack Room Ballads* by Rudyard Kipling.

The Industrial Relations Research Association for the selection from "The Aged in Industrial Societies" by Wilbert E. Moor in *The Aged and Society,* edited by Milton Derber, copyright 1950.

Henry Holt and Company for the selection from *Our Needy Aged* by Floyd Bond and associates, copyright 1954.

The Fund for Adult Education for the dramatic piece "Home Sweet Home" by Len Peterson from *Ways of Mankind,* edited by Walter Goldschmidt, copyright 1954; and for the essay by Robert Redfield from *The Educational Experience* (pp. 41-59) copyright 1955.

Houghton Mifflin Company for "On American Leisure" by Irwin Edman in *Adam, the Baby, and the Man from Mars,* copyright 1929.

The Adult Education Association of the U.S.A. for "The Mature Attitude" by Edgar Z. Friedenberg, February, 1957; "The Development of Mature Individuals" by John C. Whitehorn, January 1957; "Pre-Retirement Education" by Weldon R. Oliver, May 1957; and "Grand Rapids Learns About the Aging" by Wilma Donahue, May 1954; all from *Adult Leadership.* Also for "To Meet the Challenge of Free Choice" by Dorothy Canfield Fisher; "Art as an Avocation" by Frank L. McVey; and "To Keep Our Minds Open" by Nicholas Murray Butler; all from *Adult Education in Action,* edited by Mary L. Ely, copyright 1936.

Charles Scribner's Sons for the quotation from *Applied Imagination* by Alex F. Osborn, copyright 1953.

Alfred A. Knopf, Inc. for "Making Pictures" from *The Later D. H. Lawrence,* edited by William York Tindall, copyright 1930.

The Michigan State University Press for the selection from "The Middle-Aged Woman in Contemporary Society" by Agnes E. Meyer in *Potentialities of Women in the Middle Years,* edited by Irma Grass, copyright 1956.

Harper & Brothers for the selection entitled "The Role of Leisure" from *Creating an Industrial Civilization,* edited by Eugene Staley, copyright 1952.

Syracuse University Press for the selection "On Being Retired" by T. V. Smith from *Retrospect and Prospect*, edited by Theodore Denise and Milton Williams, copyright 1956.

Columbia University Press and the Academy of Medicine for the paragraphs from "The Retirement Myth" by Julius Hochman in *The Social and Biological Challenge of Our Aging Population*, copyright 1950.

The Graduate School of Business Administration, Harvard University for the quotation from *Some Observations on Executive Retirement* by Harold Hall, copyright 1953

The University of Chicago Press for the use of Chapter XI of *The Meaning of Work and Retirement* by Eugene A. Friedman and Robert J. Havighurst, copyright 1954.

Little, Brown & Co. for the quotation from *Good-Bye, Mr. Chips* by James Hilton, copyright 1934.

AFL-CIO for the selection from "Education for Retirement" from the *AFL-CIO Education News and Views*, February 1958.

The Special Staff on Aging, U. S. Department of Health, Education, and Welfare and Raymond Harris, M.D. for the paper by Dr. Harris which was presented at the National Leadership Training Institute, June 26, 1959.

Professor Ernst Levy, for permission to quote his letter to Barnett Byman.

Miriam L. Shrifte and Gertrude Norman, for permission to quote the letter of Piotr Tchaikovsky.

John Murray Publishers, Ltd., and Hannah Bryant, tr. for permission to publish the letter of Robert Schumann, copyright 1907.

The American Academy of Political and Social Science for excerpts from "Social Participation of the Aged in Different Cultures" by Leo W. Simmons, *The Annals*, Volume 279 (January 1952), pp. 43-51.

This book is an expansion of *Aging in the Modern World* published by The Fund for Adult Education as a part of its efforts to encourage the systematic study and public discussion of major issues in American life.

The Fund for Adult Education is an independent organization established by the Ford Foundation in 1951. Since its inception the Fund has supported a wide range of programs designed to contribute to the liberal education of American adults. It was at the invitation of the Fund that Dr. Clark Tibbitts and Dr. Wilma Donahue undertook the preparation of this volume, which has enjoyed widespread acceptance.

Now that the experimental phase of its efforts has been concluded, the Fund welcomes publication by Prentice-Hall to ensure the availability of these materials to a wider audience.

Additional information about the Fund's activities may be obtained by writing to the Office of Information, The Fund for Adult Education, 200 Bloomingdale Road, White Plains, New York.

Audio-visual materials especially developed for use with this text may be obtained from the Audio-Visual Center, Indiana University, Bloomington, Indiana.

Foreword

THIS IS A UNIQUE kind of book. Its history is unusual, for it was read and enjoyed and talked about by thousands before it was published. Its character is unusual, for it is a book about aging not written for the old. Its intention is unique, for it hopes to start you talking to yourself.

The essays and readings presented in it were first prepared and distributed in two separate volumes for group use, with the financial assistance of The Fund for Adult Education, an independent agency established by the Ford Foundation. The purpose was to stimulate group study and discussion of the materials and the problems they are concerned with. Two of America's foremost students, authorities, and teachers were the editors: Wilma Donahue, Chairman of the Department of Gerontology, Institute for Human Adjustment, University of Michigan; and Clark Tibbitts, now Assistant Director of the Special Staff on Aging of the U. S. Department of Health, Education, and Welfare.

Many groups, in all parts of the country, have met over ten-week periods to discuss the ideas and information in these readings. The groups included young, middle aged, and old people; professionals and laymen; teachers, social workers, community leaders, business men, housewives, labor leaders, ministers—all the sorts of people who recognize these problems to be deeply involved in their own personal destinies and in those of their communities.

On the basis of this proven usefulness in adult education, the present edition is offered to the general public as a book for individual reading and reflection, rather than for group use. But it inherits from the group experience a format intended to provoke thought, as well as provide material for it. Edited by John Walker Powell, with new materials, a new Introduction, and a new section on Retirement, it is here presented in a single volume, with the readings grouped beside the essays to which they relate, and with quotations and questions designed to provide a focus for reflection. This book should challenge the reader not only to think by and for himself, but to enlist his family, his friends, and his associates in the delights of talking, and reading, together about ideas of vital personal and social importance.

Preview:
What This Book Is About

THIS IS A BOOK about aging—about growing *into,* and growing *in,* maturity. Hence, it is *for* and *about* you, for and about the authors of the essays in this book; indeed it is for and about all who survive early adulthood in our rapidly changing and increasingly leisure-centered society.

In one sense the "problem" of aging is not new. While average life expectancy was only about 18 to 20 years at the height of the Greek and Roman civilizations, there were always some who lived into what we now call the middle years and some into old age. The great Greek dramatist Sophocles lived to be 90. Indeed, this has been true of the earliest human groups of which there are records, and it is still true of simple societies today. Moreover, old age early brought problems to the individual. Aristotle recognized this in his description of the character of men at different stages of life. And old people also brought problems to the family and the community.

On the whole, however, long life appears to have presented much less of a problem in earlier societies than it is presenting to us today. Few lived to be old, and the majority of those who did were able to reserve for themselves, or were assigned, functions essential to the survival of the group. Aristotle (when he was at about that age himself) suggested that the peak of mental capacity occurred at about the age of 49. And Cicero (writing in his later years) strongly implied that the very existence of the state depended upon the exercise of wisdom and prudence of old men as opposed to the free rein of rash and impetuous youth.

Today, however, the situation is vastly different. Average life expectancy has been extended to 70 years, and those who reach middle age may expect to live *on the average* another 25 years. There will soon be, in fact, *almost 50 million of us beyond 50 years of age.* Simultaneously, we are spending a smaller part of our lives in the traditional occupations of making a living and rearing children. Our growing leisure time and our ever-rising level of living are becoming available, not to a few (as in earlier historical periods), but increasingly to nearly all of us. This is perhaps the outstanding development of the North American society in which we live. And we are not alone. It is happening in other industrialized areas, too—Great Britain, Scandinavia, Western Europe, Australia, and New Zealand.

This aging of our population has created many problems, as we all know. Perhaps the greatest of all are those which confront the individual. Evidence is accumulating that the rapid succession of social and technological changes characteristic of our time is having a special impact on people in middle age, and that many of us in this age-bracket are asking new questions about ourselves and about our positions in society.

In a culture which has been heavily oriented toward work and production, it is natural that some of these questions should relate to one's position in the work economy. Work is becoming increasingly routine. How, then, shall workers find opportunity for the kind of creative expression and individuality once provided by the older agrarian-craft-small-shop economy? Others, who have carefully prepared for their occupational careers, find their skills outmoded by new methods, new machines, or shifts in consumer preferences. How shall they maintain their hard-won position in the work force? Middle age also appears to bring with it clear recognition that we either have or have not reached the level of our uppermost aspirations, so that if we are going to climb still higher, now is the last chance to start. Should we continue to strive? Should we change our occupation? Or should we taper off and look for new outside interests? Total retirement from work looks attractive in the early work years, but as the time approaches many become ambivalent about it or resist it altogether. And in an economy periodically threatened with a surplus of workers, should young or old workers be favored in new hiring?

Removal of many tasks from the home and simplifications of others raise somewhat similar questions for women. A recent symposium considered the problems facing hundreds of thousands of mothers. Is their place in the home or in an outside occupation? If both, as it is for many, how shall they manage? The question is easier for those who have no children, and for mothers whose children have grown up and left home. Yet there remain strong vestiges of tradition. How shall those who do *not* go to work spend their time when parental duties are finished? What relationships shall they have with their adult children who have been brought up to want independence and to manage their own lives? Is there community work that needs to be done, and will that give a sense of purpose adequate to sustain the interest of the older person?

Still another concomitant of middle age is recognition of the shortness of life, of declining physical power, and, often, the onset of some long-term illness. How do these events change our behavior? Do they mark the beginning of a long, slow decline? Or do they spur us to new resolutions and activity?

What shall we say of these questions? Do they mean that middle age is a turning point? Is it a period of restlessness? Or, perhaps, a period of growing pains preceding a new period of growth? Do they represent a desire to find a new sense of orientation, to develop a new set of goals? Whatever may be our answers to these questions, it seems reasonable to assume that they arise in considerable part from the profound and rapid changes that have marked the past 50 years. Perhaps they presage the emergence of a new type of society in response to the underlying technological changes —a new society growing out of unprecedented productivity, more and more leisure time, and increasing life expectancy.

If we are to have a new society, if the added years are to be meaningful, one thing is clear; we must begin to see the aging of the population as an *achievement* which has created an opportunity to be grasped, rather than as a set of problems to be solved along humdrum lines.

The present volume represents a pioneering effort within this context. It is designed, on the one hand, to enable us as individuals in the middle years to find ways of achieving meaningful personal goals and, on the other, to assist in building a more favorable climate than has existed hitherto. More specifically, it is hoped that through it men and women will be assisted

> . . . to understand the nature and significance of population aging;

> . . . to recognize the value of assessing basic *individual* needs, capacities, outlooks, interests, and conceptions of self—on which all the essayists put emphasis from one angle or another;

> . . . to identify experiences which will further the growth and development of personality and lead to new useful and creative roles which will provide a sense of life-fulfillment in our changing *society*.

AN INVITATION

You are, then, hereby invited to a new and fascinating study: *yourself*, and your *future biography*. What will it be, in physical terms? In family terms? In terms of the goal and quality and enjoyment of living? What should it include *before* retirement, to enrich its promise *after* retirement?

The answers are—in part—up to you. Within that "part," it is the purpose of this volume to be of help—as well as of interest. We sincerely hope you will join us in the attempt to realize that goal.

W. D.
C. T.

Introduction

NEVER IN HUMAN HISTORY has a society set such a rapid pace of change in the manner and means of living as our American society today. In turn, we have set in motion processes that are resulting in accelerated change in the rest of the world, from the USSR to the most primitive areas of Africa and Southeast Asia.

These changes are felt in everyone's life; though they are not always recognized or their implications understood. The automobile, for instance, made profound and permanent changes in our countryside, our cities, our personal horizons; yet none of this was foreseen, and few people today could give an accurate account of what those changes are.

A profound change is taking place today in the age-structure of the American population. Never before was being "old" so certain a prospect for so many. Never has the American people contained so large a proportion of persons over fifty. And throughout our society, from its politics to its patterns of manufacture, marketing, and entertainment, changes are being made in response to this fact. Suddenly, we American people have come to realize that we are not only living longer, but that we are spending a smaller part of our lives in rearing children, in housework, and in paid employment. More and more of our life is available to us in the form of "free" time to be employed as we choose. Gone are the conditions of earlier times in which the years of life were relatively few and in which most people were occupied in making a living as long as they survived. The new developments, coming gradually at first but now very rapidly, have raised many questions of individual financial security, economic costs to society, family relationships, maintenance of good health, and desirable living arrangements—but perhaps the most important question of all is, "How shall we use the added years of life and the freedom and leisure they are bringing?"

Extension of life beyond the completion of family and work responsibilities, in a culture marked by rising levels of living, presents unprecedented opportunity for continued personal growth, enjoyment, and service to society. Yet many people are not finding these satisfactions, and society's focus on aging is still largely on the *problems* it has created. The reason appears to be that certain aspects of our culture are lagging behind the revolutionary scientific and technological changes which are forcing us to change many of our ways of living. Personal recognition, social status, human companionship, and usefulness, for example, are still sought and achieved largely through parental and work roles, although more and more of us are now living beyond the period of life in which these roles are completed. Aging in the terms we are employing has come upon us very rapidly. We have not had time to learn that life-long household duties and work responsibilities are merely cultural overlays or ways of surviving, developed in societies in which life was short and the ways of living hard. We have yet to develop the additional overlays relevant to the later years of life. Thus far we have accepted the goal of long and leisurely life, but we have not yet adjusted ourselves to the fact that we are actually achieving it. Earlier societies, by their very nature, offer few precedents to us. We are having to pioneer. To help set this pioneering in motion is the basic objective of this volume.

To oversimplify, we could say that the American culture today is focused on two sets of people: the young adults with children, and the old. But it is those in the *middle* years who *create and manage the society for both the others.* This is why *it is to those of middle age that this book is addressed.*

In developing the materials for this book, the editors turned to the nation's most distinguished students of aging; and to distinguished writers of the past and present. Additional sources of informative and enjoyable reading are included with each chapter and in a general bibliography. The various authors, however, are not presented in the belief that they have all the "answers"; rather, they are people alert to and informed about the opportunities, the needs, the implications for personal values, of these population changes. Their objective is to *join you* in opening new vistas of experience for yourself. In the words of Oveta Culp Hobby, "Our task is . . . to build the bridge before we reach the stream, and—if possible—to build it in time for those who walk ahead of us."

Contents

PART III · SOME ASPECTS OF RETIREMENT

AGING

IN TODAY'S SOCIETY

part I

THE MIDDLE YEARS

Clark Tibbitts (born in 1903 at Chicago) is Assistant Director, Special Staff on Aging, United States Department of Health, Education, and Welfare, Washington, D.C. Close student of cultural phenomena of aging, speaker and consultant for action groups, he considers himself now to be in the new prime of life. Editor or co-editor of Social Aspects of Health in the Depression *(1938);* Living Through the Older Years *(1949);* Planning the Older Years *(1950);* Social Contribution of the Aging *(1952);* New Frontiers of Aging *(1957).*

"Anyone's success in aging will depend measurably upon facing up to these factors (i.e. the basic biological forces of life and the conditioning impact of society) in an active and participating way. And while society sets the stage, sketches out the plot of the play, and provides the conditions for more or less successful aging, the initiative must spring substantially from the individual. And where many fail, some will always succeed."

—LEO W. SIMMONS

"Social Participation of the Aged in Different Cultures." *The Annals,* January 1952. Quoted by permission.

1

Aging as a
Modern Social Achievement

CLARK TIBBITTS

WE ALL KNOW THAT the world constantly changes, but not all of us
recognize that the rate of change has speeded up tremendously in
recent times. In his book *Utopia, 1976* Morris Ernst makes the statement that American society has gone through more changes since
the nation was founded than occurred in the preceding million years
of man's existence. One of the changes, the one to which we will
give our attention in this essay, is the remarkable increase in the
number of middle-aged and older people in the population. Man's
ancient desire to live longer and better is being realized at last.

Average life expectancy at birth has increased by seventy-five
percent over the past century, and each new advance is hailed as a

---

The opinions expressed in this essay are those of the author and do not necessarily
represent those of the Department of Health, Education, and Welfare.

triumph of modern medical science. Simultaneously the problems of adjustment to longer life, described historically by Professor Simmons in his discussion of aging in other cultures, have been multiplied, and new ones are constantly being added. This is because more people are living longer in a society which is itself constantly becoming more complex. The growing number of old people challenges us to find satisfactory solutions to problems of health, family relations, housing, employment, income security, and use of free time. These problems are occupying the attention of more and more students and researchers, political leaders, the staffs of public and private agencies, and even entire communities and states. If all this energy expended on their behalf is not to fail of its purpose, older people themselves must cooperate in full measure. Older persons will not achieve satisfaction in their lives if they are but passive objects of the benevolence of experts and specialists.

The presence in the population of nearly fifty million persons beyond the age of forty-five years who are reasonably certain of a good many years of free time in the future is an unprecedented social achievement. Indeed, aging may best be defined as the survival of a growing number of people who have completed the traditional adult roles of making a living and child rearing. The years following the completion of these tasks are beginning to represent an extension of life marked by a shortening of hours of work, both on the job and in the home and, in the end, complete retirement from paid employment. In short, the extension of life has brought into being a new turning point in life which needs sharper recognition by more and more people.

If people who reach this point are wise they will find fulfillment in life by utilizing their leisure for new and different activities designed to give them new satisfactions. But there is more than a suspicion, unhappily, that many fail to recognize this and, instead, occupy their leisure with mere "busy-work" that yields little worthwhile return and that others, even more unfortunate, are overtaken by boredom and dissatisfaction.

More years of life for all! Time for enriched living? Or time for boredom? What, really, is the origin of this remarkable situation with its challenging dilemma? How has this longer life, with its promise of increased leisure, been achieved? Is it real, or merely a figment of the specialist's imagination? What, actually, does it mean for an individual person? For society at large? Can it be afforded—by society, by the individual? What is the future of this situation, and what are the answers to the questions it poses?

Some of the answers are at hand, particularly those having to do with the genesis of the situation. But the proper utilization of the opportunities opened up to those who actually achieve the longer life we are talking about is a wide-open question, in both its personal and social aspects. We are going to discuss both aspects of the matter, but on this particular occasion we are going to take a look at some of the underlying factors: the revolutionary changes taking place in our culture.

Scientific and Technological Development

Longer, healthier, and easier living is a direct outgrowth of the application of science to achieve better nutrition, medical care, and conditions of living; and to develop new forms of energy and new machines to do our work. Before this happened—before the systematic use of science became a marked characteristic of our society—the task of making a living and the carrying out of household duties occupied everybody throughout relatively short lives. This pattern of working and living persisted as normal for society for many decades of our own country's history, as Professor Simmons will show. Gradually the introduction of new tools and machines, the use of water power and steam, and improved understanding of nutrition and medicine began to create new patterns of living and to lengthen life. But only during the last fifty years or so has the full impact of the change been felt by everybody in this country.

More People, More Years

Since 1900 the number of persons beyond the age of forty-five has increased from 13 millions to 47 millions today, or to about as many people as were living in the United States in 1880. Today also there are actually more people over sixty-five than there were people of all ages in this country in 1830.[1]

Partly this is accounted for by the fact that there are more people. The total population has grown from 23 million in 1850 to 166 mil-

---

[1] The tables from which these and other statistics are taken appear at the end of this essay.

lion today. This increase, involving larger numbers of people in all the age brackets, is responsible for about half the increase in the number of older people since 1900.

A second influential factor at work here is immigration. During the last century and through the first decade of the present century, millions of people sought a new life in America. Coming largely as youths and young adults, the immigrants eventually became part of the middle-aged and older groups. They account for about twenty percent of the total increase in the upper ages since 1900.

The third factor is the improvement of the environment in terms of health: techniques for purifying milk and water were introduced, the sanitary handling of waste was mastered, vital advances in nutrition through modifications of eating habits were made, the infectious diseases of infancy, childhood, and, increasingly, adulthood were brought under control. As a consequence, more children are living into early adulthood, and more adults into their middle and later years. Life expectancy at birth has increased from about forty years in 1850, to about forty-nine years in 1900, and to seventy years today. The life expectancy of those who reach the age of forty has increased less dramatically, but still it has moved from about twenty-eight more years to thirty-four more years over the century and is expected to continue to move up.

America's aging citizenry, then, is in large part the product of population growth, immigration, medical progress, and improved environmental conditions. Since all the causes, except large-scale immigration, continue to operate, it may be predicted that around the year 2000 the population will have increased to 275 to 300 millions, with from eighty to eighty-five million persons aged forty-five years and over, of whom perhaps twenty-five million will be over three-score-and-ten. Millions now living are practically certain to live into the years assumed to be the proper years for retirement.

Patterns of Making a Living Have Changed

The way of living has also changed spectacularly. In the earlier decades of this country's history, most work was done on the home farm and in so-called cottage industries, with simple tools operated by hand or powered by animal energy. The output of each worker was relatively small—little more than enough to provide subsistence for his own family. Children normally went to work at eight or ten years of age, and most people continued to work as long as they lived. Millions were worn out by forty-five or fifty. Many died "before their time," as the expression was, and only a few lived into old age. This was the general picture.

But man was not satisfied with this hard, frugal, and short life. He strove for a higher standard of living attained with less work, and the principal means to his end was the machine. New sources of energy were brought into use: water, steam, electricity. Technological change became an outstanding characteristic of our society.

The speed of change was remarkable. In 1850 the total amount of energy produced and expended in making a living is estimated to have been 10 billion horsepower-hours, or 440 horsepower-hours for each person in the population. Around two-thirds of this was supplied by human and animal muscles. By 1950 the amount of energy used had increased to nearly 700 billion horsepower-hours, ninety-eight percent of it from inanimate sources. Today every man, woman, and child in this country commands the equivalent of 4,500 horsepower-hours of work each year, almost a ten-fold increase in but four generations.

At first the increases in output were small. People worked long hours at their machines to produce as much as they could. By around 1900, however, people began to extract other advantages from the machine. They decided to "take out" a proportion of the results in shorter hours of work. The work-week began to shorten. It shortened at the rate of about three hours every ten years. At the same time it became possible to keep children off the labor market and in school longer. And, at the other end of life, more people began to find it possible to drop out of the labor force and enjoy a few years of leisure. By 1900 about 35 percent of the older men were retired, most of them because they were physically unable to go on working in full-time competitive employment; but some had retired because they had been able to harvest the fruits of machine productivity in leisure.

It is since 1900 that the latter group, our concern here, has grown at a tremendous pace. The length of the work-week has now dropped below forty hours for many; the average age of entry into gainful employment or paid work has risen to between eighteen and nineteen; and more and more people are able drastically to reduce their hours of work, or quit altogether. Today 14 percent of all men between forty-five and sixty-four, 60 percent of those sixty-five and over, and 80 percent of those over seventy-five are not in paid employment. The proportions of older women not gainfully employed are much greater.

This remarkable change in the pattern of people's work histories —later entry into paid employment, earlier withdrawal from it—has occurred at a time when the level of living in this country has been rising. There is now being produced twice as much in goods and services *for each person* in our population of 166 million as was produced per person for the 76 million of 1900. The level of living has greatly improved, and, while prices have increased tremendously, so have wages. Real income—or the quantity of goods and services you can buy with your money income—has sharply increased. All this tends to prove the point that our society can afford the leisure it is granting its older citizens. If we continue along present lines into the future, more and more people will have the leisure we are talking about.

We are, in short, only at the beginning of this development. New varieties of energy and new kinds of machines are now coming into use. Power from atoms, energy from the sun, are moving up fast. Automation, or the skillful coordination of machines, is a living actuality. Output seems bound to increase, the standard work-week to continue to shorten. It is rather confidently predicted that by 1965 the work-week will be down another three or four hours and will probably reach thirty hours by 1975. Real income will go up twenty percent or better. Per capita purchasing power in 2000 will be double what it is now. And more people will look forward to retirement as a normal phase of the cycle of life, just as they will accept prolonged educational preparation for the earlier phases of the life cycle.

Disappearance of the Household and Its Economy

Science, technology, and factories have profoundly affected family living. In agricultural-handicraft societies the household is the unit of production, not the factory, the office, or the large store. The chief breadwinner in such societies works at or very near his home, assisted actively by his wife, children, and such relatives as are living with him. Most food and clothing are produced at home, and "exotic" foods like sugar, tea, coffee, etc. are obtained by selling the small surplus of home-produced goods, as are decorative clothing and household objects.

In such households most of the children were trained for their occupations in the household, primarily with the idea of carrying the pattern of life forward into the future. The sick were cared for at home. Even religious life was integrated into the family routine by grace before meals and Bible-reading and prayers at the close of the day. The cultural life of adults—who may or may not have had a maximum of four years at school—was what they made it through weekly newspapers and farm magazines. Recreation was created at home, even if in association with neighbors. As the seniors got older, they continued to work, but slowly shifted to lighter tasks. The traditional final place for the very old was the chimney-corner. One can get pleasurably nostalgic about all this, but as a way of life it has vanished forever for most Americans.

It has vanished as the country has industrialized and urbanized. Factories and cities have killed it. Today the head of the family, and often his wife also, works outside the home. Food and clothing are now purchased ready for use. Most educational and religious activities are carried on wholly in outside community institutions. Even recreation has, in large measure, to be sought outside the home. Only occasionally is sickness taken care of within the home; the more usual practice is to send the sick to hospitals. Houses have shrunk in size; and they are streamlined. The work in them is done as far as possible by machines: washers, vacuum cleaners, toasters, mixers, etc.

The gist of it is that the so-called economic-kinship household of our ancestors has dissolved into its component parts. Young married people, with or without children, with the aid of mass-produced and mass-distributed goods and services, have achieved a new kind of self-sufficiency, a socialized self-sufficiency. They find little need for the help of additional persons permanently resident in the home and often get along employing only a baby-sitter occasionally. There is no room for others, really. Each generation related to this new family unit tends to develop its associations with others of similar age *outside the home*. The generations tend to lead lives of their own from a relatively early age, assuming that their elders will do likewise—and continue to do so no matter how old they get. The closely knit household of kinship groups of various ages is not provided for in the new scheme of society. This new way of life is a natural consequence of modern, industrial civilization. This is what we in large measure confront today. It practically forces the older people to "make their own lives."

And this bids fair to continue indefinitely into the future. True, the population is growing rapidly, and the number of families has doubled in the last generation; but almost all the new families are modeled on the new pattern just described.

Age as Opportunity

In our society the adult years have been lengthened and may now be divided into two more or less distinct phases; or, perhaps better, *an entirely new period has been added* to life.

Early adulthood can be described as the period from twenty to twenty-five up to forty or fifty, during which the individual is occupied with creating a family, establishing a place in the community, fixing upon a career, and striving for advancement. Interest is largely focused on immediate individual needs and the family.

Middle life, or the years from forty or forty-five to fifty-five or sixty, brings many changes and is coming to be recognized as a period of transition from early to mature adulthood. Most persons are by this time well established in career occupations. Children, by and large, are now on their own, so that the pressures and responsibilities of parenthood are mainly over. Many persons at this period of life begin to realize that they have more time for the interests they were forced to set aside in early adulthood, or for entirely new interests. And most adults at this time begin to look forward to retirement.

This remarkable innovation in the life-pattern has been made possible by the amazing advances in science, leading to longer life and unprecedented productivity. Middle-life is the time when a person finds himself completing one role in life and looking for a new one. It is the stage at which opportunity for new adventures in personal growth arises and the exploration of new interests becomes possible, after long years of hard work and heavy family responsibilities.

Can the Good Life Be Found?

This situation demands careful appraisal. What is being done? Are people enjoying it? Are they using their energy and free time in ways that are satisfying? Where are they to look for new growth and adventure? What *are* the essential conditions of a really satisfying later life?

These are new and important questions. They are questions that must be answered constructively. There is little precedent to guide the individual. Expectations and duties for the earlier years are fully defined by a long tradition. There are few real choices to be made in childhood or in the early adult years. A man knows pretty much what is expected of him. But this is not true of the new phase of life we are talking about. There are few guide lines, because no society has ever before known the mass extension of life and leisure that is now upon us. Both individuals and society are embarked on uncharted seas, on a new phase of life activity, with little accumulated understanding of it.

Many people are finding their way to rich adventure. They are the pathmakers to the future. They have assessed themselves, examined their situations, potentialities, and interests, and have made their choices. Some intensify their contributions to community activities, some turn to educational activities to clarify and amplify their understanding of the life of mankind and themselves, some seek to sharpen their perceptions in the arts by cultivating an interest in literature, painting, and music. Some seek to express themselves in the arts or in crafts. Some turn to a mixture of these things and further spice it up by travel. Or they stay at home and use their talents to make it a more beautiful place than ever it was before.

Whatever they do, they are explorers, pioneers. They are the pioneers of the new "prime of life" that has been vouchsafed to so many Americans by medicine and technology. What will their explorations mean for their fellows and society at large? Are they on the way toward adding not only a new dimension to their own lives but also a new dimension to civilization in the United States of America?

Time Out for Reflection

When do you think "middle age" begins? Do you tell by years or by other criteria? Do you think men and women have different attitudes about "being middle aged"? What makes the differences?

If you look at growing old as an *achievement* rather than a "problem," does it make planning for it easier? More attractive? Do you think most Americans look on old age as a problem, and face it with dread? Why? What could change this attitude to a more positive and constructive one?

Our society has been accused of "glamorizing youth"—in its advertising, its entertainment. Do you notice any signs that movies, television, magazines, are recognizing the needs of an older audience, and changing their plots, their heroes and heroines, their product appeal—to suit these older people?

As more and more people gain more and more free time, both during their working years and after them, do you notice any changes in the ways this time is used? What opportunities does your own community offer for the constructive use of leisure—through organized activity, through service work, through learning, through creative arts and enjoyments?

What use are *you* making of your present leisure; and *how do you plan to use the freedom of the coming years?*

Figures Tell a Story

Here are some statistical tables about the changing circumstances of people growing older today. Such tables make sense most easily if you look for some particular relationship. Look, in the first five tables, at the figures for *men* and for *women* at the later ages, and think about what each table means. Then consider the five tables together: what picture do they suggest of the conditions of life of the woman over sixty? Consider the last four tables together: do they have any bearing on the kind of living that people over sixty can expect?

Growth of the Middle-Aged and Older Populations

YEAR	MIDDLE-AGED AND OLDER PEOPLE IN THE POPULATION		
	TOTAL POPULATION	*45-64 YEARS*	*65 YEARS AND OVER*
Both sexes			
1850	23,200,000	2,300,000	600,000
1900	76,000,000	10,400,000	3,100,000
1950	150,700,000	30,600,000	12,300,000
1975	235,000,000	43,810,000	21,800,000
Men			
1850	11,800,000	1,200,000	300,000
1900	38,800,000	5,500,000	1,600,000
1950	74,800,000	15,300,000	5,800,000
1975	116,000,000	20,900,000	9,300,000
Women			
1850	11,400,000	1,100,000	300,000
1900	37,200,000	4,900,000	1,500,000
1950	75,900,000	15,300,000	6,500,000
1975	119,000,000	22,900,000	12,600,000

The Growing Length of Life

YEAR	YEARS OF LIFE REMAINING AT—			
	BIRTH	AGE 20	AGE 40	AGE 60
	MEN			
1850	40			
1900	48	42	28	14
1950	67	50	31	16
1975	70	52	33	17
	WOMEN			
1850	40			
1900	51	44	29	15
1950	72	55	36	19
1975	76	57	38	21

Marital Status of Middle-Aged and Other People, 1950

AGE	PERCENTAGE DISTRIBUTION BY MARITAL STATUS					
	MEN			*WOMEN*		
	Single	Married	Widowed and Divorced	Single	Married	Widowed and Divorced
45-54 years	9%	86%	5%	7%	78%	15%
55-64 years	10	80	10	8	64	28
65-74 years	8	74	18	7	47	46
75 years and over	7	57	36	7	20	73

The Family Cycle in 1890 and 1950

| STAGE OF THE FAMILY CYCLE | MEDIAN AGE IN YEARS AT WHICH EVENTS OCCUR FOR— | | | |
| | MEN | | WOMEN | |
	1890	1950	1890	1950
First marriage	26	23	22	20
Birth of last child	36	29	32	26
Marriage of last child	59	50	55	48
Death of spouse	57	64	53	61

Couples without Children at Home

AGE	PER CENT OF COUPLES WITHOUT CHILDREN AT HOME
Under 25 years	38%
25-34 years	21
35-44 years	22
45-54 years	52
55-64 years	81
65 years and over	97

The Increasing Length of Our Working Years

| YEAR | THE YEARS WE SPEND— | | |
	in preparation	at work	in retirement
1900	14	32	2
1950	18	42	6
1975	19	44	7

Living Arrangements of Middle-Aged and Older People, 1950

LIVING ARRANGEMENTS	PERCENTAGE DISTRIBUTION WITHIN AGE PERIODS			
	45-54 yrs.	55-64 yrs.	65-75 yrs.	75 & over
All persons	100%	100%	100%	100%
Relative present	90	85	78	72
No relative present	10	15	22	28
In married couples	75	67	51	28
Man head without wife [1]	3	5	7	9
Woman head without husband [1]	7	11	16	19
As relative of head [2]	7	9	16	31
In hotels, lodging houses, institutions	7	8	9	12

[1] In about one-half of these cases the man or woman has one or more relatives living with him or her.

[2] The majority of these men and women are living with adult children.

Retirement from Work is Becoming More Common

YEAR	PROPORTION OF MEN AGE 65 AND OVER RETIRED FROM WORK
1850	5%
1900	35
1950	55
1975	70

How Machines Have Taken Over

YEAR	SOURCES OF ENERGY USED IN PRODUCING GOODS AND SERVICES		
	Human	Animal	Inanimate
1850	13%	52%	35%
1900	5	22	73
1950	1	1	98

Energy Used in Producing the Things and Services We Consume

YEAR	HORSEPOWER-HOURS OF ENERGY AND POPULATION		
	Billions of horsepower-hours produced	Population in millions	Horsepower-hours produced per person
1850	10	23.2	440
1900	78	76.0	1,030
1950	675	150.7	4,470

The Work Week Grows Shorter

YEAR	WORK-HOURS PER WEEK
1850	70
1900	55
1950	40
1975	32

Our Rising Income

YEAR	NATIONAL INCOME AND POPULATION		
	Total national income in billions of dollars	Population in millions	Income per person
1850	$ 9.4	23.2	$ 405
1900	63.3	76.0	833
1950	240.6	150.7	1,593
1975	587.0	235.0	2,500

Note: Income figures are in dollars of equivalent purchasing power.

The Seven Ages
of Man

William Shakespeare (1564-1616)

ALL THE WORLD'S a stage,
And all the men and women merely players,
They have their exits and their entrances,
And one man in his time plays many parts,
His acts being seven ages. At first the infant,
Mewling and puking in the nurse's arms.
Then the whining school-boy, with his satchel
And shining morning face, creeping like snail
Unwillingly to school. And then the lover,
Sighing like furnace, with a woeful ballad
Made to his mistress' eyebrow. Then a soldier,
Full of strange oaths, and bearded like the pard,
Jealous in honour, sudden, and quick in quarrel,
Seeking the bubble reputation
Even in the cannon's mouth. And then the justice,
In fair round belly with good capon lin'd,
With eyes severe and beard of formal cut,
Full of wise saws and modern instances;
And so he plays his part. The sixth age shifts
Into the lean and slipper'd pantaloon,
With spectacles on nose and pouch on side,
His youthful hose, well sav'd, a world too wide
For his shrunk shank; and his big manly voice

Turning again toward childish treble, pipes
And whistles in his sound. Last scene of all,
That ends this strange eventful history,
Is second childishness and mere oblivion,
Sans teeth, sans eyes, sans taste, sans everything.

A New Phase of
Spiritual Development
Edward Bellamy (1850-1898)

THE ENFRANCHISEMENT OF HUMANITY in the last century, from mental and
physical absorption in working and scheming for the mere bodily necessities, may be regarded as a species of second birth of the race, without
which its first birth to an existence that was but a burden would forever
have remained unjustified, but whereby it is now abundantly vindicated.
Since then, humanity has entered on a new phase of spiritual development, an evolution of higher faculties, the very existence of which in
human nature our ancestors scarcely suspected. In place of the dreary
hopelessness of the nineteenth century, its profound pessimism as to the
future of humanity, the animating idea of the present age is an enthusiastic conception of the opportunities of our earthly existence, and the
unbounded possibilities of human nature. The betterment of mankind
from generation to generation, physically, mentally, morally, is recognized as the one great object supremely worthy of effort and of sacrifice.
We believe the race for the first time to have entered on the realization
of God's ideal of it, and each generation must now be a step upward.

To Venus
Horace (65-8 B.C.)

O VENUS, HAVING SO LONG left me in quiet, do you begin again to raise
war against me? Spare, Goddess, I pray you, spare; I am no more what
I was under the reign of beautiful Cynara. Cruel mother of amorous desires, cease attempting to bring under your yoke a man now arrived at
his fiftieth year, and therefore stubborn to submit to your voluptuous

commands. Go whither you are called by the pressing entreaties and flatteries of our youth.

If you desire to inflame a worthy heart, and apt to receive your impressions, grow wanton in the house of Paulus Maximus, thither fly in your chariot drawn by swans. He is of an illustrious descent, distinguished by a comely and graceful port, and his eloquence is a refuge to the distressed; in a word, he is possessed of a thousand fine qualities, that will spread to a great distance the fame and glory of your empire. And, when by his powerful charms he triumphs over the rich presents of his rival, he will raise to you a marble statue, and place it in a temple near the Alban lake under a roof of citron-wood. There you shall continually smell the frankincense that shall be burnt upon your altar; and be delighted with the various hymns played upon the harp, the flute, and the Berecynthian horn. There the young boys and tender virgins, singing your praises twice a day, shall thrice beat the ground with their snowy feet after the manner of the Salii.

Neither woman or boy any longer pleases me; I am now no more delighted with the fond hope of credulous love; I contend not for the mastery in drinking, nor take a pride in adorning my head with a garland of new flowers. But why, alas! why, Ligurinus, do the tears thus trickle down my cheeks? Why does my tongue formerly eloquent now falter, and sink into a shameful silence? All the night long in my dreams sometimes I hold you in my arms; at other times, flying my embraces, I follow you, cruel as you are, through the field of Mars, and the rolling waters of the Tiber.

The Fabulous Future

David Sarnoff (1891-   )

THE DOMINANT PHYSICAL FACT in the next quarter-century will be technological progress unprecedented in kind and in volume. In relation to the total history of the human race, the last hundred years have been no more than a split second. Yet they have compassed more technological achievement than the millennia that preceded. The harnessing of electricity to the purposes of light, power, and communication; the demonstration of the germ theory of disease; discovery and application of the electron; invention of radio and television; development of anesthetics; the exploration of genes and mutations; invention of motor vehicles; evolution of the assembly line and other mass-production techniques; proliferation of organic chemistry; the splitting of the atom; development of antibiotics; the vast expansion of the known and measured universe of stars and galaxies—these are only the highlights of recent progress.

And it is not just a case of continued increase but of continued acceleration of increase. We need only project the curve into the future to realize that we are merely on the threshold of the technological age.

There is no longer margin for doubt that whatever the mind of man visualizes, the genius of modern science can turn into fact. The released energies of the atom, though born in war and baptized in destruction, are already being funneled to man's constructive purposes.

Other sources of energy—the sun, the tides, and the winds—are certain to be developed beyond present expectations. New materials by the score —metals, fabrics, woods, glass—will be added to the hundreds of synthetics already available. Fresh water purified from the briny seas will enable us to make deserts flourish and to open to human habitation immense surfaces of the globe now sterile or inaccessible. Tidelands and the ocean floors beyond, already being tapped for oil, will be increasingly mined for other materials and harvested for chemical and food resources.

Medicine can look to incalculable aid from science and technology. Similarly, techniques for learning faster and better will be opened up by color television, improved means of communication, electronic magnification, and other new processes.

We have a right to make the same kind of projection for social progress, though with far less assurance. The material triumphs now at our disposal must be translated into a happier life for mankind everywhere.

High among our goals must be greater mutual tolerance among races and nationalities. We cannot wholly weed out the primeval prejudices and fears in the jungle undergrowth of the human mind. But we can remove some and neutralize the effects of the rest.

The reduction of crime—by individuals and by nations—also deserves a priority in our hopes and plans. The ever more plentiful supplies of food and goods, higher standards of living and education and health— these should make the containment of violence easier during the coming years.

Automation and other aspects of scientific advance will, as a matter of course, put a premium on brains rather than brawn. One hopes that in the years ahead a decent education will have become as indispensable as a decent suit of clothes. Not labor but leisure will be the great problem in the decades ahead. That prospect should be accepted as a God-given opportunity to add dimensions of enjoyment and grace to life. We have reason to foresee a fantastic rise in demand for and appreciation of the better, and perhaps the best, in art, music, and letters.

In small things and large, in greater conveniences and a greater recognition of our common humanity, the quarter-century awaits us in a mood of welcome. We must resolve to fulfill its thrilling promises. Should we fail, the fault will not be with science and technology but with ourselves.

Now, perhaps the most futile intellectual exercise is the discussion as to whether an industrialized society is "desirable." We might as reasonably argue whether the tides and the seasons are desirable. The genii of science could not be stuffed back into the bottle even if we so wished.

But aside from the academic nature of the question, the claim that there is an inherent conflict between science and our immortal souls does not stand up under examination. True, the marvels of technology have come upon us so suddenly that they have created problems of adjustment. But on the whole the adjustment has been remarkably good. America, the classic land of technology, enjoys the largest freedom from destitution, ignorance, and disease, along with political rights and social improvements unique in history.

It seems to me unqualifiedly good that more and more of the weight of arduous toil will be unloaded onto the backs of machines; that the sum total of pain and agony will be further reduced by the progress of healing; that modern communications will bring peoples and nations into closer contact, leading to better understanding of one another.

The coming decades will, however, be marked by great challenges to our courage, character, wisdom, and stamina. The greatest of these challenges, of course, will be the continuing Communist drive for world dominion.

If freedom is lost, if the dignity of man is destroyed, advances on the material plan will not be "progress" but a foundation for a new savagery. Mankind cannot indefinitely carry the mounting burdens of an armaments race, and the greater burdens of fear and uncertainty.

Our supreme commitment, as we look to the crucial decades ahead, must be to win the peace—not a peace of totalitarian dominion but a genuine peace rooted in liberty.

The New Instar

George Soule (1887-   )

WHAT KIND OF CIVILIZATION lies in the further reaches of the technological revolution as manifested in the United States of America? What is it that Americans are seeking, now perhaps half consciously, in their historic concern with making and consuming more goods in less and less time, and perhaps will seek more deliberately in the future? Will their direction lead to a society that can be ranked with the great ages of the past?

No answer can be more than a series of intimations. Some of the possibilities, however, seem more likely to be realized than others.

The material basis of the new instar of Western civilization is likely to approximate the goal most fully outlined by John Stuart Mill as "the static state." Mill, like other critics of the early industrial revolution, hoped that gains of population and of production would someday cease to be regarded as the chief end of man. Competitive pushing and shoving in order to get on by accumulating material wealth, he argued, should cease to be the means by which the ends of man are achieved.

Population growth in the United States is indeed likely to diminish, or even to cease, before the land is so filled with cities, factories, and farms that there is no longer any wild shrub or plant or any place where a man can be alone. The production of the material goods that people can eat, wear, or live in has so much increased, and is likely to make such further advance, that one want after another will be satisfied; output of goods will then grow no faster than the population. Even the quantity of goods used in non-paid time (leisure or recreation) will impinge on the limitation of time itself. As material wants approach satiation, the struggle to pile up material wealth will lose much of its point.

The economists, past or contemporary, who have warned against the static state have identified it as lack of economic growth in a populous country which either had not experienced the industrial revolution at all or had faltered during its course. Adam Smith, in discussing the matter, used as his horrible examples China, where "progress" had ceased and consequently average levels of living remained low, and India, on the downgrade in production, where the pressure of population was periodically pushing the country over the brink of famine. Those prominent American economists who in the 1930s thought the United States, having reached "economic stagnation" or a "mature economy," was doomed to suffer continual and growing unemployment unless government intervened to maintain expanding output, were confronting a society in which at least 10 per cent of the labor force was unemployed and large sections of the population were "ill fed, ill clad, ill housed." John Stuart Mill's static state, on the contrary, would be one in which the industrial revolution had been pursued far enough so that all could be reasonably assured of what they needed. To achieve this state, even in the United States, will yet require decades of hard work, shrewdly considered public policy, and well-distributed increase of material output.

Mill, of course, used the words "static state" in a strictly limited material sense. He did not expect that man, or his ideas and desires, would become static. Indeed, he intensely desired the opposite. "Mankind," he wrote, was in "a very early stage of development." Technological advance itself would, he expected, continue, but would be devoted to its proper purpose—making work easier. It already has done so. The development of man would be facilitated also, he pointed out, by a marked shortening of working hours. This trend has already become well established and is almost certain to go much further.

Other potential results of technology and engineering, not anticipated by Mill, have already gone far and are likely to be more emphasized as the desirable form of the static state is approached. One is a shift in the kinds of work to be done and hence in the major occupations of the labor force. Backbreaking unskilled labor has not only been made easier; it is gradually disappearing. Monotonous, routine work in factories, farms, offices, and merchandising establishments is now rapidly being taken over by machines. There is, on the other hand, an increasing need for people with training, skills, and ingenuity in devising, building, and adjusting machinery, in the professions, in managerial posts, in dealing with other people. Work on the job, in other words, is being sorted out to impose the more machinelike, deadening tasks on machines, and to leave the more man-like, enlivening tasks to human beings.

Technology is capable of saving not only labor but material resources which are limited in quantity. It can substitute relatively abundant energy from the atom or the sun for exhaustible coal and oil. It can make more efficient the uses of whatever metals or other supplies are needed. It can multiply the output of food per acre. These and like triumphs can stretch the means of subsistence. At the same time science and its applications enable man to limit the growth of population. Limitation of population growth to a pace slower than the increase of the food supply, which looked to Malthus impossible except by heroic restraint, and to Mill desirable though difficult, has become almost an automatic accompaniment of economic growth.

Immense tasks for technology remain, not merely in augmenting production faster than population grows, but in making life as a whole more pleasant and rewarding. None of these tasks is of more moment in the near future than redesigning and rearranging the places where men live. The task has made headway in the individual home at its best; something has been done in the more fortunate suburbs, though here new problems are created almost as rapidly as old ones are solved. In the great metropolitan regions the labor seems like that of Sisyphus. Many of these areas, like New York, are rapidly strangling themselves by multiplying places to sleep and work faster than decent or efficient means of getting to and from them. Of course the problem is not technically insoluble; its solution must await a more widespread will to solve it, less opposition from vested interests, better social and political organization. The technical skill which made the skyscraper is not incapable of designing a setting for a tolerable urban community. In the meantime all those individuals who can do so—and their numbers are increasing daily—are bringing pressure on the overgrown centers to change for the better by the simple expedient of deserting or avoiding them. When great cities, like the economy as a whole, become static in terms of mere magnitude, there will arrive at least the opportunity to improve their quality, and the quality of life within them.

Easier and less work, more economic security, less rivalry for material success, seemed desirable to Mill not only in themselves but for a purpose —what he called in one passage cultivating "the graces of living" and in another learning "the Art of Life." The conditions which he thought necessary for pursuit of these ends are indeed being more closely approximated. But is finer quality really being substituted for greater quantity? Or is the dynamic thrust of a technological civilization merely being transferred from making more things for more people to doing more things in more unpaid time? Is there discernible any genuine refinement of values, any more discriminating choice of ends? Or is there, on the other hand, a deterioration, as some observers of American society fear?

Classic philosophers believed the laborers and the tradesmen unfit to exercise the duties of citizenship or to pursue literature, philosophy, and the fine arts. Laborers and tradesmen were in consequence excluded from the governing elite, or what came to be called the leisure class. The aristocratic tradition has long since succumbed to democracy: workers and tradesmen now have political and even social equality. The modern way turns out to be to diminish the labor rather than to exclude the laborer, to bestow leisure and education on all rather than to reserve them for the few.

The classical aristocrat would have expected this turn of events to debase taste, vulgarize intelligence, and make life easy for the demagogue, because he thought those engaged in work and trade were by birth inferior beings, not just adversely affected by their circumstances. Democracy would dilute the cultural brew to insipidity, perhaps even poison it. Traces of this attitude are often found in modern critics of American society, though usually these critics are too well informed—or too discreet —to put the matter in such crude terms as supposed lack of blue blood in the multitude. It is the size of the audience, not its composition, that is blamed for inferior taste; the generality of the electorate, not its lack of intelligence, that robs politics of meaning and urgency.

The old suspicion of the tradesman is now transmuted into attacks on promotional salesmanship of mass-produced articles, of mass-produced entertainment, of political candidates and parties. To produce cheaply for all it is necessary to employ expensive means. It is necessary therefore to appeal to as many as possible in as short a time as possible. The enterprise will not succeed unless one exploits the impulses that lie nearest the surface of great majorities. Crude fears, hopes, desires, excitements that may be shared by almost everyone must be emphasized, instead of the more carefully reasoned reflections and the more cultivated tastes that may be peculiar to the several numerous minorities and even more numerous individuals of which the great crowd is largely composed. So the originators, the creators, the dissenters, the leaders with worth and character, are lost in the average; often they cannot find an audience or a following at all. There is, so it is often said, in modern culture a social law like Gresham's law of money—bad currency always tends to drive good currency out of circulation. Increase of income, security, and leisure on the part of almost all do not automatically remedy this situation but may even make it worse.

In the case of books the situation has been well expressed by a publisher (The Dryden Press). Gutenberg with his movable type introduced the written word to the millions, but the ultimate outcome he scarcely could have conceived. It is now economically impossible "to publish a book that has great intrinsic value but that will appeal to a limited audience. . . . The economics of the situation are painfully simple. The modern book-printing press operates at a speed of about 3000 impressions per hour and prints 32 or 64 pages per impression. But each 'form' of 32 or 64 pages must be carefully 'made ready' before the press starts running, and this makeready may take from four to twelve hours per form, depending upon the complexity of the text. Obviously, devoting several hours to makeready when the press must run for only 30 minutes is economic insanity, although the same amount of makeready time becomes negligible on a printing of 50,000. The same ratio holds true of the other phases of book manufacture. Folding, trimming, and case-making machines turn out work at incredible rates—rates so high as to be impractical for small editions."

Many publishers, to their credit, do publish books destined for small circulation, either because they believe that the authors may come to be profitable investments in the future or because they like the books well enough to subsidize them out of their profits. A publishing house, too, may acquire prestige by including in its list distinguished books which have small sales. Yet the economics of mass production and distribution narrowly limit the freedom to indulge in this philanthropy.

The same techniques of mass production that have rendered small editions unprofitable have also made it possible to sell enormous quantities of paperbound books at low prices. These books range from sex thrillers and crime stories to great classics and excellent modern fiction and non-fiction. The great public can choose almost any kind of fare it likes—and it chooses solid food as well as the non-nutritious or even poisonous. The complaint is not that the mass of readers do not have the chance to broaden or cultivate their tastes, but that the economics of publishing tend to dry up at the source the new, the unusual, or the meritorious work which for one reason or another may appeal only to a small public, at least for a time.

The author of a book which happens to be popular may make money quickly because of a book-club adoption, movie or dramatic rights, and other subsidiary sales. If a paper-back publisher reprints a book the author may receive a substantial sum, though not usually so much as he would have been paid for work of equal difficulty and quality in some other profession. But these are the unusual cases. Meanwhile the competition of cheap reprints may make it even harder than before to sell books in hard covers that do not hit the jackpot. "Most novels," writes Malcolm Cowley in *The Literary Situation* (of the 1950s), "didn't reach a sale of five thousand; they were losing ventures for the publisher and for the author as well. The average income from writing books was below the average income of Southern mill hands, and not much above those of cotton sharecroppers. An author might work a year or more on a book, have it published and favorably reviewed, and still not earn enough royalties to cover the thousand dollars that he might have received as an advance. His next book might take another year and not be published at all." As for the poets, in the United States "only two of them earned a livelihood by writing poetry; one was Robert Frost (who also lectured), and one was Ogden Nash." After writing this Mr. Cowley discovered another one—Oscar Hammerstein, librettist of *Oklahoma!* and *South Pacific*.

The argument certainly is not that every aspiring writer ought to be assured a decent living from his literary work, or that new and good writers do not occasionally make their appearance and find a public. The argument is that mass production and mass reading put such a heavy premium on the recognized and the standardized that there is a subtle but persistent tendency to stifle the biological "sports" in literary creation who, in a simpler society, less heavily weighted in favor of the quickly favored and the popular, might have turned out to be geniuses. If in fact this is happening, we never may have a chance to discover it.

In music, as in reading, there is an enormous and growing audience, and the audience is catholic in its tastes. Democratic appreciation of music shows little sign of ruining the taste of the listeners. Those who begin with a great classic like Beethoven's Fifth go on to compare the rendition of it by various orchestras and conductors, and go on from there to listen to much less familiar works.

Yet never has it been harder for the professional musician to make his living by performing music, never more difficult for a contemporary composer to find a following—or even to get a hearing. While some $200 million worth of records are sold yearly, in 1954 only 74,000 of the 249,000 members of the American Federation of Musicians had full-time work. We need not mourn too much the disappearance of small bands in theaters and movie houses, but the professional symphony orchestras operate at huge deficits; the expansion of symphony concerts is usually at the cost of employing professionals only part time and filling in with amateurs. Some concerts are supported by the AFM Music Performance Fund, derived from a share of the proceeds of record sales.

Rent of halls is expensive—even prohibitive in large cities—except when the concert is subsidized or the seats can be filled at good prices by the attraction of a headliner. Soloists can rarely find bookings except through commercial agencies, which naturally prefer to exploit the big names instead of taking a gamble with new talent. As for the composer, he rarely derives income from either sales of music or royalty from performances unless by some lucky chance he is already well known. He is, economically, even more unfortunate than the literary man.

It is an old story that the commercial theater has suffered from competition with the motion picture. Meanwhile rents and wages of stagehands have continued upward. Only the reckless producer will take the gamble of investing the money necessary to produce a play on Broadway unless he is morally certain of full houses and long runs. And what other cities see is what Broadway has produced. The local theater in the small city—often in the past called the "opera house"—seldom if ever shows a play with live actors, let alone an opera. It has installed a screen and a projector.

As for the movies, they have long engaged in expensive productions that cannot be profitable unless booked widely. We are informed by Arthur Mayer in his "Hollywood Verdict: Guilt but Not Guilty"—a chapter in a recent book, *Is the Common Man Too Common?*—that "the average Hollywood feature film to return its investment must be seen by at least fifteen million people." There are, he writes, less than five hundred theaters that play foreign films or their few American counterparts with reasonable consistency, and they are not widely distributed. Nearly one-fourth of them are in the New York metropolitan area; "they exist in only seventy communities, and they represent less than 3 per cent of the total number of theater seats in America." Theaters in small communities, where long runs for any picture are impossible, cannot find enough "art films" or enough customers for them to afford to abandon a strictly commercial policy. There is, it appears, little opportunity for minorities of taste to see the pictures they would most like unless by some leap of nature they become majorities.

How about radio and its offspring, television, which have contributed to this sad state of affairs? We have it on the authority of Gilbert Seldes in the same volume in which Arthur Mayer writes, "that they are for the most part aimed at the same intellectual level and call for the same emotional responses, the level and the responses being relatively low." Mr. Seldes thinks the television broadcasters create the audiences for whatever they choose to present and that, like radio broadcasters in the past, they could find audiences for better things if they wanted to take the risk. But apparently they usually don't. Their costs are too high. "The pure sustaining program of radio, experimental and not intended for sale, has disappeared, and the status of television may now be described as 'commercialism mitigated by foundations.'" Philanthropic experiments *can* get time on the air—if they will pay the bill.

It is almost impossible to reproduce satisfactorily by mass methods paintings and sculpture. The difference between the original and the copy is far greater than the difference between live and "canned" music. Consequently painters and sculptors have not suffered much competition from mechanical duplication. On the other hand they have been unable to draw much income from reproductions, as have successful writers and musicians. A few lucky ones have found patrons, dealers, or museums to buy their work, as in the past. Thousands of spectators crowd the museums and art shows. But it seldom occurs to the individual consumer, even the man of some means, that he might actually *buy* a new picture, even if it is much cheaper than a new car or a mink coat. Without the guidance of advertisement or standardization, he doesn't dare to trust his judgment or indulge his taste. Of course, in the United States he never did. Mass production and mass consumption have not inhibited appreciation of visual art, but perhaps the consumer habits formed by folkways of the mass market place have made it harder for the artist to make a living—as one might expect him to do in a rich and leisured civilization.

Political democracy in the United States has been analyzed many times and in much detail; its faults are as familiar as its virtues. The present generation of critical writers has much to say about at least two democratic dangers that are new, or at least newly prominent. Both are closely germane to the subject of this book, since both stem in part from the advance of science and technology. One is the possibility that political opinions may be standardized on a low average level, as tastes may be, by mass communication. The other is that we may lose both our political competence and our liberties by official regimentation which uses fear as its whip.

The citizen used to receive his information about public affairs and his hints as to what to think about them both from his own experience and from many miscellaneous sources, varying from locality to locality. He could go to political meetings, take his pick among a number of newspapers representing a variety of editorial biases. Perhaps, even, he listened to street-corner orators. Anyone with a cause could start a periodical or at least print handbills. Public figures of many sorts, both local and national, played roles in forming "grass roots" attitudes—ministers, lawyers, barbers, anyone who could use a cogent phrase or had a mind of his own.

But expensive mass production is said to have changed all this. Only the biggest cities have more than one daily newspaper, either morning or evening. The high cost of fast modern presses, of newsprint paper, of labor, have made all but the big circulations uneconomical, and, even more serious, unattractive to mass advertisers. Whatever news the newspaper chooses to print, what it headlines on the front page, how it slants its treatment, determine the kind of news most people read. Moreover many of these newspapers belong to "chains" under one or another ownership. Virtually all of them use syndicated columns or "boilerplate" material. The columnists do often disagree with one another, but there are relatively few of them.

The same economics applies to periodicals. The opinions and interpretations supplied by the mass-circulation media cover the country; to maintain their popularity they must appeal to a wide and moderate average. Anyone can lose money rapidly by trying to start a new magazine; his "break-even" point cannot be less than several hundred thousand readers. The small-circulation or variant publications must subsist on subsidies of one kind or another. In seeking to influence public opinion, the publisher can seldom any longer start small and gradually grow big. He must be born a giant, if at all.

Meanwhile the usual voter derives most of his political know-how, not by doing anything—not even attending meetings, conversing, or reading— but by sitting in front of his television screen, seeing and hearing precisely the same things that everybody else sees and hears. No doubt he is better informed than most voters of a generation or two ago. He does see and hear opposing candidates and their spokesmen. But the criteria according to which he makes his decisions, the material for his mental constructs, now come to him ready-made—more than, as formerly, from his direct and individual experience. And when election day arrives he is as likely as not to play golf or go fishing, participating in the contest only to the extent of listening to the returns as if it were merely a political version of the world's series.

The advanced technology of warfare, at first designed to frighten enemies, has now succeeded in frightening everybody. "Security" measures, applied during World War II to prevent other nations from discovering the terrifying secrets at our disposal, did not long prevent that discovery. Spies played a part in the leakage of information, but the scientists inform us that there is no such thing as a scientific secret, or cannot be for long, since the basic knowledge and the arts of discovery are a common human property. It is of course the government's duty to frustrate spies, but we are more likely to hamper our own advance by security measures which interrupt the necessary interchange of scientific and technical information than to prevent the enemy from learning what we know. Nevertheless, now that atomic weapons are no longer anybody's secret, "security" continues to be an obsessive concern of government, some politicians, and many citizens.

In the 1920s security meant a bond or a share of stock. In the 1930s security meant some assurance against the hazards of unemployment or old age. In the 1950s security primarily means the effort of the government or even the private employer to fire, or to refrain from hiring, anyone who is suspected of having had the wrong opinions or associates. Security in this sense is supposed to protect the citizen, through his government, from foreign enemies, but as it often is applied it eviscerates his security as a political man.

So much has been said about this subject that detailed exposition of the ugly record is scarcely necessary. The relevant point for the present argument is that the resulting intimidation may induce prudent people to express no opinions about public affairs, attend no meetings, belong to no organizations, and avoid knowing anybody who someday possibly could be suspected of political activity which might fall into disrepute, lest he be cited in the files of the secret political police. Nothing could be better calculated to reproduce at home the regimentation practiced by totalitarian tyrannies, against whose poisonous influence this enormous apparatus of "security" was first erected. If that result has not occurred in the United States—and obviously it has not widely occurred—the reason is that enough Americans are just not that prudent, and still care enough about political liberty to take risks. Unfortunately, however, most of the businessmen who sponsor radio and television shows, and produce moving pictures or entertainment of other kinds, are not willing to take this kind of risk. Personally they may have no objection to employing persons against whom charges have been leveled (whether justly or unjustly), but commercially they shrink from arousing protest from any part of their audiences.

Judge Learned Hand in a recent article referred to "our constant recourse to the word 'subversive,' as a touchstone of impermissible deviation from accepted canons. . . . Contrast this protective resentment with the assumption that lies at the base of our whole system that the best chance for truth to emerge is a fair field for all ideas. Nothing, I submit, more completely betrays our latent disloyalty to this premise, to all that we pretend to believe, than the increasingly common resort to this and other question-begging words." In another passage Judge Hand comments that we might be happier "under the spell of an orthodoxy that was safe against all heresy." But, he continues, "the best answer to such systems is not so much in their immoral quality—immoral though they be—as in the fact that they are inherently unstable, because they are at war with our only trustworthy way of living in accord with the facts. For I submit that it is only by trial and error, by insistent scrutiny and by readiness to re-examine presently accredited conclusions, that we have risen, so far in fact as we have risen, from our brutish ancestors, and I believe that in our loyalty to these habits lies our only chance, not merely of progress, but even of survival." Many other leading Americans have refreshed our memories about the function of civil liberties, but Judge Hand is singularly worth quoting because it was his decision from the federal bench that opened the way to conviction of Communist party leaders for conspiracy, under the Smith Act. If he believes that government has the right to thwart Communist conspiracy against liberty, it is not because he would tolerate the undermining of liberty from any other source or in the service of any other authoritarian system.

If tastes for anything but the average and the accepted are being starved for lack of stimulation, if political life is being watered down by fear of nonconformity, if courageous leaders are not being trained, does the hope lie in education—since the time of Thomas Jefferson conceived as the means of making possible intelligent citizens and complete men? What is the condition of education, on which America has so long staked its democratic future? In spite of the large and increasing numbers in educational institutions—perhaps because of these numbers—the critics make disquieting comments on this sector also.

So small a part of our physical resources has been devoted to education that the shortage of classrooms is expected to become 450,000 by 1960. As the great army of children born in the 1940s has been advancing into the schools, the supply of teachers has actually been declining. In spite of the shortage, teachers' salaries are scandalously low. President A. Whitney Griswold of Yale states that in the fall of 1953 the projected need for additional properly trained and qualified elementary-school teachers was 160,000; our colleges in the previous year produced only 36,000. As the secondary-school enrollment rose (it will soon be doubled) the training of secondary-school teachers declined steadily in the four years 1950-53 from 86,000 to 55,000 a year.

Lack of quantity we know how to remedy, and doubtless will proceed to do so; more serious is what many believe is a deterioration in quality. Talk with faculty members of any liberal-arts college—who also are too few in number, without adequate facilities, and underpaid—and you will be told that many students are passed on to college without even the elementary skills supposed to be the basis of education. Some cannot add, subtract, or cope with the simplest mathematical reasoning. Some cannot spell or construct a grammatical English sentence, to say nothing of writing with clarity and effectiveness. Some are ignorant of the basic traditions of our culture; they are vague not just about the classics, but even about American history, to say nothing of European. Some cannot read well enough to understand or keep up with college assignments. We have it on the authority of Malcolm Cowley that "an Eastern university that chooses the best from a long list of candidates for admission gave a reading test to its students on two occasions, twenty-five years apart. The test showed that freshmen could read as well in 1925 as seniors in 1950." Lack of ability in mathematics, writing, and even reading may sometimes be patched up in college, but the need to do so is deplorable in view of the well-founded belief that good mathematicians and writers often show their highest competence in the early twenties, if not before.

In addition, many colleges and universities are not performing properly their own educational jobs. In most large institutions classes are enormous, instruction is routinized, without much personal contact between student and teacher. Curricula have run off into fringe subjects, where, under the elective system, students may browse without ever acquiring either the basis or the breadth of a liberal education. Professional schools specialize; they turn out, with graduate degrees, engineers, agronomists, economists, chemists, teachers, or what have you (not enough, to be sure), but many of these are not literate either inside or outside their specialties. One reason college students cannot write is that in their textbooks they encounter so much awkward English and almost incomprehensible jargon, produced by many of the specialists who are supposed to teach them.

Clearly mass production does not work in education. As everywhere else, an effort to strike an average curbs and deprives the exceptional. Many scapegoats have been blamed for the current state of affairs. Guesses include the allegation that children now spend too much time listening and looking instead of reading, that they are led to devote too much effort to learning to "adjust" or pursuing "frills" like social studies and art. Meanwhile defenders of the schools assert, on the basis of tests, that school-children of today are even better in the three R's than those of a generation or two ago. If, they imply, deficiency in these respects appears in college it is only because colleges now admit the culls as well as the carefully selected minority they used to cultivate.

Even the great American philosopher John Dewey and the liberal principles of education derived from his views are attacked by some critics. One gathers that these critics would like to go back to the good old days when children were supposed to learn by fear of punishment, when most of them dropped out of school before or at the eighth grade, and the favored ones who went on were drilled mainly in Greek, Latin, and mathematics. Democracy in education, they seem to be saying, is necessarily a failure and should be abandoned.

More to the point is the comment of President Griswold: "Students who have been hustled through overcrowded and undisciplined class-rooms, taught by overworked, underpaid, and improperly qualified teach-ers, and nurtured on subjects that do not constantly stretch their minds and expand their vision are poor material for college and university." Teaching is an art, to be pursued by those who like it and put into it as much skill and devotion as any fine craftsman. It cannot succeed by assembly-line methods. Education which embodies good teaching is therefore expensive; to offer it to all is doubly or trebly expensive. I speak from experience in saying that education in small classes and with a maximum of two-way communication between teacher and student can be dramatically successful with the average or even the under-average as well as with the brilliant. The United States can have both good and universal education—in time—if the people are willing to pay for it. So far they have not done so, except in unusual instances.

Some sociological writers—in particular David Riesman in *The Lonely Crowd*—argue that conformity or at least acquiescence is favored not just by special circumstances such as those outlined above, but by the broad environmental conditions which American civilization is entering. Ries-man's bold thesis is that a civilization which is approaching a static or declining population produces as a typical character what he calls the "outer-directed" man, as opposed to the "inner-directed" man who pre-vailed in the growing and pioneer America of the past. No brief summary could do justice to his reasoning—which seems to me based on insufficient premises—but the gist of the idea is that now the behavior of the typical American is influenced more by what his associates do than by any inner light derived from tradition and transmitted to him in early youth by the older generation.

An illustration is the new suburban community where the houses, though perhaps different in detail, are based on standardized designs, where most of the inhabitants are within a narrow range of income level and seldom mix with those outside it, where everybody does approximately the same thing at the same time and strives not to be conspicuous by being too different, where both social success and business promotion depend on not attracting much attention except through facility in following well-marked throughways approved by those temporarily exercising prestige. In the 1920s such a community was described by a witty writer as a place "where everybody believes that God is a Republican and works in a bank." Obviously if everybody naturally and voluntarily tries to get along with everybody else by doing exactly what his associates do civilization could stagnate.

Others have remarked what they conceive to be a growing anti-intellectualism. "Eggheads," or, as they formerly were called, "highbrows," have long been subjected to ridicule in our democratic society, but not until recently have they so often been accused of conspiring to subvert hallowed institutions. Aside from the danger that demagogues can play on such hostility for their own purposes, there could arise the more subtle but perhaps more menacing peril that a population suspicious of ideas and of those who purvey them would reject the mental food necessary for their further advance, if not their survival.

Another alarming vista is the thesis that as the technological complex necessary to sustain the population becomes more intricate and is carried on by larger units, more controls from above become necessary. The essential integration will thus surround the citizen with laws, rules, regulations, and even control of opinion, so that we may find ourselves in something like Aldous Huxley's *Brave New World* or George Orwell's terrifying *1984*.

The fact that such dangers to the flowering of democracy are not mere phantoms of a sleepless night often leads sensitive observers to a quietistic pessimism. No meaningful and creative period of American history—or any other history—has been without its shadows and its perils. If no voices arose to warn against them, to analyze their nature and origins, then a society might indeed be doomed. Complacency is the all-embracing danger, just as pride is the first of the seven deadly sins.

What the protests and the criticisms mean, on a level of meaning higher than their own content, is that the great debates about aims and policies are being renewed. Not just from foreign critics, but from Americans themselves, flows in a rising stream the very type of dissent which has been expressed by thinkers in technological civilization from the beginning. Questions are raised about the nature of man and the impact upon him of new institutions and circumstances. Little by little, issues will be joined, great debates may ensue, and pregnant decisions may be reached.

A significant shift, too, seems to be occurring in the matters most thought and argued about. The age of the great depression bred a furious concern with the material means of life and their distribution, the organization and aims of economic institutions. Controversy about such matters of course continues and is a necessary accompaniment of successful management of the economy. But it no longer arouses such intensity of feeling or such wide reverberations as in the 1930s. Probably it will not again do so unless the nation is overtaken by another deep economic crisis—an eventuality that most economists regard as unlikely because of the increased knowledge of preventive measures and the apparent will to use them.

What now seems to concern thinkers most is the future of our civilization, the values by which men live, and the cultural development of the individual personality. This is evident enough in the writings of the social critics. And there is ground for believing that it is shared by that large part of the public which reads not purely for entertainment. History, especially philosophy of history which may offer a clue to the future, commands a wide public (e.g., the works of Arnold Toynbee). At present the most popular of the non-fiction books in cheap paper editions are those on philosophy and religion—and not just the religions of the West. At least a million copies of the Koran were recently sold in the United States; there is a burgeoning interest in Buddhism.

It may be argued that all this is merely escapism; people, baffled by the seemingly insoluble problems that surround them, are seeking ways of personal salvation, systems that may provide emotional security and lift the cloud of worry and fear. In many cases this is doubtless true, yet I believe that the prevailing mood is rather like that intended by the death's head, the *memento mori*, at the feast. We live with constant reminders that not only individuals but whole nations may perish in one gargantuan act of violence. Therefore we begin to regard our own lives and the life of our civilization more seriously. How may meaning and dignity be found while there is yet time? Can the stamp of eternity somehow be imprinted on mortality? This is the kind of anxiety, called by Eric Fromm "existential," which is creative, as opposed to the neurotic anxiety induced by the ceaseless effort to sell oneself, without perhaps even having a real self at all.

If American civilization is to survive long enough so that the new instar will have begun to take recognizable form, Americans will have succeeded in living in the same world with the Soviet regime without incurring a violent catastrophe. That awe-inspiring problem is not the subject of this book. The nature of its solution, however, will condition the life of the people. It seems likely to be a sort of Missouri Compromise, tacit or explicit, delineating the boundaries between the two regimes by something corresponding to the Mason-Dixon Line. Just as the American South was under obligation not to extend slavery north of the line, while the North refrained from abolishing slavery south of it, each of the present world rivals might gain, at least for a time, reasonable assurance against interference by the other.

In the case of the Missouri Compromise, the unstable factor consisted of new territories to the West, which, through settlement and development, might become adherents of either South or North. In the new compromise similar unstable factors may be found in the "underdeveloped" regions of the world, in which neither technology nor democracy has made sufficient progress to relieve hunger, disease, and in some cases oppression. Thus the American people will be moved to understand these peoples and to strengthen the ties with them, not, as at present, mainly by military bonds, but increasingly by economic and cultural means. President Truman's "Point Four" may, in historical hindsight, appear more important than the North Atlantic Treaty Organization; certainly it could become more broadly creative. And more significant in the long run even than technical assistance or economic aid may be cultural interchange.

It has been suggested that in the next century the concern of the Western world with the continents of Asia and Africa may play a role comparable with the influence on Europe during the sixteenth and seventeenth centuries exercised by the discovery and settlement of America. The influence will of course be of a different kind. The magnetic field in which the attention of citizens of the United States is polarized always included Europe, though the lines of attraction have recently been strengthened by two world wars. Now it has been broadened even further.

The most truly international forces are humanistic leaders, ideas, and aesthetic creations. The gulf between the United States and Russia proves that similar science and technology in themselves, to which both nations are devoted, do not necessarily promote friendship. If in the future the United States produces great men of the democratic and humanistic sort, distinguished literature, music, art, and architecture, and if its political and social institutions evoke trust and admiration, it will do more to justify its civilization in the eyes of the world than any degree of military and economic power, essential though power may be.

Through the texture of daily living, non-prominent individuals may play their part. Even the artistry with which houses and their surrounding gardens are designed can arouse admiration and empathy. For example, the crowds which recently visited the replica of a Japanese house and garden at the Museum of Modern Art in New York went away with a much warmer feeling toward the Japanese than before, in many cases mixed with envy for their taste and skill.

Is America likely to win world-wide admiration, in view of the discouraging reports now heard from the critics? What of the effects of mass production on character, social and political life, the arts? Does not the necessity of salesmanship in a commercial order overemphasize a low average and stifle individuality?

In thinking of such questions one should be careful not to substitute a cultural or social determinism for the economic determinism of Marx and his followers, a determinism rejected by the judicious. Environmental conditions in human affairs are indeed powerful, but not all-powerful. What is required, if the human spirit is to triumph over almost any combination of circumstances, is not assurance of success, not inevitability proceeding from some mysterious force in the nature of things, but opportunity, however scanty, to mobilize forces on the side of growth and creation.

Not technology or its fruits limit individual development, but the way they are used. If purveyors of ideas and entertainment emphasize the average, it is because the market and salesmanship lead them to do so. The chance to emphasize the individual and the exceptional, which even now exists and may become greater in the future, can be strengthened by the slow decline of dominance by markets and salesmanship. The market culture appears to be self-limited.

As the United States has approached an adequate material base for a higher stage of civilization, the people using market mechanisms themselves, and without embracing socialism or any other named system, have emphasized a growing preference for non-market values. They have done so by unwillingness to sell all the time at their disposal. Or, to state the tendency differently, they have increasingly refused to barter as much of their time as formerly for marketable goods and services, and have instead retained much extra time for non-commercial pursuits. In this way the relative importance of the market values and of production geared to markets has begun to decline.

It is often said that although the big concerns which dominate American industry no longer compete in the same way as thousands of small producers must compete, they do engage in fierce competition, at least across industrial boundaries, for the consumer's dollar. Actually commercial producers are already competing, and will in the future still more furiously compete, for the consumer's time. After people have a moderate sufficiency of food, clothing, and shelter, their purchases turn more and more to goods or services of which they can make use in their non-paid time. It is in supplying such goods that the most rapidly growing markets now in large part exist. But even here the producers are likely to find that since the time of a given population at best is limited, the limitation of time to use and enjoy goods designed for recreation, "hobbies," and the like will eventually limit their markets. Moreover producers of finished goods are beginning to encounter competition with goods that potential consumers make for themselves, not only because in many cases the maker can in this way acquire something that he could not afford to buy outright, or could not buy at all, but also because he finds so much satisfaction in the process of making it that he prefers to spend his time that way.

Thus the market nexus of the economy, with its values, tends little by little to be de-emphasized by the working-through of the market process itself. This is a gradual and relatively painless type of change. It does not have to be realized by liquidating industrial magnates and shopkeepers and substituting for them employers who themselves are instruments of a dictatorial state, or by establishing state-controlled retail stores where the consumer can scarcely find what he really wants, except possibly at prices that he cannot pay.

In the type of culture characterizing the United States at least, advancing technology progressively allows the individual to exercise more choice as to what extent he wishes to use the market mechanism as a means of satisfying his wants, and to what extent he wishes to satisfy them by direct action of his own. It is not likely, in this culture, that markets and market values will ever disappear in the areas where the citizens show by their patronage that they wish to make use of commercial products. But in areas where commercial products cannot be had so cheaply or are not so good as the things that the consumer can make in his own time, an older type of private enterprise will flourish—the enterprise of the individual working for his own satisfaction. In satisfaction of some wants, products of any sort cannot successfully compete with non-commercial uses of time open to the individual. These include, of course, the practice of the arts, intellectual pursuits, and cooperative or social activities of many kinds.

In the early days of the industrial revolution, competition between the factory-market system and the household system of production rapidly led to the ascendancy of factories and markets because they could make and distribute more articles more cheaply. The commercial order then proceeded to draw many other operations out of the home, like laundry and even the preparation of food. But now the tide seems to be turning. It is not likely to bring back into the household many of the kinds of production that have left it, except in cases where decentralized processing can be cheaper or more satisfactory, as in the case of washing with the aid of machines. But wants that never were adequately met by factory production are finding better expression now that people have more time and means for working with their own hands and brains. This competition with markets by pure but non-commercial private enterprise ought to introduce a more healthy balance into American civilization.

As for the dedicated creators and their access to the public, their feeling of isolation is not new; it certainly preceded the advent of mass production and mass communication. At least since the time of William Morris, many serious writers, painters, musicians, and other practitioners of the arts have felt out of tune with industrial society. While the machine age destroyed the practice and spirit of craftsmanship, factory production corrupted tastes. Producers of the fine arts, and particularly the innovators among them, could only with the greatest difficulty find a market for their wares. If they were without sufficient private means, their sole recourse, aside from abandoning their calling, was to seek patronage, which could be obtained only from the rich and successful or from the state. Some found patrons, but even they were frequently subjected to limiting conditions.

An impression arose that things were better for the creative artist in the Middle Ages or the Renaissance. Then at least the classes and institutions which could offer patronage inherited cultural standards more discriminating than those of most modern businessmen. Likewise popular taste seemed to have been less corrupted by the vulgarities of the market place. This impression may be a sentimental fallacy, but there is no doubt that at least since the Victorian Age the professional practitioners of the arts have as a rule had a tough time, especially in the United States. Something in the civilization seemed to separate the creative spirits from their potential audience; they survived precariously in isolation or in precious cults, while popular taste seemed to pay no attention to them, except perhaps after they were dead and had benefited from generations of publicity spread by the critical mentors of the public.

The ultimate development of technology with its democratic leisure class, however, offers hope that the gulf between the artist and the public may be bridged. In the first place, the creative spirit, as working hours shorten and vacations lengthen, may subsidize himself modestly by occupying paid jobs which still would leave time and energy to do his proper work. In this respect he may be as well off as those in the past who were able to obtain sinecures, like John Stuart Mill as an employee of the British East India Company, or Nathaniel Hawthorne in the United States consular service. A favorite haven of this sort at present is teaching on college and university faculties. This is far from an easy or well-paid profession, but with its vacations and sabbaticals, at least it does provide opportunities for scholars to pursue their research, writers to write, painters to paint, and thinkers to think. Ingenious and highly motivated workers in the arts have already succeeded in finding varied opportunities of other kinds.

A person who wants more than anything else to write poetry, paint pictures, compose music, dance, or engage in other creative arts therefore is not obliged, and certainly has less need than in the nineteenth century, to make his living by the sale of his product. But what about his audience? Interaction between artist and reader or spectator is an essential part of the creative process. If the book is not published, the picture viewed, the musical composition, drama, or dance performed, it does not come to life. The new society of which signs are beginning to appear bears promise of better publics also. Taste improves and appreciation is sharpened most of all among those who themselves have some experience in creative work. If a large number of people are interested enough in creative arts themselves to produce or perform, the public for the more gifted is almost certain to improve both in quality and in quantity. Eventually this might cumulate in a force that would affect even the great mass-production and commercial avenues of communication.

In the meantime smaller or more local audiences may be found. Technology has even contributed to the mechanics of new printing devices that can produce, not formal books as we know them, but neatly printed and legible copies in small numbers, at negligible costs. There are local and regional art shows, theaters, concerts. Channels are opening between the creative artist and the consumer that are not encumbered by the heavy costs and cumbersome requirements of commercial mass production.

The question remains whether the creators themselves will have profundity, genius, superlative ability. Nothing distinguishes the great professional from the talented amateur more than the extent to which he pours into his work every energy and skill he can muster. The other requirement is of course that he shall have abundant resources within him. To achieve greatness in philosophy, science, art, requires dedication of a high order. What, someone may ask, does this have to do with a nation in which a democratic leisure class has turned to aesthetic or intellectual hobbies? Will not great work and great endeavor be drowned in a flood of mediocrity? Perhaps. But perhaps also average people will more and more come to regard what they can do with their unpaid time not merely as amusement or escape, but also as the serious business of life. That is what they may come to live for. Insofar as they do so, they will have absorbed the mood and the moral standards of the dedicated artist and will be better prepared to perceive and honor his superlative achievements.

As for the danger of regimentation implicit in a high development of industrial technology, we may reflect that as automation proceeds, the regimentation will be of machines and materials more than of men. Those persons who are needed in production of material goods, if they are more regimented than previously (which is doubtful), will presumably have more hours for themselves. The presence of closely packed crowds in cities already necessitates a multitude of rules governing traffic, hygiene, and other forms of behavior, but there is an increasing tendency to escape cities, and technology is making it easier to do so.

Much confusion exists in the old argument concerning centralization *versus* decentralization. It is customary to assume that these are exclusive alternatives. But, as the science of managemnt has discovered, they are, instead, complementary. By centralizing some functions that can better be performed in that way, more scope is allowed for creative autonomy in other respects. This is the principle already applied by great industrial concerns like General Motors and Standard Oil. The householder benefits from this principle also, especially in the country. He may derive his heat and power from a highly centralized electrical network, or from a gas line, or from regularly delivered oil. His food and other materials he may buy, if he wishes, at great supermarkets or shopping centers. His news comes over the air. He can talk over the telephone. But all this does not necessarily enslave him; indeed, it may make it possible for him to live in the country, since he does not have to devote so much time to the daily necessities of life while he is there. True, he is more inconvenienced if any one of these centralized services on which he relies is disconnected or ceases operation. It is more necessary than before to safeguard continuous operation of the centralized functions. Like the highly complex human body, the technically advanced society depends on its nerves and arteries. One might say that the single-celled amoeba is more free. But is it free at all, in any human sense?

Tell almost anyone that there lies in the future a time when material wants can be reasonably satisfied in a minimum of time by work that is not unpleasant, that most of life will be one long vacation in which the individual may do as he pleases, and he will express uneasiness. A sugar-and-water utopia with little place for effort and achievement, and little or no danger, may seem welcome to the tired and harassed, but after a week or two of it they want, if they are healthy, to get back into harness.

It is therefore reassuring that no future that can be foreseen is likely to be so placid. The mere fact that technology may diminish to the vanishing point the need for engaging in routine drudgery in order to have enough to eat and to wear does not imply that there will be no other jobs worth doing, no danger of any kind. On the contrary, adversity and struggle will always challenge those who wish to create something unfamiliar or better, whether in physical terms, in human relations, or in aesthetic creation.

The hardest work of all, many have discovered, is to think. This is true even in appreciation of what others have thought and felt. Jacques Barzun, writing in *Harper's Magazine* for March 1954 on "America's Passion for Culture," declares: "Whoever says that reading St. Augustine or listening to Beethoven's Opus 95 is the easy, spontaneous way to rest after a hard day's work at the office is simply lying. Habit makes artistic attention prompt and pleasurable, but attention takes mind and physical energy. When I have neither, I read detective stories like my neighbor. So in preaching culture to him I dare not promise that it will bring the recreation he really wants; I am asking him instead for more effort, more expense of every kind, even more worry about the meaning of life."

Some would say that the supreme human achievement lies in the integration of the unruly self—an integration which, to be really human, must embrace breadth, depth, variety. Those who have tried it can testify that this effort is indeed a struggle of heroic proportions. Others would say that the chief human objective must be the improvement of the relationship between the self and other persons, or society as a whole. The truth, of course, is that both aims are necessary, and that they complement each other. Without the tension between the poles of inner and outer there would never be either self or society. This magnetic field of force is what makes it possible to suffuse human life with meaning. Every added degree of freedom for the individual makes the struggle both more difficult and more meaningful.

The challenge in absence of discipline from a boss is to learn to discipline oneself. If work of one kind becomes no longer necessary, the opportunity arises to find work at something better worth doing. Nothing in history would lead to the conclusion that men and women, faced with new dangers, new challenges, new opportunities, must necessarily fail to govern them. The future offers a supreme test to individuals; it offers an unprecedented expansion of freedom, if they will grasp it, to seek the best—as it may seem to them—in their past traditions. By a new renaissance, they may live out these traditions in the new set of circumstances and values. The penalty of failure expressed long ago by Ralph Waldo Emerson in his *Days* must at some time be felt by everyone:

Daughters of Time, the hypocritic Days,
Muffled and dumb like barefoot dervishes,
And marching single in an endless file,
Bring diadems and faggots in their hands.
To each they offer gifts after his will,
Bread, kingdoms, stars, and sky that holds them all.
I, in my pleached garden, watched the pomp,
Forgot my morning wishes, hastily
Took a few herbs and apples, and the Day
Turned and departed silent. I, too late,
Under her solemn fillet saw the scorn.

The Personal Challenge
of Aging: Biological Changes
and Maintenance of Health

Edward J. Stieglitz, M.D. (1899-1958)

THE PROBLEM OF AGING is so immense that I should like to take a few moments for orientation. In order to comprehend any complicated situation involving human affairs or involving natural affairs in which human beings are concerned, such as floods, wars, volcanoes, divorce, marriage, aging, and other potential catastrophies, we need to look at it from three perspectives. If we look at it only from one or two of these perspectives, we assume a very asymmetric viewpoint. The three perspectives can be easily defined by using magnification as our basic simile. First, we must examine the problem with the naked eye. The individual is indivisible; body and mind are one. The individual is the unit. Second, with a microscope, we can take this person apart with blood counts, kidney function tests, blood pressure observations, basal metabolism determinations, and various other procedures. When we study the individual microscopically and dissect him into his biological components, the cell becomes the unit of thought, rather than the individual. Lastly, we must stand back far enough so that we may look at this individual with a telescope and see him in relation to the total environment, social and physical, economic, biological, and historical.

The science of aging, or gerontology, includes all three of these facets or perspectives. Man is the core. Our motivation for study is concern with ourselves. . . .

The second division of gerontology is concerned with the biology of senescence. Here the cell is the unit of thought. Each of us is composed of approximately two billion cells. The world population, in contrast, consists of about two billion people. The third division of gerontology is concerned with the sociologic problems of the aging in this crowded world. . . .

Aging may be defined as the element of time in living. Aging is part of living. Aging begins with conception and terminates with death. It cannot be arrested unless we arrest life. There is no elixir of eternal youth, thank goodness! It would be dreadful to remain infants all our lives. We may retard aging or accelerate it, but we cannot arrest it while life goes on, because it is essentially an element of living. Living is a continuous process, variable in its rates. Aging slows as we grow older. This is one of the compensations for later years. Aging change is rapid in youth and even more rapid prenatally in the period between conception and birth.

Aging involves two simultaneous processes which operate continuously in spite of the fact that they are contradictory to one another. On the one hand growth or evolution occurs, on the other atrophy (which means shrinkage) or involution. These processes continue throughout life, though at varying rates. We can observe illustrations of atrophy even before the infant is born in the disappearance of the gill clefts which first develop and then atrophy in the early mammalian embryo. At the time of birth, when the child begins to breathe and get its oxygen from the lungs instead of from the mother's circulation, the atrophy of certain arterial structures is indistinguishable under the microscope from the involutionary changes which we see late in life. The atrophic process is the same in the newborn infant and in the senile grandparent. A very interesting phenomenon occurs in the placenta or afterbirth. It becomes atrophic or "old" when its functional life is near termination. At nine months of pregnancy, these exists an intimate proximity and interdependence in a very young baby, a middle-aged mother, and a senile placenta. Biologically adjacent and functioning together are three widely divergent biological ages. Here is an area of study which has by no means been explored adequately.

On the other hand, growth continues late in life. The hair continues to grow throughout life, and certain hairs grow more vigorously than ever. The eyebrows become shaggy, and often about the ears there is a growth of bristly hairs that were not there in middle age and youth. The whiskers become heavier, more brittle, and thicker. The lower jaw continues to grow throughout life, according to reports of several anthropologists. These students of anatomy, however, do not tell whether the rate of this growth in later years varies with the amount of wagging that the lower jaw has done during the lifetime. It is quite possible that such functional activity is a modifying factor, as we shall see later. I am not being facetious.

Cells are the ultimate units of life. What can we learn about the aging of cells? Here the biologist in search of information is blocked, because individual cells do not age. They grow to maturity, and then divide to create two young daughter cells. Individual cells simply do not age in the sense that an individual ages. With the exception of a very few cells in our central nervous system, the brain, and spinal cord, none of the cells of our bodies is as old as we are. They are being replaced constantly with young cells. You and I are constantly rubbing off our hides and developing new skin underneath. The same process, without the friction, occurs in all other structures. So we come up against an insurmountable difficulty in studying the aging of the individual cell, because the individual cell does not age.

The classical, epoch-making studies of Carrel and his associates with tissue cultures reveal precisely the same thing as we have just deduced from general biology. Carrel started growing a bit of chick embryo heart in a flask containing a nutrient medium in 1912. In 1946, thirty-four years later, descendants of these same cells were growing just as rapidly, just as vigorously, utterly unchanged in their appearance and characteristics, as the original culture started thirty-four years previously. This period is several times the known maximum life span of a chicken. Carrel concluded that cells themselves were essentially immortal when given an appropriate environment.

The limiting proviso is a fundamental clue to the mechanism of aging. Continuation of a culture of cells is possible only if the culture medium in which it grows is sterile and refreshed every forty-eight hours. If the medium is permitted to become depleted of necessary food elements and allowed to accumulate the toxic garbage of the living, growing cells, the tissue culture quickly degenerates and dies. The essence of senescence lies not in the cellular structure, but in the matrix fluid in which they live. This intercellular medium is often spoken of as the internal environment.

Perhaps some of you do not realize that we live in two environments— an external environment of social strife, stale air, tobacco smoke, grime, grit, wind, snow, competition, sunshine, love, and hate, and an internal environment which is extraordinarily stable. The internal environment varies very little chemically and very little physically. We are by no means healthy if our temperature varies more than a degree, or more than 1 per cent of the optimum. If the concentration of sugar in the blood rises above a certain level we are no longer biologically healthy. Or if the glucose content of the blood falls below a certain level we become ill. The same applies to the many other chemical elements included in the composition of the organism. There are many elaborate mechanisms for maintaining the constancy of this internal environment. If this internal environment is not maintained within a relatively narrow range, health is impaired. We may say that an optimum internal environment is synonymous with health; that an internal environment deviating from the desirable in some respects but still within tolerable limits, is equivalent to disease, but that any intolerable deviation of the internal environment leads to death. The constants, and by that I mean such factors as body temperature, pulse, blood pressure, chemical concentrations, and many other things which are relatively constant, are not actually changed by aging. These things are not absolutely constant, but vary within narrow limits. Normal body temperature is the same at eighty as it is at eight. Pulse rate varies relatively little with age under comparable conditions of rest. Of course, the child of eight is much more active and energetic than the individual of eighty, and thus reveals a more rapid pulse when active, partly because he is more active.

The concentration of sugar in the blood is the same at eight or eighty. Though there is no appreciable change in these constants, the ability to maintain equilibrium depreciates with aging. There is great diminution in tolerance for extremes. Older individuals cannot tolerate extremes of temperature. They become ill when they are cold. An annual trip to Florida and the desire to seek warmth in winter is an admission of senility.

Similarly, the elderly do not tolerate hot weather. Each summer in the twenty-five years of practice, I have seen anywhere from one to ten persons over seventy years of age collapse during a spell of hot weather. They seem to go all to pieces. Last week I saw a gentleman of eighty-four who, after several hot days, suddenly became too weak one morning to raise his head from his pillow. He has no recollection of a period of twenty-four hours. His collapse occurred because he did not compensate for the changed external environment by necessary dietary adjustments. All he needed was some salt. Two liters of saline solution were given into his vein, and in a few hours he wanted to get up and go home. You see, as we grow older we live by habit. He had not changed his habits. The hot weather made him sweat (in Washington we not only perspire, we sweat). Sweat is salty, but he drank only pure water and did not adjust to that necessity for an increased salt intake. His collapse was due purely to salt deficiency. Habit was the major cause of his difficulty. A child, whose dietary habits are not fixed by time, will usually demand salty food in hot weather. The older person responds to habit rather than makes adjustment to the environment.

The older person is less tolerant to starvation and to overeating. The ability to maintain a normal blood sugar concentration is lessened. Thus, it is frequently desirable for the aged to eat small quantities often, rather than to attempt to eat large amounts at longer intervals.

In the aged where the reaction to any stress is lessened, symptoms are less conspicuous. The symptoms of illness are not due to injury; they are due to the reactions of the body to the injury and in later life these re-actions are less violent. We may see a man of seventy walking around, admitting he does not feel very well, but not complaining very much, despite the fact he is suffering from an extensive lobar pneumonia. . . . The older person's symptoms are much less conspicuous. Perhaps it is a blessing that illness in later years is associated with less subjective distress, but it is also a curse, inasmuch as medical attention is postponed. Too often the institution of therapy is delayed until such time that only a miracle can be expected to accomplish a cure. Pain is our friend, more precious than that dearest chum who warns us about halitosis. There are fewer accidents where there are stoplights.

The rate of aging change is by no means fixed; it is extremely variable. . . .

The asymmetry of aging is extremely significant to you and to me as individuals, as well as to the physician. First of all, there is a variation in the rate of aging at different times in the life span. For example, at puberty and the climacteric there is an acceleration of change in the structures involved in reproduction, whereas other structures do not show such acceleration of change at that particular time. There is a great variation of physical versus mental, and especially emotional maturation. For example, I am sure all of you have had experiences with individuals with old hearts but young ideas. They are likely to get into trouble because of this asymmetry; they play tennis long after they should cease. Perhaps a greater problem than being old too young, is the problem of being too young when old. Biologic age is by no means synonymous with chronologic age. They are not at all the same. They may coincide, but such parallelism is largely coincidental.

We speak with pride of our freedom, and yet we are slaves to time; it is time to get up; it is time to shave; it is time to get breakfast; it is time to get a plane; it is time to come here to a lecture; it is time for a manuscript; it is time to pay taxes. We have forgotten there are other kinds of time than sun time and chronologic time—months, years, days, and hours.

Our ordinary clocks and calendars fail us completely as tools for the measurement of astronomical or geologic time.

There is such thing as biologic time, determined by the rate of living, which may be very rapid in one individual and very slow in another. Phylogenetic time is a subdivision of biologic time. There is also psychological time. To illustrate the variations in psychological time: any military aviator knows that ten seconds of combat are the equivalent of ten minutes in apparent duration and intensity of the experience. Everyone of you needs but to contrast an hour spent in a dentist's waiting room with an hour spent in courtship, to appreciate the variability of psychological time. Nevertheless, each interval is still an hour, as measured by that infernal mechanism, the clock. The rate of living at levels lower than the mental (living which goes on below the level of awareness) is similarly variable. The rate of living is affected by use, by disuse, or by abuse. We must remember that disuse is a form of abuse, as we shall see a little later.

Unfortunately, the great majority of us are biologically older than our years. I would like to reverse the proportions and say the majority of us are biologically younger than our years. But I cannot, and remain truthful. It is my clinical impression that the average individual of sixty years is physically nearer what he should be at seventy, because of unnecessary depreciation.

The biologic age of an individual should be the basic criterion for social adjustments related to age, such as when to grant the right of voting, marriage, retirement, and the assumption and removal of privileges and responsibilities. Is it not utterly ridiculous that a man sixty-four years and 364 days is perfectly competent to carry on the immense responsibilities of an important post, and the next day he is too old to carry them? Such arbitrary retirement rules simply do not make sense.

How are we going to measure biologic age? This is an extremely difficult question, because we have to measure various ages, both structural and functional, and to try to average the estimates. Further complicating the problem is the fact that the various functions and structures are of widely differing significance to our total efficiency. Should the thickness and color of the hair or the presence or absence of wrinkles be weighed the same as visual acuity or the reserve strength of the heart?

The measurement of biologic age becomes a very complex and interesting problem, closely paralleling the challenge involved in the measurement of health, because health and the depreciations of age are closely parallel problems. The definition of health in the dictionaries today is sadly inadequate. Knowing that most medical and college textbooks are at least ten years behind the times, and that dictionaries are at least twenty-five years behind the times, we must not anticipate a revision for perhaps another decade. The antiquated definition of health, as it still appears in authoritative tomes, is that health is that state of being existing in the absence of disease. A negative and utterly inadequate definition. To me, health is that state of being in which all the reserve capacities of the organism are at their maximum. It is an ideal state, an abstraction, and, like infinity, unattainable in its perfection, but approachable.

There can be no sharp line of division between health and disease if we consider disease a depreciation of health. Health is always relative. But we must remember that disease does not necessarily imply disaster. There is not an individual in this room who is free of disease in the sense of having some depreciation of health. I have two chronic, utterly incurable diseases—one an arthritis of the hip that makes me wax profane at times and that kept me out of the Army, and the other an absolutely incurable optimism. I am perfectly willing to admit these disorders for they are not unique. It were better if all of us were aware of our defects in health and modified our lives accordingly. The adult who brags about his "perfect health" is suffering hazardous delusions. As health is always relative, there is always room for improvement.

Before leaving the subject of the biology of senescence, I should like to make one more comment regarding the theories of what aging is. As elsewhere in science, there are two opposing theories. . . . The two schools of thought regarding the basic reasons for the depreciations of aging are: (1) we wear out and (2) we rust out. One assumes that age change results from misuse or use; the other, from disuse or lack of use. The actual evidence for these two opposing concepts is so nearly equal that we may say the choice between one idea or the other depends upon the personality of the chooser. The energetic and ambitious man who bounds out of bed in the morning with vigor and enthusiasm and yodels in the cold shower says, "To age is to rust out. If I keep going, I'll go farther." The indolent, easy-going, lazy sort of chap says, "To age is to wear out. If I take it easy, I'll last longer." The actual data are just about equal. It should be kept in mind, however, that disuse, or lack of use, should be considered a form of abuse or misuse. Thus, the two theories are not truly incompatible nor mutually exclusive. Both may be correct.

But how does this theory and basic science affect you and me as individuals? To my mind, geriatric medicine is by no means limited to the senile, the aged, the decrepit, and the infirm. If it were, I would have no particular interest in geriatric medicine. The senile are the end results of senescence. What is particularly interesting is how we become senile. This morning an attempt was made at defining just when the problems of the aged begin. In many respects, the most critical phase of aging occurs in the two decades from forty to sixty. It is in this period of senescence that the changes which will ultimately disable begin and when we can hope to accomplish something by preventive measures. At that time, we have the alternative of trying to prevent unnecessary depreciation or of attempting to patch up a wreck and a ruin later on. Furthermore, there are far more aging people than there are those already old. . . .

The changes that occur with aging start far earlier than their detectable manifestations. They are silent and insidious. The superficial things, like graying hair and wrinkles, are not important. Really, what difference does it make whether the dome be covered with thatch or it be gilded? What goes on underneath is what counts, is it not? The physical implications of normal aging of personal importance are several.

First and foremost is the fact that repair after injury is slowed. We may say that for each five years we have lived it takes us an extra day to repair after a given injury, such as a sore throat or a broken leg. Little Willie, who is five years old, having suffered a sore throat, has a normal temperature after one day. . . . Physicians sometimes find it difficult to persuade an older patient to take adequate time to convalesce, because grandpa feels that the office, or the university, will collapse and go to pieces if he does not get back promptly. It is important for the maintenance of his ego that he feel indispensable. Therefore, it is often necessary to compromise and accept six days for convalescence, one day for each ten years that grandpa has lived, instead of the more appropriate twelve days.

Second, I previously mentioned the lessened reactions to injury and inconspicuousness of symptoms. In consequence of this relative silence, illness is often neglected too long. Delay in diagnosis and in institution of treatment is a definite and serious handicap in the practice of geriatric medicine. Depreciations in health must be searched for by thorough medical study if they are to be discovered early enough to permit of fully effective therapy.

Third, there are lessened reserves for stresses which become apparent with aging. Tolerance for heat and cold, overeating and starvation, dehydration, and salt depletion is reduced. We must learn to use our heads rather than our brawn for defense. . . .

We have mentioned the relativity of health and the vagueness of the borderline between health and disease. Before closing, I feel obligated to bring to your attention briefly a few facts and ideas pertaining to disease in later years. There are no specific diseases of age. Practically any illness may occur at any age. But certain disorders increase in frequency after the peak of maturity. These disorders, while not limited to senescents, are nevertheless characteristically geriatric. These disorders, by reason of their frequency, their insidious onsets, slow but persistent progressiveness, and immense toll of lives, constitute the major problem of clinical medicine today. Of all deaths 66 per cent are now due to chronic illness, and most of these are included in the so-called degenerative disorders.

Included in this important group are several vascular problems, such as arteriosclerosis, high blood pressure, and heart disease. Arteriosclerosis has many consequences. It may involve vessels of the brain, predominantly, to cause the mental disorder arteriosclerotic dementia, or affect the heart, primarily, to produce coronary disease, or the pancreas where it induces diabetes mellitus. Also included in the disorders of later years are several metabolic disorders: diabetes mellitus, the male and female climacterics, gout, anemia, obesity, the arthritides, and many types of cancer. . . .

These disorders all have certain generic characteristics which are significant. First, their causation is characteristically endogenous. They arise from within, not from external factors. Typically, their causation is a series of superimposed insults, comparable to the various straws that ultimately broke the camel's back. It is significant that the straws, or insults, are not necessarily identical in any two instances. For example, high blood pressure may be due to entirely different factors in each of a dozen cases. No one will ever discover "the cause of" hypertension or of cancer, for there are always many accumulative factors, differing in different instances. Contrasting this clinical problem with those presented by smallpox, typhoid fever, or diphtheria, which are always due to specific and identical infecting organisms, reveals how vastly more complex are these chronic disorders of later years.

Second, the onsets or beginnings of these disorders are without symptoms. These are fifth column disorders that sneak up on us, silent saboteurs that do not ring a bell or wave a red flag and say, "Here we come."

Third, they are chronic, slowly progressive, and characterized by a truly diabolical persistence in their progression. They do not protect the individual by inducing immunity, but rather increase his vulnerability to other disorders. And last, there is observed infinitely more individual variation than in the disorders of youth.

What about the future? What can be done? . . .

The essential requirements for their prevention and/or early treatment are, first, that initiative and effort be contributed by the individual. We can give health to no one any more than we can give or buy true respect. Both have to be earned. Health is not a fundamental human right. It is a privilege, and, as a privilege, it entails the equivalent responsibility for its maintenance. Thus, the initiative and effort must be made on the part of the aging individual to maintain his own health. Herein lies the greatest obstacle to full application of existing knowledge. Advice which is not followed is useless. . . .

Whose responsibility is maintenance of health? It is yours and mine. Our greatest hope lies, I feel, in research and education. Medical research will be relatively futile, however, without the backing of broad public or lay education. First is the need to emphasize the importance of individual responsibility. Second, education is needed in how to use, rather than abuse, our endowment of healthy bodies in youth. Third, education should be directed toward preparation for senescence. It is truly extraordinary that though we all are in full agreement that youth must spend some of its time in preparing how to become an adult, it is assumed that preparation for senescence is unnecessary. The number of young adults who give thought to their own future is pitifully small. I was once told by Mr. James, then secretary of the Carnegie Teacher's Annuity and Life Insurance Association, which insures university professors, high-school teachers, and the like, that when they wrote to their policyholders: "Dear Professor So and So, You are due to retire in six months. How would you like your pension fund paid, and can we be of any assistance to you?" 75 per cent of their policyholders replied in this vein: "An exception is going to be made in my case. I have made no plans for retirement; I wouldn't know what to do if it was forced upon me." These replies came from people who are supposed to have foresight and who devote their lives to teaching. I think we should be ashamed of ourselves, and I say 'we' because for twenty years I taught medical students.

Finally, I should like to give you the thought that the longer men live, the more time there is to think; to think is to grow; and to grow is to live.

Mental Hygiene of Old Age

Moses M. Frohlich, M.D. (1901-   )

THE PSYCHOLOGICAL PROBLEMS OF OLD AGE usually are associated with the readjustments the person who is growing older has to make to the changes which commonly, or well-nigh inevitably, overtake him. . . . What I should like to do at present is to inquire into the emotional impact and the psychological meaning that readjustments to changed situations have for the aged. It is obvious that when anything disturbs the equilibrium of our adjustment we react in a manner more or less characteristic of our personality. We usually repeat our previously established methods of dealing with conflicts or problems. It is also obvious that the equilibrium of different people will be disturbed to different degrees, by the same changes in situation, and that this disturbance will depend on what the specific change means to the individual involved. In other words, the significance to an aging person of any change in his situation, and his mode of reaction to it, will be directly related to his previous history. His present adjustment is the resultant of his constitutional endowment and his physical and functional growth and development, of his past successes and failures, and of his previous modes of adapting his physical, emotional, and social needs to his inner and outer environmental situations.

The very marked individual variations merely emphasize the fact that the person growing older is still the same person, and that the traces of his infancy and childhood, adolescence and maturity, will, of course, be found in his later years. Though his reactions to the various changes in old age will be directly related to his previous life, we can make some successful attempts at generalizations. . . .

How is he apt to react to [aging]? A man who, throughout his life, has prided himself on his physical prowess and who has constantly, though not necessarily consciously, attempted to protect his bodily self will certainly react much more violently than one who had no strong fears in regard to his physical integrity. So will a woman to whom her beauty and appeal or physical health and capacity were of particular psychological importance. Men or women who have striven throughout their lives from childhood on to balance their feelings of inadequacy by success, will certainly be strongly affected by the realization of their failing capacities. People who have always felt insecure are also likely to have a marked situational reaction at this time. Those who have denied themselves various satisfactions because of feelings of guilt, or other fears, are now likely to become panicky and disturbed and may frantically seek to compensate themselves. Aging, and all it may imply to them, may be completely rejected by them, at least temporarily. They may attempt to deny the fact of their growing older, refuse to acknowledge any illnesses or give heed to any weaknesses. Not only that, they may over react, affecting manners and clothes of a much younger age, and attempting to achieve successes in their profession, in their social life, and particularly in the sexual sphere, in competition with much younger people. This sort of reaction is quite common. Mild anxiety is quite frequent too, but it may become very marked and show itself in sleeplessness, irritability, or in various fears, especially in regard to health or in regard to the future. Attempts may be made to alleviate these anxieties by excessive care or by almost ritual-like precautions. Depending on their previous modes of reaction, people may extrude the knowledge that they are growing older and their resentment of the younger generations which are making them aware of it, and attach their feelings to others about them. They become suspicious and even paranoid, feeling that they are persecuted and treated unfairly. There may be some truth in this at times, and they make the most of it. Finding satisfactions at their mature level blocked, they may turn to earlier, childish, or even infantile, methods of gaining pleasures. They may act and behave in a helpless, childish manner, unconsciously seeking a return to a more satisfying period of their lives. This may manifest itself in a milder form as an attempt to stop the progress of time by insisting that all things remain as they were, with intolerance for any change or for any new-fangled ideas and with an increased, rigid resistance to any new adaptations. These people may then collect trifles or even trash and store them as if they were something valuable. The realization of being older may be a catastrophe to some, before which they give up the fight and passively submit. They may become markedly depressed in the face of it, further deprecating themselves, being pessimistic, in fact, entirely hopeless about the future, and even committing suicide. Some of these reactions may be relatively mild and transitory. In others they may, however, assume the proportions of a psychosis when the person loses contact with reality to a very considerable extent, or they may become neurotic illnesses often superimposed on a diminished intellectual functioning as a result of some brain damage. These reactions may be temporary and usually are, especially if they occur in association with serious economic, social, or occupational changes, and if the previous adjustment of the person and his previous life satisfactions were adequate. In rarer instances, when the past and present conditions are unfavorable, they may be extremely persistent and even become permanently incapacitating, in spite of any treatment.

Of the changes outside of himself which the aging person has to face, the loss of his occupation is usually extremely disturbing. The loss of a job through discharge, or the loss of one's daily work through retirement, may be sudden and carries with it the implication of economic dependency, unemployability, etc., only too often. In a woman, the loss of her occupation is usually also associated with complete disruption of routine and generally with the need of a serious social readjustment since it is often the result of the death of her husband and the loss of her home. How important the mere routine of some activity may be, can be seen from the numerous instances of older people who find and maintain regular activities of some kind to substitute for the work they have lost. Minor chores around the house, walks to certain places in town, or meeting and inspecting the afternoon train each day assume a tremendous importance. It is as if this regularity itself were an insurance against all the dire but unknown danger which they feel threatening them. But the job itself has much more meaning than this. Our feeling of well-being is always dependent to some extent on how we judge ourselves and how others judge us on the basis of our accomplishments. We derive some of our feeling of well-being from our importance and the power we have, from the usefulness we feel, from the approval of others, as well as from the economic and social status which goes with our occupation. As we get older and the direct satisfactions of our physical, primarily sexual, drives lessen, we seem to depend much more on those things which heighten our self-esteem and which are often associated with our work. It is for this reason partly that older people are so insistent that respect be shown to them and so sensitive to any change which is likely to endanger their established position.

The reaction to the loss of a job will again depend on a great many factors in the person's previous development. It will also depend on how well he was prepared for and how much he had anticipated this particular change. If he was prepared for it, he may still resent it, become mildly anxious or depressed, but is likely to have something ready to substitute for his old work. It may be another, more suitable, job, or some hobby, or study or travel. His reaction and adjustment will also depend upon how much functional capacity he still retains and how much ability to change and to adapt himself to new situations remains with him. A baseball player who is old at forty is in an entirely different situation from that of a factory worker who is discharged from his job or retired at sixty or sixty-five. The baseball player has usually anticipated the end of his active playing days and has been able to prepare some plans for his retirement. He is still young and healthy enough to be able to adjust to some new occupation. The housewife who has lost the work in her home at the age of sixty-five will have fewer capacities for readjustment, especially if, as so often happens, she has withdrawn from social contacts, has limited her interests, and has devoted herself increasingly to her household as her years advanced. Our reactions to loss of job do depend to a very large extent on how rich our life has been before. The fewer satisfactions we had previously, the more disturbed we are likely to get. The fewer friends and interests and hobbies we have, the harder it will be to find a substitute for our jobs. The financial or economic status may make a considerable difference, especially in those people who have through their lives feared and combated an unconscious desire to be dependent and to be taken care of by others. Such people may become markedly disturbed by the prospect of having to succumb to this forbidden desire. Some people may finally give in completely and become excessively childlike, demanding of attention and solicitude now that dependency has become acceptable to them because of their old age.

To summarize, a person's reaction to the loss of his work will depend not only on his previous adjustment, most especially his need for self-esteem, but also on how suddenly this loss came upon him and on what interests and activities he can substitute for his work. During the critical period of readjustment, he will react, depending on his habitual modes of dealing with problems, with anxiety or depression, with irritability or ideas of persecution, with apathy, or at times with sickness. As you know, the reaction or response not infrequently is either a frank and obvious suicide or one which is less apparent but just as effective by means of a so-called accident, or a mysterious but marked and rapid deterioration of health. Luckily, most of the disturbances of readjustment are not only mild but also temporary.

With advancing years, social or interpersonal relations are apt to be changed by the loss of children, husband or wife, or of friends. The children grow up, become independent, move away, and the house becomes empty. This used to happen fairly early in people's lives, and the children did not go very far. The readjustment to it was then relatively easier. Now people marry later and children stay home longer, and both their occupations and their new locations are often much farther removed from the parents. The loss of children from the home is getting to be a problem of later years and therefore harder to cope with. When much effort and energy and interest have been concentrated on the children, the adjustment to their departure is also more difficult. Too frequently, children have special psychological meanings to their parents, which complicate matters. A mother may have transferred all of her affection from her husband to her children, or to some one child. She will resent and fight against any independent life of this offspring and strongly react to her abandonment by him. The father may attempt to retain his youth and to perpetuate himself and his power through his children and insist on their working with him to serve his interests. He will then become critical and bitter when they choose to do otherwise. These, and some other special types of reaction to the departure of the children from the household, are fortunately not too common.

The loss of a spouse at an advanced age, more commonly the loss of a husband, is likely to result in a marked psychological reaction. It often results in a serious economic change, the loss of a home, and brings forth the specter of a future in a dependent situation. It carries with it an implied threat of the nearness of our own end. Above all, it calls for a readjustment of one's emotional relationships to people. The surviving person must reinvest his feelings of tenderness and affection in someone else and must find other sources to supply his own needs for love and friendliness. At least for a while, life is likely to be empty, frightening, and depressing. People try to ignore or deny the loss of their spouse by retaining the house or the furniture as a symbol of their marriage. They continuously talk of their past life and of the departed husband or wife. We can forgive them if at times they exaggerate and forget some unpleasant difficulties of their past marital life. In their effort to regain an emotional relationship with someone, they may again turn to their children, other relatives, or even strangers, to shower them with solicitude, often interfering and unwelcome, and to demand from them attention with frequently annoying persistence. Their striving to find substitutes in friendships or in the care of children or grandchildren may never prove satisfactory, when it is tried, and their grief may persist. A mental or physical illness coupled with a lack of desire to live not too rarely ends the survivor's life before long.

The difficulties in readjustment after the loss of a spouse, the loss of a job, or the loss of health, are accentuated when our friends become fewer as we grow older. Our own increasing rigidity and insistence on regularity often limit our social contacts. Physical difficulties make the maintenance of friendship difficult. When we lose our jobs, we lose many social contacts. We or our friends are likely to move away and there are fewer and fewer old people around. If we have lost our homes, it is more difficult to entertain and more difficult to meet new friends to replace those who have gone. Younger generations crowd the older people, who are likely to develop a class consciousness and feel resentful toward the whole class of younger people by whom they feel themselves displaced. They become hostile and suspicious and withdraw more and more, becoming increasingly impoverished as far as external satisfactions are concerned and less able to make a readjustment. When economic situations permit it, old people tend to migrate to Florida or California. There the concentrations of old people are high, and this, perhaps even more than the climate, draws them to these places.

The loss of a home, because of economic circumstances or because of the physical or emotional incapacity of the older person to maintain himself independently, brings problems of its own. To live with one's children may be an excellent solution but often brings with it many emotional and psychological difficulties. The parent who attempts to deny his increasing age and his loss of power or independence may not only seek to resume his previous authoritative relationship to his children but may exaggerate it to the point of tyranny. He is made unhappy by any display of independence or difference of interests in his children. He will interfere with all activities and insist on special prerogatives and privileges as an older, wiser, and respected person. He may attempt to exact filial obedience to the point of complete subjugation. Old jealousies are revived and increased and the aged mother may compete with her children for the affection of her grandchildren, of the servants in the house, of the "in-laws," or even of the neighbors. Old hostilities are revived and aggravated on both sides, with the children who had felt themselves rejected or thwarted in their childhood, attempting unconsciously, or even consciously, to get revenge on their parents. In addition to the usual irritations, this may arouse guilt feelings in the children and disturb their emotional equilibrium. When the condition of the parent demands much care because of chronic illness or debility, the problems are likely to become so severe that, to prevent illness on the part of the children and serious emotional disturbances on the part of the grandchildren, other living arrangements must be considered. The struggle between the older parent and his children may resolve itself with the parent becoming submissive, withdrawn, and quite unhappy. The parent may become completely dependent, demanding attention to the point of developing illnesses and exaggerating pains and incapacities. Often this is the only satisfaction the parent gets in a situation in which he feels thwarted, and where his own personal interests and activities are markedly circumscribed by, probably, an unconsciously hostile oversolicitude of his children. What happens when an older mother or father comes to live with a married child, of course, again depends on his previous relationship with this child, on his previous adjustments, and on his present interests. Not only must his own welfare be considered, but also that of the rest of the family, most especially that of the youngsters growing up in the household. On the basis of the individual situation, or perhaps on the basis of a trial, it may prove that the best adjustment is permanent residence in the child's home, or that a transitory stay only is advisable there. Living with children will often succeed, but if it does not and if factors are present which cannot be changed, and which will doom the attempt to failure, then living in the home of a stranger or in a special institution for the aged should be resolutely advised and worked for. Wherever the aged one may live, he will fare much better if he has a room of his own. We know that prisoners of war were hopeless and apathetic when first captured and that their hopes and interests revived as soon as they could hang a picture of their own, or have a bunk or a little corner which was theirs. With all persons it is important, but much more so with the aged, that they have a place which they can keep in any kind of state they wish, where they can accumulate and hoard, within reason, the little symbols of their past power and their present security. Their own rooms represent to them psychologically much more than we are likely to think when we are younger.

Physical illness is to an older person a serious threat and a real threat.

Certain injuries, like a fracture of the neck or a femur, and certain incapacities, like those following a stroke or due to a heart disease, may require a great deal of care over a long period of time. These are serious risks but excessive limitation of the activities of an older person in order to avoid these risks to his physical health may be even more detrimental to him through their ill effect on his emotional health. No one can get much satisfaction from living in a cage lined with cotton batting. Even though it may entail some risks, an old person with a weak heart should not be kept strictly in bed nor completely inactive. Even in illness, some activities must be provided and some social contacts must be maintained. When, however, the illness becomes too great a burden on the household, too difficult to care for, hospitalization or care in a nursing home is the wisest thing.

As mentioned previously, older people may exaggerate their physical handicaps in order to gain, by this means, satisfaction through attention, solicitude, dependency, or even the expression of their hostilities. This must be treated, like other attention-gaining mechanisms, by friendly indifference and by attempts to supply other satisfactions. Should such treatment fail, it might again be wiser for the older person and healthier, both for him and the others, if he lived away from his family. He may complain and be bitter for a while, but it is likely that he will eventually develop new interests and satisfactions and become quite happy through at times still complaining.

I have discussed at some length the various psychological situations one is apt to encounter in older people. This review of some of their emotional problems may leave you with the unfortunate impression that all, or that most of the aged, have serious emotional disturbances. It is true that we all have to readjust in old age as our situations change, but we have to readjust through every change to which we are exposed by the vicissitudes of our lives. The stresses we encounter in old age are perhaps most comparable to the stresses in our adolescence, which is another period of emotional turbulence in which our adjustments are likely to be more strenuous even than in old age. Most of us get by adolescence and most of us are quite likely to keep our equilibrium within fair balance through the process of getting old. The point I want to reiterate is that the severity of our problems, our reactions to them, and our solutions of these problems, depend on our previous life. They are predominantly individual and to a large extent different in each person. Our adjustments are affected by external and internal factors, by cultural, economic, and social situations as well as by the inevitable fact that everything living is constantly aging and dying. Mental hygiene of old age is related to many things which require social or political action. Various educational measures or programs can be helpful in improving mental health of the aged, and social case work can help individual instances. The progress of physical medicine is likely to multiply though not necessarily increase the problems of old age. Many questions relating to the psychic functioning of old people are still unanswered. The practical present-day measures of mental health in old age are part and parcel of the mental hygiene of all ages. The adjustment of the aged is a direct continuation of his adjustment from infancy on. More immediately, our latest adjustment depends on the richness and the satisfaction we have achieved before we reach old age. It depends on how well we have matured and how well we have reaped the fruits of our maturity in our relations with our spouses, our children, and our friends. It depends on how well we have achieved emotional security, independence, and the satisfactions of various interests and activities which go with maturity. With better mental hygiene through our earlier life, the problems of old age will be minimized. The better our previous mental health, the more readily we will accept old age, the better we will be prepared for it, and the more easily we shall find pleasures in new things to substitute for those no longer available to us. The problems and difficulties of our later adjustment are largely continuations of our precarious adjustments in earlier years. Those of us who have lived fairly satisfactory lives need not have any fears or doubts about our old age. Our earlier satisfactions will be the foundation and the guarantee of our emotional and psychic well-being in later years.

On Freedom

Albert Einstein (1879-1955)

I KNOW THAT IT IS a hopeless undertaking to debate about fundamental value judgments. For instance if someone approves, as a goal, the extirpation of the human race from the earth, one cannot refute such a viewpoint on rational grounds. But if there is agreement on certain goals and values, one can argue rationally about the means by which these objectives may be attained. Let us, then, indicate two goals which may well be agreed upon by nearly all who read these lines.

1. Those instrumental goods which should serve to maintain the life and health of all human beings should be produced by the least possible labor of all.

2. The satisfaction of physical needs is indeed the indispensable precondition of a satisfactory existence, but in itself it is not enough. In order

to be content men must also have the possibility of developing their intellectual and artistic powers to whatever extent accords with their personal characteristics and abilities.

The first of these two goals requires the promotion of all knowledge relating to the laws of nature and the laws of social processes, that is, the promotion of all scientific endeavor. For scientific endeavor is a natural whole, the parts of which mutually support one another in a way which to be sure, no one can anticipate. However, the progress of science presupposes the possibility of unrestricted communication of all results and judgments—freedom of expression and instruction in all realms of intellectual endeavor. By freedom I understand social conditions of such a kind that the expression of opinions and assertions about general and particular matters of knowledge will not involve dangers or serious disadvantages for him who expresses them. This freedom of communication is indispensable for the development and extension of scientific knowledge, a consideration of much practical import. In the first instance it must be guaranteed by law. But laws alone cannot secure freedom of expression; in order that every man may present his views without penalty there must be a spirit of tolerance in the entire population. Such an ideal of external liberty can never be fully attained but must be sought unremittingly if scientific thought, and philosophical and creative thinking in general, are to be advanced as far as possible.

If the second goal, that is, the possibility of the spiritual development of all individuals, is to be secured, a second kind of outward freedom is necessary. Man should not have to work for the achievement of the necessities of life to such an extent that he has neither time nor strength for personal activities. Without this second kind of outward liberty, freedom of expression is useless for him. Advances in technology would provide the possibility of this kind of freedom if the problem of a reasonable division of labor were solved.

The development of science and of the creative activities of the spirit in general requires still another kind of freedom, which may be characterized as inward freedom. It is this freedom of the spirit which consists in the independence of thought from the restrictions of authoritarian and social prejudices as well as from unphilosophical routinizing and habit in general. This inward freedom is an infrequent gift of nature and a worthy objective for the individual. Yet the community can do much to further this achievement, too, at least by not interfering with its development. Thus schools may interfere with the development of inward freedom through authoritarian influences and through imposing on young people excessive spiritual burdens; on the other hand schools may favor such freedom by encouraging independent thought. Only if outward and inner freedom are constantly and consciously pursued is there a possibility of spiritual development and perfection and thus of improving man's outward and inner life.

Suggestions for Further Reading

The Affluent Society, by John K. Galbraith. Boston: Houghton, Mifflin Company. 1958.

> An economist takes a deep look at our economy of abundance and urges that it is time to shift more of our attention from the production of goods to the increase of services which will enable the individual to lead a happier, healthier, fuller life.

Longer Life, by George Soule. New York: The Viking Press, 1958.

> A leading economist discusses the health, income, employment, and social status of older people and concludes that present social policies are detrimental to the wellbeing of both older people and society.

The Older Population of the United States: The Characteristics and Contributions of the Nation's Older People, by Henry S. Sheldon with concluding chapters by Clark Tibbitts. New York: John Wiley and Sons, 1958.

> A comprehensive and scientific analysis of the older population of the United States which brings into question some of our popular notions and helps to set the record straight on why there are more older people, what occupations are favorable to long employment, why workers retire, levels of income, and so on.

Professor Leo W. Simmons (born in 1897 at Kingston, North Carolina) is in the Department of Sociology at Columbia University, New York City. Professor Simmons has collected voluminous data on the aging and aged in pre-industrial and modern societies, much of which he has used in writing The Role of the Aged in Primitive Societies *(1945) and a number of articles on aging in other cultures and in our own. He has also written* Sun Chief: The Autobiography of a Hopi Indian *(1942) and* Social Science in Medicine *(1954). Professor Simmons follows the 2000-year-old prescription of Cicero and spends much of his leisure time in farming.*

". . . One could probably demonstrate beyond all possibility of reasonable doubt that the relative position of the aged reaches its maximum in the most highly developed rural civilizations. This is to say that, when the rural mode of existence rules supreme, the lot of the aged is probably far superior to what it is in pre-rural (primitive) groups, on the one hand, or in the more highly industrialized civilizations, on the other."

—T. LYNN SMITH

"The Aged in Rural Society." Quoted by permission from *The Aged and Society.* Industrial Relations Research Association, 1950.

2

Aging in
Pre-industrial Cultures

LEO W. SIMMONS

A SUCCESSFUL LATER LIFE IS something to be attained by planning and effort; it is not as a rule a free gift. Whenever it is attained, it comes largely through the efforts of older people themselves to safeguard and fulfill their own interests within the range of opportunities and restrictions of their particular environment. It is a two-way relationship that involves the initiative of the individual and the character of the society in which he lives. This has been true, generally speaking, throughout history.

Interests in Aging

In general terms, the purposes which older people seem to share and cherish everywhere are roughly as follows:

1. To live as long as possible, at least until life's satisfactions are

overbalanced by its difficulties, or until the advantage of death outweighs the burden of life.

2. To get more "rest," or a release from the compulsion of weari-some exertion at humdrum tasks, and protection from too great exposure to physical hazards, with a view to safeguarding and conserving waning physical energies.

3. To maintain nevertheless active participation in personal and group affairs, either as an actor or manager.

4. To safeguard and strengthen, if possible, acquired rights, and the authority and the prestige that go with them.

5. The right to withdraw from life, should necessity require it, to an honorable and comfortable position with the prospect of a satisfactory future.

But the fact is that the way in which aging has been viewed and experienced in actuality has varied widely. It appears that old age has begun early or late in life, and that it may last a short or a long time. Its coming has been resented and resisted, or welcomed and treasured. It has been regarded as a period of fruitful activity, and a time of idleness and uselessness. It has brought promotion to a position commanding homage; it has brought demotion and degra-dation. It has passed quickly, interestingly, and zestfully; and it has dragged itself out in dull boredom. In one society individuals may look forward to a full and ripe old age; in another, to next to none at all. From place to place and time to time, aging has been re-garded, on the one hand, as a curse; on the other, as a challenge and potential blessing. But most people actually experience old age on some middle ground.

Social and Cultural Determinants

Nature in the raw has never been particularly kind to old age. Everyone has to get older and die. It is the social and cultural factors that have been central in determining the types of adjustment avail-able to those who escape early death.

The mastery of fire is an example of how the material culture early benefited the aged. When fire was brought under control and used as a defense against the climate and wild animals, applied to the preparation of food and the manufacture of implements, and made a stabilizing factor in family life, a new day dawned for the older people. Indeed, fire was soon so closely associated with benefit to the old that, even when the necessity arose of abandoning an old and enfeebled individual—as it very often did in early times—it became widely the custom to leave with the victim some food, a fire, and some fuel, a final compassionate gesture.

But it is plain that life for the aged has been barely possible and really quite intolerable without a sustaining social order, no matter what the stage of material evolution. Old age security has depended to a marked degree upon satisfactory reciprocal relations between the generations. Let us therefore examine such relationships within the broadest range of social and cultural differences and note what effects they have had on older people.

Although we have much more information about primitive and contemporary societies than is available on the middle span of history, the gap may be bridged with some materials from the agrarian and handicraft economies of the Middle Ages and those which still survive in backward rural regions today.

Some generalizations may be attempted even before detailed comparisons are made. The greatest contrast in the social role of older people is between primitive and modern Western societies. The agrarian economies represent the transition between these extremes. Under primitive conditions, older people generally gained in influence and security with the gradual establishment of permanent residence, the achievement of a stable food supply, the rise of agriculture and grazing, and the development of the closely-knit family. Their security was further enhanced by the growth of magical and religious practices and by the accumulation of general knowledge and technical skills. Under agrarian economies, it was usual to provide for a gradual accumulation of prerogatives as one aged; and the assertion of them was a protection in old age. But it is clear that, with the evolution and elaboration of social systems, a gain at one point was often counter-balanced by a loss at another.

It will be instructive, therefore, to follow some of the more important prerogatives of age through the shifting currents of historical and contemporary societies. With this in mind, the following topics will be glanced at: employment of older people; their property rights; their family privileges; and their opportunities for leadership and prestige.

Influence and Security Through Employment

Employment has long been regarded as a primary source of influence, almost regardless of age or changes in the social milieu. Opportunities for participation through work, however, have varied greatly from society to society, and especially for aging persons. It has been found that, in the early and very rudimentary forms of social life, the aged had relatively few and uncertain opportunities for major productive efforts. Under the pressure of necessity, older persons did struggle on at certain tasks as long as they could and, not infrequently, until they died in their tracks. But with the tribe's meager reserves, its very crude tools, and its undeveloped techniques, the frailties of age usually resulted in early death.

Opportunities for the old to work were relatively few among tribes that wandered to gather their food. Such opportunities were greater among hunters and fishers, and still greater among those who kept herds of animals. But the greatest chance for prolonged and useful employment was among the cultivators of the soil. Here the old shifted so gradually to lighter and lighter tasks that they rarely lacked, into old age, fruitful occupation, seldom suffered abrupt retirement, and usually were able to turn their hands to useful undertakings until very near the end of their days.

In the agrarian and handicraft economies of the Middle Ages, aging persons were afforded ample opportunity for useful employment. Indeed, agriculture and household handicrafts have characteristically insured individuals with even modest reserves of energy and skill fairly certain security against enforced idleness. The general situation can be illustrated by reference to contemporary Ireland, often described as an old person's country. Agrarian life there tends to set the norm of life for the whole country, certainly with respect to the status and opportunity of the old. On the farms gainfully employed men over seventy are reported to be one in fourteen, as contrasted with one in fifty-six for general town occupations, and one in seventy-five in the professions.[1]

It is among farm holders that opportunities for employment reach

---

[1] C. M. Arensberg and S. T. Kimball, *Family and Community in Ireland*, p. 161. Cambridge: Harvard University Press, 1940.

furthest into later life. It is, also, among the small farm owners that the greatest proportion of aged survive and remain employed. "On the small farm, then, the old people do not retire." [2]

The Irish countryside provides probably the highest life expectancy in the world. Many causes have been advanced to account for this, but our authors' theory is that "they live long because they have much to live for. In their own sphere of life, they are honored. They have power." Neighbors described an old man: "He is a saint, and there isn't a thought against anyone in him. . . . He and Roche (a neighbor) are two level-headed farmers, and they have met every sort of trouble. If you are in doubt about any farm advice, you can go to them and they will give you as good advice as you can get, because both of them have been successful farmers. It would pay a young man to listen to them." [3]

The self-employment of agrarian systems has probably been the most secure occupational status that society at large has yet provided for the majority of the aged. Traditional agrarian life preserves more of the assets of age than any other economy. But our contemporary large-scale and mechanized farming, under which the vast majority of workers have become wage employees, subjects its workers to much the same occupational hazards as factories.

Older people who are able to continue in some kind of regular work, or even with odd jobs, or hobbies, are better adjusted than those who do not or cannot. One observer has put it: "If old people are to be happy and well-adjusted, they must be busy. . . . When aged people get to the place where they can no longer prove their worth, or when they are deprived of their work, they become discontented and unhappy. Thus it would seem that, if a society is to deprive its aged citizenry of work at a certain time, it must go further than just offering financial assistance. It must provide a program which will keep the aged content by enabling them to feel that they still have a useful place in society." [4] The essential thing is that the older person *fit into society;* it is not enough that he be

---

[2] *Ibid.*, pp. 163-164.
[3] *Ibid.*, pp. 167-168.
[4] J. T. Landis, "Social-Psychological Factors in Aging," *Social Forces,* Vol. 20, No. 4, 1942, p. 470.

merely "taken care of." There may be a real danger, however, in coddling, protecting, and humoring any age group without providing opportunity for the individuals to function as normal, self-reliant people.

A person who has gone in for amateur gardening, carpentry, or even stamp collecting, working even at an old man's pace, has found incentive to show what he can do and often surprises both himself and others, both by accomplishment and in terms of personal satisfaction. It is an old saying that "the only thing that matters is that one have a passion for something." Frequently a very simple pastime is sufficient, even for those who have labored at great undertakings when younger.

Property Rights

A method of prolonged and effective participation in life is the exercise of rights and privileges won over a lifetime. A long life affords an opportunity to establish them securely, and they then can be used like arms—to reach out and hold onto life's affairs. Property ownership is an excellent example. It is among the most flexible, impersonal, and effective means of influencing others with a minimum of physical effort. Where such rights are firmly fixed, they generally enable the long-lived to profit from them.

With a backlog of such rights, the holder is in a favorable position to influence others along lines of his, and probably their, interests, long after he is too enfeebled to accomplish much on his own. It is almost a certainty that wherever these rights are well-developed in society, there is a marked difference between growing old with property and growing old without it.

It would appear that property rights, as an assurance of influence and security for the aging, had a very simple beginning and have increased in importance with the growth of more complex social systems. Of course property holding is much influenced by the way in which property is distributed among individuals in a society. Too great concentration of property in a few hands leaves the many without the opportunity to secure the benefits of owning property. If concentration of property ownership is carried too far, large numbers of old people will become very dependent in an otherwise rich society. This situation can be successfully met only through an adequate system of income redistribution, as under an efficient social-security system.

Status and Security in the Family

In primitive and agricultural societies, another way in which the aging may exercise their rights is in family relationshps. Within the bonds of kith and kin, the obligations of youth to age are so nearly universal that they cut across cultural differences and transcend historical eras. Not infrequently aging persons use such ties to very great advantage, finding in them not only support but also opportunities for participation in on-going life that reach far into senility and even beyond death, by way of a will. It is quite evident, therefore, that aging individuals must endeavor to fit themselves effectively into these family relationships; and it is equally clear that such opportunities should be sustained by social approval and perhaps coercives of a legal kind.

A relationship of special interest is the close association of the very old with the very young. Frequently they are left together while the able-bodied members of the family sally forth to secure the family "living." The older people protect and often instruct the children, while the children serve the old as "eyes, ears, hands, and feet." In a sense, the aging thus recover their youth, while finding a useful occupation for the older years; and the children are likely to benefit from their wisdom and discipline.

The position of the patriarch in Roman society illustrates the ultimate expression of the authority of the old. As Cicero put it: "Appius being, beside his extreme old age, also blind, ruled and kept in awe his four tall sons, five daughters, his family, and household (which was great), and extended the patronage of his suppliant clients. For he had his mind bent like a bow, and never shrunk from his years, neither suffered he old age to have the victory over him. He reserved and kept his authority over all them that were under his charge, and his family was ready at his beck and commandment; his servants feared him, his children honoured and revered him, and all men entirely loved him. In his household the customs of his noble pedigree and ancestors, and the discipline of his country, took place effectually. For herein is old age honest and honourable, in defending and maintaining itself, in retaining and keeping its authority, in saving itself free from bondage and servitude, and in exercising rule and authority over them that are under his charge, even until the last hours of death." [5]

Under such a system the collective resources of kith and kin have backed up the individual, particularly when he, or occasionally she, has occupied a position of leadership and authority. Even in senescence, when younger relatives have taken over the active responsibilities, the elders hold their place in the household, "entertaining and instructing the grandchildren, helping with the work around the house, watching a baby, mending broken tools, and, if nothing more, giving their children a great sense of responsibility in watching over the health of their aged parents, humoring them even at the expense of conflict with other family members." [6] It is such family structures, with their entrenched "power rights of parents," that have characterized the social systems of many different agrarian civilizations. They flourished in the Middle Ages, in China, Japan, ancient Greece, Rome; and they survive to some degree in isolated rural areas today, remnants of a world now largely vanished.

Describing the patriarchal family of the nineteenth century, Floyd Dell wrote: "The old parents, finding ample means of subsistence in the nature of their locality, are able to gather around them four generations of their own blood. The father of the family, whose power is justified by his long experience, possessed the necessary ascendency to hold both youth and ripe age in submission to the Decalogue and to custom." [7] Thus was built up a solid concept of the responsibility of children for their parents. Tradition required that the parents remain with their children, or that the children provide for their parents in homes of their own.

Intergenerational responsibility was the keynote of the family, and it embraced all age groups, the waxing and the waning alike. Such a family system guaranteed probably the greatest sense of security that aging persons have yet known. Mr. Tibbitts has indicated what has happened to it in recent times.

---

[5] Cicero. *De Senectute, De Amicitia, De Divinatione,* translated by W. A. Falconer, pp. 104-105. London: Wm. Heinemann, 1928.
[6] Landis, "Social-Psychological Factors," p. 465.
[7] Floyd Dell, *Love in the Machine Age,* pp. 18, 45. New York: Farrar, 1930.

Other Avenues of Influence

The "crowning glory of old age," according to Cicero, is its "influence." In earlier cultures, both primitive and agrarian, prestige and power were found in chieftainships, official councils, regulative organizations, clubs, and secret societies. These and similar organizations provided effective positions of influence for enterprising older people, particularly those who had already demonstrated competence and responsibility in the heyday of life.

Older people could maintain high levels of prestige, particularly in regard to ranges of knowledge, political functions, and magical and religious rites. Qualifications and vested interests in positions in these areas gave them opportunity to prolong their control over a wide area of affairs. They were able to discipline, supervise, instruct, and counsel. They were in a position officially to launch undertakings critical to the well-being of the community, such as wars, or truces after wars; and in emergencies they were called upon to mediate between their fellow men and the supernatural powers which were believed to bring good luck or misfortune. The aging—particularly the gifted aging—were thus in frequent demand for treating diseases, exorcising evil spirits, divining the future, controlling the weather, and safeguarding the community in dangerous or delicate situations. They were the expected officiators at ceremonies marking birth, initiation, death, and burial.

Since relatively few persons then managed to survive past their prime, those who did usually possessed wide experience, were at least imputed seasoned judgment, often had fertile memories, and possessed "mysterious powers" acquired by virtue of their long lives. They were generally considered to be important, even indispensable, to their groups. They were rich repositories of the facts and wisdom of life; in them the past survived as in a living record; from them came the prescriptions for success upon which people relied and by which they tried to live.

In primitive and agrarian societies it was standard practice for younger people to turn to their elders for guidance and support; and the older people, whose lives had given them experience and, presumably, wisdom, knew it was wise to give freely of themselves, for thereby they wielded great influence. Indeed, because few persons in these societies reached any great age, those who did had an enhanced value to their groups. Modern libraries and other store-houses of accumulated knowledge, and rapid means of communication, make it difficult for us fully to appreciate the nature of the pervasive influence of the old in earlier cultures.

Implications for Modern Society

Human beings met and solved the problems of a fruitful and satisfying old age long before there was the opportunity for many to grow old. Modern civilization, as we have learned, promises longer life to more and more people; but the earlier and rewarding adaptations, with which we have been concerned here, have been disrupted and discarded to a surprising degree.

Perhaps the most important lesson that can come to us out of the earlier cultures is that *successful aging rests upon the capacity and opportunity for individuals to fit into the social framework of their own societies in a way that will insure security and influence.* The modern world is challenged to rediscover secrets long ago learned and long ago lost. We need new adaptations, designed to fit a radically different society from those we have here discussed, which will draw from our aging people, naturally and inevitably, the creative contributions which ripe old age makes possible.

Time Out for Reflection

Is *respect* for older people "natural" in the young, and the lack of it "unnatural"? Or are these attitudes determined by the structure and manners of particular societies? How?

Do you think older people have to *earn* the respect of the young? Can the young understand what it is in the elders that deserves respect?

The security and influence of older people appears to be at its highest in agricultural societies. Is this because of the continuity of the land-based family? Is the lack of this in our own society making things harder for the old? What could take its place: social security? If you don't think so, why not?

In these land-based cultures, the old could wisely advise the young because things did not change rapidly. Is the pace of change in our time making old people obsolete? What things that they have learned do *not* change? How can they communicate these?

Consider for a moment (a) your own family, (b) your own community. What functions do the old people have? What ones do they want? What ones are they offered? What, in short, is it assumed they are "good for"?

READINGS

CHAPTER 2

Youth, Age, and
The Prime of Life

Aristotle (384-322 B.C.)

LET US NOW CONSIDER the various types of human character, in relation to the emotions and moral qualities, showing how they correspond to our various ages and fortunes. By emotions I mean anger, desire, and the like. . . . By moral qualities I mean virtues and vices . . . as well as the various things that various types of men tend to will and to do. By ages I mean youth, the prime of life, and old age. By fortune I mean birth, wealth, power, and their opposites—in fact, good fortune and ill fortune.

To begin with the Youthful type of character. Young men have strong passions, and tend to gratify them indiscriminately. Of the bodily desires, it is the sexual by which they are most swayed and in which they show absence of self-control. They are changeable and fickle in their desires, which are violent while they last, but quickly over: their impulses are keen but not deep-rooted, and are like sick people's attacks of hunger and thirst. They are hot-tempered and quick-tempered, and apt to give way to their anger; bad temper often gets the better of them, for owing to their love of honour they cannot bear being slighted, and are indignant if they imagine themselves unfairly treated. While they love honour, they love victory still more; for youth is eager for superiority over others, and victory is one form of this. They love both more than they love money, which indeed they love very little, not having yet learnt what it means to be without it. . . . They look at the good side rather than the bad, not having yet witnessed many instances of wickedness. They trust others readily, because they have not yet often been cheated. They are sanguine; nature warms their blood as though with excess of wine; and besides that, they have as yet met with few disappointments. Their lives are mainly spent not in memory but in expectation; for expectation refers to the future, memory to the past, and youth has a long future before it and a short past behind it: on the first day of one's life one has nothing at all to remember, and can only look forward. They are easily cheated, owing to the sanguine disposition just mentioned. Their hot tempers and hopeful dispositions make them more courageous than older men are; the hot temper prevents fear, and the hopeful disposition creates confidence; we cannot feel fear so long as we are feeling angry, and any expectation of good makes us confident. They are shy, accepting the rules of society in which they have been trained, and not yet believing in any other standard of honour. They have exalted notions, because they have not yet been humbled by life or learnt its necessary limitations; moreover, their hopeful disposition makes them think themselves equal to great things—and that means having exalted notions. They would always rather do noble deeds than useful ones: their lives are regulated more by moral feeling than by reasoning; and whereas reasoning leads us to choose what is useful, moral goodness leads us to choose what is noble. They are fonder of their friends, intimates, and companions than older men are, because they like spending their days in the company of others, and have not yet come to value either their friends or anything else by their usefulness to themselves. All their mistakes are in the direction of doing things excessively and vehemently. They disobey Chilon's precept . . . '(do) nothing in excess,' 'don't overdo anything,' by overdoing everything; they love too much and hate too much, and the same with everything else. They think they know everything, and are always quite sure about it; this, in fact, is why they overdo everything. If they do wrong to others, it is because they mean to insult them, not to do them actual harm. They are ready to pity others, because they think every one an honest man, or anyhow better than he is: they judge their neighbour by their own harmless natures, and so cannot think he deserves to be treated in that way. They are fond of fun and therefore witty, wit being well-bred insolence.

Such, then, is the character of the Young. The character of Elderly Men—men who are past their prime—may be said to be formed for the most part of elements that are the contrary of all these. They have lived many years; they have often been taken in, and often made mistakes; and life on the whole is a bad business. The result is that they are sure about nothing and *under-do* everything. They 'think,' but they never 'know'; and because of their hesitation they always add a 'possibly' or a 'perhaps,' putting everything this way and nothing positively. They are cynical; that is, they tend to put the worse construction on everything. Further, their experience makes them distrustful and therefore suspicious of evil. Consequently they neither love warmly nor hate bitterly, but following the hint of Bias they love as though they will some day hate and hate as though they will some day love. They are small-minded, because they have been humbled by life; their desires are set upon nothing more exalted or unusual than what will help them to keep alive. They are not generous, because money is one of the things they must have, and at the same time their experience has taught them how hard it is to get and how easy to lose. They are cowardly, and are always anticipating danger; unlike that of the young, who are warm-blooded, their temperament is chilly; old age has paved the way for cowardice; fear is, in fact, a form of chill. They love life; and all the more when their last day has come, because the object of all desire is something we have not got, and also because we desire most strongly that which we need most urgently. They are too fond of themselves; this is one form that small-mindedness takes. Because of this, they guide their lives too much by considerations of what is useful and too little by what is noble—for the useful is what is good for oneself, and the noble what is good absolutely. They are not shy, but shameless rather; caring less for what is noble than for what is useful, they feel contempt for what people may think of them. They lack confidence in the future; partly through experience—for most things go wrong, or anyhow turn out worse than one expects; and partly because of their cowardice. They live by memory rather than by hope; for what is left to them of life is but little as compared with the long past; and hope is of the future, memory of the past. This, again, is the cause of their loquacity; they are continually talking of the past, because they enjoy remembering it. Their fits of anger are sudden but feeble. Their sensual passions have either altogether gone or have lost their vigour; consequently they do not feel their passions much, and their actions are inspired less by what they do feel than by the love of gain. Hence men at this time of life are often supposed to have a self-controlled character; the fact is that their passions have slackened, and they are slaves to the love of gain. They guide their lives by reasoning more than by moral feeling; reasoning being directed to utility and moral feeling to moral goodness. If they wrong others, they mean to injure them, not to insult them. Old men may feel pity, as well as young men, but not for the same reason. Young men feel it out of kindness; old men out of weakness, imagining that anything that befalls any one else might easily happen to them . . . is a thought that excites pity. Hence they are querulous, and not disposed to jesting or laughter—the love of laughter being the very opposite of querulousness. . . .

As for Men in their Prime, clearly we shall find that they have a character between that of the young and that of the old, free from the extremes of either. They have neither that excess of confidence which amounts to rashness, nor too much timidity, but the right amount of each. They neither trust everybody nor distrust everybody, but judge people correctly. Their lives will be guided not by the sole consideration either of what is noble or of what is useful, but by both; neither by parsimony nor by prodigality, but by what is fit and proper. So, too, in regard to anger and desire; they will be brave as well as temperate, and temperate as well as brave; these virtues are divided between the young and the old; the young are brave but intemperate, the old temperate but cowardly. To put it generally, all the valuable qualities that youth and age divide between them are united in the prime of life, while all their excesses or defects are replaced by moderation and fitness. The body is in its prime from thirty to five-and-thirty; the mind about forty-nine.

Guardians of the Republic

Plato (427?-347 B.C.)

THERE CAN BE NO DOUBT that the elder must rule the younger.

Clearly.

And that the best of these must rule.

That is also clear.

Now, are not the best husbandmen those who are most devoted to husbandry?

Yes.

And as we are to have the best of guardians for our city, must they not be those who have most the character of guardians?

Yes.

And to this end they ought to be wise and efficient, and to have a special care of the State?

True.

And a man will be most likely to care about that which he loves?

To be sure.

And he will be most likely to love that which he regards as having the same interest with himself, and that of which the good or evil fortune is supposed by him at any time most to affect his own?

Very true, he replied.

Then there must be a selection. Let us note among the guardians those who in their whole life show the greatest eagerness to do what is for the good of their country, and the greatest repugnance to do what is against her interests.

Those are the right men.

And they will have to be watched at every age, in order that we may see whether they preserve their resolution, and never, under the influence either of force or enchantment, forget or cast off their sense of duty to the State.

And he who at every age, as boy and youth and in mature life, has come out of the trial victorious and pure, shall be appointed a ruler and guardian of the State; he shall be honoured in life and death, and shall receive sepulture and other memorials of honour, the greatest that we have to give. But him who fails, we must reject. I am inclined to think that this is the sort of way in which our rulers and guardians should be chosen and appointed. I speak generally, and not with any pretension to exactness.

And, speaking generally, I agree with you, he said.

And perhaps the word 'guardian' in the fullest sense ought to be applied to this higher class only who preserve us against foreign enemies and maintain peace among our citizens at home, that the one may not have the will, or the others the power, to harm us. The young men whom we before called guardians may be more properly designated auxiliaries and supporters of the principles of the rulers.

De Senectute

Cicero (106-43 B.C.)

And if, Titus, I somehow aid, your heart somehow relieve
Of the care that carps, the sting that rankles,
What my reward?

I MAY FITLY ADDRESS YOU, my dear Atticus. . . . My present purpose is to dedicate to you an essay on old age. It is my desire to lighten the burden impending or at any rate advancing on us both; though in your case I am very sure that you support it and will support it with calm and philosophic temper. Upon resolving to write on this theme I thought of you as the proper recipient of a gift which might profit us both alike.

To me, at any rate, the composition of this book has been so delightful that it has not only wiped away all the annoyance of old age but has rendered it easy and agreeable. Never can philosophy be sufficiently praised; the man who hearkens to its precepts is enabled to pass every season of life free from worry.

But on such topics I have said much and shall often say more; this book which I send you is on old age. I have put the whole discourse not, as Aristo of Ceos did, in the mouth of Tithonus—a mere fable would not carry conviction—but in that of Marcus Cato when he was an old man, to give it greater weight. I represent Laelius and Scipio at his house expressing surprise at his bearing his years so well, and Cato responding to them. If he shall appear to argue more learnedly than he himself was wont to do in his books, ascribe it to Greek literature, of which it is known that he became an eager student in his later years. But why need I say more? Cato's own conversation will unfold my sentiments on old age.

scipio. Time and again, in conversation with Laelius here, I have marveled, Cato, at the eminent, nay, perfect, wisdom displayed by you indeed at all points, but above all because I have observed that old age never seemed a burden to you, whereas most old men find it so irksome that they declare they support a load heavier than Etna. cato. It is no very difficult feat that arouses your admiration, Scipio and Laelius. Men who have no inner resources for a good and happy life find every age burdensome; those who look for all happiness from within can think nothing evil which the laws of nature entail. Old age is first in that category; all men wish to attain it, and yet grumble when they have done so—so inconsistent and perverse is folly. They say it steals upon them faster than they expected. In the first place, who compelled them to calculate wrong? Does old age steal upon youth more quickly than youth upon boyhood? Would old age be less irksome if they were in their 800th rather than in their 80th year? However long the past, when it had gone it could never solace or soothe a foolish old age. If then you are accustomed to admire my wisdom—and would it were worthy of your good opinion and of my surname Sapiens—I am wise in that I follow that good guide nature; it is not likely, when she has written the rest of the play well, that she should, like a lazy playwright, skimp the last act. There had to be an ending, just as fruits and crops come in the course of time to a period of fall and decay. No wise man will resent this. What is warring against the gods, as the giants did, other than fighting against nature? laelius. And yet, Cato, you will oblige us greatly (I venture to speak for Scipio as for myself) if, since we all hope or at least wish to become old men—you would allow us to learn from you in good time the principles by which we may most easily support the weight of increasing years. CATO. I shall certainly do so, Laelius, especially if, as you say, you both find it agreeable. LAELIUS. We do wish, Cato, if it is no trouble to you, to see what sort of place you have reached after the long journey upon which we too must embark.

CATO. I will do my best, Laelius. I have often listened to the complaints of old men—like consorts with like, as the old proverb has it— men like Gaius Salinator and Spurius Albinus, consulars and virtually my contemporaries, who lamented that they had lost the pleasures of the senses, without which life is a cipher, and that they were neglected by people who used to court them. Their blame seemed to me misdirected. If the fault were of old age, the same misfortunes would have befallen me and other older men; but I have known many who made no complaint, who were not grieved to be loosed from the thralldom of the passions and were not looked down upon by their friends. In all complaints of this kind, the fault is in the character of a man, not his age. Temperate old men who are neither testy nor ill-natured pass a very tolerable old age; discontent and ill-nature are irksome at any age. LAELIUS. It is as you say, Cato. But perhaps someone may suggest that it is your large means, wealth, and high position that make you think old age tolerable; very few enjoy such good fortune. CATO. There is something in what you say, Laelius, but by no means the whole story. For instance, the tale is told of Themistocles' answer when he was quarreling with a certain Seriphian, who asserted that Themistocles owed his brilliant position to his country's reputation and not his own. "If I had been a Seriphian," said he, "even I should never have been famous, nor would you if you had been an Athenian." The same may be said of old age. Not even to a philosopher could old age be easy in the depths of poverty, nor could a fool find it anything but burdensome even amid ample wealth. The arms best adapted to old age, Scipio and Laelius, are the attainment and practice of the virtues; if cultivated at every period of life these produce wonderful fruits when you reach old age, not only because they never fail— though that too is an important consideration—but also because the consciousness of a life well spent and the recollection of many virtuous deeds afford great satisfaction.

I was as fond of Quintus Fabius Maximus, who recovered Tarentum, as if he had been of my own age, though he was old and I was young. His dignity was seasoned by affability, nor had age altered his disposition. He was an elderly but not really an old man when I began to cultivate his acquaintance; his first consulship fell the year I was born. When he was consul for the fourth time and I only a lad I served under him in the expedition to Capua, and five years later in that to Tarentum. Four years later, in the consulship of Tuditanus and Cethegus, I became quaestor; and he, now quite old, urged the passage of the Cincian law on fees and gifts. When he was quite old he conducted wars with the spirit of youth, and his perseverance checked Hannibal's youthful impetuosity. Well did my friend Ennius say of him:

> One man by delay restored our fortune;
> Safety he valued above the people's applause,
> Hence his glory brighter shines and will shine.

What vigilance, what prudence did he show in retaking Tarentum! It was in my hearing, indeed, that he made the famous retort to Salinator, who had retreated into the citadel after losing the town. "You recovered Tarentum by my instrumentality," Salinator boasted. "Unquestionably," Fabius said with a laugh, "for if you had not lost it I should never have recovered it." Nor was his civil career less eminent than his military. In his second consulship, unsupported by his colleague Carvilius, he resisted to the utmost of his power the efforts of the tribune Caius Flaminius to make allotments of the Picene and Gallic territory in defiance of the senate's will. As augur he dared to say that whatever was done in the interests of the state was done under the best auspices and that measures inimical to its interests were undertaken with adverse auspices. Much that was remarkable have I observed in that old man, but nothing more admirable than the way he bore the death of his son, an illustrious man who had held the consulship. When we read the eulogy, which is still in circulation, we feel that he surpassed the philosophers. Nor was he great only in public and in the eyes of the community; in private and domestic life he was even more outstanding. What conversation! What maxims! What broad knowledge of antiquity, and what expertness in augural lore! He was widely read, too, for a Roman, and knew by heart the history of all wars, domestic and foreign. I availed myself as eagerly of my opportunities of conversing with him as if I had already divined, what proved to be true, that when he should pass away I would have no one from whom to learn.

Why so much about Maximus? Because you must now see that it is monstrous to call such an old age miserable. Not everyone, it is true, can be a Scipio or a Maximus and have stormings of cities, battles by land and sea, general commands, and triumphs to recall. But there is also the calm and serene old age of a life passed peacefully, simply, and gracefully. Such, we have heard, was Plato's, who died at his desk in his eighty-first year; such was Isocrates', who was ninety-four when he wrote his *Panathenaicus* and lived five years more. His teacher Gorgias

of Leontini rounded out one hundred and seven years without suspend-
ing his diligence or his pursuits. When he was asked why he was willing
to live so long, he replied, "I have no fault to find with old age"—a noble
answer and worthy of a scholar. It is their own vices and faults that fools
charge to old age; not so Ennius, whom I just now mentioned:

> As the gallant steed who oft in the last lap
> Conquered, and now foredone with age reposes.

His age he compares to that of a spirited and successful racehorse. You
might well remember him, for the present consuls, Titus Flamininus
and Manius Acilius, were elected nineteen years after his death, which
took place in the consulship of Caepio and Philippus (the latter in his
second term); I was sixty-five at the time, and was urging the Voconian
law with a strong voice and sound lungs. At seventy—such was Ennius'
span—he bore the two burdens which are esteemed the heaviest, poverty
and old age, and almost seemed to take pleasure in them.

When I reflect on the subject, I find that the reasons why old age is
regarded as unhappy are four: one, it withdraws us from active employments; another, it impairs physical vigor; the third, it deprives us of
nearly all sensual pleasures; and four, it is the verge of death. Let us see,
if you please, how much force and justice there is in these several reasons.

"Old age withdraws us from active employments." You mean, do you
not, those that involve youth and vigor? Are there no old men's employments which are carried on by the intellect even when the body is feeble?
Was Maximus not employed? Was Lucius Paulus, your father, Scipio,
and my excellent son's father-in-law, not employed? Were old men like
Fabricius, Curius, Coruncanius not employed when their wisdom and
influence were preserving the commonwealth? Appius was blind as well
as old, and yet when the inclinations of the senate favored peace and a
treaty with Pyrrhus he did not hesitate to utter what Ennius has put into
verse:

> Whither have your minds which used upright to stand
> In folly turned away?

And so on, in most impressive style. You know the poem, and the actual
speech of Appius is extant. He delivered it seventeen years after his
second consulship, though ten years had intervened between his two
consulships and he had been censor before he was consul. This will
show you that at the time of the war with Pyrrhus he was a very old
man; yet this is the story handed down to us. There is nothing, then, in

the argument that old age is devoid of useful activity. To say that is like saying that a steersman sitting quietly in the stern and holding the tiller contributes nothing to sailing the ship, for others climb the masts, run up and down the gangways, man the pumps. He may not be doing what younger men do, but what he does is better and more important. Large affairs are not performed by muscle, speed, nimbleness, but by reflection, character, judgment. In age these qualities are not diminished but augmented. Or perhaps you think that a military man like myself, who fought in various wars as private, captain, general, commander-in-chief, is now unemployed because he is not off to the wars. But I direct the senate on what wars are to be fought, and how; against Carthage, which has long been plotting mischief, I have declared war far in advance. I shall not cease to fear Carthage until I know it is utterly destroyed. That victory may the gods reserve for you, Scipio, so that you may complete the task begun by your grandfather. Thirty-two years have passed since his death, but all succeeding years will cherish his memory. He died the year before I was censor, nine years after my consulship; in my consulship he was elected consul for the second time. If he had lived to a hundred, would he ever have regretted old age? He would of course not have been practising running, jumping, spear hurling, sword play, but he would be using reflection, reason, judgment. Unless these faculties resided in old men, our ancestors would never have called their supreme council senate. In Sparta the highest magistrates are called, as they in fact are, elders. If you would turn to foreign history you will find that the mightiest states have been overthrown by the young and supported and restored by the old. In Naevius' *Wolf* there is a question: "How lost you, pray, your mighty state so soon?" There is a long answer, but the chief point is: "A crop of new advisers, silly striplings." Of course rashness belongs to blooming youth, prudence to old age.

But the memory is impaired. No doubt, unless you keep it in practice, or if you happen to be naturally dull. Themistocles had learned by heart the names of all the citizens of Athens; do you suppose he addressed Aristides as Lysimachus in his old age? I myself know not only living people but their fathers and grandfathers too; and in reading tombstones I am not afraid, as superstition has it, that I shall lose my memory, for their reading actually recalls the memory of the dead. I have never heard of any old man forgetting where he had hidden his money. The old remember everything that concerns them—appointments in court, who owes them money, to whom they owe money. What about lawyers, pontiffs, augurs, philosophers who are old? What a multitude of things they remember! The old retain their intellectual powers provided their interest and inclination continue, and not only in the case of men in high and distinguished positions, but also in private and peaceful pursuits. Sophocles wrote tragedies up to extreme old age, and when this preoccupation was thought to impair his attention to business matters, his sons brought him to court to prove imbecility, on a law similar to ours which deprives a householder of the management of his property if he has proved incompetent. The old poet is then said to have read to the jury the *Oedipus at Colonus*, which he had lately written and was revising, and to have asked whether it seemed the work of an imbecile. After the reading he was acquitted. Did old age silence this man, or Homer, Hesiod, Simonides, Stesichorus, or Isocrates and Gorgias whom I have mentioned, or the founders of the philosophic schools, Pythagoras, Democritus, Plato, or Xenocrates, or, later, Zeno and Cleanthes, or the Stoic Diogenes, whom you lately saw at Rome? Did not the activity of each of these men terminate only with his life? To pass over these lofty pursuits, I can mention Roman farmers in the Sabine district, neighbors and acquaintances of mine, without whose presence scarcely any important farm work is done, whether sowing, harvesting, or storing produce. In field crops this is not so surprising, for no one is so old but that he expects to live another year; but they also bestow labor on what they know cannot affect them. "He plants trees to profit another age," as our own Caecilius Statius says in his *Comrades*. If you ask a farmer, however old, for whom he is planting, he will reply without hesitation, "For the immortal gods, who intended that I should not only receive these things from my ancestors, but also transmit them to my descendants."

Statius' lines on the old man making provision for a future generation are better than this other passage: "Verily, old age, if thou bringest with thee no other bane, this one is enough: by living long one sees much he likes not." And perhaps much he likes, and youth too encounters what it does not like. But the same Caecilius has something even more objectionable: "This I reckon old age's worst bane: old men feel they are tedious to the young." Agreeable rather than tedious! Just as intelligent old men take pleasure in young men of parts and find their old age ameliorated by the courteous attentions of the young, so do young men take pleasure in the maxims of their elders, by which they are drawn to the pursuit of excellence. I do not feel that my company is less agreeable to you than yours to me. But you see that so far from being listless and inert old age is always busy with work and plans, usually of the sort which occupied earlier years. Old men even learn new things; we find Solon boasting that he learned new things as he grew old. I myself have learned Greek as an old man, and grasped it as greedily as if I were trying to satisfy a long protracted thirst. That is how I learned the things you now see me use as illustrations. When I heard what Socrates had done about the lyre I should have liked for my part to have done that too, for the ancients used to learn the lyre; but at any rate I worked hard at literature.

Nor, again, do I now miss the bodily strength of a young man (for that was the second head in the disadvantages of old age) any more than as a young man I missed the strength of a bull or an elephant. What one has, that one ought to use; and whatever you do, you should do it with all your strength. Contemptible indeed was Milo of Croton's exclamation. When as an old man he was watching athletes exercising on the track he is said to have looked at his arms and to have remarked with tears, "But these are now dead." ·Not your arms, silly man, as much as yourself; it was not yourself that made you famous but your chest and biceps. Sextus Aelius never uttered such a remark, nor Titus Coruncanius in the old days, nor Publius Crassus more recently. All advised their fellow citizens in jurisprudence, and their competence continued to their last breath. The orator, I fear, does lose vigor by old age, for his craft involves not the intellect alone but lungs and bodily strength. Yet as a rule the musical ring in the voice somehow gains brilliance with age; I have not lost it, and you see my years. It is the subdued and unemotional style that best becomes an old man, and the calm and mild discourse of a veteran often wins itself a hearing. And if that cannot be managed, still there are Scipios and Laeliuses to be taught! What is more charming than an old age surrounded by the enthusiasm of youth? Shall we not concede old age even strength to teach the young, to train and equip them for the duties of life? What can be nobler? For my part I used to consider Publius and Gnaeus Scipio and your two grandfathers, Lucius Aemilius and Publius Africanus, fortunate men when I saw them attended by a throng of noble youths. No teachers of the liberal arts should be considered unhappy, however much their physical vigor may have waned and failed. And even that failure is more often chargeable to the follies of youth than of age; a voluptuous and intemperate youth bequeaths an exhausted body to old age. Xenophon's Cyrus, for instance, speaking on his death bed in high old age, said that he never felt his old age was feebler than his youth had been. From my boyhood I remember Lucius Metellus, who held the office of pontifex maximus for twenty-two years after receiving it full four years after his second consulship; to the end of his days he enjoyed such physical vigor that he never felt the loss of youth. I need not speak of myself, though that is an old man's habit and allowable at my age.

How frequently Nestor speaks of his own merits in Homer! He was living through a third generation, and had no fear that in speaking truth of himself he would appear impertinent or garrulous. As Homer says, "from his lips flowed discourse sweeter than honey"—for which he had no need of physical strength. And that famous general of the Greeks nowhere wishes he had ten men like Ajax, but like Nestor; if he had them he is sure Troy would quickly fall. But I return to my own case. I am eighty-three, and could wish I might make Cyrus' boast; but so much I can say: though I am not so strong as I was as a private in the Punic War, or as quaestor in the same war, or as consul in Spain, or as military tribune under Glabrio four years later, still, as you see, old age has not wholly unstrung my nerves or shattered me. Neither the senate, nor the rostrum, nor my friends, nor my clients, nor my guests miss the strength I have lost. I have never agreed to that hoary and much-lauded proverb that you must become an old man early if you wish to be one long. I would rather not be old so long than be old before my time. No one has wanted to meet me to whom I have denied myself on the plea of age. I have less strength than either of you, it is true, but neither do you have the strength of the centurion Titus Pontius; is he then the better man? Provided one husbands his strength and does not attempt to go beyond it, he will not be hampered by lack of requisite strength. At Olympia Milo is said to have walked the course with an ox on his shoulders: would you prefer such physical power or the mental power of Pythagoras? In a word, use your physical strength while you have it, and do not bewail it when it is gone—unless you believe that youth must bewail the loss of infancy or early manhood the passing of youth. Life has its fixed course, and nature one unvarying way; to each is allotted its appropriate quality, so that the fickleness of boyhood, the impetuosity of youth, the sobriety of middle life, and the ripeness of age all have something of nature's yield which must be garnered in its own season. You must have heard, Scipio, what your grandfather's foreign friend Masinissa does to this very day, though he is ninety. When he begins a journey on foot he will not mount, nor dismount if he begins on horseback. No rain or chill can induce him to cover his head. His sinewy body enables him to perform the duties and functions of a king. Exercise and temperance can preserve some of a man's vigor even in old age.

Is there no strength in old age? None is expected of old age. Hence both by law and custom our time of life is exempt from public services which require physical strength. Not only are we not forced to do what we cannot do; we are not even obliged to do what we can do. Yet, it may be urged, so feeble are many old men that they can perform none of life's duties or functions at all. But that weakness is not peculiar to old age; it belongs also to ill health. How feeble, Scipio, was your adoptive father Publius Africanus! His health was so weak as to be non-existent.

But for this he would have shone forth as our second great political luminary, for to his father's greatness of spirit he added a richer culture. What wonder, then, that the aged are sometimes weak when even young men cannot escape infirmity? My dear Laelius and Scipio, old age must be resisted, and its deficiencies supplied by taking pains; we must fight it as we do disease. Care must be bestowed upon health; moderate exercise should be taken; food and drink should be sufficient to recruit, not over-burden, our strength. And not the body alone must be sustained, but the powers of the mind much more; unless you supply them, as oil to a lamp, they too grow dim with age. Whereas overexertion weighs the body down with fatigue, exercise makes the mind buoyant. When Caecilius speaks of "dotards of the comic stage" he means credulity, forgetfulness, languor, and these are faults not of old age but of lazy, indolent, and drowsy old age. As wantonness and licentiousness are faults of the young rather than of the old, yet not of all young men but only of the depraved, so the senile folly called dotage is characteristic not of all old men but only of the frivolous. Four stout sons, five daughters, a large household, numerous dependents, did Appius manage, though both old and blind, for his mind was alert, like a bent bow, and did not succumb to old age by growing slack. He maintained not merely in-fluence but absolute command over his large household. The slaves feared him, the children respected him, all held him dear; beneath his roof the usages and discipline of our forefathers were in the ascendant. Old age is respectable so long as it asserts itself, maintains its rights, is subservient to no one, and retains its sway to the last breath. I like a young man who has a touch of the old, and I like an old man who has a touch of the young. A man who cultivates this principle may be old in body, in mind never. I am now engaged on the seventh volume of my *Origines*. I am collecting all records of antiquity. I am just now revising the pleadings I delivered in famous cases. I am dealing with the augural, pontifical, and civil law. I read a good deal of Greek. Following the Pythagorean method, each evening I run over what I have heard and done during the day, for the sake of exercising my memory. These are my intellectual calisthenics, the running track of the mind, and when I sweat and strain at them I do not greatly miss bodily strength. I appear in court for my friends, I attend the senate frequently and introduce proposals I have pondered long and earnestly; these I support with intellectual, not physical, energy. If I were too feeble for these functions, my couch would afford me the entertainment of imagining the very operations which I was now unable to perform. But what makes me capable of doing this is my past life. For a man who is always living amid such studies and pursuits as mine is not aware of the stealthy approach of age. Life draws to its end by slow and imperceptible degrees; there is no sudden rupture but a gradual extinction.

The third charge against old age is that it lacks sensual pleasures. What a splendid boon if age takes from us youth's greatest blemish! Listen, my dear young friends, to what the great and eminent Archytas of Tarentum said in an ancient speech which was communicated to me when I was a young man serving with Quintus Maximus at Tarentum. "No more deadly curse," said he, "has nature inflicted on men than sensual pleasure. To gratify it our wanton appetites are roused beyond all prudence and restraint. It is a source of treason, revolution, clandestine commerce with the enemy. There is no crime, no wickedness, to which the lust for pleasure does not impel. Fornications and adulteries and every vice of that stripe are initiated by the enticements of pleasure and by that alone. Intellect is the best gift of nature or God; to this gift nothing is so hostile as pleasure. Where lust holds sway there is no place for temperance, nor where pleasure reigns can virtue find footing. To realize this more clearly, imagine a man aroused to the highest conceivable pitch of sensual pleasure. None will doubt that as long as he is in such a state that man cannot use intellect or reason or thought. Nothing is therefore so detestable and pernicious as pleasure, for if it is violent and enduring it darkens all the light of the soul." My Tarentine host Nearchus, who remained loyal to Rome, told me that he had heard from his elders that Archytas spoke these words to the Samnite Pontius, father of the man who defeated the consuls Spurius Postumius and Titus Veturius at the Caudine Forks. Plato is said to have been present at the conversation; I find that Plato did visit Tarentum in the consulship of Lucius Camillus and Appius Claudius. What is the point of all this? To show you that if reason and wisdom did not enable us to reject pleasure, we should be very grateful to old age for depriving us of the desire to do what we ought not. Pleasure hinders thought, is a foe to reason, and, so to say, blinds the eyes of the mind. It has no dealings with virtue. I was reluctant to expel Lucius Flamininus, brother of the gallant Titus Flamininus, from the senate seven years after he had been consul; but I thought that his licentiousness must be stigmatized. When he was commanding in Gaul a courtesan prevailed on him at a banquet to behead a prisoner condemned on a capital charge. In the censorship of his brother Titus, my predecessor, he escaped; but so profligate and abandoned an act of lust Flaccus and I could never allow to pass, for it involved disgrace to the empire as well as personal infamy.

I have often been told by men older than myself, who said that they had heard it as boys from old men, that Gaius Fabricius was in the habit of expressing astonishment at having heard, when envoy at the headquarters of King Pyrrhus, from the Thessalian Cineas, that there was a man of Athens who professed to be a 'philosopher' and affirmed that all our actions were to be referred to pleasure. When he told this to Manius Curius and Publius Decius their remark was that they only wished that the Samnites and Pyrrhus himself would hold the same opinion; it would be easier to conquer them when they had given themselves up to pleasure. Manius Curius was intimate with Publius Decius, who, in his fourth consulship and five years before Curius held that office, had immolated himself for his country's salvation. Fabricius and Coruncanius had known Decius also, and from their experience and Decius' heroic deed they inferred that there does exist something intrinsically pure and noble which is sought for its own sake and is the objective of all good men who spurn and despise pleasure. Why so much on pleasure? Because it is not only no reproach to old age but even its highest merit that it does not severely feel the loss of bodily pleasures. It must dispense with sumptuous feasts, loaded tables, oft-drained cups; it dispenses too with sottishness, indigestion, broken sleep. If some concession must be made to pleasure, its charms being so difficult to resist —Plato aptly calls it the bait of sin, for by it men are caught like fish—then old age, though it dispenses with immoderate feasting, can yet find pleasure in modest festivities. When I was a boy I often saw the venerable Caius Duilius, the first victor over the Carthaginians at sea, returning home from supper. He took particular pleasure in being escorted by torch and flute-player; though the privilege was unprecedented for a private citizen, his military glory allowed him the license. But why mention others? I return to my own case. In the first place, I have always had my club—it was in my quaestorship that the clubs were instituted, when the Idaean rites of the Great Mother were received in Rome. I used to dine with the brethren, moderately on the whole, yet with something of the joviality that belonged to my earlier years but which the progress of time gradually diminishes. I did not calculate the pleasure of those banquets by the pleasures of the body so much as by the gathering and conversation of friends. Our ancestors were quite right to style that presence of guests at dinner-table—seeing that it implies a community of enjoyment—a *convivium* or "living together." It is a better term than the Greek words which mean "a drinking together" or "an eating together." These seem to give the preference to what is really the least important aspect.

For my own part, owing to the pleasure I take in conversation, I enjoy even banquets that begin early in the afternoon, and not only with my contemporaries, of whom few survive, but also with men of your own age and with yourselves. I am heartily thankful to old age, which has increased my appetite for conversation and removed that for food and drink. But if anyone does enjoy these—let me not seem to have declared war on all pleasure, for some is justified by nature—I am not aware that old age does not appreciate them. I enjoy the ancestral custom of appointing a master of ceremonies, and the talk, which begins at the head of the table in the old-fashioned way, and small and dewy cups, like those in Xenophon's *Symposium,* and the cool breeze for the dining room in summer, and the sun or fire in winter. Even on my Sabine farm I keep up these customs, and daily fill my table with my neighbors, prolonging our varied talk to the latest possible hour.

But you may urge that there is not the same tingling sensation of pleasure in old men. No doubt; but neither do they miss it so much. Nothing for which you do not yearn troubles you. It was an excellent reply that Sophocles made to a certain man who asked him, when he was already old, if he still indulged in the delights of love. "Heaven forbid!" he said. "Indeed I have fled from them as from a harsh and cruel master." To men fond of such things it is perhaps disagreeable and irksome to be without them; but to those who are sated and cloyed with them it is more pleasant to be in want of them than to possess them; though indeed a man cannot "want" that for which he has no longing, and therefore I assert that the absence of longing is more pleasant.

But even granting that youth enjoys these pleasures with more zest; in the first place, they are insignificant things to enjoy, as I have said; and in the second place, such as age is not entirely without, if it does not possess them in profusion. Just as Ambivius Turpio gives greater delight to the spectators in the front row of the theater, and yet gives some delight even to those in the last row, so youth, looking on pleasures at close range, perhaps enjoys them more, while old age, on the other hand, finds delight enough in a more distant view. But what a blessing it is for the soul to be with itself, to live, as the phrase is, apart, discharged from the service of lust, ambition, strife, enmities, and all passions! If it has any scholarly interests stored up as it were provender, nothing can be more enjoyable than an old age of leisure. I used to see Gallus—your father's friend, Scipio—studiously charting heaven and earth. Dawn would overtake him when he had begun some problem at night, and night when he had begun in the early morning. How he enjoyed predicting eclipses of sun and moon far in advance! In studies less recondite but still requiring acuteness, what pleasure Naevius took in his *Punic War* and Plautus in his *Truculentus* and *Pseudolus!* I even saw old Livius Andronicus; he presented a play in the consulship of Cento and Tuditanus, six years before I was born, and lived on till I was almost a man. Why speak of Publius Licinius Crassus' devotion to pontifical and civil law, or of that of the contemporary Publius Scipio, who was lately made pontifex maximus? All these men I have named we have seen ardently engaged in their several departments in old age. Marcus Cethegus too, whom Ennius justly styled Persuasion's Marrow—what zeal I saw him display in his oratory even as an old man! How can the pleasures of feasting, games, and harlots be comparable to these? All of these involve learning, which, in wise and cultured men, increases with age. Creditable is the verse of Solon I have quoted, "I grow old learning many new things." There is no greater pleasure than the mind's.

I come now to the pleasures of agriculture, in which I find incredible delight. To these old age is no impediment, and in them I think a man makes the nearest approach to the life of the sage. The farmer keeps an open account with the earth, which never refuses a draft, never returns a deposit without interest, sometimes, indeed, at a low rate, but generally at a high. Yet it is not the revenue which charms me, but the very nature and properties of the soil. When it has received the seed into its softened and prepared bosom it keeps it *buried* (whence our word *harrowing* is derived), and then by its pressure and the moisture it yields it cleaves the seed and draws from it the verdant shoot, which, sustained by its root fibres, grows till it stands erect on its jointed stalk, enclosed in a sheath as if to protect its downy youth, till, emerging, it yields the grain with its orderly arrangement in the ear, defended against predatory birds by its bearded rampart. Why should I tell of the planting, burgeoning, growth, of vines? Of this pleasure I can never have too much—to let you into the secret of what gives my old age repose and amusement. I pass over the inherent power of things generated from the earth, which, from so tiny a grape or fig seed, or from the minute seeds of other fruits and plants, produces such massive trunks and shoots, sprouts, cuttings, divisions, and layers enough to afford wonder and delight to any man? The vine, indeed, drooping by nature unless supported, is weighed down to the ground; but to raise itself it embraces with its hand-like tendrils whatever it can lay hold upon; and then, as it twines with intricate and wild profusion, the vine-dresser's art trims it close with the pruning knife, lest it run to wood and spread too far. So in early spring the joints of the branches that are left sprout buds from which the incipient grapes appear; these grow by the moisture of the earth and the heat of the sun, and though at first bitter to the taste, they sweeten as they ripen; its shelter of leaves allows it sufficient warmth, yet keeps off the intense heat of the sun. What can be more delicious or more beautiful? It is not only the vine's utility, as I have remarked, that pleases me, but also the process of its cultivation and its very nature—the rows of stakes, the lateral supports, the tying up and training of the vines, the pruning of some of the twigs (as I have said) and the grafting of others. I need hardly mention irrigation, trenching, and frequent hoeing to increase fertility. Of the advantages of manuring I have spoken in my book on agriculture. The learned Hesiod, though he writes on agriculture, has nothing on this subject, though Homer, who preceded him, I think, by many generations, represents Laertes as relieving his longing for his son by cultivating and manuring his farm. Cornfields, meadows, vine-yards, woodlands are not the only satisfactions of the rustic life; there are also orchards and gardens, grazing and bee-keeping, and the infinite variety of flowers. And besides planting there is also grafting—the most ingenious invention in agriculture. . . .

But in all I say remember I am praising an old age whose foundations have been laid in youth. This implies what I once said, with universal approval, that it was a wretched old age which had to defend itself by speech. White hair or wrinkles cannot usurp influence; this an early life well spent reaps as the fruit of its age. Attentions which seem trivial and conventional are marks of honor—the morning call, being sought after, precedence, having people rise for you, being escorted to and from the forum, being consulted—courtesies carefully observed with us and in other states so far as good manners prevail. The Spartan Lysander, of whom I have just spoken, used to say that Sparta is the best domicile of age, for nowhere else is age so deferred to and respected. There is a story that when an elderly man entered the theater at a festival in Athens none of his countrymen in the large assembly gave place to him, but when he approached the seats reserved for the Lacedaemonians as am-bassadors, all of them rose and invited the old man to sit down. When the whole assembly greeted the act with repeated applause, one of the Spartans said, "The Athenians know what is right but will not do it." There are many excellent rules in our augural college, but especially is the one whereby each member has precedence in debate according to his age, and the oldest are preferred not only to those of higher official rank but even to functioning magistrates. What pleasures of the body can then be compared to the prerogatives of influence? Those who have employed it with distinction appear to me to have played the drama of life to its end, and not to have broken down in the last act like unpractised actors.

But old men are said to be peevish and fretful and irascible and dis-agreeable; they are miserly too, if we care to look for such. But these are faults of character, not of age. But peevishness and the rest may be extenuated if not justified. Old men imagine they are scorned, despised, mocked; and when the body is frail the slightest blow is irritating. But good habits and education can ameliorate these faults, as we can see in real life and in such a play as Terence's *Adelphi* with its two brothers. How grim one is, how genial the other! So it is: neither every wine nor every disposition sours with age. I approve of gravity in old age, but, as in all else, in moderation; of sourness not at all. The sense of avarice in an old man I cannot conceive; can anything be more absurd than to multiply luggage as one nears the journey's end?

There remains the fourth reason, which more than the others seems to make my time of life anxious and perturbed—the approach of death, which certainly cannot be far removed from old age. Wretched old man, not to have learned in a long life that death is to be despised! Death is wholly negligible if it extinguishes life altogether, and even desirable, if it conducts the soul where it will be immortal; surely no third possibility is imaginable. Why then should I fear death if I shall be not unhappy or else be happy? Even so, is anyone so foolish, however young he be, as to be sure he will live till evening? Youth has many more chances of death than age. The young are more liable to disease, their sickness is more serious, their cure more difficult. Few reach old age; were it not so life would be better and wiser. Intelligence and reason and prudence reside in the old, and but for them there could be no community at all. But to return to the imminence of death—can it be urged as a charge against age when you see that it is shared by youth? The death of my own excellent son, and of your brothers, Scipio, men born to the highest expectations, taught me that death is common to every age. Yet a young man hopes to live long and an old man can entertain no such hope. The hope itself is foolish; what can be more stupid than to take things uncertain for certain, false for true? "An old man has nothing even to hope." There he is in better case than the young, for what the one hopes the other has attained; one wishes to live long, the other has lived long.

And can we, in heaven's name, call anything human long? Grant the very latest term of life; suppose we reach the age of the king of Tartessus —it is recorded that Arganthonius of Cadiz ruled eighty years and lived a hundred and twenty—still nothing that has an end is long. When the end comes what has passed has flowed away, and all that is left is what you have achieved by virtue and good deeds. Hours, days, months, years, glide by; the past never returns, and what is to come we cannot know. With whatever span is allotted us we should be content. There is no need for an actor to perform the whole play to give his audience satisfaction; enough to play his own role well. Nor need the wise man continue to the last curtain. A short span is long enough to live well and honorably; if you live on you have no more reason to mourn your advancing years than have farmers, when the sweetness of spring is past, to lament the coming of fall and winter. Spring typifies youth, and points to the fruits to come; the other seasons are appropriate for harvesting and storing the crop. The harvest of old age, as I have often said, is the memory and abundance of blessings previously acquired. Moreover, all that falls out according to nature must be reckoned good, and what accords better with nature than for old men to die? Nature struggles and rebels when the young die. When they die it is as if a violent fire is extinguished by a torrent, but the old die like a spent fire quenched of its own accord and without external effort. Unripe apples must be wrenched from the tree, but fall of their own accord when ripe and mellow; so from the young it is force that takes life, from the old, ripeness. So agreeable is this ripeness to me that as I approach death nearer I feel like a voyager at last in sight of land and on the point of reaching harbor after a long journey.

Old age has no fixed term, and one may fitly live in it so long as he can observe and discharge the duties of his station, and yet despise death. Fearless of death, old age may transcend youth in courage and fortitude. Such is the meaning of Solon's answer to the tyrant Pisistratus, who asked the grounds of his bold resistance; "old age" was Solon's reply. That end of life is best when, with mind and faculties unimpaired, Nature herself takes apart what she has put together. The builder of a ship or house is best able to tear it down, and so Nature who compacted man can best effect his dissolution. What is newly compacted is hard to tear apart, old fabrics come apart easily. It follows that old men should neither be avid of their brief remaining span nor desert it without cause. Pythagoras forbids us to desert our post and charge in life without the order of our commander, God. A couplet of the wise Solon expresses the wish that his death be attended by the grief and lamentation of his friends. He wants, I suppose, to be beloved by them. But I prefer Ennius' sentiment:

Let none honor me with tears, nor at my funeral
Make lamentation.

For these reasons, Scipio, old age sits lightly on me—that is what you and Laelius wondered at—and I find it not irksome but actually agreeable. If I err in believing men's souls to be immortal, I err willingly, and as long as I live I do not wish an error which gives me such satisfaction to be wrested from me. If I shall have no sensation in death, as some paltry philosophers think, I have no fear that the dead philosophers will ridicule my error. But if we are not going to be immortal, it is desirable for a man to be erased in proper season; nature imposes a limit upon life as upon all else. Old age is the closing act of life, as of a drama, and we ought to leave when the play grows wearisome, especially if we have had our fill.

Such are my views on old age. I pray you attain it, so that you can verify what you have heard from me by experience.

The Superannuated Man

Charles Lamb (1775-1834)

IF PERADVENTURE, READER, it has been thy lot to waste the golden years of thy life—thy shining youth—in the irksome confinement of an office; to have thy prison days prolonged through middle age down to decrepitude and silver hairs, without hope of release or respite; to have lived to forget that there are such things as holidays, or to remember them but as the prerogatives of childhood; then, and then only, will you be able to appreciate my deliverance.

It is now six-and-thirty years since I took my seat at the desk in Mincing Lane. Melancholy was the transition at fourteen from the abundant playtime, and the frequently intervening vacations of school days, to the eight, nine, and sometimes ten hours a day attendance at the counting-house. But time partially reconciles us to anything. I gradually became content—doggedly contented, as wild animals in cages.

It is true I had my Sundays to myself; but Sundays, admirable as the institution of them is for purposes of worship, are for that very reason the very worst adapted for days of unbending and recreation. In particular, there is a gloom for me attendant upon a city Sunday, a weight in the air. I miss the cheerful cries of London, the music, and the ballad-singers—the buzz and stirring murmur of the streets. Those eternal bells depress me. The closed shops repel me. Prints, pictures, all the glittering and endless succession of knacks and gewgaws, and ostentatiously displayed wares of tradesmen, which make a weekday saunter through the less busy parts of the metropolis so delightful—are shut out. No book-stalls deliciously to idle over—no busy faces to recreate the idle man who contemplates them ever passing by—the very face of business a charm by contrast to his temporary relaxation from it. Nothing to be seen but unhappy countenances—or half-happy at best—of emancipated 'prentices and little tradesfolks, with here and there a servant-maid that has got leave to go out, who, slaving all the week, with the habit has lost almost the capacity of enjoying a free hour; and livelily expressing the hollowness of a day's pleasuring. The very strollers in the fields on that day look anything but comfortable.

But besides Sundays, I had a day at Easter, and a day at Christmas, with a full week in the summer to go and air myself in my native fields of Hertfordshire. This last was a great indulgence; and the prospect of its recurrence, I believe, alone kept me up through the year, and made my durance tolerable. But when the week came round, did the glittering phantom of the distance keep touch with me, or rather was it not a series of seven uneasy days, spent in restless pursuit of pleasure, and a wearisome anxiety to find out how to make the most of them? Where was the quiet, where the promised rest? Before I had a taste of it, it was vanished. I was at the desk again, counting upon the fifty-one tedious weeks that must intervene before such another snatch would come. Still the prospect of its coming threw something of an illumination upon the darker side of my captivity. Without it, as I have said, I could scarcely have sustained my thraldom.

Independently of the rigors of attendance, I have ever been haunted with a sense (perhaps a mere caprice) of incapacity for business. This, during my latter years, had increased to such a degree that it was visible in all the lines of my countenance. My health and my good spirits flagged. I had perpetually a dread of some crisis, to which I should be found unequal. Besides my daylight servitude, I served over again all night in my sleep, and would awake with terrors of imaginary false entries, errors in my accounts, and the like. I was fifty years of age, and no prospect of emancipation presented itself. I had grown to my desk, as it were; and the wood had entered into my soul.

My fellows in the office would sometimes rally me upon the trouble legible in my countenance; but I did not know that it had raised the suspicions of any of my employers, when, on the fifth of last month, a day ever to be remembered by me, L——, the junior partner in the firm, calling me on one side, directly taxed me with my bad looks, and frankly inquired the cause of them. So taxed, I honestly made confession of my infirmity, and added that I was afraid I should eventually be obliged to resign his service. He spoke some words of course to hearten me, and there the matter rested. A whole week I remained laboring under the impression that I had acted imprudently in my disclosure; that I had foolishly given a handle against myself, and had been anticipating my own dismissal. A week passed in this manner—the most anxious one, I verily believe, in my whole life—when on the evening of the 12th of

April, just as I was about quitting my desk to go home (it might be about eight o'clock), I received an awful summons to attend the presence of the whole assembled firm in the formidable back parlor. I thought now my time is surely come; I have done for myself, I am going to be told that they have no longer occasion for me. L——, I could see, smiled at the terror I was in, which was a little relief to me,—when to my utter astonishment B——, the eldest partner, began a formal harangue to me on the length of my services, my very meritorious conduct during the whole of the time (the deuce, thought I, how did he find out that? I protest I never had the confidence to think as much). He went on to descant on the expediency of retiring at a certain time of life, (how my heart panted!) and asking me a few question as to the amount of my own property, of which I have a little, ended with a proposal, to which his three partners nodded a grave assent, that I should accept from the house, which I had served so well, a pension for life to the amount of two thirds of my accustomed salary—a magnificent offer! I do not know what I answered, between surprise and gratitude, but it was understood that I accepted their proposal, and I was told that I was free from that hour to leave their service. I stammered out a bow, and at just ten minutes after eight I went home—for ever. This noble benefit—gratitude forbids me to conceal their names—I owe to the kindness of the most munificent firm in the world—the house of Boldero, Merryweather, Bosanquet, and Lacy.

Esto perpetua! [*May it last forever!*]

For the first day or two I felt stunned—overwhelmed. I could only apprehend my felicity; I was too confused to taste it sincerely. I wandered about, thinking I was happy, and knowing that I was not. I was in the condition of a prisoner in the old Bastile, suddenly let loose after a forty years' confinement. I could scarce trust myself with myself. It was like passing out of Time into Eternity—for it is a sort of Eternity for a man to have all his Time to himself. It seemed to me that I had more time on my hands than I could ever manage. From a poor man, poor in Time, I was suddenly lifted up into a vast revenue; I could see no end of my possessions; I wanted some steward, or judicious bailiff, to manage my estates in Time for me. And here let me caution persons grown old in active business, not lightly, nor without weighing their own resources, to forego their customary employment all at once, for there may be danger in it. I feel it by myself, but I know that my resources are suf-ficient; and now that those first giddy raptures have subsided, I have a quiet home-feeling of the blessedness of my condition. I am in no hurry. Having all holidays, I am as though I had none. If Time hung heavy upon me, I could walk it away; but I do *not* walk all day long, as I used to do in those old transient holidays, thirty miles a day, to make the most of them. If Time were troublesome, I could read it away; but I do *not* read in that violent measure, with which, having no Time my own but candlelight Time, I used to weary out my head and eyesight in bygone winters. I walk, read, or scribble (as now) just when the fit seizes me. I no longer hunt after pleasure; I let it come to me. I am like the man

—*"that's born, and has his years come to him,*
In some green desert."

"Years!" you will say; "what is this superannuated simpleton calculating upon? He has already told us he is past fifty."

I have indeed lived nominally fifty years, but deduct out of them the hours which I have lived to other people, and not to myself, and you will find me still a young fellow. For *that* is the only true Time, which a man can properly call his own—that which he has all to himself; the rest, though in some sense he may be said to live it, is other people's Time, not his. The remnant of my poor days, long or short, is at least multiplied for me threefold. My ten next years, if I stretch so far, will be as long as any preceding thirty. 'T is a fair rule-of-three sum.

Among the strange fantasies which beset me at the commencement of my freedom, and of which all traces are not yet gone, one was, that a vast tract of time had intervened since I quitted the Counting-House. I could not conceive of it as an affair of yesterday. The partners, and the clerks with whom I had for so many years, and for so many hours in each day of the year, been closely associated—being suddenly removed from them—they seemed as dead to me. There is a fine passage, which may serve to illustrate this fancy, in a Tragedy by Sir Robert Howard, speaking of a friend's death:—

—*" 'T was but just now he went away;*
I have not since had time to shed a tear;
And yet the distance does the same appear
As if he had been a thousand years from me.
Time takes no measure in Eternity."

To dissipate this awkward feeling, I have been fain to go among them once or twice since; to visit my old desk-fellows—my co-brethren of the quill—that I had left below in the state militant. Not all the kindness with which they received me could quite restore to me that pleasant familiarity, which I had heretofore enjoyed among them. We cracked some of our old jokes, but methought they went off but faintly. My old desk, the peg where I hung my hat, were appropriated to another. I knew it must be, but I could not take it kindly. D——l take me, if I did not feel some remorse—beast, if I had not—at quitting my old compeers, the faithful partners of my toils for six-and-thirty years, that soothed for me with their jokes and conundrums the ruggedness of my professional road. Had it been so rugged then, after all? or was I a coward simply? Well, it is too late to repent; and I also know that these suggestions are a common fallacy of the mind on such occasions. But my heart smote me. I had violently broken the bands betwixt us. It was at least not courteous. I shall be some time before I get quite reconciled to the separation. Farewell, old cronies, yet not for long, for again and again I will come among ye, if I shall have your leave. Farewell, Ch——, dry, sarcastic, and friendly! Do——, mild, slow to move, and gentlemanly! Pl——, officious to do, and to volunteer, good services!—and thou, thou dreary pile, fit mansion for a Gresham or a Whittington of old, stately house of Merchants; with thy labyrinthine passages, and light-excluding, pent-up offices, where candles for one half the year supplied the place of the sun's light; unhealthy contributor to my weal, stern fosterer of my living, farewell! In thee remain, and not in the obscure collection of some wandering bookseller, my "works"! There let them rest, as I do from my labors, piled on thy massy shelves, more MSS. in folio than ever Aquinas left, and full as useful! My mantle I bequeath among ye.

A fortnight has passed since the date of my first communication. At that period I was approaching to tranquillity, but had not reached it. I boasted of a calm indeed, but it was comparative only. Something of the first flutter was left; an unsettling sense of novelty; the dazzle to weak eyes of unaccustomed light. I missed my old chains, forsooth, as if they had been some necessary part of my apparel. I was a poor Carthusian, from strict cellular discipline suddenly by some revolution returned upon the world. I am now as if I had never been other than my own master. It is natural for me to go where I please, to do what I please. I find myself at eleven o'clock in the day in Bond Street, and it seems to me that I have been sauntering there at that very hour for years past. I digress into Soho, to explore a bookstall. Methinks I have been thirty years a collector. There is nothing strange nor new in it. I find myself before a fine picture in the morning. Was it ever otherwise? What is become of Fish Street Hill? Where is Fenchurch Street? Stones of old Mincing Lane, which I have worn with my daily pilgrimage for six-and-thirty years, to the footsteps of what toil-worn clerk are your everlasting flints now vocal? I indent the gayer flags of Pall Mall. It is 'Change time, and I am strangely among the Elgin marbles. It was no hyperbole when I ventured to compare the change in my condition to passing into another world. Time stands still in a manner to me. I have lost all distinction of season. I do not know the day of the week or of the month. Each day used to be individually felt by me in its reference to the foreign post days; in its distance from, or propinquity to, the next Sunday. I had my Wednesday feelings, my Saturday night's sensations. The genius of each day was upon me distinctly during the whole of it, affecting my appetite, spirits, etc. The phantom of the next day, with the dreary five to follow, sate as a load upon my poor Sabbath recreations. What charm has washed that Ethiop white? What is gone of Black Monday? All days are the same. Sunday itself—that unfortunate failure of a holiday, as it too often proved, what with my sense of its fugitiveness, and over-care to get the greatest quantity of pleasure out of it—is melted down into a weekday. I can spare to go to church now, without grudging the huge cantle which it used to seem to cut out of the holiday. I have time for everything. I can visit a sick friend. I can interrupt the man of much occupation when he is busiest. I can insult over him with an invitation to take a day's pleasure with me to Windsor this fine May morning. It is Lucretian pleasure to behold the poor drudges, whom I have left behind in the world, carking and caring; like horses in a mill, drudging on in the same eternal round—and what is it all for? A man can never have too much Time to himself, nor too little to do. Had I a little son, I would christen him, NOTHING-TO-DO; he should do nothing. Man, I verily believe, is out of his element as long as he is operative. I am altogether for the life contemplative. Will no kindly earthquake come and swallow up those accursed cotton-mills? Take me that lumber of a desk there, and bowl it down

"As low as to the fiends."

I am no longer——, clerk to the Firm of, etc. I am Retired Leisure. I am to be met with in trim gardens. I am already come to be known by my vacant face and careless gesture, perambulating at no fixed pace, nor with any settled purpose. I walk about; not to and from. They tell me, a certain *cum dignitate* air, that has been buried so long with my other good parts, has begun to shoot forth in my person. I grow into gentility perceptibly. When I take up a newspaper, it is to read the state of the opera. *Opus operatum est.* I have done all that I came into this world to do. I have worked taskwork, and have the rest of the day to myself.

Suggestions for Further Reading

Family and Community in Ireland, by Conrad M. Arensberg and Solon T. Kimball. Cambridge: Harvard University Press, 1940.

> Relations among the generations under the social and economic conditions and customs of modern Ireland.

The Old Man and the Boy, by Robert Ruark. New York: Henry Holt and Company, 1953.

> An autobiographical account of a warm relationship between a boy and his grandfather, in pre-industrial America.

Love in the Machine Age, by Floyd Dell. New York: Farrar and Rinehart, 1930.

> A psychological study of the change from attitudes of the patriarchal past to those of modern times.

Dr. Wilma T. Donahue (born in 1900 in Iowa) is Chairman of the Division of Gerontology, Institute for Human Adjustment, University of Michigan, Ann Arbor. Student, writer, speaker, researcher, consultant, convener of annual University of Michigan conferences in the field of aging. Editor or co-editor of Planning the Older Years *(1950)*, Growing in the Older Years *(1951)*, Rehabilitation of the Older Worker *(1953)*, Housing the Aging *(1954)*, Education for Later Maturity *(1955)*, Earning Opportunities for Older Workers *(1955)*, Free Time: Challenge of Later Maturity *(1958).*

"There is, without question, a revolution going on not only in technology but in every aspect of living. By inviting people to join together to explore and discover the meaning of the new ideas and ways of thinking that are now bringing about this revolution we give them a new and exciting opportunity to continue learning. Thereby they will stay alert, active, and participating in the emerging new climate of opinion. Here, as Ortega y Gasset has pointed out, we may live at the 'height of our times', probably the most exciting period in all human history, instead of being 'living fossils' who continue to exist but who cannot share in the great events now taking place."

—LAWRENCE K. FRANK

"Education for Aging." Quoted by permission from *Education for Later Maturity*. Whiteside Inc., 1955.

3

The Human Machine
at Middle Life

WILMA DONAHUE

AGING IS AS OLD as the phenomenon of life. Ever since the origin of life, the process of aging has played a tremendous role in evolution.

With conception, a marvelous series of events is set into motion. A simple protozoan divides into two cells. A second division produces a creature composed of but four cells. The third, fourth, fifth, and sixth divisions bring the number up to 8, 16, 32, and 64 cells respectively; in 32 divisions the number has risen to something over 2 billion living cells. In the process of division the human embryo also undergoes a progressive metamorphosis in which two billion years of evolution are repeated. The individual organism passes from stages like those of the protozoa to those of the metazoa, from those like invertebrates to those of vertebrates, from fish to primate to man. Gills come and go, a tail grows and is later absorbed. All this happens in a period of nine months. Never shall we age so rapidly again. In our embryonic development we literally age two billion years in less than a single year.[1]

The individual, denied the consciousness of the rich experience of this two billion years of exciting evolution, is given, for good measure, an additional gift of post-natal life amounting to three-score-and-ten years or more. During this period of years he is able to exploit his talent for self-development and the enjoyment of life. In *Man for Himself* Eric Fromm makes the point that "Birth is only one particular step in a continuum which begins with conception and ends with death. All that is between these two poles is a process of giving birth to one's potentialities, of bringing to life all that is potentially given in the two cells . . . the development of the self is never completed; even under the best conditions only part of man's potentialities is realized. Man always dies before he is fully born." [2] Increased longevity and the new way of life achieved in our modern world, described by Clark Tibbitts, may provide man at last with enough years of life to bring himself to the highest level of self-realization.

Wise men and women, reaching the midstream of life when their responsibilities for the perpetuation of the on-coming generation are discharged and when their awareness of the passage of time is becoming acute, should reappraise their physical and mental equipment for the achievement of a new order of purposes.

The Physical Machine

In planning our earlier adult years, it is seldom that much thought is given to the physical machine that is to be used in the achievement of our aims. The durability of the physical organism is taken for granted. In youth, when we are so richly endowed with the biological factors required to maintain and restore the capacities of the body, we assume that the physical ability to meet the demands for effective living will always be the same. The fact is, however, that the functional efficiency of these protective factors diminishes progressively, until, by middle age, almost all of us experience some

---

[1] Considerable credit for the point of view expressed in this paper is due to the late physiologist, Dr. Robert Gesell.

[2] Erich Fromm, *Man for Himself*, p. 91. New York: Rinehart & Company, 1947.

of the cumulative consequences of aging in the form of lessened energy and vigor. When this happens, our personal interest in the nature and effects of aging is aroused, and we begin to ask questions.

We want to know all about this "business" of aging, and we become interested in evaluating its implications for our future life and plans. Why, we ask, do we require more rest in order to carry out our daily tasks with no more than the usual amount of fatigue? Why does any display on our part of athletic, gastronomical, or bacchanalian prowess have such disastrous and lasting consequences? Why do we age? What is aging, anyway? Are illness and aging different aspects of the same phenomenon? When does one begin to grow old? How rapidly do age changes progress, once they have become apparent? What, if anything, can be done to retard or compensate the physical effects of aging?

Answers to these and similar questions help us to accept with better grace our growing older, because we are able to relate aging to the over-all biologic perspectives of the human species. As Dr. Carl Weller has pointed out, man grows old naturally and, in so doing, is fulfilling the biologic destiny of all living matter. Viewed thus, aging can be accepted as the impersonal outcome of the privilege we have of living out a lifetime.

Aging is one aspect of the growth and maturation of the organism, and there are several bodily changes indicative of the progressive nature of the process, all of which extend from birth to death: decrease in metabolic energy; decrease in water content of the tissues; decrease of tissue elasticity; decrease in the ability of cells to divide and thus repair the normal wear and tear in using the body or to restore injured tissue; and a decrease in all other factors that protect the physical well-being of the individual. If we consider the development of the physical structure and functions of the various body systems—muscular, skeletal, circulatory, respiratory, gastrointestinal, skin, endocrine, and neural—we find that most, although not all, grow in strength and size during the early years of life, and that only in the later decades do they appreciably decline. In general, then, we may say that the pinnacle of physical development and efficiency occurs between the ages of twenty and twenty-five, and that following this period there is a very gradual decrease in most abilities until late in life, at which time the age changes become accelerated. Misinterpretation of the meaning of these physical changes can lead to a failure to make the most of life.

Examination of a number of physical characteristics will serve to illustrate these general trends. It will also emphasize the variability of the time of their onset and the rate at which they progress. The skeletal musculature, for example, continues to increase in bulk and density until the age of fifty and does not show degenerative changes before age sixty, yet muscular strength is at its maximum around the thirtieth year. Motility and motor coordination, which are dependent upon the skeletal muscles and the maturity of the nervous system, are most efficient at an earlier age. Most careers in the 100-yard dash, prize-fighting, and channel swimming must be suspended well before the beginning of the fourth decade. Middle-aged people are better suited to physical tasks requiring endurance than to activities calling for great expenditures of physical energy. Unfortunately, too few persons learn soon enough to adapt their activities to their changing physical status.

Unlike the skeletal musculature, the smooth muscles which are essential to the vegetative functions, and to the maintenance of life itself, show practically no change with age. These smooth muscles make up the walls of the blood vessels, respiratory organs, stomach and other parts of the gastro-intestinal tract, and urinary organs. Thus the vital organs, if properly treated and nourished, can remain effective machines until the end of life itself.

Of special interest is the metabolic function. At birth, the body is maximally efficient in its ability to combine food and oxygen to produce energy. Its metabolic capacity diminishes thereafter for the rest of life, especially when the growth period is completed. Beginning with the thirties, most people begin to require increasing amounts of rest to maintain their energy reserves at levels high enough to meet daily needs. As we grow still older, we may be well advised to curtail the number of our activities and to ration our available energies in order to achieve those things we consider of greatest merit.

Another area in which occur age-changes that are of particular importance to the individual's adaptation to and continued mastery of his environment is that of the senses. The only way in which we can keep touch with the external world is through the media of our sense organs, all of which undergo characteristic changes with age. In fact, one of the most common sensory changes that occurs with amazing regularity at about the age of forty-five in persons with normal visual apparatus is presbyopia. Holmes has called this the "arm length age" because the reduction in the elasticity of the crystalline lens of the eye has progressed to the point where the lens can no longer change its curvature sufficiently to allow accommodation for near points of vision. Until we are fitted for glasses with convex lenses, we may have to stand outside a phone booth in order to read the directory inside! Fortunately, there is now little of the stigma that was once attached to wearing glases, and more people are accepting gratefully the visual aid provided by them, thereby preserving their eyesight or preventing undue eyestrain.

Presbyopia is, however, only one of the visual changes associated with aging; all the components of the eye undergo structural changes to some degree. The cornea—the clear outer coat—tends to lose some of its transparency, and the pupil, beginning at about age thirty, decreases in size, thus admitting less light and causing visual difficulty under conditions of poor illumination. Adequate compensation for this defect can usually be made by increasing illumination without increasing glare.

The retina—that portion of the eye in which lie the sensitive visual cells—undergoes changes which result in reduced visual acuity, decreased sensitivity of the eye in the dark, and restriction on the periphery of the visual fields. Since these changes are normal and are not the result of pathological or disease processes, the individual at middle age is scarcely aware of them or may easily adjust to them. In addition to the correction provided by lenses, these retina changes may call for more caution in driving after dark, waiting a little longer after the lights are put out before attempting to go into a darkened room, or turning the head further to see what lies on the outer edges of the visual fields. Most of these adaptations, made unconsciously, are of concern only in insuring safety and proper visual communication.

Hearing, like vision, is a most important sense, in bringing about understanding; and, like vision, the auditory apparatus undergoes, with age, a number of changes in structure. Most important of these is the gradual atrophy or hardening of the auditory sensory cells and nerves, which causes practically everyone to experience some loss in auditory acuity.

Deafness which is identified with age—that is, when it is not pathological in origin—involves primarily the higher tone freqencies. Before the age of sixty or over, there is very little loss in hearing acuity for tones in the voice range or lower. Presbycusis—progressive loss of hearing for higher tones—begins, however, in early adulthood and shows greater and greater loss as age increases. It is interesting to note here that there are marked sex differences in auditory sensitivity. Women and men show no difference in acuity up to frequencies in the middle ranges (2048 cycles) but, for frequencies above this point, females of all ages are able to hear high tones much better than can males.

With the advent of transistors and other electronic devices, hearing losses are becoming increasingly susceptible of compensation by efficient and inconspicuous sensory aids. Acceptance of the loss as a normal change occurring with age makes it easier for many of us to adjust to it by being fitted with proper hearing aids. The implication of such adaptation, when our losses are of such magnitude as to interfere with our work or with our continued participation in the normal activities of our friends, are obvious.

Among the functional age changes which have the most far-reaching consequences during middle life are, perhaps, those associated with reproduction. During childhood, the sex glands grow slowly but are functionally immature until about the age of twelve. From puberty onward, the reproductive function increases in strength continuously until it reaches a maximum at about the age of twenty-five. After that it declines sharply until, in women, it disappears altogether sometime between the ages of forty-five and fifty years.

Although still a controversial point, it is usually conceded that men experience a similar "climacteric," though at a somewhat later age. In both sexes, the slow atrophy of the sex glands after the age of twenty-five causes a gradual lowering in the amount of male and female androgens (sex hormones) secreted. This atrophy is responsible for bringing the reproductive period of the female (whose androgen output at all ages is less than that of the male) to a close, and for diminishing the sexual interests and activities of the male.

In the mores of our past culture this climacteric often gave rise to a number of psychological symptoms. The menopausal woman dwelt on her "hot flashes," was wont to faint and call for her smelling salts, sometimes took to her bed and became mildly depressed. She was nervous, lacked energy, and was always tired. A man, experiencing a similar biologic state, was mentally depressed, tired, and deeply worried about his lack of drive toward sexual activities. It was assumed by both sexes that these profound changes and the end of the reproductive period were necessary concomitants of hapless old age. Fortunately, modern men and women are putting less emphasis upon the symptoms commonly associated with the climacteric and are, as a result, enjoying better mental and physical health.

In some ways, life is easier than it was in the past. The physical demands of work have been so lightened and so shortened that the level of health has been favorably influenced. People are better informed and have come, through education, to understand the meaning of physiological changes. Neither sex feels guilty or embarrassed when natural physiological attractions wane and other interests begin more and more to engage its attention. It is now common knowledge that, with the cessation of the reproductive function and drive, there is a release of responsibility from continuing demands of procreation of the race. Moreover, there is ample evidence that men and women continue to enjoy excellent physical and mental health, that most of them live twenty-five or more years to reach old age, and that they become increasingly endowed with time in which to pursue their own projected purposes.

Professor Havighurst has placed the new prime of life at this period when freedom from certain biological demands becomes a new dimension in living. Aristotle would not agree that it is a "new" prime but would insist that it is "the" prime of life. In considering the various types of human character in relation to age, he expressed the opinion that "the body is in its prime from thirty to five and thirty, the mind about forty-nine." (Aristotle is thought to have been about forty-nine when he set these limits.) "It is evident," he said, "that the character of those in the prime of life will be the mean between that of the other two, if the excess in each case be removed.

. . . Speaking generally, all the advantages that youth and old age possess separately, those in the prime of life possess combined: all cases of excess or defect in the other two are replaced by due moderation and fitness." [3] Aristotle's conception clearly suggests that the different periods of life have different uses; and that the wise man carefully explores these uses.

The Psychological Machine

We have reviewed the various changes that take place in the physiological and biochemical functions of a maturing individual. We have seen that physical aging is a natural process, that it proceeds continuously from the beginning to the end of life, and that the rate of change varies among different individuals and for different functions within the individual himself. We have seen, also, that without growth and development, there can be no physical maturity, and that, without such maturity, there can be little accomplished.

What is true of the physical machine is equally true of the psychological functions of the individual, with one possible and extremely important difference. The peak of growth, strength, and effective physiological function, as we have seen, is attained by the age of twenty to twenty-five; following this point there is a very gradual decline in the physical capacities of the individual until late in life, when the change may become somewhat more rapid. That this is true may depend, at least in part, upon the fact that the purely biological functions mature and age more rapidly than do the psychological and spiritual capacities.

It is possible, however, for *mental* function to be maintained at maximum performance or even to be increased for many years. Cerebral capacity begins to weaken only in later years and then relatively slowly. At the age of seventy, a person is still as capable as at fifty. At eighty, the intellect is the equivalent of that of the twenties. At ninety, the return is back to the teens, a period often considered the best of life.

It has long been known that a man or woman needs some years of adult experience to achieve mature judgment and to become "exceeding wise," but it has only been within the last few years that

---

[3] W. R. Roberts and I. Bywater, *The Rhetoric and Poetics of Aristotle.* Oxford: Clarendon Press, 1940.

we have been able to demonstrate objectively that the general intelligence of the middle-aged person, as well as his judgment and wisdom, is greater than it was at a younger age.

How is this increase in general intelligence and cerebral capacity brought about when the brain, like other parts of the physical organism, is undergoing involutional changes with age? The answer to this question has not been demonstrated conclusively. The brain is a remarkable structure. It is unquestionably the most comprehensive and interesting phenomenon that nature has created. It is the only structure that possesses such strange attributes as consciousness, feelings, emotion, intellect, and ideas. It is among the latest evolutionary acquisitions of the animal kingdom. The extraordinary development of the brain of man distinguishes him from all his fellow creatures and makes him ruler of the inanimate inorganic world and of the plant and animal kingdoms.

It happens, then, that man has been placed in a position of tremendous responsibility. By the time he has completed his functions of procreation and the training of his progeny and is thus free to expand his fields of interest, his mind has matured until it has become a tool of great strength and precision. Cerebral function is the most dependable servant that can be called upon over a long span of years. The brain virtually becomes the sanctuary of the middle and later years. This remarkable organ can be the greatest source of pleasure, amusement, and satisfaction. No toy has ever yielded more enjoyment. No toy, if properly used, can improve so much with age. And here lies the secret of life.

Knowing this secret, do humans make use of it? Some do, of course, but all too few. It may be argued that everyone must think all of the time in order to carry on his daily tasks and that, therefore, there should be no decline in intellectual ability through lack of use of mental capacities. That this argument is fallacious may be shown by the fact that, although we learn and remember daily, we are generally, when older, plagued with difficulty in learning new and varied ideas. This does not mean the loss of ability to learn and recall, because, when a middle-aged or older person engages in retraining, he regains his original proficiency. For example, when an adult re-enters an educational program, he usually experiences considerable difficulty during the first weeks of his class work in recalling in detail the materials he reads or hears. This is frequently so dismaying that many people are discouraged from continuing the learning process long enough to become efficient again. Practice and refreshing of the learning skill has the same beneficial effect upon the skill as, for example, practice has upon proficiency in golf. Many middle-aged women are finding that, with a few weeks of intensive retraining, they are able to refurbish their knowledge of shorthand and their skill in typing. These women, regaining experience in their ability, are re-entering the labor market and, since there is a great shortage of good typists and stenographers, are making an important contribution to the economy.

Some older people who are required to retire from their regular occupations are finding that they, too, can turn to new fields of endeavor with great success. When recently a professor of history was retired because of age, he turned to the development of a new business in a field in which he had had no previous experience. He reports that learning the new facts needed to conduct his business, and applying the skills acquired over the years, brought as great personal satisfaction as the preparation for his first vocation had brought. And why should not this be the case? Growth, development, the expression of latent potentialities, and the achievement of one's aspirations are, at any age, "heady" wine, indeed. One may better inquire why so many of us, although we recognize the rewarding vista from the hill to be climbed, deny ourselves the pleasure of the quest. Perhaps we are "valley bound" by a too-ready willingness to accept, as one of the heritages of our culture, the belief that middle and old age are periods of mental senescence, instead of recognizing that these years yield opportunity and freedom for perfection of our talents.

John Addington Symonds, in his biography of the poet Shelley, makes the point that psychological potentialities need maturity to bring them to full fruition. "It is worse than useless," he writes, "to deplore the irremediable; yet no man, probably, has failed to mourn the fate of mighty poets, whose dawning gave the promise of a glorious day, but who passed from the earth while yet the light that shone in them was crescent. That the world should know Marlowe and Giorgione, Raphael and Mozart, only by the products of their early manhood, is indeed a cause for lamentation, when we remember what the long lives of a Bach, a Titian, a Michelangelo, and Goethe, held in reserve for their maturity and age. It is no use to persuade ourselves, as some have done, that we possess the best work of men untimely slain. Had Sophocles been cut off in his prime, before the composition of Oedipus; had Handel never merged the fame of his forgotten operas in the immortal music of his oratorios; had Milton been known only by the poems of his youth, we might with equal plausibility have laid that flattering unction to our heart. And yet how shallow would have been our optimism, how fallacious our attempt at consolation. There is no denying the fact that when a young Marcellus is shown by fate for one brief moment, and withdrawn before his springtime has brought forth the fruits of summer, we must bow in silence to the law of waste that rules inscrutably in nature." [4]

Symonds' eloquent evaluation of the contribution of maturity, and of the time of life when one's mental endowments can be given their fullest expression, leaves little doubt about the effectiveness of the psychological machine at middle age. What is essential, of course, is the willingness to exercise and use one's psychological equipment in order to accept, and adapt to, the physical limitations and emotional changes imposed by age and exposure to environmental vicissitudes. But, given this willingness, the middle-aged person should find within himself the resources of personal experiences, knowledges, skills, and spiritual living that can be used to achieve a continuing pattern of effective living for many years to come.

Conclusion

It should be stressed again, in conclusion, that aging is a natural phenomenon and a basic characteristic of all living matter and is, therefore, not to be confused with disease. Aging is best understood as a continuous process of progressive change in all structures and functions of the body. As the efficiency of its physical and psychological machines decreases, mankind is forced to make certain adaptations and adjustments in its way of life; but, once these adjustments are made, the majority of humans are capable of accomplishing many worthwhile things. The candle is decidedly worth the burning.

While youth has the advantages of physical strength and agility,

---

[4] John A. Symonds, *Shelley*. New York: Harper & Brothers, 1905.

it also has the responsibility for perpetuating the species and must, in addition, spend prodigious amounts of energy in acquiring the abilities and experiences that will be helpful to its middle age. Maturity of fifty years, on the other hand, brings with it judgment, a consciousness of the magnitude of the world and the place of the individual in it, and increased opportunity for self-expression and pursuit of knowledge. No longer does energy have to be used to insure the biological survival of the race. Consideration can now be given to the improvement and transmittal of the culture of the times. The human mental machine is now, at last, ready for its prime performance. Its careful and thoughtful use can only bring an increase in its precision and skill.

Time Out for Reflection

In older times, few people lived past fifty—the time, we now think, when mental powers achieve their height. Does this mean that most of the mental potential of those societies was lost, and that in our own it is saved? How are we using it? Do you think we could do better?

Athletes generally reach their peak in the 20's, creative people often in their 30's; executives (such as U.S. presidents) tend to average in their 50's on taking office. Does this have any implications about the age at which—

men can be called on to serve as soldiers?

young adults should be given the vote?

people make the most effective parents?

Mental powers, like physical, flourish when they are given consistent exercise. What invitations to their exercise does our culture give to people in their middle years? What restraints does it impose on people who want to cultivate independent powers of thought or of creativity? What more could you yourself be doing to develop the powers that you will enjoy throughout your later years?

READINGS   CHAPTER 3

The Philosophy of Stress

Hans Selye

WHATEVER WE DO and whatever is done to us causes wear and tear. Stress is not the specific result of any one among our actions; nor is it a typical response to any one thing acting upon us from without; it is a common feature of all biological activities.

When stress is defined as the "rate of wear and tear in the body," the close relationship between aging and stress becomes particularly evident. Stress is a kind of "speedometer of life."

There is a great *difference between physiologic and chronologic age.* One man may be much more senile in body and mind, and much closer to the grave, at forty than another person at sixty. Vitality is like a special kind of bank account which you can use up by withdrawals but cannot increase by deposits. Your only control over this most precious fortune is the rate at which you make your withdrawals. The solution is evidently not to stop withdrawing, for this would be death. Nor is it to withdraw just enough for survival, for this would permit only a vegetative life, worse than death. The intelligent thing to do is to withdraw generously, but never expend wastefully.

Many people believe that, after they have exposed themselves to very stressful activities, a rest can restore them to where they were before. This is false. Experiments on animals have clearly shown that each exposure leaves an indelible scar, in that it uses up reserves of adaptability which cannot be replaced. It is true that immediately after some harassing experience, rest can restore us almost to the original level of fitness by eliminating acute fatigue. But the emphasis is on the word *almost.* Since we constantly go through periods of stress and rest during life, just a little deficit of adaptation energy every day adds up—it adds up to what we call *aging*.

Apparently, there are *two kinds of adaptation energy:* the superficial kind, which is ready to use, and the deeper kind, which acts as a sort of frozen reserve. When superficial adaptation energy is exhausted during exertion, it can slowly be restored from a deeper store during rest. This gives a certain plasticity to our resistance. It also protects us from wasting adaptation energy too lavishly in certain foolish moments, because acute fatigue automatically stops us. It is the restoration of the superficial adaptation energy from the deep reserves that tricks us into believing that the loss has been made good. Actually, it has only been covered from reserves—and at the cost of depleting reserves.

To Die of Old Age

What makes me so certain that the natural human life-span is far in excess of the actual one is this:

Among all my autopsies (and I have performed quite a few), I have never seen a man who died of old age. In fact, *I do not think anyone has ever died of old age yet.* To die of old age would mean that all organs of the body would be worn out proportionately, merely by having been used too long. This is never the case. We invariably die because one vital part has worn out too early in proportion to the rest of the body.

The lesson seems to be that, as far as man can regulate his life by voluntary actions, he should seek to equalize stress throughout his being, by what we have called *deviation,* the frequent shifting-over of work from one part to the other. The human body—like the tires on a car, or the rug on a floor—wears longest when it wears evenly. We can do ourselves a great deal of good in this respect by just yielding to our natural cravings for variety in everyday life.

A human being can do much, through voluntary choice of conduct, to get as far as possible with a given bodily structure and supply of adaptation energy, under given social conditions. For instance, he can live and express his personality at a tempo and in a manner best suited to his inherited talents, under the prevailing social conditions. The two great limiting factors—which are set once a man is born—are: his supply of adaptation energy and the wear and tear that the weakest vital part of his body can tolerate. So, actually, we can accomplish a great deal by living wisely in accordance with natural laws.

A Way of Life

Can the scientific study of stress teach us the wisdom to live a rich and meaningful life which satisfies our needs for self-expression and yet is not marred or cut short by the stresses of senseless struggles? I believe that the mere fact of understanding the general rules about the way stress acts upon mind and body, with a few remarks about the way this has been used as a basis for one man's personal philosophy, can help others, better than fixed rules, to formulate their own solutions.

I found it helpful to subdivide my aspirations into three kinds: short-range aims, long-range aims and the ultimate aim.

Short-range Aims

Man's short-range aims are designed for immediate gratification—you merely let things act upon you which give you a pleasant feeling and you do things you like to do.

But man's mind is capable of much *more lasting and profound passive satisfactions.* These are not so readily accessible, because they presuppose a carefully developed, acquired taste. We must plan these; they are not fully developed by our heredity. I think that people in all practical walks of life should keep in mind that, deep in their hearts, they need the pure enjoyment of impractical pleasures to live a balanced life.

Let me explain. Anybody who likes music can enjoy at least a simple folk song; no special schooling is needed for this. But a person who has a real understanding for the art of combining tones can appreciate really great music much better than the casual amateur. The same is true of literature and of painting. Anyone can enjoy the universe by looking at the stars or life by looking at flowers and animals. The profound pleasure of studying nature comes from our understanding—however superficially—the lawfulness which governs it.

The appreciation of art and the admiration of nature has another advantage over the simple pleasures of the flesh: its afterglow lasts longer. The more you learn to appreciate detail the more you get in return.

Long-range Aims

Man's long-range aims are designed to permit future gratification. Some people hope to find such aims in the acquisition of wealth, power and social position; others in religion or philosophy. Yet others have instinctively realized that they are unable to solve this problem. They just give up and drift from day to day, trying to divert their attention from the future by some such sedative as compulsive promiscuity, frantic work, or simply alcohol.

That none of these things can assure lasting happiness is self-evident. Of course, there are many better guides to it: love, kindness, or simply the desire to do some good. These are often very successful; but it seems to me that they all have common roots in *man's innate, though often subconscious, desire to earn gratitude and to avoid being the target for revenge.*

The relationship between long-range aims and stress is so evident that it hardly justifies more than a fleeting comment. Mental tensions, frustrations, the sense of insecurity, and aimlessness are among the most important stressors. As psychosomatic studies have shown, they are also very common causes of physical disease. How often are migraine headache, gastric and duodenal ulcer, coronary thrombosis, arthritis, hypertension, insanity, suicide, or just hopeless unhappiness actually caused by the failure to find a satisfactory guide for conduct?

But neither short-range nor long-range aims are actually the ultimate aim of man: the objective which would furnish a basis for all our actions.

The Ultimate Aim

As I see it, man's ultimate aim is *to express himself as fully as possible, according to his own lights.*

The goal is certainly not to avoid stress. Stress is part of life. It is a natural by-product of all our activities; there is no more justification for avoiding stress than for shunning food, exercise, or love. But, in order to express yourself fully, you must first find your optimum stress-level, and then, use your adaptation energy at a rate and in a direction adjusted to the innate structure of your mind and body.

The study of stress has shown that complete rest is not good, either for the body as a whole, or even for any organ within the body. Stress, applied in moderation, is necessary for life. Besides, enforced inactivity may be very harmful and cause more stress than normal activity.

At the risk of sounding facetious, let me present a little motto which I developed while analyzing stress in my experimental animals, in my colleagues, my friends, and myself.

> *Fight always for the highest attainable aim*
> *But never put up resistance in vain.*

Everyone should *fight* for whatever seems really worthwhile to him. On the other hand, he should aim only for *things attainable* to him, for otherwise he will merely become frustrated. Finally, *resistance* should be put up whenever there is reasonable expectation of its succeeding, but never if we know it would be *in vain.*

It is not easy to live by this motto; it takes much practice and almost constant self-analysis. Any time during the day, in discussions, at work and at play, when I begin to feel keyed up, I consciously stop to analyze the situation. I ask myself: "Is this really the best thing I could do now, and is it worth the trouble of putting up resistance against counter-arguments, boredom, or fatigue?" If the answer is no, I just stop; or whenever this cannot be done gracefully I simply "float" and let things go on as they will, with a minimum of active participation (e.g. during most committee meetings and unavoidable interviews with crack-pots).

Probably few people would be inclined to contest the soundness of this motto. The trick is to follow it! But that is where my assistance must stop. That is where you come in. We all must live our own lives. No self-respecting person wants to go from cradle to grave sheepishly following the directives of another man.

Success Formula?

One of the main points of this whole discussion is that *there is no ready-made success formula which would suit everybody*. We are all different. The only thing we have in common is our obedience to certain fundamental biologic laws which govern all men.

The philosophy of stress has helped me enormously in achieving equanimity and a personally satisfactory program for the way I want to go through life. I rather think if you tried it, it might help you too.

Biological Aspects
of the Aging Process
Carl V. Weller, M.D. (1887-1956)

WE GROW OLD NATURALLY. That is a statement which has no unpleasant connotation. It is a simple statement of a truth, the appreciation of which is essential if the process of aging is to be understood, accepted, and utilized for the benefit of man. If the order of the words is changed to "naturally, we grow old," the implication becomes less pleasant. Far different concepts of old age are entertained by the child, the young adult, the middle-aged, and those in late middle life. Those who say "naturally, we grow old" speak without complete understanding. They do not realize that they were growing old before they were born. I propose to show that the process of growing old is as normal and as natural as life itself.

That man grows old naturally is evident from the pattern of life. Man is one of the long-lived animals. Despite popular belief to the contrary, only giant tortoises have a longer life span. Sixty years is the longest authenticated life for an elephant and fifty-four years for a parrot, both of them belonging to species to which great longevity is popularly attributed. A dog at fourteen years is said to be as old as a man of eighty, and our familiar laboratory white rats are senile at four years. Thus, for each species there is an ultimate life limit which not all members of the species reach. Within the life span of the individuals of each species a pattern of life has been established which, through a long period of trial, has proved most successful for the perpetuation of that species. We cannot escape that pattern. It is indelibly stamped into the living nuclear substance which determines heredity. That the pattern is different for each species is evidence enough that it can be modified, but alteration of the life pattern is an unbelievably slow process. For man, change in the life pattern and therefore in the ultimate life limit, if it is occurring at all, is at too slow a rate to be recognized in the lifetime of any observer. It is doubtful if there has been any clearly recognizable change in the human pattern in the few thousand of years which comprise the historical record of our species.

For each species of animal or plant the established life pattern is wholly an expression of the biological mechanisms for securing perpetuation of the species. That purpose is never out of sight. Consequently, the pattern can always be interpreted as purposeful. It makes not a particle of difference to my thesis, or to the wholesome appreciation of the aging process which I hope to impart to you, whether you write "nature" with an initial capital and think of God, the Creator, as the directing force in human life; or whether you think of nature in terms of evolution and involution, and of the life pattern as the result of processes of trial and error extending through ranges of time known only to the geologist and the astronomer. Whichever, or whatever, your personal philosophy may be, it is equally applicable to a genuine understanding of why and how we grow old naturally.

The impelling, dynamic drive to secure the continuity of the species determines the pattern of life, but the factors concerned are numerous, and the duration and intensity of the instinctive urge for procreation is but one of them. Another is the length of the period of gestation during which the developing infant remains unborn. For man, this is about ten lunar months. Still other factors are the number of young born at one time, their degree of development at birth, the length of the period of physical growth, the age at which procreation becomes possible, the length of the training period for the acquisition of knowledge and skills, the extent of the period of fertility, and the duration of the need for parental (particularly, maternal) care before the succeeding generation can, in turn, assume an independent role in the pattern of life. Innumerable examples of the varying devices by which nature makes adjustments for these biological needs can be found. The adult guinea pig and the adult rat are of approximately the same size. For the guinea pig the period of gestation is about sixty-three days, and the average litter is between two and three young. For the rat, the period of gestation is about twenty days, and the average litter is about nine. But note the compensatory factors for these marked differences! The newborn guinea pig has its eyes open, it weighs about eighty grams, it is capable of active locomotion, and it takes some food other than its mother's milk. The newborn rat is a tiny, hairless, blind infant, capable of wriggling motion only, and entirely dependent upon the maternal food supply for many days. Each pattern is successful in maintaining the species. "Pigs Is Pigs" caught the popular fancy a generation or so ago; and the brown rat is an almost worldwide pest, although the ingenuity of man is constantly pitted against him.

Applied to man, intra-uterine life extends for about 280 days, fully dependent infancy lasts about two years, and partly dependent childhood for another decade or more. Physiologically, reproduction usually becomes possible at twelve to seventeen years of age, but our highly technical culture requires a longer period for the acquisition of knowledge and skill. After the training period, there is a further interval before economic independence is assured. Thus, parenthood is usually delayed until the middle of the third decade. Since maternal care is desirable for fifteen years or more after a child is born, the reason for the cessation of female fertility at about forty-five years of age at once becomes evident. The normal life expectancy must provide for maternal care after the birth of the last child. The paternal part in bringing the infant to the stage of independent living is far less intimate, as we all realize. We are not surprised, therefore, to find that there is no fixed limit upon male fertility. Many men of advanced years retain the possibility of fatherhood.

There is still another phase of the life pattern, both for the lower animals and for man. In securing the perpetuation of the species, nature must utilize the individual, but when the end has been served the individual is no longer needed. To be sure, those of advanced years may be of value to the tribe because they can impart their knowledge and skill to the young hunters and warriors. The maturity of judgment gained by experience makes the aged of use as counselors. Their main task has been accomplished, however, and soon they are to be removed from the scene. The tempo of the aging process increases, the initial energy charge is finally expended, and death may be physiologic if disease does not intervene.

From this rapid survey of the biologic pattern of life it should be recognized that the entire process is natural, it is purposeful, and it is for the good of our species. The aging process is a part of the master scheme of life. The process of aging is racially altruistic!

How natural it is to grow old becomes evident at once with the not unpleasant discovery that we commence growing old before we are born. Nature is economical. Useless structures undergo atrophy and disappear, or are otherwise disposed of. Those who have some familiarity with embryology will recall that in the development of the human egg cell, the ovum, three-fourths of the nuclear material is discarded. The tail of the spermatozoon is absorbed after the spermatozoon has entered the ovum. The placental blood vessels show senile changes at the time of birth. Throughout the entire development period these involuntary processes take place. The roots of the milk teeth are absorbed and the thymus gland and the tonsils diminish in size. These and many other alterations are part of the process of growing old, even in childhood and adolescence.

After adult stature has been attained the aging process continues. It influences the character of the diseases of middle life and of old age, but we are not now discussing individual diseases. There are recognizable tissue changes which become more and more evident as the years advance. Reasonably enough, these are of the same character as those found in the mature (senile) placenta which was discarded when the person was born. These are the basic changes in physiologic involution. They fall into three groups:

1. Reduction in size of organs and of the organism as a whole. This is physiologic atrophy and is brought about in part by reduction in number of cells and in part by reduction in size of cells. Replacement and repair, effective in earlier years, have become inadequate to offset the attrition of use.

2. Changes in the intercellular and supporting tissues of the body which increase the proportion of connective tissues as compared to the more actively functioning elements. These same supporting tissue elements become less cellular and more dense and hyaline. Elasticity is diminished, and there is a strong tendency toward the deposition of calcium and magnesium salts—calcification.

3. Alterations in the blood vessels characterize the aging process more than any other general feature. Normally, arteries have elastic walls which expand as the pulse wave comes along and contract upon the

contained blood after it passes. These large elastic vessels serve to equalize and control blood pressure in much the same way that the air compression chamber of a force pump gives a steady stream from the nozzle. In the aging process and as a part of the major involution which is to remove the unneeded organism from the scene, blood vessels lose much of their elasticity; their walls become thicker; muscle and elastic fibers are replaced by nonelastic hyaline substance; lime salts are laid down in the wall; and the lumen, through which the blood flows, becomes progressively more narrow.

These changes in the blood vessels constitute the process of vascular sclerosis, popularly known as hardening of the arteries. Similar, if not identical, changes occur in certain blood vessels of babies, which must be obliterated in making over the fetal circulation into the postnatal pattern. No one thinks of these infantile adjustments as disease. There is no more reason for thinking of the vascular changes of late middle life and old age as disease. Yet they exact certain penalties from the human body, and many of the ailments which are considered as more or less peculiar to advanced years are the functional expression of impaired blood supply to important organs as a result of these same, apparently physiologic, vascular changes. The results are noted particularly in the musculature of the heart, in the kidneys, and in the brain. While these retrogressive changes in the blood vessels appear to be as natural and as inevitable for the involutionary period as growth is for the earlier decades of life, it is not too much to hope that medical science may discover more effective methods than are now available for postponing their onset or retarding their development. But this is a difficult task, since it means modifying processes which are a part of the hereditary pattern of life itself.

Just as life and the aging process, which is a part of life, exhibit a pattern which is peculiar to the species, so, also, do the functional components of human activity. They show varying phases of emphasis in respect to age that are most desirable in securing the perpetuation of the species. The curves for nutrition and metabolism, motility, reproductive power in the female, and cerebral and spiritual development can be drawn in relation to the decades of life. The ascent and decline of these vital functions reflect biologic needs, the satisfaction of these needs, and the effects of involutionary changes. The function of nutrition and metabolism is at its highest pitch at birth, declines rapidly until about twenty years of age, remains at a nearly constant level until about seventy, and then gradually falls again until the end of life. We are better machines for taking in food, building bodies, and producing energy at birth than we will ever be again. The function of motility, having in mind both the magnitude and velocity of motion and also motor skill, is exhibited at a low level at birth and rises rapidly after infancy to reach a broadly rounded summit in the third decade. Athletes and coaches know that at a period varying from about twenty-five to thirty years motor skill and the precise control of motor activity begin to decline. This decline continues to advanced years. The curve of reproductive function, as the biologic requirements lead us to anticipate, rises abruptly at puberty from the zero level of birth to reach its acme at about twenty-six years of age, with a return to the zero line (for the female) at the average menopausal age of forty-five. In a monogamous social arrangement the reproductive function is thus concentrated in a period of about two or two and one-half decades. For reasons which I have already stated, this is as it should be for the good of the species, and it is purposeful and not accidental. We should not have children until we are physically and spiritually ready to care for them, and children should not be born so late in parental life that there is no normal prospect of parental care continuing until they become independent. The curve of reproductive function meets these needs with the single exception that the physical capacity for reproduction develops too early for our complex and exacting economy.

The curve of cerebral function and spiritual development deserves special attention. With a very rapid rise from shortly after birth, the ascent is continuous but at a decreasing rate until late middle life or early old age. That the curve can and does, in many persons, continue to rise until fifty, sixty, or even sixty-five years of age is of the greatest importance. Those who are in that period can still acquire new knowledge, can develop greater power in the synthesis of facts, can temper judgment with experience, and, through the years, can gain in appreciation of that which is good and beautiful and in the understanding of spiritual values. Contemplation of the four curves of major vital functions leaves no doubt wherein lie the possibilities for gracious living on the part of those who are in the later years of life. . . .

It is true that growing old is a natural process, the purpose of which is ultimately to remove those whose major usefulness to the species has come to an end. But usefulness to the species includes much more than the creation of children and rearing them to an age at which they are physically competent to make their own contribution to the endless stream of life. If it were not so, we would count each generation as fifteen or twenty years instead of a third of a century as is true for all practical purposes today. Even with primitive man, whose food needed only to be gathered and not to be produced, those of advancing years were of value to the community as demonstrators of how the procurement of food could best be achieved, and as counselors whose past experience made it possible for them to interpret the significance of changing seasons and of other features of a constantly varying environment.

It is still more true today than it was one hundred thousand years ago that the aging have further biologic usefulness after childbearing has been completed. The present social and economic pattern calls for the extension of parental care for many years after offspring have passed the pubertal period. Education is prolonged, skills must be acquired, shelter must be found, economic independence must be reasonably secure. For such reasons marriage and childbearing are delayed and offspring come late. Longer years of parental aid and counsel are needed. Or, if the second generation marries before independence is assured, grandparents become useful in assuming responsibilities for care and maintenance to a degree which may be somewhat at variance with the general pattern of life but leaves no doubt in the grandparental minds that their biologic duty is not yet ended.

It is particularly in those activities which depend upon maturity of cerebral function, memory of accumulated experiences, and increased skill, tact, and forbearance in human relations that the aging retain and augment their usefulness. They function as counselors and guides, and as the determiners of policy. With child-rearing completed, time and strength remain for an active share in civic affairs, in politics, in the church, or in the fraternal order. For some time the totality of cerebral function increases, and the opportunity for its use is at hand.

The first and the most important ingredient in the prescription for growing old graciously and happily is understanding—understanding of the naturalness of the process of growing old. This inevitable involution, which begins even before we are born, is but the fulfillment of biologic destiny. In growing old we are equally a part of the patterned life of the species as when we are rearing children. With this view accepted, the mind is left free to make the most of the declining years. . . .

Knowledge of the biologic significance of the aging process makes possible the acceptance of its manifestations with understanding. With this foundation laid, it is possible to avoid or, at least, to mitigate, many of the annoyances and inconveniences of the later years of life. At the same time it is possible to augment the satisfactions of that period—to capitalize, as it were, the special assets of later maturity.

With understanding, we, the aging, can agree with Cicero in *De senectute:* "Whatever is natural must be accounted good."

A Period of
Second Flowering

Anne Morrow Lindbergh (1907-   )

THE PRIMITIVE, PHYSICAL, FUNCTIONAL pattern of the morning of life, the active years before forty or fifty, is outlived. But there is still the afternoon opening up, which one can spend not in the feverish pace of the morning but in having time at last for those intellectual, cultural, and spiritual activities that were pushed aside in the heat of the race. We Americans, with our terrific emphasis on youth, action, and material success, certainly tend to belittle the afternoon of life and even to pretend it never comes. We push the clock back and try to prolong the morning, overreaching and overstraining ourselves in the unnatural effort. We do not succeed, of course. We cannot compete with our sons and daughters. And what a struggle it is to race with these overactive and under-wise adults! In our breathless attempts we often miss the flowering that waits for afternoon.

For is it not possible that middle age can be looked upon as a period of second flowering, second growth, even a kind of second adolescence? It is true that society in general does not help one accept this interpretation of the second half of life. And therefore this period of expanding is often tragically misunderstood. Many people never climb above the plateau of forty-to-fifty. The signs that presage growth, so similar, it seems to me, to those in early adolescence: discontent, restlessness, doubt, despair, longing are interpreted falsely as signs of decay. In youth one does not as often misinterpret the signs; one accepts them, quite rightly, as growing pains. One takes them seriously, listens to them, follows where they lead. One is afraid. Naturally. Who is not afraid of pure space—that breath-taking empty space of an open door? But despite fear, one goes through to the room beyond.

But in middle age, because of the false assumption that it is a period of decline, one interprets these life-signs, paradoxically, as signs of approaching death. Instead of facing them, one runs away; one escapes—into depressions, nervous breakdowns, drink, love affairs, or frantic, thoughtless, fruitless overwork. Anything, rather than face them. Anything, rather than stand still and learn from them. One tries to cure the signs of growth, to exorcise them, as if they were devils, when really they might be angels of annunciation.

Cycles and Turning Points
Everett C. Hughes (1901-   )

EVERY CULTURE DEVELOPS a calendar; some cycle of days, moons, positions of sun and stars, or rain and drought, heat and cold, of plenty and want; of germination, growth, and harvest of plant; of breeding, birth, growth, and migration of the animals upon which they depend. These cycles of nature are interlaced with man's cycle of work and play and with his movements from place to place. Anthropologists have given us a rich body of descriptions of these cycles among the peoples of the world and of the myriad rites, festivals, exorcisms, and the like which mark their turning points. They tell us of cycles of mood as well as of natural occurrence, of periods of black despair followed by gay renewal of life and hope. . . .

All cultures also recognize and mark in various ways the biological life-cycle of the human individual. Birth is attended by rites which acknowledge the social existence of the infant, and make him a member of his kin-group and of his community. At the same time, his parents are ritually made into father and mother and assume responsibility for developing and training their offspring into good members of the community. Further rites often occur at puberty, when membership in one sex or the other becomes a more fateful matter; or when a boy is ready to go to sea, to war, or to the hunt with adult males. Entering upon a trade, marrying, growing old, and dying are also celebrated. These are all cases of passage from one status to another, from one patterned combination of duties and privileges, with its attendant perils and joys, to another. After the phrase of van Gennep, they have come to be called *rites de passage,* rites of transition. Sometimes the transition from one status to another is considered of such import that the candidate is given special instructions in the canons of conduct appropriate to his new estate. He may be sent upon a lonely journey in search of a vision, separated from other people and ordinary activities for a time, subjected to severe ordeals and bound by solemn vows. He may be made symbolically to die as a child and to be born again as a man. Finally he may appear again in the world transfigured, in a new costume and like St. Paul, bearing a new name.

Not only is the biological life-cycle of the individual thus related to the corresponding social cycle of his standing in society, but account is also taken of occasional cycles of mood and condition, that is, of the things which, while not so fixed in their order as are birth, puberty, aging, and death, are pretty sure to happen to all men, life and human nature being what they are. One may violate a tabu, commit a sin, or do an injury to another. A man may have been ill and in his fever may have seen the spirits of the dead. A woman may be bereft of the man whose bed and board she shared so closely that they were as one life. These things alienate one from other men and womn, and from the routine and banality of life. . . .

Many societies have institutionalized this alienation. In India the widow jumped into the funeral pyre and joined her husband in death. More commonly, there are rites for bringing the person, in due time, back into the world. Thus, the familiar example of ceremonial mourning. In French Canada, it is worked out in fine detail. A young widow mourns her young husband for a long time, starting with the severest of black costume and gradually returning to one which suggests that though she be a woman with a sorrow, her youth, attractiveness, and fruitfulness are not to be wasted. There is a period and a depth of mourning appropriate to every age and state of the mourner and the mourned, and to every degree of kin relations between them. In some societies, mourning is brought to an end after a stated period, and in a ceremonial way. The bereaved arises, puts on new garments, and goes among men again.

How well, in each case, does the proper institutional expression suit the felt grief of the bereaved individual? How often is it a hypocritical cover? How often a woefully insufficient expression of deep feeling? How often does the fixed penance for sin really liquidate the sense of guilt? How often is the rite gone through with defiant unrepentance? These are appropriate questions, but one cannot answer them in the mass. I suppose that if the instituted rites no longer correspond fairly well to the cycles and degrees of feeling accompanying the crises they are intended to carry one over, one would have to say that something is out of joint in society; that is, if the psychological reality and the social institution are no longer in some good functioning relation to one another. However that may be, there is one great thing to be said for conventional and instituted rites for carrying people over such crises, and for passing them on from one state of life to another; namely, that so long as the rites are practised there is no attempt to deny the realities of the human life-cycle, and the contingencies and changes of status that occur during it, and there is no pretence that the rhythms of mood, of guilt, of unhappiness, and grief do not occur. I am afraid that many of us, in our culture and in our time, do try to deny these things, to exorcise the reality by the negative rite of looking firmly in the opposite direction so as to pretend nothing is happening.

The number of phases of the social life-cycle varies from society to society and may be altered by social changes of many kinds. The passage from one phase to another may be obscured or prolonged. In our society, the ages of entering and leaving school and of going to work and supporting one's self have been undergoing great change. We are far from the simple state of rural Quebec where a boy is a man when, for the first time, he goes to the field and handles a team of horses. On that day, when he comes in to dinner he eats with the men and, before returning to the field, hauls down a pipe from the rack near the kitchen stove and smokes a pipeful of home-ground, home-cured tobacco, even if it nearly kills him. With us, a man's graduation from college or professional school may be attended by his own children. A physician, on the average, does not make ends meet until he is past thirty years of age.

It is difficult to say when childhood ceases, when adolescence begins and ends, when one is really adult. The onset and the risks of middle age are altered by technological change; the great contingency has become that of having a job, not the older one of being hurt or killed at one's work. The functions of old age are perhaps less clearly defined than ever before, in spite of the fact that there is an increasing tendency to standardize the age of retirement from work and the movement to provide pensions and thus economic security for all people.

What Is Middle Age?

James Slotkin (1913-   ) as reported by Sid Ross and Ernest La France

IS THERE a "middle age"?

When do we reach it? At 35? 40? 45?

Is it the same age for everybody?

What is the "middle-aged feeling" like?

How do most people react to it?

New light may be thrown on the least understood period in life through a special study by James Slotkin, Associate Professor of Social Science at the University of Chicago.

"Middle-aged" (42) himself, he recently began asking people the questions above—and found that, with the exception of popular descriptions and scientific papers on "middle age problems," there is little known about the period itself.

Borrowing methods he had used as an anthropologist to study the

Menominee Indians of Wisconsin, Slotkin tackled the basic idea of defining middle age. His conclusion: except in terms of life span, there probably is no such thing.

Since Shakespeare's time, most people have divided man's social life cycle (in most societies) into seven "ages": birth, infancy, childhood, adolescence, marriage, parenthood, and old age. Middle age, as such, is missing.

Turning for a clue to the Menominee Indians, Slotkin noted that they have no such thing as a "middle age problem." This traces to one fact: among the Menominees, the lifetime goal is growing old and having grandchildren.

Our Own "Carrot"

"Every society," Slotkin points out, "has some sort of carrot to dangle before you as a lifetime goal. This is 'normal.' Psychopaths don't have a lifetime goal. Among the Menominees, you don't get the carrot until you are an old person. In our society, you can get the carrot when you are still middle-aged in point of years. Finally, it struck me that that is the key to helping us define what we mean by 'middle-aged.' Actually, what we have to do is examine ourselves in terms of striving for our goals, rather than in chronological age."

Slotkin found a yardstick in studies made in the 1930s by Viennese psychologists, who divided adult striving into five stages. As revised by him to fit competitive American society, they are:

1) *The exploratory stage*—between the ages of about 15 and 27, when we've finished school and are trying to decide on our lifetime goal.

2) *Selective maturity*—between about 28 and 42, when we decide on our goal and put all our efforts into trying to achieve it.

3) *The testing stage*—beginning at about 43, when we start to reflect on our lives to determine whether we have achieved our goal, and to wonder if things have turned out as we had planned.

4) *The indulgent stage*—beginning at about 48, when we try to concentrate on getting the maximum satisfaction and gratification out of the "prime" of life.

5) *Completion*—from about 65, when we look back on life, begin to live in the past and usually stop seeking a further goal.

Interviewing many "middle-aged" people in the 42-and-up brackets, Slotkin tried to fit their lives into the proper categories. He found some discrepancies. Many Americans (baseball players and movie stars, for instance) hit their peak years at an age when most people are still trying to find their goals in life. By "middle age," they are already past their prime. Others (doctors, lawyers, professors) may be just getting started when the baseball players are facing retirement and often keep going when athletes and entertainers are forgotten. Still others (artists, the self-employed) have no timetables but themselves.

Because Stage 3 has commonly been associated with middle age through books like Walter Pitkin's *Life Begins at 40,* Slotkin examined it minutely. "For most people," he maintains, "middle age is a *role.* You can look at it chronologically, but what middle age means in our society is *not* your chronological age, but rather the time you begin thinking in terms of ending your occupational career. You have worked like a dog in the second, or selective, stage. Now you begin to think, 'Am I getting what I was looking for? Is this what I wanted?'"

To one degree or another, the individual starts evaluating his life. Broadly speaking, he will find himself falling into four categories: successful, partly successful, failure, or undecided.

"I want to stress that it's not only the objective factors that count but the subjective as well," says Slotkin. "A person who is considered successful by every standard of our society may decide that the whole thing isn't worthwhile, that the game isn't worth the candle. Or, on the other hand, he may decide that he is sitting on top of the world."

Success and Failure

According to Slotkin, only about 5 per cent of us feel that we are outright successes or failures. The rest are unable to decide.

Among the 5 per cent, only a small number are right, judged objectively. Some years ago, a top baseball player committed suicide. He was batting over .300, but in his own mind, he was a "failure."

How do most people react? "Failures," claims Slotkin, "are of two main types: those who acknowledge failure and those who take a grandiose attitude towards their failure to reach the goal." "Few people," he says, "have the guts to acknowledge failure. They try to escape and 'adjust' one way or the other. It is a lot more comfortable to look for another 'life goal'—in effect, to revert back to the exploratory and selective stages of earlier life." In competitive American society, this isn't easy.

The grandiose failure, typified by a mediocre painter Slotkin interviewed, becomes embittered, has a grudge against the world—and keeps it for the rest of his life. He never develops either the courage or the ability to really examine himself. He grows older spitefully.

The successful and the partly successful make up the rest of the 5 per cent. "The successful," says Slotkin, "fall into two types: the satisfied and the dissatisfied. The satisfied success is the individual who believes that he has achieved his original goals, and that these goals are gratifying. He has gotten what he wants. It fits him to a 'T' and he enjoys it." He has no "middle age problem."

The dissatisfied success can be as puzzled as the failures. "He is the poor devil who reaches the top and finds that all is ashes in his mouth," says the Professor. "He's made a mistake in his original life goals. His dominant desires still remain ungratified." He, like the failure, can wind up with serious neuroses, go back to find another goal, or (more usually) go ahead to Stage 4 and concentrate on finding an answer in pleasure. He has found it relatively easy to pursue his life course. It is too late to change.

Ninety-five in a hundred of the estimated 25,000,000 Americans who find themselves at the chronological "middle age" of the 40s fall into Slotkin's *inconclusive type.* "Most Americans like these," he says, "think that they will finally get that new car, that new home, security, the chicken in every pot, success in their job or profession. They keep plugging away after the carrot.

"The inconclusive person doesn't try to evaluate what he has. If he did, he'd have to evaluate what he *doesn't* have. He almost always feels that he 'still has a chance'—that he'll get through to his original life goals even though they somehow continue to elude him."

How an Actress Adjusted

If he becomes embittered, despairs of ever getting what he wants, desperately looks for a new start, or gives up trying, he is no longer middle-aged but actually in another "age" group.

Slotkin, who has already written a study of human adjustment (*Personality Development*—Harper & Bros.), thinks that someday he can complete research that will help make middle age adjustment easier for all.

Meanwhile, the best adjustment may be that of a middle-aged actress. "I wanted to be a big star," she told him, "but now I won't be. So I just want to be a darn good character actress."

"That's the only healthy adjustment," says Slotkin. "If you can't be a star, settle for a planet!"

Suggestions for Further Reading

Happiness, by William Lyon Phelps. New York: E. P. Dutton & Company, 1927.

A delightful and amusing essay on the relation of happiness and growing older, which points out the value of experience and accumulated knowledge.

Potentialities of Women in the Middle Years, edited by Irma H. Gross. East Lansing, Michigan: Michigan State University Press, 1956.

A notable symposium representing a determined search for answers to the perplexing questions of position, status, roles, problems, and life-fulfillment of middle-age women in twentieth century changing society. The chapters by Havighurst, Lawrence Frank, and Agnes Meyer are particularly appropriate to the topic of the essay you have just read.

The Second Forty Years, by E. J. Steiglitz. Philadelphia: Lippincott & Co., 1946.

Presents in popular style a great geriatric physician's views on the characteristic physical and mental changes associated with aging, with many sound suggestions.

Professor Robert J. Havighurst (born in 1900 at De Pere, Wis.) is Professor of Education at the University of Chicago. He was formerly Chairman, Committee on Human Development, University of Chicago. His research activities have been in the social psychology of adolescence and later maturity. Co-author of Who Shall Be Educated? *(1944),* Father of the Man *(1947),* Personal Adjustment in Old Age *(1949),* Older People *(1953),* The Meaning of Work and Retirement *(1954). He has been President of the Gerontological Society, Inc. and is UNESCO Educational Consultant to Brazil.*

"The issues are those which make the difference between defeat and opportunity, between frustration and fulfillment, in the everyday lives of average persons. They have to do with education, with medical care, with more equal opportunities for minority groups, with the better planning of our cities and our suburbs, with slum clearance and decent housing, with the improvement of life for the sick and the aged, with the freedoms of speech, expression, and conscience, with the bettering of our mass media, and the elevation of our popular culture—in short, with the quality of civilization to which our nation aspires in an age of ever-increasing abundance and leisure."

—ARTHUR SCHLESINGER, JR.

"The Future of Liberalism." *The Reporter*, May 3, 1956. Quoted by permission of the author.

4

Middle Age—
the New Prime of Life?

ROBERT J. HAVIGHURST

WHEN IS THE PRIME of life? This is a personal question which different people answer differently. Still, there is a general agreement
among people in America today that the prime of life is somewhere
between 40 and 60. Businessmen are likely to place their prime between 40 and 50 and to say that a man gets his top job by about 45.
Professional men may place their prime at 50 or even 55, while
manual workers regard the prime of life as between 30 and 40.
Women vary in their notions about the prime of life more than men
do, some women thinking of their thirties as their prime, when their
children were young, while others place the prime of life in the fifties,
after the children are grown and have left the home.

It seems likely that people now think of the prime of life as coming later than they did a century ago. The latter half of life now

seems more inviting, and also something (as Mr. Tibbitts has explained) more to be counted on, than was true a century ago.

While there are still many who moan and groan inwardly when they reach their 40th birthday, there are a growing number who ignore 40 and rejoice when they reach 50, because they feel they can begin to enjoy the fruits of the first 50 years of life.

A few years ago a Paris newspaper held an essay contest with the title "The Best 10 Years of Life." The prize was won by a Frenchman who said that the decade from 50 to 60 was the best, for the following reasons:

1. A man's daughters, if he has them, are married off and their dowries paid.
2. A man's business competitors are either too old to be effective, or too young to be experienced.
3. Inherited wealth has come, if there is to be any.
4. A man can really enjoy his leisure-time interests.

What this man saw at 50 was a set of changes which, on the whole, made life more interesting and rewarding to him.

Changing Social Roles

A good way to look at the changes that come with middle age is to think of life as consisting of a set of *social roles* and to see how these roles change in importance and in their claim on the time of a man or woman. Life for a middle-aged person involves meeting one's self-expectations and the expectations of other people in the following roles:

1. The Parental Role. As children grow up and establish themselves in jobs and homes of their own, the parental role becomes less demanding. The successful parent has set his children free and become more free himself in the process. As for grandchildren, the grandparents can usually enjoy them without feeling responsible for them.

2. The Home-Maker Role. With children grown and out of the home, there is often a chance to move to a less pretentious dwelling, usually smaller, more modern, and easier to keep up. Leisure time can be used in gardening and fixing up the interior; and people may take particular pride in the physical condition of their homes.

3. The Role of Spouse. Husband and wife are likely to spend more time together. Not only do their children need them less as parents, but, as spouses, they may need each other more. They may feel the need of greater mutual emotional support.

4. The Worker Role. As a man (or woman) reaches the peak of his career, the worker role changes its significance. He may relax and take his work more easily; or he may do just the opposite—strive to better himself in a hopeless struggle against his own aging. A good many women in middle age take up the worker role again, finding that they have time on their hands.

5. The Association Member. A variety of changes may take place in one's participation in clubs, churches, labor unions, fraternal or professional organizations. One may drop out of certain organizations, such as the Parent-Teacher Association, and one may join some social club for which he finds both time and money. One may take leadership in clubs, or one may give up leadership. About all that can be said with certainty is that this period of life gives a person a chance to take stock of his associational activities and to change them if he wants to do so.

6. The Citizen Role. Plato thought that a person should reach the prime of citizenship around the age of 50. By this age his youthful impetuosity would be replaced by the wisdom of experience, and he would act in the best interests of society. Some people today do develop into the best of citizens in their later adult years, combining wisdom with greater freedom from other demands on their time, to fill the role of citizen in a really distinguished way.

7. The Friend Role. Friendships are likely to become somewhat more important at this time, largely because there is a gain in leisure time, and perhaps there is more of an investment of interest in people outside the family as involvement with one's children decreases.

8. The Role of User of Leisure Time. This is potentially one of greatly increased importance since there is usually more leisure time available, free from the demands of one's family, and because there is promise of even more leisure in the future. Some people deliberately cultivate new leisure activities, or reactivate old ones. Other people drop into a rut with a few time-killers, while they cease doing other things for which they no longer have physical energy or motivation, such as dancing, athletics, or keeping up with a social club. Although the happy use of leisure should be a most important gain of middle age, some people cannot find satisfaction in their leisure, because they cannot give leisure the same validity that they give to paid employment, housework, or care of children.

Thus we see that the roles which make up life are apt to change a great deal at about the age of 50. But they may change for the better or for the worse.

The Turning Point of Maturity

Complicating the changing roles of middle age is the acute awareness that one is growing older—an awareness that comes to most people within a few years of fifty, either before or after. This awareness is marked by three things:

1. *Physical changes that are uncomfortable.* These changes are dramatized for women by the menopause, but they are present for both sexes in other forms. Men and women acquire the "middle-aged-spread" and put on fat around the waist. The eye lens loses elasticity, and people have to wear reading glasses or bifocals. Unusual exertion, such as running, playing tennis, or mountain climbing, may result in sprained ankles, torn ligaments, and physical exhaustion. Men who have been physically active and even athletic suddenly find that their adolescent sons can outdo them. Men experience a decrease of sexual drive.

2. *Recognition that one has reached the top of one's career.* After years of promotion, increases in salary, and growth in status and power, a person realizes that he has reached a plateau. There will be no further rise, and eventually he must go downhill.

3. *Realization that the future is not of unlimited duration.* There comes a time in every person's life when he realizes that he does not have a limitless amount of time ahead of him. Before this time, he can make plans and take on responsibilities without asking himself how many of these things he can accomplish in his lifetime. After this point, he realizes that there will not be time enough in his life to do all the things he would like to do. Therefore he must assign some priorities, decline some opportunities, and parcel out his remaining years so as to get the most important things done.

All three of these things may come on gradually for some people, while they come sharply for others. Few people think much about them before the age of 50. During the period from 50 to 55, however, most people come to terms with all three things and alter their outlook on life accordingly.

This might be called the turning point of *maturity*. Maturity might be defined as recognition that a person has reached the peak of his career, passed his physical prime, and has only a limited time left to do all the things he would like to do.

The Wisdom of Middle Age

At the turning point of maturity, one is in a position to change one's roles so as to make a satisfying life for the next 25 or 30 years. This requires a kind of wisdom which consists of self-analysis and self-development along several lines.*

1. Valuing wisdom versus valuating physical powers. Decrease in physical vigor and attractiveness must result in feelings of failure and inadequacy unless one learns to accept this as a natural consequence of growing older, and learns to give a higher value to the foresight and judgment that arise from the experience of living. The principal means of coping with life shifts from the use of physical energy to the use of wisdom. By employing this shift, one can actually accomplish more than younger people, for one can now concentrate on things that are really important.

2. Emotional expansion versus emotional constriction. Middle age is the period when, for most people, parents die, children leave home, and the circle of friends and relatives of similar age begins to be broken by death. Also, this is the period when sexual activity begins to drop off for the male. All this can mean an impoverishment of emotional life—fewer friends and fewer family members to love and enjoy. But the successful person learns to reinvest his emotions in new friends and other pursuits. When the primary bonds to parents and children are broken by death and departure, there is either emotional constriction or the forming of new emotional bonds. While it may be true that some people are so deeply bound to their parents that they never completely recover from their deaths and thus doom

---

* This analysis of development in middle age is taken largely from a paper by Robert F. Peck "Psychological Developments in the Second Half of Life," which appears in *Psychological Aspects of Aging*, John E. Anderson, editor. Washington: American Psychological Association, 1956.

themselves to a later life of emotional constriction, this hardly seems true of many middle-aged people today.

There is certainly a possibility of forming new friendships and investing emotional capital in new pursuits, for a person at this age generally has a wide circle of acquaintances and has the freedom and the time and financial means to do new things.

3. Mental flexibility versus mental rigidity. By middle age one achieves a relatively stable and publicly known set of attitudes on a variety of public and private matters, which automatically govern one's behavior and give it a fixed and rigid quality. Since, by this time, one has usually achieved a degree of worldly success, there is a temptation to coast along on this success, making no effort to examine new circumstances for possible new answers. In other words, one tends to become mentally rigid.

Yet the changing circumstances of our society call for a degree of open-mindedness and flexibility, both on public and private issues.

4. Expansion of interests beyond the work role. The work role is the principal source of satisfaction and feeling of worth for men and many women in our society. Some women adopt the work role after 50 as a substitute for the mother role. But the work role generally lasts only to age 65 or 70 at the most, and its rewards fall off after the age of 60 for most people. Consequently it is important in middle age to expand one's interests beyond the work role so as to get out of other activities satisfactions which formerly came largely through work. This may be done through the development of leisure activities, or through putting more investment into clubs, church, civic life, home-making, friendships, or some form of creative expression.

The main problem is that of finding sources of self-respect outside of the work role. Americans are so thoroughly work-oriented that it is difficult for some of them to achieve self-respect through competence in any other area of life. A man of 64 said: "I have asked our pastor, when he prays; will he pray that St. Peter will give me a good job when I die. That's all I want, a good job in heaven." Somehow one must find some other definition of heaven than that of possessing a "good job." Otherwise one is not likely to enjoy his last years on earth.

5. Body transcendence versus body preoccupation. The lessening of physical vigor and attractiveness that accompanies middle age comes as a blow to most people, because they have invested a great deal of emotional capital in their physical appearance and physical well-being. This blow may be made more devastating by some chronic disease which causes pain or limits activity. It is only sensible that people should maintain their health and physical attractiveness by getting medical advice, by watching their diets, by getting exercise, and by dressing carefully. This much preoccupation with the body is desirable in middle age. But along with it should go a new definition of happiness and comfort, in terms of satisfying human relationships and creative mental activities which will survive the physical decline of the body.

The Freedom of Middle Age

Just before the prime of life, when a man or woman is working most efficiently and meeting the demands of life most successfully, it is true in a paradoxical way that he is least free. One's life is "cut out" for him at such a time, by the multitude of expectations which make up the roles of worker, parent, spouse, homemaker, citizen, church member, and association member. One's very success in these roles is a measure of the demands they make upon him. He has little freedom.

When the roles become less demanding, at the turning point of maturity, one has, for the first time since childhood, a real freedom to dispose of his time, to choose what he will do and will not do. One has a chance to redesign his life, to take up new roles and to alter old ones. The prize for the new design of life is happiness for another 25 or 30 years.

It is exhausting and even painful for a man or woman to try to hold on to the old roles and to live on in them when new and younger aspirants are pushing in to take them up. It is even more of a tragedy for a man or woman to give up the rewarding roles of the 40's and take nothing in their place, drawing into himself and getting less from, and giving less to, the world around him.

There is no need for people to live such a tragic life after the age of 50. There is no need for them to wear themselves out trying to live as if they were 40.

People can be happy and free and young in spirit in their middle age and for a long time afterward if they do some personal stocktaking and planning for this period of their lives.

Time Out for Reflection

Think of people you know who have made the adjustment to middle age successfully, and some who had difficulty making it. What factors seem to influence the ability to make it:

> do men make it more easily than women?
> does the presence or absence of children make a difference?
> the age of the children?
> the nature of the occupation?
> the example of the older parents?
> the presence or absence of money?

What can people do better at 50 or 60 than they could at 20?

Do people change the emphasis they put on different "roles" as they gain the middle years? e.g., as parent, homemaker, association member, entertainer, civic participant, etc.?

What changes do you notice in your own, or your friends', use of leisure time as you gain middle age?

Can people in middle age set *new goals* for themselves, or must they go on seeking (or lamenting) the ones they had in youth?

The transition periods of life may not be very clear-cut as we live along from day to day. Two careful observers of life processes, Dr. Maurice Linden and Dr. Douglas Courtney, have described five periods of the adult life span:

The Family Creative Period is, of course, the time when men and women are developing their family units.

The Social Creative Period is entered when the parents become aware of the family's position and responsibility in the community and when they try to integrate their offspring with social requirements.

The State Creative Period emerges at a still later date when the children are grown and set out on their own. At this period, the parents' vision is extended to the problems and requirements of the larger world in which their children will now live and participate.

The Moral and Ethical Reaffirmative Period follows when the older generation evaluates its world and tries to manipulate the state and its institutions for the well-being of oncoming generations

The Retrospective Examination Period comes finally when the person becomes concerned with system, order, and the meaning of human experience.

Do you agree that these five periods represent a logical sequence of life development in our present society? Would you combine any of these? Or add others?

Reflect on the experiences of older friends or relatives you have known intimately for a long time. Do you feel they are bearing out the Linden-Courtney hypothesis?

The Human Life Cycle

Maurice Linden, M.D. (1915-   )
and Douglas Courtney (1916-   )

A REVIEW OF THE LITERATURE will lead the student of later maturity to discover 2 general tendencies, one of method, the other of attitude: (1) an effort to understand the whole of man through isolated criteria and (2) a tendency to regard adulthood as a more or less continuous state of maturity terminated by progressive decline and death.

An individual at any time in his life is the aggregate and interaction of many functions, some in development, some at peak, and some in decline. Any approach toward comprehending the nature of man that uses for measurement a single function, or even a group of functions, such as sensory acuity, motor response, intelligence, vocabulary, etc., succeeds in describing merely a dissected part of a totality. A society such as ours, which appears to place a heavy emphasis on the attributes of youthfulness, physical agility, and the behavioral constellation surrounding reproduction, makes the same error on a cultural scale that the researcher makes on a laboratory scale, *i.e.*, it fails to integrate enough human variables into a realistic life scheme, and views human growth with lopsided values, so that adult life is popularly regarded as the simple achievement of an ambiguous maturity followed by a general decline.

This paper is an introductory effort to organize some observations and tentative conclusions made on the basis of psychiatric clinical experience with several hundred older patients of many diagnostic categories in and out of a mental hospital, and to develop methods and some criteria for testing the hypothesis * that has evolved and is to be described.

* The authors wish to express their gratitude and indebtedness to Arthur P. Noyes, M.D., and Lawrence C. Kolb, M.D., Superintendent and former Assistant Superintendent, respectively, of Norristown State Hospital, for their help and valuable criticism in the preparation and development of the hypothesis.

Background for a Theory

A point of view regarding stages of maturation requires an analysis and resynthesis of the factors playing a part in personality organization. For simplicity these may be separated into 3 general groups: biologic, physiologic, and psychosocial. Focusing attention on one area yields unilateral conclusions.

Biologists have long considered the adult stage of all living organisms as the period of procreation and parenthood. Since the primary function of all living things will have been achieved by reproduction and subsequent life for the adult will be an *anticlimactic* outliving of usefulness, it follows that after rearing of the young the most logical sequential step must be termination of individual existence.

The physiologic investigators with an apparent biologic orientation seem to have been bent on finding means for sustaining juvenescence, keeping alive sexual-reproductive interest, and thus postponing individual terminus as they view it.

Little place is found in a mobile and aggressive society, except fortuitously, for individuals in the postreproductive phases of life. The popular and scientific concepts of *climacterium* and *involution* that relegate postclimacteric existence to an ignominious level in the pattern of civilization have been stultifying and restrictive. The absence of an adequate conceptual scheme, meager information, and perhaps a lack of interest and attention have hampered a changing view.

The authors are of the conviction that the human life span is in fact a predetermined, inexorable cycle in which genetic and instinctual endowments are the motivators. The beginning and end points of this cycle are not birth and involution but conception and death.

The biologic dogma is applicable, probably, to most other forms of life in the animal kingdom, but seems singularly untrue in the human animal: An innate endowment for social organization in animals is very likely the genetic conveyance of the results of eons of trial-and-error adaptation, but from generation to generation their societies are relatively immutable. While animals do appear to have societal organization and do appear to have cultures, it is in the transmission of these cultures that a difference is perceived between man and animal. Some ancient prompting deep in the genetic development of the animal guides his activities, whereas the human culture is transmitted postnatally quite specifically to each individual and by elders as a rule. The human culture is so complex that the transmission process requires extensive recording systems with the attendant complexities necessary to maintain the communication network. On this basic difference between animal and human societies depends much of the relative difference in the function of the aging human being and the aging animal. The aging human individual is just beginning some of his most important functions when parenthood ceases.

Structure of a Holistic Conceptual Framework

The approach of no single scientific discipline is sufficient to account for the behavior of the complete organism. Every step in behavioral progression is dependent on biologic diatheses, physiologic preparation, psychologic integration, and social demands. Man in action is the composite of these basic factors and his behavior is their expression. A study of observable behavior ought to disclose the functions of a total organization at any stage in progression.

It may well be that the additional function of the adult of preserving culture, of maintaining the annals of history, of keeping alive human judgment, of maintaining human skills, of preserving and skillfully contriving the instruments of civilization, and of conveying all this to on-coming generations, is the postreproductive work of the human organism and that this realistic and valuable quality of the human mind is uncovered or manifested in the senescent individual.

The authors are not unaware of the numerous arguments that are stimulated by a hypothesis of this type. It may be pointed out that the function of cultural maintenance is not unknown to the earlier stages of human development, and that procreativity does not preclude socially oriented thought and cultural precept. Obviously, these and related arguments must be accepted, but they do not refute the hypothesis. Personality development is a continuum. Factors present in fractional quantities in early periods of growth become preponderances in later stages, while the reverse is also true.

The initial observation giving rise to this theoretic formulation is that there appears to exist the same kind of conflict in the shift at middle life that exists during the adolescent shift. Traditionally, the youth at adolescence is rebellious. Under the pressures of pubertal change he seeks independence, self-expression, and freedom of action. The pronouncements of his elders, usually parents, are rejected out of hand as outworn solutions not applicable to himself.

We see a striking recurrence of this internecine strife at middle life. For convenience let us divide the life cycle into halves and let us name the young side of the middle of life as *evolescence*, with the older side *senescence*. We may now speak of the "E's" and the "S's." We can perceive the rebellion of the E's against the S's. Some of this rebellion is the frustration that comes in recognizing the older wisdom, a recognition of the irreality of one's own wishes. Some of it comes from within. The individual perceives his own metamorphosis from an E to an S. He fights the change because our society has placed all its values in evolescence and has not voiced or even recognized the more subtle inherent values in senescence.

The S counter-rebellion is a continuous restatement of old ideas, a tenacious attachment to the established and proven solutions, a reluctance to countenance social revolution, and an increasing awareness of the value of the past as a predictor of the future and an instrument of judgment.

The S segment of life, rather than being a merely tolerated period before the organism's demise, is very likely a socially necessary phase following the mid-area in the human life cycle and continuing until the individual ceases to exist or until destructive processes supervene. It is probable that the psychophysiologic events that characterize involution are less significant as the termination of the reproductive function and are more important as preparation of the individual for subsequent social functioning.

Personality may be regarded as a series of peak achievements, and for every faculty that passes its prime a further developing faculty becomes dominant that has yet to reach its level of highest integration. Thus the conclusion is reached that adult life is not one continuous plateau of maturation, but is a series of merging stages, regarded for convenience as early, middle, and late and their subdivisions. For the sake of clarity a definition of maturity is necessary at this juncture.

The Maturity Concept

The comprehension of maturity as a level of psychologic development is too involved an area of study for a brief account. However, a thread of consistency is found to run through all efforts to understand it. The common denominator of varying points of view regarding maturity is *integrated environmental orientation*.

The freshly conceived organism lacks maturity, but it does possess unbridled forces in its infantile state. What is to become of these forces, or how they are to be expressed as the organism goes forward is determined in large part by counterforces that derive both from an internal environment, the psyche, and an external environment, reality. Counterforces are obstacles. The presentation of an obstacle yields conflict.

Solution of conflict is experience. The integration of experience is organization. The most efficient organization is maturity. *Maturity, therefore, is the achievement of efficiently organized psychic growth predicated upon the integration of experiences of solving environmentally stimulated conflicts.*

Most of the demands upon forces within the individual are made by the external environment. (This can still be regarded as true when the external environment is internalized.) Since the most potent environment is the society in which he lives, it is seen that an individual's conflicts are in the main socially incurred. Thus, a concept of maturity requires the realization of a psychosocial organization, or what may be termed *cultural direction.* This means that the individual is understood largely through his ways of relating to and comparing with the group, its experiences, and its mores.

The essential difference between evolescence and senescence is to be found in the cultural direction of conflict solution. The E portion of the life cycle begins as nearly complete dependence and is characterized by progressive private rebellion against dependence. Dependence is mainly upon the S culture against which the E bid for independence is expressed as egocentric strivings for gratification of instinct-urges, or pleasure-seeking, regardless of its manifold disguises.

It is axiomatic that the union of groups of no matter what dimensions depends upon the intensity of *sharing of conflict solution* by the participants. Since pleasure-seeking is private and selfish, it is probable that the E state of cultural direction is negative to some degree and tends toward group fragmentation. This would eventuate in cultural disintegration were it not for the S culture with its public orientation, which tends to contain and to restrain individual instinct-pleasure seeking.

The S viewpoint causes many E strivings to be regarded as dangerous, because if fulfilled they threaten group integration. It is therefore seen that *the S attitude is simultaneously directed toward protection of the E's against social perils and toward the preservation of a culture.*

The development of his civilization and the maintenance of its culture are probably man's loftiest ideal. Such an ideal is of the widest possible social scope and requires for its realization the progressive renunciation of E egocentricity and the development of S protectiveness and altruism. It is therefore hypothesized that the attainment in the individual of S functioning despite its many modalities represents the achievement of a broad cultural vista. Contrary to popular views holding that older people are more restricted in their psychic interests, this study suggests their general outlook is actually broader and less selfish than that of younger, or less mature, people.

Stages of Maturation

The definition of psychic maturity given earlier suggests that the process of maturation may be measured as a resultant of 2 vectors: selfish (instinct-gratifying) drives and culture-directed (protective and altruistic) drives obtaining at any point along the life course.

Infancy starts as a period of instinct-supremacy and is followed by a series of relationships between the infant-child and his environment, producing experiences that have been called *"the education of the instincts."* The renunciation and alteration of instinctual drives lead to further social learning in the child as he attempts to achieve a progressive mastery over his own impulses and orients his new-found ambitions toward accomplishments in reality. This increase in cultural orientation that characterizes earliest adolescence is interrupted by bio-physiologic puberty. The psychologic effect of puberty is a resurgence of temporarily concealed drives, a regression toward instinct-supremacy. The process of coping successfully with such insistent energies leads to further personality organization in adolescence with the emergence first of *self-identity* and later rudimentary parental attitudes. This proceeds into *pairing*, a psychologic device that allows for the mutual working out of problems of identification and develops attitudes relating to the smallest possible social unit—a group of 2 people of opposite sexes.

The capacity for intimacy growing out of adolescent pairing and the idiocentric psychologic attitudes directed toward the fulfillment of pleasure urges culminate in the *mating and reproduction* of early adulthood. A later phase of early adulthood is then characterized by the beginnings of larger group formations. This may be termed a *family creative* period. The psychosocial organization at this level is relatively small, constricted, and confined to the development of the home-family unit.

Middle adulthood, or middle maturity, then appears as a stage of widening social interest in which the family-society becomes increasingly oriented within the framework of its responsibility toward a greater society. This may be termed a *social creative* period. It is during this period that the progeny are traversing earlier phases of evolescence and in which parental attention is directed toward assisting in the integration of offspring wishes with social requirements. Clinical experience gives the impression that people at this phase of maturation are concerned with the social development of the family and the community collective of families.

The involutional disturbance is self-limited and is followed by personality reintegration with the advent of the third or late phase of maturity.

Later maturity appears to be roughly divided into 3 sequential segments. The predominant mature point of view in the first segment may be regarded as a *social-political* one, or *culture-organizational*. By this time of maturity the progeny have reached an early adult phase and are themselves in a family creative period. A ruling and protective sovereignty befalls the mature adult at this level as he assumes the parental hierarchical leadership over his family of families. Thus, the scope of interest here becomes wider and is concerned with the creation, ordering, and maintenance of a larger society, or what may be called the state. Thus, in a sense, the first segment of late adulthood may be called *state creative*.

The second segment of late maturity is ushered in by a set of conditions requiring the establishment of social, moral, and ethical standards. It may be said that at this regulative level in the life cycle it is necessary for the establishment of pacific relationships among the oncoming generations that the parental ruling body draw upon cumulative experience to render decisions, assist in planning, erect social guideposts, and to select subordinate leaders. The judgmental functions of the human mind may be found to be most highly developed during this period. Judgment is created out of actual and vicarious experience with conflict solutions and out of cultural learning. Since cultural standards are established, archetypical, and have withstood the tests of historical application, the necessity for judgment functioning produces a kind of rediscovery of old values already found effective in cultural maintenance. For this reason, the second segment of late maturity may be called a *moral and ethical reaffirmative* period.

The integration of the mature personality at this level yields a profound concern for system, order, and meaning in human existence and engenders an almost newly found kinship with past (parental) leaders and regard for the current standard-bearers of all the disciplines of culture (technologic, scientific, etc.).

The need to correlate the present with the past to determine the true nature of accomplishments, errors, and rediscoveries ushers in the last phase of late psychic maturity. The area of cultural vision at this level is at its broadest possible development embracing one nearly complete life cycle and its interrelatedness with a multitude of other life cycles throughout its span of existence. The individual at this level compares and contrasts his values with cultural values to which he has been longitudinally exposed, and through a process of conscious reasoning and intuition he evaluates meaning and purpose. Intuition is probably unconscious statistical analysis of experience. Hence, this latest period becomes one of *retrospective examination,* and an increased interest in the history of human development may be found at this level.

It may be said that whereas the early evolescent views himself as a potential ambitious and dauntless master of a dimly conceived mankind, the late mature senescent, by contrast, views himself with real humility as at most a contributor or at least a participant in the improvement of his society.

Life's Changing Tasks

John Walker Powell (1904-   )

MIND IS A PRODUCT of life; and living, at least for men, is shaped in turn by the way they put their minds to work upon it. Thinking is another of Man's vocations; it, too, is a form of doing. But there still is a difference in our meanings when we think of *the thing being done* and of *the person doing it.* In *doing,* a man is an instrument, a skilled and specialized tool, serving a purpose. As *person,* it is he who has the purpose, who chooses that this shall be done and in this way. These are, if you like, the realms of know-how and know-why. Know-how has been America's specialty, as has the schooling that produces it. Our need, now in maturity, is in the other realm, in the development of ourselves as persons rather than as instruments. And this, to me, is the realm of education.

I say "to me," but I mean also to a growing number of those who plan for education in maturity. This recognition is, in fact, one of three reasons why I say that adult education is itself beginning to come of age.

A second is the even wider recognition that the achievement of maturity through education is a never-ending process. Our language habits had trapped us into making education into a noun, a thing. You either "had" an education or you hadn't, or you went somewhere to "get one." In times of profound unrest and concern over our economy and our country's role in the world, "educated" adults would say to us, when we proposed group readings of Veblen and Smith or of Beard or Toynbee, "Oh, I don't need economics, I don't need history; I *had* them in college." You would have thought history was a form of measles. But the discovery that has become accepted throughout the adult field is that educating oneself is a process, not a package. The goal is not to acquire a set of ideas but to maintain the power of the thinking muscles, to keep the *process* of understanding ever alert.

The key recognition of all, finally, is that there is an *adult* mind, different from those of the youth and the undergraduate; that the grownup has a qualitatively different way of using his mind, of relating ideas to experience, of weighing and using knowledge. It is for this distinctively grown-up mind that education in maturity is now, increasingly, being planned. . . .

Recent research in what is called "human development" has also been highlighting some of the major differences between the tasks faced by the individual at different stages of his living: in the tasks, and in his performance of them. Out of these studies there emerges a sort of theory about the Seven Ages of Man in American society. The first three decades are largely taken up with getting accepted as a grown-up member of the society: getting his schooling, finding his vocation, finding a mate and building a nest. It is not until he is over 30 that the usual American has time to take breath, to take stock, to look around him for help in learning the tasks he faces next. The children are still in school, the house is not paid for, the head of the household is a very junior executive in his job. In the forties, things change. The children are taking their own memberships in a wider society; the vocation is more securely held; the nature of the marriage is changing, the grandparents need more help, living is at a different pace. There is time, and need, for asking questions.

The next decade faces new kinds of decision. The children are getting launched; the vocation is expert, and individuals are respected in their grasp of it; they have memberships and positions in community organizations carrying more active responsibility; they are being eyed as successors to the retiring, and will soon pass from parenthood to grandparenthood. And the prospect of reaching retirement and old age is becoming an uncomfortable reality instead of a statistical possibility. In the seventh decade, it will take place, along with other kinds of new experience, enjoyable or uncomfortable, but all of it wanting interpretation and help in understanding.

It is not by accident, therefore, that the statistical norm for *entrance* into voluntary adult learning is at about age 35. For by this age, the accumulated changes in circumstances of living have added up to a qualitative change in the personality needs. The man or woman of 35 has at least three points of difference from the youth. He has had *experience* of living as a responsible member of the adult world; he has fashioned a *situation* in which his responsibilities are well defined; and he has solidified some phases of the *self-knowledge*, or at least the *self-picture*, which will govern his actions from now on.

Education now means an enlightening of this experience, an interpretaton and evaluation of these responsibilities, an enlarging and deepening of his self-understanding. He seeks now not teachers but companions in the search for greater wisdom. Where the undergraduate grasps at new ideas for the sake of liberating himself from his childhood stereotypes and limitations, the adult grasps at ideas as illuminating what he is already doing and committed to do. . . .

So the difference is not merely in the age. More pertinently, it is in the curriculum, and in the needs on which it is built. For schooling, the core curriculum was always the three R's—reading, 'riting, and 'rithmetic —with their accompanying languages and tools. The goal of schooling is *competence*, at whatever age it is sought.

For this other kind of education, we might describe the curriculum in terms of three C's: Curiosity, Creativeness, and Comprehension.

If you think of these three C's as they operate naturally in children, they will not need much explanation. And also you will notice how different they are from the three R's. The saddest fact about schooling is the uniformity with which it kills, in children, the three C's. In our mature years, then, we have to leave time and provide opportunity for them to re-emerge. They are the substance of adult intelligence.

Curiosity is a motive, creativeness a process, comprehension a goal. There is joy in each of them, and together they make up most of the enjoyment of living. They all involve judgment, discrimination, decision-making; and "judgment" is our common synonym for intelligence, decision our test of its rightness. And all of these apply in all of the life-tasks we perform as adults.

Because each area does involve roles that must be performed, it calls for competence in the appropriate skills. Because it involves us in relationships with others, it requires comprehension. Because it calls for choices of values and actions, it requires creativity. And because it demands knowledge, it appeals to curiosity. On the other hand, because each is a major field of activity within an organized society, society has developed certain institutions, regularized patterns or ways of organizing men's behavior within each cluster of interests—the family, for instance, with all its connections to institutions of marriage, of property, of name and succession, of law and right and obligation. And finally, because things change, each of these fields of activity is also subject to changes: the family is beset by changes in living and housing patterns, by increasing longevity of its older members, by the growth of professional services like schools and health and recreation and welfare; modes and mores in marriage and child-rearing become altered; and the whole field is subject to the stresses between forces trying to keep it as it was and forces tending to alter it toward a new pattern.

Oh, yes, indeed; these major clusters of our adult concern and performance are no rote tasks to be taught. They are small universes calling for
the utmost intelligence each of us can muster. This fact has led educators
into the trap of planning for what people "need," as though understanding
were a vitamin pill. All I am trying to point out here is that these concerns are areas in which people are already using their intelligence, and
want to understand better than they do. What is my evidence for this
rash assumption?

The evidence against me is considerable. Much of our reading is trash.
Most of our conversation is trivial. And—here is an extraordinary fact
that dawned on me only recently—never in any American novel or story
or play that I have read does any character take any time to seek education about the problems the novelist has involved him in: from Hawthorne to O'Hara, our writers see us as people with consuming problems
and no urge to get help in understanding them. . . .

It is only as you get the American engaged in serious conversation that
his underlying desires begin to be revealed. In years of working with
adult students I have come to believe that the American does a lot of
private thinking (which he is shy about revealing) on the subjects of his
concern: his country, his community, his neighbors; his parents, his children, and his relationships as child of one and parent of the other; his
relation to, and his destiny in, the universe; his private interests and
hobbies; his friendships and enmities, and his successes and failures in
getting along with people and in understanding himself. The interest is
there. But many a latent citizen is discouraged about acting because he
feels powerless to affect the course of events; and many a potential student remains inert because he feels diffident about "exposing his ignorance" or about his ability to manage a book or contribute to a discussion.
Education's problem is that of invitation, motivation, the giving of success-
experiences in its occasions.

I Began to Get My Breath

Girolamo Cardano (1501-1576)

THE SUCCESSIVE PERIODS of our lives bring about changes in our customs,
in the bodily form, in temperament, and in appearance. I have heard it
said that in childhood I was fat and rosy; in boyhood I was scrawny, with
a long face, fair complexioned and flushed, and I grew so rapidly that by
my sixteenth year I had almost completed my growth, and I seemed as

tall as I am now; my disposition was inclined to sadness. In youth I was sandy haired, in deportment and temper nothing unusual, cheerful, given to pleasures, especially to music.

In the period of my life falling between my thirtieth and fortieth years there was little change. I had troubles which disturbed me—poverty, with a wife and children, an infirm state of bodily health, and rivals so bitter that when I cured Bartolommea Cribella, a noble lady, and following her, her brother, this same man, as he was convalescing, made mock of me. To him I said, "What would you all be doing"—for others had joined his mockery—"if he had not been cured?"

Was it not then to be expected that after all this—but not before my thirty-ninth year—I began to get my breath? Nevertheless, during the next four years, that is, from the first of September 1539 to the first of November 1543, I did nothing else except strive, by private means and public measures, to the end that I might be freed from my embarrassment and given the honor due me as a doctor. The first year of changed fortune was, accordingly, my forty-third. From that time up to my seventieth year almost twenty-seven years intervened—the duration of the Peloponnesian War—in which I composed all those books. From my seventy-first to my seventy-fifth year, four years have glided by during which I wrote twelve works, consisting of eighteen books. . . .

During those early years I devoted seven years to pleasures—music and others—to gambling and to fishing, the latter especially. Later I trained myself for debate, and at the same time found myself still more lacking in bodily health. My teeth ached and a few of them fell out. Gout invaded me, but did not, however, torture me. The attack was generally of twenty-four hours' duration, and whatever pain remained tended toward a gradual moderation. Up to my sixtieth year my vitality did not diminish, so that it appears my strength failed rather because of mental anguish than because of my age. From that year on I have made it my business to attend to my domestic affairs, but so many discouragements have cast their baleful light upon me that it is a marvel that I have been able to live until the present. If anyone should enumerate my struggles, my anxieties, my bitterness and grief, my mistakes in conducting my life, the claims of my personal interests, fear of poverty, sleeplessness, intestinal trouble, asthma, skin disease and even phtheiriasis, the inconstant character of my grandson, the sins of my son, would that man not be surprised that I still survive?

The Enviable Time of Life

Edward Bellamy (1850-1898)

THAT EVENING I SAT UP for some time after the ladies had retired, talking with Dr. Leete about the effect of the plan of exempting men from further service to the nation after the age of forty-five, a point brought up by his account of the part taken by the retired citizens in the government.

'At forty-five,' said I, 'a man still has ten years of good manual labor in him, and twice ten years of good intellectual service. To be superannuated at that age and laid on the shelf must be regarded rather as a hardship than a favor by men of energetic dispositions.'

'My dear Mr. West,' exclaimed Dr. Leete, beaming upon me, 'you cannot have any idea of the piquancy your nineteenth century ideas have for us of this day, the rare quaintness of their effect. Know, O child of another race and yet the same, that the labor we have to render as our part in securing for the nation the means of a comfortable physical existence is by no means regarded as the most important, the most interesting, or the most dignified employment of our powers. We look upon it as a necessary duty to be discharged before we can fully devote ourselves to the higher exercise of our faculties, the intellectual and spiritual enjoyments and pursuits which alone mean life. Everything possible is indeed done by the just distribution of burdens, and by all manner of special attractions and incentives to relieve our labor of irksomeness, and, except in a comparative sense, it is not usually irksome, and is often inspiring. But it is not our labor, but the higher and larger activities which the performance of our task will leave us free to enter upon, that are considered the main business of existence.

'Of course not all, nor the majority, have those scientific, artistic, literary, or scholarly interests which make leisure the one thing valuable to their possessors. Many look upon the last half of life chiefly as a period for enjoyment of other sorts; for travel, for social relaxation in the company of their life-time friends; a time for the cultivation of all manner of personal idiosyncrasies and special tastes, and the pursuit of every imaginable form of recreation; in a word, a time for the leisurely and unperturbed appreciation of the good things of the world which they have helped to create. But whatever the differences between our individual tastes as to the use we shall put our leisure to, we all agree in looking forward to the date of our discharge as the time when we shall first enter upon the full enjoyment of our birthright, the period when we shall first really attain our majority and become enfranchised from discipline and control, with the fee of our lives vested in ourselves. As eager boys in your day anticipated twenty-one, so men nowadays look forward to forty-five. At twenty-one we become men, but at forty-five we renew youth. Middle age and what you would have called old age are considered, rather than youth, the enviable time of life. Thanks to the better conditions of existence nowadays, and above all the freedom of every one from care, old age approaches many years later and has an aspect far more benign than in past times. Persons of average constitution usually live to eighty-five or ninety, and at forty-five we are physically and mentally younger, I fancy, than you were at thirty-five. It is a strange reflection that at forty-five, when we are just entering upon the most enjoyable period of life, you already began to think of growing old and to look backward. With you it was the forenoon, with us it is the afternoon, which is the brighter half of life.'

My Rival

Rudyard Kipling (1865-1936)

I go to concert, party, ball—
    What profit is in these?
I sit alone against the wall,
    And strive to look at ease.
The incense that is mine by right
    They burn before Her shrine;
And that's because I'm seventeen
    And she is forty-nine.

I cannot check my girlish blush,
    My colour comes and goes;
I redden to my finger-tips,
    And sometimes to my nose;
But She is white where white should be
    And red where red should shine—
The blush that flies at seventeen
    Is fixed at forty-nine.

I wish *I* had Her constant cheek:
    I wish that I could sing

All sorts of funny little songs,
    Not quite the proper thing.
I'm very gauche and very shy;
    Her jokes aren't in my line;
And, worst of all, I'm seventeen,
    While She is forty-nine.

The young men come, the young men go,
    Each pink and white and neat,
She's older than their mothers, but
    They grovel at Her feet;
They walk beside Her *'rickshaw*-wheels—
    They never walk by mine;
And that's because I'm seventeen
    And She is forty-nine.

She rides with half a dozen men
    (She calls them "boys" and "mashers");
I trot along the Mall alone.
    My prettiest frocks and sashes
Don't help to fill my programme-card,
    And vainly I repine
From 10 to 2 A.M. Ah me!
    Would I were forty-nine!

She calls me "darling," "pet," and "dear,"
    And "sweet retiring maid."
I'm always at the back, I know;
    She puts me in the shade.
She introduces me to men,
    "Cast" lovers, I opine,
For sixty takes to seventeen,
    Nineteen to forty-nine.

But even She must older grow
    And end Her dancing days;
She can't go on for ever so
    At concerts, balls, and plays!
One ray of priceless hope I see
    Before my footsteps shine:
Just think that She'll be eighty-one
    When I am forty-nine!

Suggestions for Further Reading

The Harvest Years, by Janet H. Baird. New York: Doubleday, 1951.
> A collection of essays by various observers, being a realistic guide toward achievement of a long and active maturity.

Moments of Personal Discovery, by Robert M. MacIver. New York: Harper and Bros., 1952.
> Sermons and articles by noted persons, with a central theme of discovering oneself and developing a full life.

Growing in the Older Years, edited by Wilma Donahue and Clark Tibbitts. Ann Arbor: University of Michigan Press, 1951.
> Preceded by *Living Through the Older Years* (1949) and *Planning the Older Years* (1950), the three constituting a trilogy aimed at discovering the personal and social requirements for a new prime of life.

Dr. Evelyn Millis Duvall (Mrs. S. M.) (born in 1906 at Oswego, N. Y.) is a teacher, consultant, counselor, and world student in the field of family relations. She has served as Director, Association for Family Living and as Executive Secretary, National Council on Family Relations. Mrs. Duvall has a lively style of writing which is em- ployed in her books on Facts of Life and Love *(1950)* Family Living *(1950);* In-Laws: Pro and Con; Family Development *(1956); and others. The Duvalls have two married daughters, a grandchild, and have extended their parentship to include an adopted Korean boy.*

"At present the United States is in the throes of conflict be- tween marital and family norms bred from the rural social conditions of the past century and new modes of conduct spawned by present industrial urbanization, which are not as yet well controlled by new social norms. The conflicts create issues of great social importance involving not only personal happiness but also social well-being. The need is great to understand these issues to the end that some rational control may aid and accelerate the slow natural processes of read- justment."

—RUTH SHONLE CAVAN

The American Family, © 1953. Quoted by permission from Thomas Y. Crowell Company.

5

New Family Roles
in Middle Life

EVELYN MILLIS DUVALL

IT WAS CUSTOMARY until relatively recently for several generations to share a common household as a "big old-fashioned family." In such a home the middle-aged man or woman occupied an important place as head of the house and boss of the home industries. This situation no longer obtains in America. Previous essayists have described the changing pattern of life and the virtual disappearance of the elaborate household economy of our grandfathers and great-grandfathers. Factory-made goods now largely replace those laboriously produced in the homes of our forefathers. Fewer women nowadays make their own clothes or those of their children—at least do not make them because they have to—and prepared foods have shortened the time spent in the kitchen. Electric washing machines have taken the sting out of wash-day Monday, and other labor-saving devices have lightened general housework.

Education and religious instruction have been delegated almost entirely to the schools and churches, as have the protective functions to the police and fire departments. With the sharply decreased incidence of sickness, mothers are no longer so active as "doctor and nurse" as formerly. The family as a self-contained, self dependent unit has largely disappeared.

No retooling of industry has been so full of problems and promise as the twentieth-century shift in the roles of the members of the family. This shift, while it may have destroyed the cohesiveness and companionship of the old days, has provided the leisure and opportunity for new emphases. Released from much of the drudgery of maintaining a home, parents can now more consciously, and more conscientiously, concentrate on fostering an emotional climate that is favorable to the individual development of each member of the family. Today's challenge to the family is to develop patterns of interaction among its members and persons outside the home that will give fuller expression to the human spirit.

New Vitality in the Middle Years

There was a time when a person of forty, fifty, or sixty years of age was generally considered "old." Whistler's mother, her hands quietly folded in her lap, was a popular symbol of motherhood in the days when a woman was worn out by the time her family was grown. Indeed, parents jestingly referred to themselves as the "old folks" as soon as their children were married and on their own.

Today's middle-aged men and women are literally at the prime of life when their fostering parenthood roles are over. The American is today assured not only a longer life than his grandfather knew but also increased vitality and better health into later life. Parents today characteristically have only two to four children in contrast to yesterday's big families of nine, ten, or even more. In grandfather's day, when the older boys and girls were ready to go to work or to set up their own households, there were youngsters still at home. Not so today very often. When parents reach their silver wedding anniversary, all their children have normally left home, and they are alone as a couple for possibly another dozen years or more.

Challenges of the Middle-aged Family Today

Young people today leave home for college, work, or marriage while their parents are still at robust maturity. Likewise, the age of marriage has declined during the twentieth century. At the turn of the century, the typical young man married a girl a couple of years younger than himself when he was somewhat beyond his twenty-sixth birthday. Today half of our American girls are married by the time they are twenty to boys but a year or two older than themselves. Such practices launch remarkably young people into a multiplicity of roles—workers, students, spouses, and parents. With so many roles to perform, young people are frequently eager to enlist the services of parents in ways new to both generations.

Military service has increased the uncertainties of the young people, and it brings many a parent back into active duty for its duration. The young husband away, the wife is either left alone, tries to follow him from camp to camp, or makes her home with her or his family. When the baby comes, she is apt to become dependent upon parents or in-laws. His or her parents find that, as grandparents, they must assume some of the responsibilities of parents all over again.

Often the parents must supply funds to make possible the continuance of schooling, even after marriage and the birth of children. Such situations bring new dimensions to the role of parents whose children are grown, but not completely independent; gone, but still very much a part of the family—all in ways that require many innovations and great flexibility both on the part of the parents and the young people.

But the parents we are talking about have tremendous resources uncommon in earlier generations and even in earlier stages of the life cycle. After years of experience a person smoothly carries responsibilities at home and at work. The home is well-established by the time the children are grown. Income is relatively high when family expenses begin to decline as the children become self-supporting. The parents are now in a position to create a rich, full life for themselves.

New dimensions in companionship with their mates open up for the mature man and woman today. Now is the time that a married pair can call its own, for the first period in their life together. Always before they have been cramped by the responsibilities of home, family, and child-rearing. Now they are free as a couple to enjoy life on their own terms, without the bother and expense of baby-sitters, or waiting up for latch-key children. They can freely develop new interests and hobbies, even if such hobbies take time, money, and extended practice. They can travel where they like for as long as they like. One professional husband-wife team enjoyed a joint assignment around the world the year their last child left for a home of her own. Such a jaunt may be more expensive than many a couple can manage or desire, but almost any middle-aged pair can take off for a few weeks to practically any spot it chooses.

Home may look unusually good, now that it is so peaceful and quiet. Gone are the messiness of childhood, the noise and clutter of adolescence, the goings-and-comings of young adulthood. Now that a man and his wife can call their home their own, they can refurbish it, remodeling an old bedroom into a den or workshop, adding facilities for this activity or that, carrying out projects long dreamed of.

Yard and garden may now come into their own. There is time for planning, planting, and caring for growing things outside the house. Trampled areas belonged to the busy, bustling stage when the children were young. Bicycles gone and the last jalopy out of the yard, gardening interest can be cultivated as never before.

Entertaining takes on new satisfactions. Now that the house has been brightened up and remains clean for predictable periods of time, it is a pleasure to invite friends for gracious hospitality. Whether it is beer and cheese over cards on the kitchen table, or a fancy buffet in the dining room, is not the point. Significance lies in hospitality and fellowship with friends.

The home is now a happy place for family festivals and festivities. Married children are expected to come home for the holidays and to brng their children for christenings, birthdays, anniversaries, and other family occasions. This helps give solidity and continuity to traditions and fosters happy memories through meaningful family rituals. Family stability is supported by hospitality and good fellowship. To the younger generation, "going to Grandma's" establishes an imperishable tie with older days, and Grandma's (or Grandpa's) stories to still older times.

There is also opportunity to cultivate good relationships with the families brought into the circle through the marriages of the children. For every child who marries there are two new families to take into account—the married child's and that of the child's spouse. Harmony among in-laws depends, in part, upon the congeniality of the families united by marriage, but mostly, according to recent studies, upon mutual respect and acceptance. When one set of parents genuinely accepts the young person entering their family by marriage, they can make a real effort to accept the other parents involved and include them freely in the family circle.

New depths of fellowship with grown children are a source of satisfaction for many a mature couple. When children have outgrown the dependence of childhood and have emerged from the edgy independence of adolescence, mutual acceptance and interdependence becomes possible. Two mature, autonomous families in close relationship can provide rich rewards for both. It is true that the patterns of help are largely one-way for a while—as they must be, when there is so much that the young couple needs, so much that the parents can provide. The parents willingly step in to help the young folks through a crisis, such as the birth of a baby, illness, or temporary homelessness. Their financial help is perhaps available for a down payment on a car or new furniture, or to continue education. If the married children have attained emotional maturity, they reciprocate with the genuine affection, companionship, and thoughtful attention so meaningful to older people.

The secret of success in relationships between the generations seems to lie in achieving and maintaining autonomy as persons, whatever one's age or generation. As young people are encouraged to live lives of their own, to make their own decisions, and to work out their own careers, they no longer are provoked to rebel against what they feel to be the smothering love of their parents. As mature people find life meaningful apart from their roles as parents, they no longer feel the impulse to be possessive, but become more freely loving and lovable. As the children grow up, these patterns are best established by parents who develop interests and activities of their own that are compatible, but not identical, with their role as parents.

One recent study indicates that mothers with part-time jobs have better relationships with their adolescent children than do full-time homemakers, the reason being that the woman with too little to do may meddle with her growing children so that mother and children cannot harmoniously engage in common enterprises. The mother with some outside activities and responsibilities does not have to get all her emotional satisfactions from her growing children. Another study indicates that parents whose major emphasis is on the growth and development of both their children and themselves are more often successful in their relationships with their grown children than more traditional parents who have "lived for nothing but their children."

Encouraging Self-sufficiency

Many of the changes of recent decades have encouraged economic self-sufficiency. Social security, sickness benefits, hospitalization insurance, unemployment compensation, compulsory savings plans, pensions, old-age compensation, G.I. allotments and allowances, veterans' benefits, and other social policies and practices have gone far to help men and women, both young and old, to anticipate a satisfactory future without dependence upon others. There is the widespread feeling among the middle-aged and older persons that adequate retirement and insurance plans are important safeguards against having to rely on others for support when it is no longer possible for these older ones to work or when they wish to retire. Young people generally prefer to make ends meet by their own efforts and resources rather than continue to receive help from their parents.

The current emphasis on economic independence, fortified by impersonal institutional arrangements, has not done away with all forms of intergenerational assistance, as we have seen. There are indications, rather, that the giving and receiving between the generations today may be freer and more acceptable because of the assurance that "it is only for a while." Because there are so many institutional supports available for the individual unable to provide for himself, other family members need not feel indefinitely burdened, and therefore are more willing to make occasional contributions for special needs. It may well be that, in many families, the modern social aids promote better relationships between the generations, by removing the threat of continued dependency, a state irritating to the giver, humiliating to the receiver.

Living Under One Roof

Ideally, in this country, each family unit of husband, wife, and children has a separate domicile. There are times, however, when it becomes necessary or expedient for two or more generations to "double-up." Parents today often provide a home for a married son or daughter during military service, education, or vocational training, while building a house, or when a baby is due. Sometimes it becomes necessary for an older man or woman to make his or her home with a married son or daughter. Intervals of "doubling up" may extend over a few days or for many years.

How can the time together be spent with great satisfaction and the least stress and strain? Investigation of those families that have satisfactorily joined forces under one roof suggests four practices conducive to interfamily harmony:

(1) definite agreement as to "who does what" in the household
(2) satisfying outside interests and contacts with other people
(3) respect for each other's privacy, activities, and friends
(4) generous interchange of personal favors, helpfulness, and gracious good will

Each of us at times must lean on others, and at times must help bear the burdens of others. If the giving is spontaneous and the receiving is with appreciation, the relationship can be strengthened by its interdependence.

All Alone in the Prime of Life

If couples with children feel themselves alone after the children have gone, what of the childless couples, and what of the millions of men and women who actually and literally find themselves alone in the prime of life? About one-sixth of the married couples in the United States never have children. Beyond these there are persons who have not married (one in ten of people forty-five years old), the divorced or separated, and the widows and widowers. These people consider their predicament—if they see it as a predicament—as special, or at least different from that of parents who have weathered the chances and changes of life in a family. Those who are separated or widowed may have grown, and growing, children, of course. And this is the time for such parents to examine their relationships with their children as the other parents we have been talking about are doing and to proceed also to cultivate creative interests appropriate to middle-aged adults. But let us assume that many do not have children and therefore cannot approach the task in parental terms at all. Let us think for a moment about the truly childless.

In a world so often described as "child-centered" perhaps the most obvious suggestion for those who have no children of their own is that they manage to acquire some surrogate (or substitute) children! This suggests a very wide range of relationships, from formal adoption, where that is feasible, to "taking a special interest in" nieces and nephews or the children of friends—or even of strangers. Such a move tends to draw a couple or an unattached person into something like a family circle—working with children, as in the Boy and Girl Scout movements, serving as story-teller at the local library, or taking a hand as a volunteer in a recreational or "social work" program for children.

Not all the rewards that come from satisfactory relations between adults and children are reserved for parents. Those without children who bar themselves from the pleasures of helping intimately in the maturation of young people are making a personal choice, not accepting an inevitability. Children are usually remarkably receptive to proffers of friendship and often, long after they have become men and women, are loyal to such friends. There is hardly a man alive who cannot identify at least one adult, not his parent, who deeply influenced his life when he was a child.

Beyond establishing a substitute for the child-centeredness our society values so highly, the problem of the childless is comparable in kind to that of the parents whose children have left home. If they are couples, they have one another; if they are unattached, they nevertheless share the need for discovering sustaining interests and activities which bring individual satisfactions. There is hardly a suggestion made in the discussion we are carrying on which does not apply as exactly to single individuals as to the individuals composing couples. In fact, there is no assumption, implicit or otherwise, that a couple is firmly a unit in these matters, that what satisfies one of the couple must inevitably satisfy the other partner; but rather let it be assumed that each individual—single or one of a married couple—finds his own satisfaction by cultivating his personal potentialities.

The Hazard and the Possible Rewards of Maturity

The real threat to the middle years is the dry rot that immobilizes so many of us. The first enthusiasm for accomplishment may diminish. Earlier ambitions may not have been fulfilled with the success envisaged. Children grow up and leave home. The exacting demands for survival are tempered, and, all too often, cherished purposes lose their appeal. As one escapes the pressing demands of life, he feels bereft, useless, left-behind, abandoned. Those who have children may cling to them and become dependent upon them. Those without children may bemoan their fate. Whatever the later years hold for them, most human beings are responsible for what the future brings to them.

The middle years, it would seem, bring a challenge to redefine our roles as men and women, as fathers and mothers, as husbands and wives, or as unattached individuals. Maturity today offers new resources in time, energy, and opportunity never equaled before in the history of the race. The middle-aged person today is not old. He is literally in the prime of life with fully half his adult years still ahead of him. How he spends these decades depends in large measure upon how he sees himself in the multiplicity of roles open to him as a mature person intent on further development. The world of today calls for flexible persons who keep on growing through the years.

Time Out for Reflection

In our society the middle-aged or older man often has the opportunity to work along with his wife in shopping, preparing food, housekeeping, gardening, entertaining, and baby sitting. Are men being "feminized" when they share these tasks? Is there any real reason why such jobs should be considered appropriate for women only? Do men you know enjoy these roles?

What do maturing and mature families need to learn and practice that will put life into the "empty-nest" period of family living, after the children are grown?

Dr. Duvall lists four principles to guide older men and women who are living with their adult children. As you consider your acquaintances who are living happily in three-generation families, would you say that they are observing these principles? Have they added any others to the list? You probably know some families of adult children and older parents who are not getting along well. Which of Dr. Duvall's principles are they overlooking?

Married Couples
in Middle Age
Anne Morrow Lindbergh (1907-)

THE TIDE OF LIFE recedes. The house, with its bulging sleeping porches and sheds, begins little by little to empty. The children go away to school and then to marriage and lives of their own. Most people by middle age have attained, or ceased to struggle to attain, their place in the world. That terrific tenacity to life, to place, to people, to material surroundings and accumulations—is it as necessary as it was when one was struggling for one's security or the security of one's children? Many of the physical struggles have ceased, due either to success or to failure. Does the shell need to be so welded to its rock? Married couples are apt to find themselves in middle age, high and dry in an outmoded shell, in a fortress which has outlived its function. What is one to do—die of atrophy in an outstripped form? Or move on to another form, other experiences?

Changing Family
Patterns: Why?
Wilbert Moore (1914-)

PERHAPS THE FUNDAMENTAL problem of the aged in industrial societies is that they have no definite place in the social structure. That is, there are no regular, institutionally sanctioned responsibilities for their care and social participation which square with both traditional values and the requirements of an industrial system. To test these assertions, rather careful attention must be given to the place of the family in industrial societies.

The family system of the modern Western World approaches one extreme along a range that extends from complete emphasis on extended biological kinship (the consanguine family) at one pole to complete emphasis on the marital relationship and its immature progeny (the conjugal family) at the other. Along this range the family in industrial societies is clearly nearer the conjugal type, and the degree of its approximation to the pure type stands in some proximate relation to the degree to which the various societies approach the pure type of urban industrialism as a mode of social organization. The most frequent appearance of the pure conjugal family appears to be in the United States.

The significance of this family type for the role of the aged may best be seen through comparison and contrast with other kinship systems. It is the universal function of the family to provide sanctioned sexual relations and legitimate reproduction, to educate the child in attitudes and at least partly in facts, and to establish the child as a member of society as a whole. A child is a member of society only by membership in an effective kinship unit, or in some substitute unit recognized as such.

In most societies, however, the immediate family of reproduction is part of an extended kinship system, so that the child is *structurally* related to siblings and parents but also to grandparents and collateral relatives descended from common ancestors (uncles and aunts, cousins of various degrees). *Structurally* related is emphasized because that form of kinship system sets definite patterns of social rights and responsibilities among kinsmen, varying with their relationship as defined in the structure. A most important attribute of the consanguine system in the present context is that it retains its forms of social relationships throughout the life of any member, shifting only by change of status from child to parent or grandparent (and their collateral equivalents) as a normal part of growing older. The important point is that the child remains a member of the same extended kinship group, with definite and continuing rights and responsibilities, even through marriage, parenthood, and old age. Neither adulthood nor marriage severs ties with the parental family and its broader kinship liaisons. The aged in such a system tend to acquire increasing power and responsibility, with correlative security, at least as long as they retain their normal faculties.

The extreme conjugal family stands in marked contrast to such a system. As in any system, the conjugal family is the nexus between the child and society. But the family into which a child is born and the family into which his children are born are two quite different units, only tenuously related through the single individual. In the conjugal system when an adult married person refers to "his" family he must perforce mean his wife and immature children and not his parents or brothers and sisters. In short, the conjugal family in the type case involves a radical separation of the generations, and of adult brothers and sisters. They are all members of different families. Each married adult male has a wife who also no longer belongs to the kinship unit into which she was born.

The implications of this system for the role of the aged are clear and far-reaching. Old people have *no* definite claim upon an extended kinship group for support and social participation. The primary obligation of each brother and sister is to his or her *own* family, *and the same is true for married children.*

The increasing incidence of the conjugal family type in industrial societies is often interpreted in terms of "loss of functions" to more specialized agencies (government, factory, church, school, organized recreation). With this interpretation there are commonly explicit or implicit overtones of moral condemnation for those who have allowed timeless principles of kinship obligations and solidarity to fall into neglect. These interpretations usually rest upon a fundamental misapprehension of the structural requirements of modern industrial societies.

The conjugal family makes possible and indeed fosters the determination of adult status upon the basis of qualities and achievements of the individual as they are developed through childhood and maturity. This system of filling adult occupational and other positions is quite different from the determination of adult status at birth on the basis of criteria such as kinship group and birth order, over which the individual has no control. The efficiency of the industrial system rests upon the recruitment of individuals as individuals, for their technical competence and not for their membership in a kinship system. An adult can be assigned a status appropriate to the system and various rewards for his own performance in the occupational sphere only if he is not directly and completely dependent upon the success of his parents and siblings. This mode of occupational placement and reward requires also a substantial amount of movement from place to place and between occupations, and the necessary motivation to seek enhanced opportunities. Changes of this sort are most easily accomplished if the family is sufficiently small and free from entangling alliances with kinsmen.

The family universally prepares the child for adulthood, with or without the help of other agencies. It follows from the thesis presented here that the conjugal family supports the industrial system by preparing the child for adult independence of his parents and siblings.

Once this relationship between family and society becomes clear, considerable light is thrown on many contemporary problems associated with the aged. For example, the care of the aged is often discussed in terms of urbanization and urban housing. But urbanization simply gives a geographical dimension to the basic phenomenon of occupational change. And housing is merely a symptom and not a very reliable one at that. Comparisons of the ease of housing the aged in rural communities as contrasted with the cramped space in urban apartments are likely to involve unrecognized comparisons through time and across social strata. Not all rural families live in large, rambling dwellings where aged parents may be given a room and a corner in a spacious living room. The spacious dwelling unit is a rarity in rural as in urban communities; crowding is common in both.

The hidden comparison through time is that between the standards and expectations typical of the semi-isolated rural community at the turn of the century and those of urban dwellers (but also of many of their contemporaries) at the present time. Crowding is resented only when it is recognized as such, and it is increasingly alleged precisely because the basic structure of the modern family encourages spatial as well as social separation of the generations. Married children have both the right and the duty to "lead their own lives."

The hidden comparison across social strata is that between low-income farm families, where more traditional types of kinship relations are likely to prevail, and white-collar and professional groups in the cities, which are precisely the most mobile as compared with parental occupations and status and as compared with the aspirations and expectations of other occupational strata. It is for the competitor in the urban occupational sphere that the separation of generations is most effective.

The unwillingness of the young married adult to make serious sacrifices for the benefit of his parents is then something different from a general attrition of morals. If he makes such sacrifices he not only prejudices his own legitimate aspirations but also jeopardizes his responsibilities to his own children.

The foregoing structural analysis is, however, a little too neat. The conjugal family is *not* universally adhered to in industrial societies. In major sectors of the social systems of Western Europe, where change has been somewhat more gradual, and in older rural communities and among the very poor and families representing several generations of wealth in the United States, the generations and collateral kinsmen retain a variable but important range of social ties. These areas and sectors of the social order are precisely the least mobile in terms of generational change and of movement within a single career. It is therefore not accurate to refer to the pure conjugal family as *the* kinship system of industrial societies, but only as the kinship system best integrated with urban industrialism.

This lack of uniformity in practice is also reflected in the normative system. The conjugal family is *not* completely institutionalized, even in the United States. An adult married person may be criticized both for continuing to consider himself a member of his parental family and for failing to provide for his aged parents. Age-respect, honor to one's father and mother, and indeed intimate affectional bonds between generations are traditional values that do not mesh neatly with intergenerational mobility and achievement of social status. Parents are expected to provide maximum opportunities for their children, but without commensurate assurances for themselves.

Persons now in or approaching inactive old age were reared before the end of the last century, quite probably in a rural environment and certainly when urban industrialism was less firmly entrenched. They are likely to be kinship-oriented to a degree that disturbs their children and bewilders their grandchildren. Here the lack of clarity and uniformity as to the nature of the American family system may have acute consequences: the total incompatibility between the expectations of aged parents and their children as to their mutual obligations. Of the two, the children are the more likely to be ambivalent because of the inconsistency between the older expectations and the newer ones.

It is important to emphasize that this ambivalence is not one between moral obligation and crude self-interest. It is a moral obligation to the middle-class breadwinner to respect his primary responsibility to his own immediate family.

Only on the most superficial view can the sloppy sentimentality surrounding Mother's Day be attributed to clever commercialism. Its emotionalism is also cultivated and sanctified in urban churches. But the basic factor is surely the widespread prevalence of uneasy consciences about aged parents cut off from their adult offspring.

At the same time there are manifold signs of a sense of frustration among the aged. As Professor Talcott Parsons suggests, it is highly probable that the demand for pensions, especially as represented in pension clubs, is only partly a search for financial security. Emotional security is perhaps the acute need of the aged, and this can be assured only by stable and fairly intimate relationships that are regarded by participants as good in themselves and not as inferior substitutes.

There is a kind of deep tragedy in the vagaries of the normative patterns as they now stand. Parenthood, far from being "old age insurance," is a type of sacrificial duty. In the urban environment large families generally hamper both generations in competition for status. But even the small family does not assure the position of the parents after their children reach adulthood. The parents' freedom from responsibilities is likely to be too late for effective utilization for enhancement of the parents' social status of the money, time, and effort formerly spent on the young. Even more important is the lack of satisfying social participation, as the available activities substituted for those centering around the family are likely not to provide the emotional sense of belonging and being needed. The aged are in effect members of no family except their own truncated one. If that is further severed by death of one member, the awkward question of living arrangements arises. And there are few definite and approved patterns for filling the gap.

The tragedy, however, does not consist primarily of the separation of the generations. Rather it arises from the differing expectations of the aged and their children as to rights and responsibilities. This in turn derives from the incomplete institutionalization of the conjugal family. Failure to recognize this situation accounts in large measure both for the lack of attention to the social participation of the aged and for the apparent feeling of the aged that available activities are inferior substitutes for kinship bonds.

The same complex process loosely called "urbanization" and "industrialization" has made it possible for more people to reach old age and has made it difficult or impossible for the aged to be used and supported in conformity with older patterns and values. It has been argued here that continued efficiency and technical innovation in the industrial system will require modifications in the organization of productive assignments and definite provisions for dealing with the obsolescence of skills of the older worker, probably through adult retraining. It has also been argued that the type of family system best fitted to the industrial order is incompletely supported by social norms. This fact has further implications not only for the expectations of the aged but also for the scant attention society has given to the emotional as well as financial security of old people and to the types of social participation which will be within the capacities and expectations of the aged.

The problems of the aged will be alleviated but not solved by pensions or other forms of financial security. The reintegration of the aged into an extended kinship system would entail tremendous sacrifices in the organization of industrial societies with their attendant norms—sacrifices of such degree and complexity as to result in a quite different form of productive organization. A solution consistent with the industrial order would require new activities and organizations *appropriate* for the aged, appropriate being defined not only in terms of their capacities and interests, but also in terms of ethical principles commonly held in the society at large.

Financial Support of Parents:

Some Attitudes and Opinions

From California

Floyd Bond (1913-   ) and associates

WHAT ARE SOME OF these attitudes? How do the aged—both those who need aid and those who do not—look upon the salient features of the state's assistance program? How do their grown children view the prospects of passing on to the state all or part of the responsibility for their parents' care? How do those charged with administering the program regard both groups? How adequate or inadequate do they consider the law under which they work? What changes, if any, would they like to see made? . . .

Three factors that are having profound effects upon family organization and functioning are: (1) the trend toward earlier marriage, (2) the decreasing size of family, and (3) the increasing span of life. Marrying early, young people are usually out of the home before their parents are old or in need of help. By the time this occurs (if it does) the young people normally will have had a good many years of living unburdened by any obligation to support their parents, and therefore will often be psychologically unready to accept such a responsibility, even though they might have accepted it almost as a matter of course had there not been the long hiatus of freedom. Coupled with the fact that greater longevity now means more years after retirement, there is increasing likelihood that children will be called upon for help, unless (1) parents make more successful provision for their own later years, (2) social insurance becomes more nearly universal and adequate, (3) suitable employment opportunities are provided for elders who can work, or (4) society relieves the children of their obligations through public old age assistance programs.

Four fifths of the aged in California have living children and more than three fourths of these have children living in California. How do the parents feel about receiving help from their children? Nine tenths of them say their children would be *willing* to help support them if they needed help, but only half think they would be *able* to help. . . .

Would the parents be willing to let their children help support them? Some 40 per cent of the OAA (Old Age Assistance) recipients and 45 per cent of the non-recipients say they would be willing to accept such help.

Some interesting differences in the replies of men and women showed up. Far more women than men, both among those on and those not on assistance, (1) think their children would be willing to help, (2) think they would be able to help, and (3) would be willing to let them help. For example, three times as many women as men on OAA believe that their children are able to help support them. Among those not on OAA the difference is not so great, but still the women run far ahead of the men in believing that their children would be able to help them if they needed it. Likewise, in both groups, the women are far more willing than the men to accept such help.

The reported ability of the children to help support their parents varies with the parents' educational level. Of parents with only a grade-school education, 44 per cent think their children are able to help them if necessary; of those with a high-school education, 55 per cent; and of those who were college educated, 64 per cent.

What are the attitudes of adult children regarding their parents' applying for OAA? Among the 39 per cent of the parents who say their children have expressed an opinion on the matter, 45 per cent state that the children have urged them to go on and 36 per cent say that the children are willing for them to apply or not, as they wish. In other words, in four fifths of the cases in which opinions are known, the children either desire or are willing to have their parents go on OAA, in spite of the fact that in only one half the cases are the children considered by their parents to be unable to help. Of those able to help, 32 per cent have urged their parents to apply for OAA and 36 per cent more are willing for them to do so—that is, two thirds of the children, in spite of their ability to help, are ready for others to assume the responsibility for part or all of the support of their parents.

It will be remembered that only 43 per cent of the parents say they would be willing to accept aid from their children, yet even in this group 50 per cent of the children whose opinions are known have urged the parents to go on OAA—a higher percentage than among those cases in which the parents are *not* willing to let the children help them. Again the desire to be relieved of part or all of filial responsibility is apparent, even among those presumably able to assume it. . . .

There is an interesting relationship between the educational level of the parents and the children's attitude toward OAA. [It is safe to assume that the children's education, on the average, is better than that of their parents.] Of those persons on OAA whose children's opinions are known, the percentage whose children had urged them to apply for aid drops sharply as the education of the parents increases, being 52, 31, and 17 per cent respectively, for the grade-school, high-school, and college groups. Conversely, the percentage whose children had urged them *not* to apply rises regularly with education, being 10, 19, and 26 per cent respectively, for grade-school, high-school, and college groups. . . .

The matter of urban or rural environment during childhood also seemed to be related to attitudes. The children of the city-bred were more desirous (46%) that their parents apply for OAA than were the children of those reared on farms (33%). There may be something to the common belief that rural folk are usually inclined to be more self-reliant than urban folk.

One other angle of the matter of filial support deserves attention. On the question of whether adult children should be required by law to contribute to the support of aged parents who are in need, 36 per cent of the old folk say "yes," 55 per cent say "no," the balance having no opinion. However, of those on OAA, only 29 per cent take the affirmative, but 40 per cent of those not on OAA do so. In both cases, relatively more men than women think that children should be required to help their parents if in need. This is interesting, in view of the fact (shown above) that in both groups the men are considerably less willing to accept aid from the children than are the women. Does this show an unconscious conflict between principle and behavior? Are they merely insisting upon the *right* to support by their children in time of need, but actually are unwilling to accept it from them?

Finally, it is somewhat surprising that the proportion of children (whose opinions are known) *urging* their parents to apply for OAA is about the same in the group of parents who think children should be required to help support needy parents (42%) as in the group who think they should not be required to do so (45%). . . . Evidently the opinions of parents regarding such filial obligations have little effect on the desires of their offspring. . . .

Because it is sound in principle, both morally and economically, we favor the retention of relatives' responsibility, verification of income through the State Franchise Tax Board, and bringing out-of-state relatives within the circle of responsibility as far as possible.

There is a moral responsibility, even higher than the legal, for children to help their needy parents. The forces tending toward the disintegration of strong family bonds are already too numerous; for the state deliberately to add to them by removing any filial obligations would be to weaken still further the most basic and revered of all our social institutions.

Family Patterns:
China and the USA

Len Peterson (1918-   )

OF ALL THE GROUPS we belong to, the family is the most important. This is true in every culture. But what the family is, how it is organized, who is important to it—these things are different in different cultures. And the way the family is organized is very important to the way people feel and act. . . .

When we marry, we generally take a house or apartment separate from our parents and our in-laws. But some people never do this. In some societies the bride moves into the household of her husband, as in the Chinese village family. In some the groom moves into his wife's family. Usually, where there are such arrangements, the small family is thought of as merely a part of the larger group of kin. Then it is the large family that matters, and the parents on one side or the other are a part of the family—while those on the opposite side are not. Arrangements of this kind are spoken of as lineages (as with the Chinese) or as clans. This is another way in which families vary. . . .

It is also important to appreciate that the family organization is influenced in many ways by the economic life of the people. Nearly everywhere that farming is carried on as a peasant activity, we find a lineage system held closely together by its landholdings. In these families, work is carried on by the larger family group as a single enterprise. In our society usually only one member earns the living. Where two or more family members are working, they will usually be working for separate wages or salaries. This tends to divide their interests and make them more independent of each other.

Each family system has its sources of strength and weakness. If we compare the Chinese peasant family with our own, we can see this. The Chinese family emphasizes unity and gives strength and support to its members, but the freedom of each person is lessened by the demands of family ties. The American family is discontinuous, it is small, and it offers less strength and support to each member. If a man dies, his widow may be put entirely on her own, and children do not regularly support their aging parents. But the system does give more freedom of action—particularly to the youth—and allows them more opportunity to find their own way and serve their own interests. We might well argue over which system is the better scheme for personal satisfaction; but it is hardly doubtful that our family pattern is better adjusted for life in America, with its rapid changes and need for free movement. . . .

GEORGE. *I was in China just after the war on a special food commission: livestock and poultry diseases. And I came to Nantao, the village where my father was born. It was a mythical place to me—the home of my ancestors. I was well received in Nantao.*

FU. Then we are cousins, George. George—that is a strange name.

GEORGE. It's an American name, Cousin Fu.

FU. But you have kept the family name, Wang.

GEORGE. Yes.

FU. I have heard stories of your father who went away to America. He did not come back, but you come.

GEORGE. Never thought I would.

FU. You and I have the same grandfather. See, here is his name and his accomplishments on this plaque. Died at the age of sixty-eight.

GEORGE. You have quite an impressive family shrine here in your house, Cousin Fu. Are these offerings to ancestors, these bowls of fruit, incense, flowers?

FU. Yes, and to the gods. You will want to see the clan temple too. Over half the people in Nantao belong to our clan.

GEORGE. Well! Could we wander around and meet some?

FU. Yes. And I will show you our family graveyard.

GEORGE. Fine, fine.

FU. There is my father. I thought he might be down here at the graveyard. His tomb has just been finished. He is very proud of it.

GEORGE. His tomb?

FU. Yes. Come along and meet him.

GEORGE. Fine and healthy-looking old gentleman.

FU. My dear father.

HENG-SHEN. Fu, the inscription on my stone looks well.

FU. We have a visitor, a son of Ping who went to America.

HENG-SHEN. Son of Ping?

FU. George Wang. . . .

GEORGE. *The talk was light-hearted and lively beside Heng-shen's tomb. He asked a stream of questions about the Wangs in America, and in turn related a good deal about our common ancestors, whose tombs lay all about us under the trees. It began as an idyl, that stay at the home of my cousin in Nantao. My work hadn't started, and the Communist sweep had not yet reached that far. Life was casual; I had time on my hands. I loafed about, absorbing the warm summer sun and the past and a new sense of family. Oh, I was very aware of family.*

FU. Do you want me to hide you away, George? Are you growing tired of all the Wangs hunting you out and bombarding you with questions?

GEORGE. No, I am enjoying it. In America we ask about relatives, too, but here they are much more serious about it, even about relatives eight or ten times removed. The American family circle used to include more relatives, but now generally speaking only the man and his wife and their children are included; and sometimes even some of those feel on the outside of the circle.

FU. The man's father and mother are not part of the family? The man's ancestors?

GEORGE. (*Chuckles.*) Ancestors? Americans are a people on the move. They can't be bothered lugging their ancestors around with them. My father stuck to Chinatown in San Francisco. I am the halfway child. My children are real Americans. It has taken three generations; that is a long time to Americans. My children speak only English. They don't want to know anything about their ancestors.

FU. You are unhappy about it?

GEORGE. After all, they are Americans. Why shouldn't they live as Americans? I'm American—more American than Chinese.

FU. Yes, you seem to be.

GEORGE. Sometimes lately I have felt like a man without any family, completely without ties. The only thing that mattered has been my work.

FU. I cannot imagine that. . . .

HENG-SHEN. Fu, you will take those hens to market in the morning?

FU. Yes, Father.

HENG-SHEN. And bring back some paper to mend the windows.

FU. Ch'in thinks we are rich enough to put glass in some of the windows.

HENG-SHEN. Fu, you are listening too much to that wife of yours. Her parents have no glass in their windows. Bring back wax paper for the windows.

FU. Yes, Father.

HENG-SHEN. Have you fed the ox yet?

FU. (*Leaving.*) I was about to do so, Father.

HENG-SHEN. My daughter-in-law has been influencing Fu too much since my wife died and she became the woman of the house. Up until now Fu has been a dutiful son.

GEORGE. How differently you would fare in my country, Uncle Heng-shen. There the young people boss the old, and the women—ah, it is a woman's country. Seventy per cent of the wealth in America is in women's hands.

HENG-SHEN. It sounds like the Communists—everything for the young, women behaving like men. There is no sense to it: upheaval, upheaval, unrest, no stability. If you were looking for wisdom would you look among women? Would you look among children?

GEORGE. (*Only half seriously.*) I suppose among old men of experience.

HENG-SHEN. Where else on this earth?

GEORGE. Some will argue that was fine when things changed little from generation to generation, but we're astride a runaway jet today. A man of forty doesn't stand much chance giving advice to a youth of twenty; a man of seventy attempting it is considered ludicrous. . . .

HENG-SHEN. And what of your family—the Wangs in America? Where are they going? You haven't told me much about that.

GEORGE. We don't think in America of families going anywhere—it's more the individual.

HENG-SHEN. Oh, yes, I have heard that in America (it is the same in Europe, is it not?) the family means only the man and his wife and their children. When the man or woman dies, or they part, that is the end of the family. It seems very strange. Can it possibly be like that?

GEORGE. I'm afraid it is. . .

HENG-SHEN. With us it is very different. The Chinese family is buttressed against misfortunes that happen to individuals in the family. There is continuity. The family includes the dead, the living, and those not yet born. The land and other property belong to the family, not to individuals. At the core of the Chinese family is the father and son. . . .

GEORGE. In your family there doesn't seem to be the isolation between generations that plagues us, Uncle Heng-shen. In my world the children, adults, and old people lead different lives. Of course, in a society rooted to the land the work keeps you all together. But in the shifting industrial and commercial society in our cities there is a terrible isolation. I feel my children are strangers to me; and my father is a stranger. It is easier to grow old here than in America.

HENG-SHEN.   Everywhere with age there come aches and pains.

GEORGE.   But for the old men of China there are compensations: respect from the young, obedience. When I think of my father—I wish I could do something for him.

HENG-SHEN.   Can you not?

GEORGE.   *This association with the old patriarch Heng-shen made me think a lot about my father. He was not as old as Heng-shen, but already he was a cast-off; there was no place for him in our family. He was alone; all his children had set up establishments of their own, and my mother had died in 1939. It used to hurt me, his gratitude whenever we invited him over for a meal or suggested that he stay for the night.*

FATHER.   You are sure it will not put you out too much? You are sure it won't inconvenience you? I don't want to be any trouble. I—I can't stay longer than the one night. I must go tomorrow—business. I wish I could stay longer, but business—You're sure I won't be in the way?

DORIS.   No, of course not, Dad. I'll get the bed made up for you.

FATHER.   You are very good to me, Doris.

GEORGE.   *He knew he was not welcome, except for short visits. He stifled his pride and came. But I couldn't stifle my sense of shame, or the touch of contempt I felt for my wife's selfishness, the time I suggested he come for a longer visit.*

DORIS.   Why should we look after him?

GEORGE.   You won't have to look after him, Doris; he can look after himself. You know he'll contribute more than his share.

DORIS.   But he'll be in the way. If I can't have my household to myself—

GEORGE.   I think it's the least we can do.

DORIS.   Why? George, you know it wouldn't work. It hasn't worked with any of the families I know. I'm doing your father a favor by avoiding bad feeling later on.

GEORGE.   That's a neat argument, I must say.

DORIS.   We have nothing in common with him; you know that. What can we talk to him about? The things that we're interested in would just bore him stiff. And our friends—what has he got to say to them? It'd be uncomfortable all around. Be sensible!

GEORGE. Doris, I owe my father a great deal. He didn't have to give me as much schooling as he did.

DORIS. Pay him back some other way. I want my own house to myself.

GEORGE. All right, have the house to yourself, then.

DORIS. It's no reflection on your father. I like him, and I want you to do something for him. But having him live with us for a while just wouldn't work.

GEORGE. But that's all he cares about—the family, the kids.

DORIS. All right, invite him to come and live with us; but I won't be responsible if it doesn't work.

GEORGE. That's a fine basis on which to invite him. No thanks.

DORIS. Suit yourself.

GEORGE. *I think I've got a good wife; we've had a pretty good life together. But the stand she's always taken toward my father bothers me. Like all American husbands, I have felt that the wishes of my wife have had to take precedence over the wishes of my father. With Fu in Nantao, the wishes of his father came first.* (With a sense of personal defeat.) *The wishes of my children too come before mine—and before my wife's. . . .*

DORIS. The children have got their friends; you've got your work. But here I sit.

GEORGE. Doris, you can do anything you want to.

DORIS. What, alone? (*Forlorn.*) Yes, that's a great stimulus for doing something, isn't it?

GEORGE. *I was tempted to say to Doris: "Well, this is the loneliness that goes with the kind of independence you've always wanted." But I never have said it. Who am I? Doris's predicament is no different from that of a lot of American wives and mothers I know. On the other hand Fu's wife's situation—at the age when Doris was beginning to feel that her life was over, Fu's wife was coming into her own.*

CH'IN. I am a grandmother. (*The baby enters jabbering.*) Oh, listen to this talkative one, Hsiaomair! This one made me a grandmother, and in a few days I shall be twice a grandmother. But this time to a boy—I have been to a fortune teller.

FU. (*Entering.*) You are looking over the family shrine again, George?

GEORGE. Yes; and comparing your family and mine, Cousin Fu. Yours has a more solid foundation. You've more rigid traditions and customs defining the relationship of all the members of your family; this seems to make life run more smoothly for you day to day. And the peak in your lives, especially of your women, comes not in the middle years, but well along in life—something to look forward to. And there's this sense, wonderful sense of continuity: your life is not isolated, but bound to the past and to the future. Every age has links with every other age.

FU.   George, we have our difficulties too.

GEORGE.   Oh, I'm sure; but they can't be any greater than ours. The American family is restless these days. We ask: What do we want? How should it be, the family? Where are we going? I like the quiet, settled atmosphere around here.

FU.   It was, it was—but it's changing. We listen with great intensity now to how other people do things; we wonder how we would like it.

GEORGE.   *My dream began to fade. Nantao, the mythical place in my heart, all-good, all-sense, all-harmony, began to be replaced by the Nantao of reality.*

FU.   Ah, the old fool, the old fool!

GEORGE.   *(Comes in casually.)* Well, you sound upset, Fu, What's up?

FU.   He does not know Asia is on the march!

GEORGE.   Who?

FU.   Heng-shen, my revered father.

GEORGE.   You have had a quarrel with him?

FU.   No, I am a dutiful son, but I may not be dutiful forever.

GEORGE.   Why, what's wrong, Fu?

FU.   The inoculation measures against disease you suggested to me for our cattle he will have nothing to do with. Unnatural, he said—it will not work, it will kill all our cattle. With every suggestion I make, it is the same; if he has not done it that way in the past, then it is no good. We had the same argument a month ago over a gasoline pump I wanted to install. In America you do not have to wait for the greybeards, do you? If the younger generation wishes to make a change, progress, they go ahead?

GEORGE.   Yes. Frequently.

FU.   There is a part of me that is not Chinese, not the old Chinese. I do not wish to wait until I am a greybeard—though I am close to it—before I improve things around here. I cannot wait for the slow advance my father is content with. Sometimes I almost feel I do not fear disobedience to my father. If my ancestors were alive today, they might well do what I want to do themselves! . . .

GEORGE. *Every day, I became aware of more and more stress and strain in my Nantao family; it was there when I looked for it. By the time I was ready to leave, my family setup back home in San Francisco didn't look so bad. The Nantao family had the kind of long-term stability we sometimes yearn for—but at the expense of a lot of elbow room for the younger people, and for the women, and for the individual generally. If I came from Mars I don't know which kind of family setup I'd prefer; they both have advantages and drawbacks. But being American, and having grown into the American mold, I guess I'm for the American model, with all the stresses and strains peculiar to it. I need elbow room more than stability.*

Suggestions for Further Reading

The Family Life of Old People: An Inquiry in London, by Peter Townsend. Glencoe, Ill. The Free Press, 1958.

> A detailed inquiry into the intergenerational family relationships, with special reference to mutual exchanges of help and to the satisfactions and dissatisfactions accruing to the older generation.

American Families, by Paul C. Glick. New York: John Wiley and Sons, 1957.

> A new and brilliant documentation of changes during the family life cycle: family composition, income, social characteristics, changes in modern society. Documents the need for shifting social roles, personal planning, and special housing.

Family Development, by Evelyn Millis Duvall. Philadelphia: Lippincott and Co., 1957.

> Part III of Dr. Duvall's book deals with the "Contracting Families." The married pair are followed from the departure of their young adult children, through the middle-age years, both as a couple and as individuals.

Technology and the Changing Family, by William F. Ogburn and Meyer Nimkoff. New York: Houghton Mifflin Company, 1955.

> America's pioneer and persistent student of social change, sociologist William F. Ogburn, together with a close student of family life, Meyer Nimkoff, examines the impact of industrialization and urbanization on the family. This scholarly and highly readable survey describes the changes that are taking place in family functions and shows how they grow naturally and inevitably out of underlying scientific and technological advances.

You and Your Aging Parents, by Edith M. Stern and Mabel Ross, M.D. New York: A. A. Wyn, Inc., 1952.

> A comprehensive examination of relationships among the adult generations. Illustrated with numerous case sketches, and designed to help adults work out satisfactory social, financial, and housing arrangements within the family constellation.

part II

THE OPPORTUNITY YEARS

C. Hartley Grattan (born in 1902 at Wakefield, Massachusetts) has been in practice as a "general writer" since 1924 when he began to contribute to the national magazines. In 1929 he began to publish books. As a magazine writer he has contributed prolifically to journals at home and abroad, notably at home to The American Mercury *under H. L. Mencken,* Scribner's *under Alfred Dashiel, and* Harper's *under Frederick Lewis Allen. As to his books, he prefers to be known for* Why We Fought *(1929),* The Three Jameses: A Family of Minds *(1932),* Introducing Australia *(1942 and 1947), and* In Quest of Knowledge: A Historical Perspective on Adult Education *(1955). But there are others. In 1953 he was awarded an honorary D. Litt. by his own alma mater, Clark.*

"Liberal adult education is ordinarily concerned with the humanities and the social sciences and should also include the natural sciences, music, and the plastic arts. Its primary objective is to deepen the understanding of the human predicament and put men in the way of making relevant judgments and sensitive discriminations among values. It is not concerned, in the first instance, with improving the prospect of greater pecuniary rewards like most vocational education, nor with improving competence in recreation, nor with information of any specialized kind, but with those varieties of knowledge and understanding that somehow underpin wisdom. Liberal adult education is calculated to assist the maturation of the individual as an individual—not simply as a factor in the economic equation or as a political citizen, but as a Man."

—C. HARTLEY GRATTAN
In Quest of Knowledge, 1955.
Quoted by permission from Association Press.

6

Curiosity, Creativeness, Comprehension

C. HARTLEY GRATTAN

The Root Is Curiosity

WHEN JOHN WALKER POWELL selected the three C's—Curiosity, Creativeness, and Comprehension—as basic to adult education, he also defined a trinity peculiarly meaningful to persons who have reached middle life and are attempting to reassess their personal resources, interests, and prospects. This is the time of life at which all three can be given freer play than ever before, not encumbered by considerations of vocational training nor limited by the sense of inexperience which normally afflicts youth.

The Greek thinkers long ago concluded that there were ranges of knowledge more fruitfully to be explored by adults than by adolescents. We have thus far profited little from that insight; but surely the time has come to do so, what with leisure ever becoming more freely available in later life. Moreover, our civilization normally allows but little scope for the free expression of creativeness in the occupations open to most people during young adulthood. Middle life, less weighted down by the hard necessities of earning a living, can take time out for it. All one needs, to do these things, is Curiosity; and fortunately in most people it survives in some measure, or can be stimulated without too much difficulty.

Curiosity is a key characteristic of man as he confronts the world in which he lives. From the vaguest and most transient wonderment at the way the world wags, to the most specific and searching question about the same thing, Curiosity is at work. It is what prompts us to demand "answers" to the problem of what life is all about. Everyone's life is sustained by answers of one kind or another, even if one is unable to bring them to consciousness and phrase them with exactitude. They may simply be the answers enforced on one's mind—sunk into one's unconscious—by one's family or one's peers. But at middle life, the compulsive tasks of parenthood and career largely carried through—as the writers in this series have pointed out—the answers which have sustained one more or less satisfactorily so far seem to demand reassessment, amplification, confirmation, denial, or reaffirmation through enlarged understanding. The answers need to be "pawed over" so that life "makes sense"—if there is any sense to be made of it. At this point one's Curiosity about "the answers" is acutely active, and one has enough accumulated experience to make a mature judgment. Education re-enters the picture.

Education: To Be or Be Something?

A dangerous word, "education." It has a variety of meanings, including that which you yourself associate with it. To you it may chiefly conjure up a visual image of a more or less pleasant teacher who imposed tasks on you in the fourth grade, or it may recall to mind that memorable character—man or woman in high school or college—who first made you realize you had a mind and could use it easily and well. But by education as it is relevant to the middle years of life, I mean simply any ways and means you discover to assist you in winning comprehension of life as a great, if mysterious, experience. You now want to examine your life, as Socrates long ago said all men should; and in examining it you will necessarily want to take a look at the larger circumstances of life in our time and place. You may do this by solitary reading of books borrowed from the library or bought, or in company with your fellows in classes or discussion groups. *How* you do it is your own choice, but *do it* you quite certainly will; for it is reasonably certain that we all, to a greater or lesser degree, aspire to a sense of orientation in life; and, to gain this, we try to construct a "frame of reference"—a scheme of understanding of the world in which we can define a satisfactory place for ourselves.

Henry James the Elder—the father of Henry the novelist and of William the psychologist-philosopher—drew a distinction which is highly relevant here. He advised his boys to *be* before trying to *be something*. Most of us reverse the process and only get around to try to *be* after we *have been something* for a good many years. Our American world has always had a strong bias toward insisting that all of us *be something*—bookkeepers, executives, doctors, lawyers, indian chiefs. The tradition that every man should unfailingly be able to earn a living has enforced this demand. Therefore there has been a lesser emphasis on *being*—so little that many of us are at a loss to see what it means. To *be* means, I think, to cultivate one's capacities in such a fashion that one is a "marvelous person" quite aside from the *something* one happens to be. We acknowledge this as a valid aspiration when we say that so-and-so is "far more than" whatever his occupation defines him as, whether carpenter or Supreme Court justice. Conversely we sometimes say that somebody is "rather less of a person" than his job appears to require. When we can say that a man is "far more than" his job seems to imply, we know that he has troubled himself to *be* as well as *be something*.

Now the big question is how one gets to *be*. The state of *being*—as apart from *being something*—is a subtle combination of personality qualities and wisdom, neither of which can be snared in formulae and passed around in a dish like candy. Men develop personality and wisdom by *living*. But all who *live* do not develop striking personalities or outstanding wisdom. The secret apparently lies in the *quality of living;* and the quality appears to be related to knowledge, insight, comprehension.

And so, circuitously, we come back to education—or at least education when it is distinguished from training; the part devoted to training people to *be something*. This portion of education is roughly the variety called liberal. Liberal education, as I see it, is built upon the humanities, the social sciences, science, and the arts. It does not *guarantee* that one will know how to *be* without some acquaintance with it. As I have remarked, there is no ascertainable formula for making people *be*. It can only be gotten at by indirection. Let us try to illustrate.

A liberally educated person has some conception of the persistent issues of human life and the solutions proposed for these issues. Both the issues and the solutions can be presented to adolescents— and they are, regularly, as we all know—but the Greeks, as remarked earlier, concluded that they should be, if not reserved for the consideration of mature adults, at least re-presented to them. The idea is that the issues are more real to adults because in the ordinary course of life adults have actually confronted many of them. And the solutions are better evaluated by adults because they have, having lived, a better comprehension of the implications of the alternatives. They are better able to see whether a given formulation really makes a difference, and whether the difference is live or inert, good or bad. Mature adults, that is to say, can better comprehend what is at issue as well as better evaluate the solutions offered to the dilemmas posed. Out of a systematic investigation of what wise men have said about the issues of life one can, in middle age, slowly fortify a position of one's own toward life.

As remarked, this exploration of the great and wise writers of the past can either be an individual adventure—the chosen method of the self-starters—or it can be done in association with others of the same mind in a discussion group where one will be stimulated by the clash of opinions. *How* such exploration proceeds is probably less significant than the fact of undertaking the task at all. But unless one has been a self-starter all one's life, the group approach has much to recommend it, for the reasons Professor Burgess adduces.

The writers one can profitably take a look at are exceedingly numerous, and any selection among them is difficult unless one aims to enforce a particular point of view. Until one feels that one's outlook is "jelling"—until the discipline of seeking to understand other men's minds has given one a sense of an individually satisfactory comprehension of the answers to the issues of life—diversity is the best rule. Reading only writers with whom one is pretty sure to agree may make one feel good, but it won't sharpen one's wits or clarify one's personal insights. One should probably read in Plato, Aristotle, and Plutarch; in the Bible, in Machiavelli, and Milton; Tocqueville and Marx, Thoreau and Tolstoi, St. Augustine and Rousseau, John Stuart Mill and Mark Twain, Confucius and Nietzsche, Kant and John Woolman, William James and St. Thomas Aquinas—in other words, explore secular and religious thinkers with equal diligence.

The names cited correctly imply that, in our search for Comprehension, we will read what thinkers have to say and what literary artists have to say also. It is a stirring moment in anybody's life when it is perceived that a novel can be more than merely a good yarn well told: that it can also be vicarious experience so expertly presented and interpreted as to illuminate life deeply and subtly. And that poetry and drama also do this and have been doing it longer. The discovery of literature as an illuminator of life is one of life's great experiences, and to miss discovering it is one of life's great deprivations. Its discovery, or rediscovery, in middle life can mean the difference between spiritual rebirth and spiritual ossification.

The social sciences also figure in our rebirth in middle life. Some of these social sciences have long histories, and the thinkers already mentioned have contributed to them; but others are fairly recent creations, and the insights they offer are best obtained from the writings of contemporary writers. There are two ways of looking at the social sciences—at all intellectual disciplines for that matter: either one can concentrate on the conclusions the writers have arrived at, or one can seek to master the method employed to arrive at the conclusions.

A social science is, among other things, an apparatus of the mind designed to handle certain ranges of social facts, in a rewarding fashion. Most of us at middle life will be satisfied to look at the conclusions of a few of the outstanding writers, but it is possible that we may want both to look at the ideas of, say, a few distinguished contemporary economists, and also to try to grasp *how* economists reason. There is nothing to stop us, if we have the curiosity and the will.

Nor is there anything to stop us from similarly investigating the ancient art of history, or the modern disciplines of anthropology, sociology, or psychology (individual and social).

As to science, it seems to me we should be concerned to do more than pick up the latest information from whatever field attracts our attention, though such data should never be ignored. Rather our special purpose should be to get a grasp on how the scientist approaches his problems, on how the mind trained for scientific investigation actually works. This is by no means easy; but if we lack all comprehension of science, we perforce seem to live in a world of inexplicable wonders conjured up by magicians. If you think we *really* do, then you do not understand the scientific mind and method and are, to that extent, not living at the peak of your time and your own potentialities. It is as simple—and as complex—as that!

And so we come to the arts, not because they are properly to be given last place in our regimen but simply because the accidents of exposition have placed them last. The arts might well come first if you believe, as I do, that they are the quintessence of civilization. The arts are, of course, literature (already discussed), painting, music, sculpture, architecture, and the lesser forms of aesthetic expression. It is through our comprehension of the arts—or of those we find ourselves equipped by nature to grasp and appreciate—that we educate and sophisticate our subtler feelings and more delicate perceptions, and in so doing deepen our sense of the infinite resources of man in exploring, reporting, and evaluating the world and all that is therein. A great picture greatly understood gives us more of a sense of this than endless reiteration of it in words—and similarly a great musical composition, or a noble piece of sculpture, or a fine building.

The Greeks felt strongly that things seen and heard were important educators, and so have most peoples who have attained high civilization. Walt Whitman said that great artists need great audiences; so there is honor in being of the audience. By an irony that all should try to appreciate, in the long run civilizations are best and most widely remembered by what survives of their arts; and it is the manifestations of the aesthetic impulse that have a way of surviving for later generations. Archaeology could hardly exist without the evidence derived from decorated pottery.

It would be a peculiar kind of folly to imply—and a worse one bluntly to state—that the middle years are the time to turn to the arts, inasmuch as I have suggested that people in their middle years have a special affinity for the *reflective* disciplines. The arts belong to *all* of us *all* the time, if we have the luck to encounter them and the good sense to claim them for our own. But we can honestly say that the arts, like the reflective disciplines we discussed earlier, are great openers-up of new avenues of thought and feeling; and they therefore beckon the middle aged to explore, or re-explore, them in the hope that they will stir old fires or kindle new ones. The arts contribute to that "renewal," of which my fellow essayists have spoken in their different papers.

How High to Set Our Sights

We now come to two large questions, neither of which we can fully explore here. Whole books have been written about them. (Indeed this entire essay is but a hop-skip-and-jump over subjects any one of which needs a book fully to discuss.) I refer to the vexing question of the *level* of difficulty at which the humanities, the social sciences, science, and the arts should be approached; and to the question of where, in this galaxy of imposing fields of knowledge suggested for exploration, the individual can participate as creator. It is Curiosity that inspires our quest. Comprehension is what we seek. And Creativeness gives our comprehension expression.

First, the level of difficulty. We touch here upon the invidious distinctions usually made by referring to low-brows, middle-brows, and high-brows. People often assign themselves to these categories, but more often they are thrust into them by others. Which one fits you is entirely up to you; but remember there are phonies in every one. The thing to do is to be yourself and not to be tempted to underestimate your resources. There is really no moral distinction involved—only a reference to the quantity and quality of the experience and understanding you have happened to acquire. You aren't assigned to one category or another at birth; the category into which you fall is thrust upon you by life; and there is nothing whatever to prevent your migration from low- to middle- to high-brow except lack of will and opportunity. Similarly you can, possibly, drop down the scale by virtue of a failure to cultivate your powers and refine your perceptions. Many people are surprised at one moment or another in life to find that they have miscategorized themselves, or been miscategorized; that actually their taste is better than they thought, and their powers of comprehension greater than they imagined. The point to keep in mind is not where you think you are, but how far you are prepared, when challenged, to stretch your mind to reach a satisfactory maximum of understanding.

For the big point of all that is being said here is that really to get on top of the challenges of middle life, outlined for us by the other writers of essays, is to stretch our minds and talents to their maximum in our search for Comprehension and satisfaction.

This is using our powers creatively. Thinking *is* Creativeness. Mathematicians and philosophers, literary artists and sociologists, *create* as surely as the makers of things. But, to round out our picture, let us take a look at the creativeness that results in *things* rather than *thoughts*.

Here again we come up against that vexing problem of *level*. Obviously, we can't all be "masters." We can't all paint masterly pictures, compose music that will become classic, or write books that will be read down through the centuries. Nobody ever sat down deliberately to do any of these things anyhow, except pretentious clowns with diseased egos. The quality called "classic" is in part a quality isolated by the winnowing of time, during which process many, many other examples are down-graded and discarded. There are "also-rans" in the arts as well as politics. So subtle—or so difficult —are the discriminations involved, that only a supremely lucky connoisseur will be able to pick out the classics created in his own time. Not that that is any reason for any of us to give up trying to create them!

More to the point, however, is the observation that the impulse to create can be satisfied in a wide variety of ways. Those who sort out the arts use various terminologies to discriminate among them, but all the schemes recognize both the "high arts" and the "crafts," or the popular arts. Nobody of true perception and sensitivity ever looked down his nose at the crafts because they were simpler and within the capacities of more people than the high arts. Rather they are looked down upon when they are bad works of craftsmanship. Discriminations apply in both realms.

It is symbolic of the true position of the crafts that a Museum of

Contemporary Crafts was recently opened on West 53rd Street in New York City, near the Museum of Modern Art and the Whitney Museum of American Art. The line between the high arts and the crafts is a fuzzy one, as this geographical association implies. The Museum of Modern Art, as a matter of fact, has exhibited pictures by "popular" (or "Sunday" or untrained) painters who are closely related to the craftsmen,[1] as well as articles of everyday use selected for their excellence of design. So fervent a defender of the most advanced modern painters as Sir Herbert Read has also written a highly regarded work on industrial art.[2]

The point about the crafts—or the popular arts, or whatever you choose to call them—is that whichever is cultivated: pottery, silverwork, weaving, rug-making, furniture-making, woodworking, or "Sunday" oils or watercolors, should be carried on at the highest level of expertness that can be achieved technically and in as good taste as the aesthetic sensibilities of the worker allows. "Whatever is worth doing at all is worth doing well."

As a matter of fact, you may well decide that a craft should have a conspicuous role in your regimen. The doors are wide open to you, and the opportunities to learn are rather more abundant than if you choose to take up deep thinking or high art. In either case you will be giving expression to your creative impulses, and that is what matters.

But in working out a regimen for yourself, be sure you do not underestimate your resources, something many middle aged people are tempted to do. If you underestimate your powers, you may put together a regimen that fits you very comfortably but which is hardly a challenge to you. Henry David Thoreau once said that most men start out to build a castle in Spain and end up building a henhouse. He did not reason from this that most men should curb their ambitions and start out to build a henhouse, leaving castles in Spain to the vain and the foolish. Rather, Thoreau was himself a notable builder of a castle in Spain, which in the end brought him imperishable fame.[3] What he was getting at, I think, was that most men seem

---

[1] And published a book about them, *Masters of Popular Painting* by Cahill, Cassou, Gauthier, and Miller. New York: 1938.

[2] *Art and Industry*. London: 1954.

[3] Henry David Thoreau (1817-1862), author of *Walden, A Week on the Concord and Merrimack Rivers, An Essay on Civil Disobedience,* etc. See the biography, *Thoreau*, by H. S. Canby. Boston, 1939.

to find good, but hopelessly mistaken, reasons for abandoning their high ambitions, seem to underestimate their resources, and then have to settle for a henhouse because they have adopted the henhouse outlook.

It is taken for granted in what I have had to say that the henhouse attitude has been rejected. We may not all achieve a castle in Spain—not even a split-level, air-conditioned, ranch-type dwelling with a huge picture window actually opening on a magnificent view. Nevertheless we won't settle for anything less than a well-founded, weatherproof home of our own, of which we can justly be proud.

Time Out for Reflection

Do you think the mind at middle life is flexible enough to take up new interests and to develop new powers of creation?

Among the people you know, is "leisure" a time for free enjoyment, a time of obligation to do something useful, a time to be idle? Is "idleness" good or bad?

Let's take an inventory:

How far did your schooling go? What subjects are still of interest to you? What ones have you pursued? What ones would you like to resume?

What have you read in the last six months? What topics of reading or conversation do you find most absorbing? What matters of interest are you postponing "until you have time?" Why?

What do you do that is creative (the list ranges from cookery to crafts, from needle arts to fine arts, from decorating to designing)? What would you *like* to start doing—and why don't you?

What does your *family* do with its leisure? Do you do things *together,* for fun? For growth? What do your *friends* do that you share in—for curiosity, for creativeness, for comprehension?

Contemplation Is His Bliss

William Cowper (1731-1800)

He is the happy man whose life e'en now
Shows somewhat of that happier life to come;
Who, doom'd to an obscure but tranquil state,
Is pleased with it, and, were he free to choose,
Would make his fate his choice; whom peace, the fruit
Of virtue, and whom virtue, fruit of faith,
Prepare for happiness; bespeak him one
Content indeed to sojourn while he must
Below the skies, but having there his home.
The world o'erlooks him in her busy search
Of objects more illustrious in her view;
And, occupied as earnestly as she,
Though more sublimely, he o'erlooks the world.
She scorns his pleasures, for she knows them not;
He seeks not hers, for he has proved them vain.
He cannot skim the ground like summer birds
Pursuing gilded flies; and such he deems
Her honours, her emoluments, her joys.
Therefore in Contemplation is his bliss,
Whose power is such, that whom she lifts from earth
She makes familiar with a heaven unseen,
And shows him glories yet to be reveal'd.
Not slothful he, though seeming unemploy'd,
And censured oft as useless. Stillest streams
Oft water fairest meadows, and the bird

That flutters least is longest on the wing.
Ask him, indeed, what trophies he has raised,
Or what achievements of immortal fame
He purposes, and he shall answer—None.
His warfare is within. There unfatigued
His fervent spirit labours. There he fights,
And there obtains fresh triumphs o'er himself,
And never-withering wreaths, compared with which
The laurels that a Caesar reaps are weeds.
Perhaps the self-approving haughty world,
That as she sweeps him with her whistling silks
Scarce deigns to notice him, or, if she see,
Deems him a cipher in the works of God,
Receives advantage from his noiseless hours,
Of which she little dreams. Perhaps she owes
Her sunshine and her rain, her blooming spring
And plenteous harvest, to the prayer he makes
When, Isaac-like, the solitary saint
Walks forth to meditate at even-tide,
And think on her, who thinks not for herself.
Forgive him, then, thou bustler in concerns
Of little worth, an idler in the best,
If, author of no mischief and some good,
He seeks his proper happiness by means
That may advance, but cannot hinder, thine.
Nor, though he tread the secret path of life,
Engage no notice, and enjoy much ease,
Account him an encumbrance on the state,
Receiving benefits, and rendering none.

On Sterility of Action

Robert Louis Stevenson (1850-1894)

EXTREME BUSINESS, whether at school or college, kirk or market, is a symptom of deficient vitality; and faculty for idleness implies a catholic appetite and a strong sense of personal identity. There is a sort of dead-alive, hackneyed people about, who are scarcely conscious of living except in the exercise of some conventional occupation. Bring these fellows into the country, or set them aboard ship, and you will see how they pine for their desk or their study. They have no curiosity; they cannot give themselves over to random provocations; they do not take pleasure in the exercise of their faculties for its own sake; and unless Necessity lays about them with a stick, they will even stand still. It is no good speaking to such folk: they *cannot* be idle, their nature is not generous enough; and they pass those hours in a sort of coma, which are not dedicated to furious moiling in the gold-mill. When they do not require to go to the office, when they are not hungry, and have no mind to drink, the whole breathing world is a blank to them. If they have to wait an hour or so for a train, they fall into a stupid trance with their eyes open. To see them, you would suppose there was nothing to look at and no one to speak with; you would imagine they were paralyzed or alienated; and yet very possibly they are hard workers in their own way, and have good eyesight for a flaw in a deed or a turn of the market. They have been to school and college, but all the time had their eye on the medal; they have gone about in the world and mixed with clever people, but all the time they were thinking of their own affairs. As if a man's soul were not too small to begin with, they have dwarfed and narrowed theirs by a life of all work and no play; until here they are at forty, with a listless attention, a mind vacant of all material of amusement, and not one thought to rub against another, while they wait for the train. Before he was breeched he might have clambered on the boxes; when he was twenty, he would have stared at the girls; but now the pipe is smoked out, the snuff-box empty, and my gentleman sits bolt upright upon a bench, with lamentable eyes. This does not appeal to me as being Success in Life.

On American Leisure

Irwin Edman (1896-1954)

THE BEST TEST OF the quality of a civilization is the quality of its leisure. Not what the citizens of a commonwealth do when they are obliged to do something by necessity, but what they do when they can do anything by choice, is the criterion of a people's life. One can tell much about a man by noting the objects and pastimes to which he spontaneously turns for joy. The same may be said of a nation. It was a suggestive comment of Maxim Gorky's on visiting Coney Island, "What an unhappy people it must be that turns for happiness here." The most serious criticism leveled against American civilization is not that its work is standardized and its business engulfing, but that its pleasures are mechanical and its leisure slavish. It is not that we have not time. Foreign observers are repeatedly astonished at the number of hours an ever-increasing number of Americans have to themselves. It is not time we lack, but leisure.

Leisure is indeed an affair of mood and atmosphere rather than simply of the clock. It is not a chronological occurrence but a spiritual state. It is unhurried pleasurable living among one's native enthusiasms. Leisure consists of those pauses in our lives when experience is a fusion of stimulation and repose. Genuine leisure yields at once a feeling of vividness and a sense of peace. It consists of moments so clear and pleasant in themselves that one might wish they were eternal.

For traveled Americans, at least, the best illustrations and memories of such experiences will come from abroad. For one it will be the recollection of keen but casual conversation at tea on a lawn in Sussex or Surrey. For another it will be the image of two friends chatting over coffee and liquors at an *al fresco* table on a boulevard in Paris. Another will remember a stroll in an Italian piazza or the long, dignified peace of an evening in a London club.

It is not that one cannot find domestic images, too, of a quality of leisure that seems to be passing almost completely out of the American scene. Many a middle-aged American, in the midst of a life crowded with social as well as business or professional obligations, will recall some rare hour that in its golden and gratuitous irrelevance seems to belong not in the realm of time but in the careless length of eternity, an afternoon spent browsing without purpose in a library or walking without the thought of time or destination on the quiet windings of an unfrequented country road. One recalls conversations lightly begun after dinner and meandering through wreaths of smoke into unexpected depths and intensities until long after an unnoticed midnight. One remembers some incredibly remote year when one wrote by hand a letter that flowed on as if ink and paper and ideas would never end.

But for Americans the word "leisure" has distinctively Old World associations. That is partly because some Americans have there known it best. Cut off from the pressure and compulsions of their normal occupations at home, they have moved with freedom amid the grace of a leisurely tradition. But there is a deeper reason which lies in the contrast between that European tradition and our own. The quality of leisure in Europe is partly the heritage of a long leisure-class tradition, partly the patience of peoples that have the sense of age and are not obsessed with hastening toward the new and building the possible in a hurry. In our own civilization, originally and in spirit partly pioneer, there is a working- rather than a leisure-class tradition, and the impress and atmosphere of work have come to control our lives even when we are not working. To be busy has been with us a primary virtue, and even our play has had to find a place for itself as a kind of business.

A number of years ago Professor Veblen in his *Theory of the Leisure Class* tried to point out how the traditions and interests of a leisure class had shaped our tastes and our morals. A quite plausible volume might be written on the thesis that the pursuit of leisure in our civilization is determined by our traditions of work; we carry the morals and ideals of an essentially industrial, essentially business civilization over into our play. Leisure—a quiet and emancipated absorption in things and doings for their own sake—has always seemed to us effeminate and exotic. We wish leisure for relief, for release, for escape; for instruction, enlightenment, or advancement. There is something immoral about moments that are good in themselves. There is probably no other country in the world where idleness is one of the deadly sins.

With us, therefore, leisure has been a melodramatic escape into self-improvement. We oscillate between night clubs and outlines of culture. Every one has at some time or other been present at a determinedly gay party. He has seen ordinarily quiet, intelligent people become wilfully noisy and stupid. He has seen men and women, separately delightful and entertaining, prance about loudly, screaming vulgarities, acting the "grown-up babies of the age." And his pain has been increased by a sense that none of these people cared to do the silly things they were doing. They drank more than they really wished to, and uttered hiccoughing nonsense that they themselves despised.

Every one, likewise, has listened to a group of people at dinner or afterwards, talk with obligatory boredom about the modish books and plays and ideas. Spontaneity, which is of the essence of any truly spiritual life, flies out of the conversation and out of the window, when "culture" becomes deliberate. We settle down as grimly to being serious as we settle down to being silly. Between the foolish and the funereal we have managed to find no middle course.

Of escapes from the pressure of an increasingly mechanized life to occasional outbursts of excitement or triviality there is much to be said. At least it may be said for them that they are natural, perhaps needful, refuges from a world whose tightly woven days would otherwise be unbearable. It is perhaps a sad commentary on the angular and constricted lives we lead that we should have to seek lurid or futile ways to peace. But it is not to be wondered at that, living in such a world of routine, we should plunge ever so often into the loud nonsene of inane parties, wallow in the absurd pathos and comedy of the screen, or fall enraptured victims to successive crazes of footless puzzles and dull games. We may be forgiven our excursions to musical comedies without wit or music, and conversational evenings without humanity or ideas. The contemporary citizen is vexed beyond his own realization by the humdrum unthrilling pressure of his days; he craves naturally now and then an opportunity to be trivial, irresponsible, and absurd.

But the irony of our situation lies in the fact that even when we try to escape into triviality or foolishness we make a serious and standardized business of it. One can pardon occasional madness in a sober civilization, but there is something pathetic, almost ghastly, in soberly making madness a routine. The half-drunken gayety that has become the accompaniment of much respectable social life is a sad determined business. Orgy has become a social obligation; dissipation a prescription to the weary, the repressed, and the disenchanted. It becomes as much a social obligation to play a new game or have a new thrill as to read a new book or wear a current collar or hat. Any number of "nice" people go systematically about becoming on occasion trivial, foolish, or mad. It is as if the American could not stop being efficient when he wanted to, and had to be gay or trivial or ecstatic with the same thoroughness and strained energy with which he might build a business or a skyscraper.

There are other reasons besides our own solemn efficiency that have been transforming our attempts to amuse ourselves into pale and standard routines. The same forces that have gone into the big business of providing our necessities have gone into the big business of providing our amusements. One may glamorously state the possibilities of the radio, the universalization of beautiful music and distinguished thought. One may talk as one will about the possible high art of the moving picture, marvel as one will at the new mechanical perfections of the phonograph. There is no question but that these are at their best mechanical. They turn our leisure into a passive receptivity of standard mediocre amusement. They provide almost nothing of that spontaneous sense of individual living which is part of the repose and stimulation of leisure. It is not pleasant to realize that our leisure is taking on the color—or colorlessness—of the rest of our lives; that we are becoming stereotypes in our play as in our work. The most serious spiritual danger of the Industrial Revolution is that it has come to mechanize and industrialize not merely things but the spirit as well.

When a man is at leisure we like to say he is free to be himself, but if his freedom consists in efficiently amusing himself according to the standard formulas or subjecting himself to the passive reception of standard amusements, he is not free at all.

But while leisure has in one direction gone toward conventional amusement and stereotyped triviality, in another direction it has become a kind of elegant overtime work. The latest use we have found for leisure is to make it useful. Its usefulness, which might have been supposed to be that it was a good in itself, has been transformed into its possibility as a means of systematic self-improvement. Correspondence courses, outlines of knowledge, scrapbooks of learning—agencies not always disinterested—have been trying to teach us what we might do with our unharnessed moments if only we would harness them. A little less carousal and a little less bridge, and we might become heirs to all of Western culture, or experts in philosophy or French. There is a revealing irrelevance in the reasons assigned for turning the casual moments of our lives to the pursuit of knowledge. It is not that knowledge will render us self-possessed and whole, that it will give wings to our imagination and give a larger, clear, and sweeter horizon to our lives. It is that knowledge, or a smattering of it, will make us successful or respected, that a veneer of garbled French will reveal our breeding, or a parade of the names of philosophers testify to our intellectual curiosity. There is possibly no clearer index to the remoteness of a native American culture than the eager indiscriminate voracity with which Americans gobble up tabloid versions of fields of expert knowledge. Far from meaning that we have turned to the love of wisdom, it means that we have turned our idle hours into the hurried business of getting short cuts to knowledge. Outlines simply are a way of applying efficiency to culture as well as to business. Their very essence is to say that here is all philosophy or history or literature for those who have not the patience or sympathy to explore any corner of any of them with disinterested delight. Worst of all, they have taken from leisure its saving essence—the sense of doing some lovely thing for its own lovable sake.

There are aristocratic pessimists in our midst who hold that leisure in the sense of a fine spontaneous use of free time is increasingly impossible in America. They point to the facts cited in the foregoing and to other equally distressing social habits. The omnipresence of the automobile is not simply a temptation to literal speed, but has come to be a symbol for speed in spiritual matters as well. The only excitement in any activity, even in the pursuit of truth, is the excitement of going fast. It is for that reason, they insist, that there is no country where ideas become popular so fast as in America, no country where, half-learned, they are so quickly outmoded and forgotten. A book is the book of a month or at most a season, and the rapid-transit reader comes to forswear books for the reviews of them, and forswear reviews for excerpts from them in a synthetic magazine.

It is pointed out again, and with justice, that the mutiplication of physical luxuries and physical distractions is a constant intruder upon that collectedness of spirit in which alone leisure can come to being. Serenity and integrity are menaced as much by the telephone as by any single invention of the last century. Long quiet waves of time have become almost impossible in evenings shattered by radios, by movies, and by the constant seduction and noise of the automobile. Speculation begins in a dreaming fantasy; meditation in reverie. In our contemporary urban world one almost never has a chance to achieve that half-drowsy detachment in which fantasy and reverie begin. We are kept too wide-awake ever to be really at peace or in thought. Finally, in a country where there is still a glamorous sense of unlimited opportunity, the desire for first place makes almost impossible that freedom and detachment, which leave one free to follow an impulse for its own self-rewarding delight.

The desire for speed, the desire for luxury, the desire for first place—these are indeed three deadly enemies of leisure. In the current movement of American life there is not much prospect of radically overcoming them. But there are portents of a change in our point of view that may portend a radical change in our practice.

There are growing evidences of a hunger for quiet and unhurried living among an increasing number of Americans. One cannot—nor would one—abolish the telephone or the automobile. There is no use in sighing for an anachronistic Paradise. It is impossible to transform life in New York in the twentieth century into the retirement of a rectory in Kent in the eighteenth. One cannot in the noise and hurry of a Western metropolitan winter pretend one is living in the timeless unconcern of an Eastern tropical island.

But part of our difficulty lies not in the impossibility of our circumstances, but in the blindness of our philosophy. If we once learned to rediscover the values of quiet spaces in our lives we should find a way to find them. There is time to be had even in New York or Chicago, and solitude even among crowds. One need not follow Thoreau into the wilderness to practice his isolation, nor Buddha into the desert to achieve his meditation. There is peace in a city apartment if one will but stay at home an evening to find it, and Nirvana to be found at home in one's own mind.

Ultimately the lack of leisure is lack of spiritual integration. We flee to society, dull though it be, through the fear of the greater dullness of being alone. We hurtle along at a breakneck speed, physically and spiritually, for fear of the drabness and futility we might feel if we slowed down. Any number of people are suddenly becoming aware of that situation and, honest with themselves, are beginning to realize how much leisure one might have if one had enough faith in one's own resources. One need not let life be shattered into a splintered busyness by a routine absorption into social evenings which give one a standard good time. The rediscovery of solitude is being made by Americans, and with that rediscovery come many other delightful things: the chance to do nothing at all, not even talk, and the chance out of that interlude to follow a fancy or meditate a dream. Many a good citizen, given a chance to be alone with himself for an evening, might discover for the first time the quality of his own character, the contours of taste and interest that make him a personality as well as a jobholder and taxpaper. In such an interval a man may discover a hobby that will be for him a substitute for creative genius. He may not paint, write, or compose, but he may learn to do something indelibly himself and make something incredibly his own.

But in the golden days of leisure, in the spacious and graceful society of the Renaissance or the English country house, obviously men and women did not retire into their own souls away from the stimulation of other people. Good conversation is certainly one of the most enlivening ways of leisure, and good conversation is something between solemnity and absurdity. In America, of late, we have had to choose between talking on "subjects" solemnly and schematically, or babbling nonsense, doing anything rather than talk. We are, I think, beginning to learn again the joy of conversation, a light and easy play of minds and tempers over common human themes. We have grown a little weary of talk that is all smart and burnished; we have grown tired, too, of talk that sounds like the overflow program of a literary club. We are learning again that the meeting of minds and moods is one of the sweetest and most amiable fruits of human society. It has its own novelties and excitements no less than the automobile, radio, and bridge.

Not but that these last have their own special value as the pure gold of leisure. Even the mania for speed has about it something of the quality of poetry. No one who on some moonlight night has sped along a country road will deny the sheer poetical appeal there is in the ease and freedom of speed. But the automobile has made the more peaceful kind of leisure possible as it never was before. It has brought the city dweller within easy reach of green and solitude. It has made neighbors of involuntary hermits. The radio, too, for all its blare of tawdry music, has put millions within the reach of formerly impossible musical beauty. It has brought Beethoven to the farmer and to apartment dwellers who could never be lured to Carnegie Hall. And bridge, sniffed at by the cultured moralist, has its own justification. It is a diverting and harmless adventure of the mind and has for its devotees its own glories of wonder and conflict and surprise. If all these things are less interesting ultimately than conversation it is because we are social minds rather than aleatory machines.

There is, paradoxically enough, an incredible romanticism in our efficient impatience with leisure. We chase as madly as any early nineteenth-century German poet the Blue Flower of Happiness always beyond the hill. It is for that reason that we cannot take our idleness for the happiness it is; we try to turn it into an instrument toward the happiness it may bring. It may bring all knowledge into our province, or all salaries into our reach. It is for that reason that we have turned to outlines of knowledge and courses in success. But here, too, a change in spirit is notable.

There are men one knows who have made the surprised and delighted discovery that it is possible, if not to become hastily omniscient at least to become patiently at home in some small field of knowledge or some tiny technic or art. It is not easy or particularly joyous to go into the whole vague history of mankind; but it is possible with pleasure to know one period or one decade of American history, or the story of one man or one movement. Only an octogenarian genius can master the whole of comparative literature; but any one can carve out a little pathway of poetry or prose, make one author, one genre, one theme his own, be it Trollope or sonnets, whaling or ballades. It is not possible for every man to be an artist; but almost any one can learn to draw or model, to play an instrument or plant a garden. In England one meets omniscient people no more than in America; nor are artists in every lane. But there are thousands of unpretentious lawyers or business men who have made some intimate little field of knowledge or thought their own, or learned to do one modest small hobby well.

We may talk much about the future of America, and think to measure its destiny by statistics of its educational, economic, or political changes. But the outlook for our country lies in the quality of its idleness almost as much as anything else.

Shall we then always alternate between trivial escapes into foolishness and solemn plunges into exploitation of our moments of repose? For us, as for Aristotle, there must be a golden mean. We may learn still to be at peace long enough to think and dream after our own fashion. We may learn to be together and be gay without being rowdy. We may learn to be expert in some little territory of art or thought or science without losing the amateur touch. We may still find time to live rather than time to kill.

If we do, we shall have learned what the spiritual life really means. For it means nothing more than those moments in experience when we have some free glint of life for its own sake, some lovely unforced glimmer of laughter or reason or love.

Some Areas of Adult Concern

John Walker Powell

MANY STUDENTS OF OUR SOCIETY have tried to define the "life-tasks of the adult," the roles he is called upon to perform. To me, this language of sociological abstraction seems to have an unhappy way of leaving out the livingness, the personalness, of the experiences it is describing. "Tasks" and "performance" have the ring of grim duty; but being a member of a family, or a man working at his job, or a citizen excited over an issue like racial integration, these are really just huge swatches of a man's living, full of fascination and feeling and fury and fun. I should rather describe these major areas of our living as constellations of relationship with other people, and as realms of value-choice and action-choice. They involve ambition and striving, and frustrations and problems, and problem-solving and satisfactions. From the individual's point of view, perhaps the best single word for these areas of "task" and "role" is the old Quaker word, *concern.* When someone in a Friends' meeting says he "has a concern," it means that he has a live and urgent interest in a matter he believes important and wants something done about.

The American in his lifetime has very many concerns. But, as adult, they can be seen as clustering around a few major constellations of concern: his membership in a community, in a family, in a vocation; and the arts of enjoying the world he lives in, and of having good relationships with others.

These concerns, because they comprise many of the deepest interests of our people, can therefore be thought of as suggesting a sort of "core" for an adult *curriculum.* This is a hard word to define. After years of making up sequences of books for adult groups to read, I came to the conclusion that a curriculum is a set of learnings so intimately related to each other that *each* of them seems to be prerequisite to *all* of them. And this *is* the intimacy of relation among our five fields of interest. For each of them is in reality a set of relations with other people; and which-ever set you start to think about, one of the others will seem to need understanding first. This is what leads men into becoming specialists; and the relationships among their specialties sketch the profile of a program for adult learning.

Let's look at these areas, now, a little more carefully. At the periphery, so to speak, are the questions and obligations involved in being *a member of a community* that is part of a nation which is working at its role among a world of nations. The mature American is a householder; he votes, locally, statewise, and nationally; he is a producer and a consumer; and he is likely to be involved in some movement or organization to advance the welfare of the community or the nation or the world of mankind, along some particular line. In being all these, he wants to understand our own history, to have available what Van Wyck Brooks called "a usable past." He has to think about politics, and about the nature and problems of our economic system—and about those of other nations as well. He is called on to make choices—informed ones, if possible—about local and national policies on a myriad issues. His choices involve guesses about world conditions, about the international currency in human values, and about how our actions affect the world and vice versa, including the effect of other countries' actions on the security of his own community. Law and the Constitution and how laws are made and how courts interpret them are necessary parts of his understanding. He has to reckon with the urbanization of American culture as opposed to the agrarian cultures of our neighbors; and to have some acquaintance with the alien practices of other folk, their customs and ways of thinking and languages and literature. He cares also, however, about slums and schools and tax rates and traffic and sidewalks and police and insurance rates in his home town. In short, this is the area in which the individual handles the web of threads that link him to his city, the nation, and the world. . . .

The area of *family membership* is even more intimately pressing. Growing to independence; making a marriage; making a home; raising children: familiar goals and roles, pressed by motivations from within and expectations from without, shot through with dubious choices that never end. The role of child, for example, begins as a relation of dependence, goes through a long struggle for independence, and ends by taking care of dependent parents. Before this is completed, the child has had children of his own who go from dependence toward independence; and he must look forward to his own renewed dependency. These are tough transitions to make. It is hard, for example, to accept dependence on one whom we still think of as dependent on us: one of our family's favorite stories is of the 93-year-old neighbor who said to her 70-year-old daughter who was starting upstairs carrying a lamp, "Clara Lyon Peters, give me that lamp! You know you're not old enough to carry it up those stairs."

Growing up, as anyone in a family can tell you, is largely a matter of meeting the expectations of other people. And families fall easily into what Hollywood calls "type casting": you get known in one kind of role, and it's hard to break out of it because people go on expecting you to be that again. It's not easy to keep our expectations of a child geared to what the child is really *ready* to be. Here is where we need curiosity, about the real person in the child; creativeness, in making circumstances that bring that person out of the type-cast child; and comprehension of what the process means, why it is important, and what our role in it is. . . .

The "tasks" that cluster around our *vocations* are not simple: skills on the job, and skill in relating our own job to the larger enterprise of which it is a part; trade memberships, perhaps expressed through unions or professional organizations, involving the need to understand the meaning and purpose of the trade we're in, and our own role in it and contribution to it; and many threads of relationship to fellow workers, to employers, to employees, to the consuming public. The rapid introduction of technological miracles, electronic controls and the like, is calling for a rapid re-education of large sections of the labor force. Management, too, has recognized new needs and demands; the development of replacements for present management has become a major field of education in the last ten years, with universities and adult education agencies increasingly involved. And, significantly, what management is looking for turns out to be the development of men with curiosity, creativeness, and comprehension. A good head of an accounting department is not, they find, automatically a good vice-president or president. Training is not enough; education is required. Labor union executives, another kind of Management, are coming to the same findings. I don't mean to suggest the millennium; and there are immense problems of democratic participation left unsolved in both areas. All I mean to say is that the earning task, the role of worker, is changing at such a rate that the old stereotypes will not suffice any longer to guide our expectations about it.

From the periphery of social membership we have worked our way in to *the individual himself*, first in his knowledge and enjoyment of his relation to his world, and finally in his understanding of his relation to his fellows. While the first of these takes in an infinite territory, to me its chief feature is the enjoyment of living, the enrichment of life—the realm of play, so to speak, as against the sober realms of obligation. In this area I, myself, would include the intellectual pursuits, as well as the arts. Here too, I would include religion, both as philosophy and as worship; for it, like the arts, is an affirmation of ourselves in relation to the universe: the affirmation that *the universe is capable of intimate response to me, and I to it.*

The other realm, the last of the suggested five comprehensive ones, I call the realm of *self-understanding.* I choose the self as focus, though I mean to include all efforts to comprehend human beings and human relations and the curious ways of mankind; for in all my study of other people, the object I am searching for is myself. But "I" am elusive. There seem to be several of me, and some of me approve what makes others of me angry, and each of me finds some reflection of itself in the other people I live among, work among, and read about. I am a little Society, a group— in short, a human being. All of my life I shall, like others of my kind, be trying to discover the ways in which I correspond to the society of my fellows, and it to me. For here, again, I am met by the expectations of others, by their notions of what I am or ought to be, even by my own picture, borrowed from them, of what I am and what I ought to be.

In all these major areas of adult relation and performance, my "task" is confused both by my many roles and by the stress between old and new demands—my own upon myself and others upon me. Without the freedom to search, and the effort to learn, I could still fall into easy slavery to those demands, into acquiescence in stereotyped roles. Unless education, at adult levels, helps us to focus our minds on these problems of task and role, we may suffer more and more from the lag between our expectations, our old stereotypes based on what used to be, and our new realities. Left to itself, society might even freeze all roles into a set of expectations from which no one could break free. . . .

Ours, however, is a loose-jointed society, full of diversity and contradictions. But it is also knit together by the interrelations between the realms of adult action, and among the institutions that try to govern these. The "citizen" is a working family member; the "worker" is a voting family member; the family head is a worker and community member; and in all three roles he is also a person who has opinions, makes judgments, approves some values over others, and tries to understand himself and his neighbors—and his enemies. If "institutions" became rigid, we too would become a monolithic society; it has happened to other great nations in our time. The whole measure of a *free* society is that it plays by rules that keep the players—as ballplayers say—"loose." The coach is not dictating every play; the function of individual judgment is still paramount. Therefore, the only true mark of a free society is that it provides to its members the opportunity to keep their minds active, their information objective, their commuications open: in a word, *education*.

We have been discussing education in relation to the principal "roles" that the mature American has to play, and to the problems that arise within and among these roles. Now the question is: Is there a field of knowledge that we can acquire in order to solve all these fluid dilemmas? What *super*-role does society offer us, to resolve all the rest under one kind of mastery? Is there a schooling for this?

There is a schooling for each role; but that is where the danger lies. To be sensitive to many roles, to be able to make *appropriate* judgments about them and about the roles of other people, takes something different. Usually, we just call it *intelligence*.

Intelligence, not knowledge, is the aim of education. Rather, it is the subject of education, the material it works on; for intelligence is an activity, a muscle, an organ of sensitiveness. Knowledge can't be transferred from field to field: your ability to plot an end-around play on the football field won't help you much with mathematics; your knowledge of chess is little help in learning bridge. But intelligence, as Dr. Flexner wrote in a book on education many years ago, is "capable of being applied in any field whatever." A man may be an *intelligent* student of social questions, music, and baseball. Or, he may just have *opinions* about them, stereotypes like "longhair" and "red" and a distaste for men who chew tobacco.

Now the job of education, it seems to me, is that of keeping intelligence so alert, so tuned to many pitches of experience, so sensitive to other people and other ideas and other ways, that its possessor can live in many worlds at once, and be at home in all of them. He can make judgments with his feelings, as well as with his mind, that are appropriate to the subject. He may not be a civic leader, or a performer in organized activities; but he can at least be an intelligent spectator; and every team, including the Congress of the United States, plays better to an informed gallery.

Most important, intelligence is not a *collection* of skills. Intelligence is YOU thinking, making judgments about and in the course of and among your different roles and realms of action. Your intelligence is the guarantee that you are *one* person, after all. "At the center of his multiple memberships stands the individual himself. Where all the lines of training intersect, there is a person." At the core of your many selves, there is "the Watcher, the Witness."

You see why this is so important for our conversation. Knowledge and skill will serve each of our concerns; but education has to center on the person himself whose living is fulfilled through all the realms he lives in: on his intelligence, his discrimination and judgment and richness of resource and maturity of decision. We need schooling, so that we can do what we must. We seek education, so that we can be what we will.

Education for the

Freedom Years

Norman Cousins (1912-   )

FREQUENTLY, IN RECENT YEARS, I have had the opportunity of talking to people in other countries about life in the United States. No recollection of these excursions is more vivid than an experience I had in a village some twenty miles from Colombo, Ceylon.

As is customary with visitors, I was seated in a straight-backed wooden chair and then was garlanded by one of the village elders. The wreath was remarkably similar to the Hawaiian lei that has become the routine ceremony of greeting for visitors to Honolulu from the mainland. The village elder announced that I brought greetings from the people of the United States and that I had accepted his invitation to talk about America.

There was an immediate burst of enthusiastic questions. It was clear the people of the village didn't want a speech; they wanted direct information to satisfy their excited curiosity about America and Americans. And so I dispensed with my talk and spent almost two hours answering their questions as best I could.

What impressed me most about the experience was that more than half the questions had to do with education in the United States. Few aspects of American life are considered more revolutionary by the Asian peoples than the educational opportunities available in this nation. For to most Asians education is still a miracle. The illiteracy rate in the villages of Ceylon is more than 85 percent. In Pakistan, the government recognizes that no problem is more basic than is represented by the illiteracy rate of 87 percent. In India, the illiteracy rate is dropping but is still close to 80 percent. And Communism directs its appeal in Asia not merely to empty bellies but to hungry minds. For nothing is more dynamic in Asia than the promise of free education for children.

"Are you sure you are right when you say that even poor people are allowed to send their children to free schools?" I was asked that day in Ceylon by a man whose age I judged to be about fifty.

I nodded.

"I am a very old man," he continued, "and a very poor one. I have three children who are living and they have ten children of their own among them. Are children like these allowed to learn to read and write and study things?"

"Not only allowed but required to do so," I replied, going on to explain how compulsory education operated in the United States. Then I gave a brief picture of higher education in the United States, pointing out that the large majority of American students paid very small amounts for their college schooling and, indeed, that many students who attended the large state universities paid no tuition at all.

As I said that, I observed the people closely. They looked at each other in stark wonderment.

"Until what age is it permitted that a person may study?" one of them asked.

I said that there was no age limitation. Any person who was qualified to do so and had the means to do so could study in a university, regardless of age. I added that many universities had extension divisions in which anyone could enroll, and that it was not necessary to take a full or formal higher education in order to study in such extension courses the special things in which one might be interested. I told how, only a few years earlier, I had enrolled in an extension division course so that I might learn about the new developments in science that had occurred since I had been an undergraduate.

The effect on my listeners was electric. It was as though I had just told of seeing the alchemist's dream come to reality. For almost a minute there was the silence of amazement and incredulity.

"Well, then," said the man who had earlier spoken of his children and grandchildren. "Well, then, if this is true, why would anyone ever stop learning? I would suppose that no one would ever want to do anything else."

To him, free education was like gold in the streets; and it seemed a waste of time not to pick up every bit of it so long as one had the physical strength to do so.

When I replied that a large number of adult Americans, but still only a minority, took advantage of the educational opportunities available to them, it became clear that I had said the one thing that defied rational explanation. How was it possible that every single person would not snap up the riches which were there for the taking?

I made no attempt to answer that particular question, but I have been thinking about it ever since. . . .

Similarly, the failure to educate beyond youth and beyond the classroom can become our most dangerous weakness.

The purposes of education, generally speaking, are twofold: first of all, to enable the individual to know what to do with his time, in terms of both skills and interests; second, to enable the individual to understand the world around him and to make his own contribution to the general welfare. This involves preparation for both a career and for citizenship.

In terms of today's world, however, formal education by itself is no longer adequate to meet these needs. In the past quarter-century alone, the world has known the equivalent of at least two centuries with respect to change. The metabolism of history is no longer governed by gradual change but by vast, sudden leaps. Formal education is doing its best to keep pace, but it is slowed down by two dominant facts. One is that there just isn't enough classroom time to pack in all the information relating to fast-accruing knowledge. The other is that the school cannot reach out after its graduates to bring them important new knowledge. Therefore, no man can call himself truly educated unless he exercises his own initiative in the years beyond formal schooling to make the necessary changes or additions which can keep his education from becoming obsolete.

For the professional man—especially those in the sciences—this becomes stern necessity. But even for those whose work imposes the need to keep up to date, the same reasons that held for formal schooling hold for education by personal initiative in maturity. If an individual places any value on his status as an educated man, then a diploma today becomes less important than the continuing pursuit of the miracle of education.

Working knowledge, however, is not the ultimate good. Beyond knowledge, there is the matter of the fullest possible development of the human individual. No waste of resources can possibly be so costly as the undeveloped or untapped mental resources of man. The uniqueness of human life can be fully realized only as an individual can bring his full potentiality into being. Education is not the only means to this end, but it is still the most effective means yet devised.

To Keep Our Minds Open

Nicholas Murray Butler (1862-1947)

WE MAKE PROGRESS TOWARD clear thinking only when we are careful about our use of terms. Therefore, it is my preference to keep the word education for the one major process that it connotes and to use other words for those other undertakings to which the term education is sometimes applied. For me there is no such thing as legal education, or medical education, or vocational education, or professional education. I see all these efforts as instruction, or perhaps as preparation, but not as education. The process to which alone I choose to apply the term education is that of conscious and purposeful adaptation of the human organism to its environment. This process is of the very essence of human existence; it begins with birth and goes on, or it may go on, to old age. The problem of those who are studying and promoting adult education is how to continue that process of adaptation, or education, as long and as far and as usefully as possible.

If there were no such thing as the plasticity of the infant there could be no education. When a creature comes into the world full-fledged, ready to take its place among those of its kind, it can not be educated. Its instincts, its habits, its natural reactions furnish both the guidance and the instruments of its activity. But as soon as there is a prolonged period of infancy, formal education becomes possible, and after a time the school comes into existence.

One of the difficulties that I find in discussing education in a broad and philosophic sense arises out of its having become too largely confounded with school instruction. All over the world we are asking the school to bear a burden that does not belong to it and that it can not carry. We are seeking to excuse the family from its fundamental responsibility. We are overlooking the responsibility of society itself and are losing sight of the particular part of this responsibility that the churches ought to bear. All these agencies must do their share if the plastic infant is to have a chance to come into his full inheritance; to find ways and means of expressing his own personality and of adding something, however small it may be, to that complex of activities and ideas and institutions that we call civilization.

As soon as we begin to think of education in a larger sense, as involving much more than instruction and as covering much more than the period of infancy, just so soon, I think, do we come to a point of view where adult education begins to fall into its proper place and to take on that large and important meaning that certainly attaches to it.

My own observation is that every human being comes into the world with a certain initial velocity, intellectual and spiritual, and that the curve of that velocity tends to fall to earth before he reaches forty years of age. There are very few human beings whose personal, intellectual, and spiritual velocity is still rising at forty. Again, it is my observation and experience that a very small minority of human beings continue to grow intellectually after they reach the age of twenty-three or twenty-four. The initial force supplied by the school, or school and college, or school and family and college together, seems by that time to have virtually exhausted itself. Men and women then settle down to fixed habits of mind, fixed points of view, definite appreciations, permanent likes and dislikes; they build about themselves walls within which they continue to dwell as long as life lasts. But in our modern democratic society that sort of thing will not do. We are all face to face with the grave responsibility for carrying forward our political organization, for straightening out our economic and social difficulties, and for meeting emergencies as they arise. How can these things be done save by those who are open-minded, who still have elasticity of temper?

The larger aspect of adult education, as I see it, has two objectives. First, it must try to reach the individual at a time when his curve of possible growth and accomplishment is still rising and give him new power and ambition. If adult education functions as it should, there ought to be, fifty years from now, a noticeably greater number of persons whose curves of ability will still be rising at forty.

The second objective of adult education should be the preservation of open-mindedness, of plastic sympathies, of elastic temper to a much later period than is now customary with the great mass of mankind.

Men say that they were born into this political party or that, into this form of religious belief or that, into this social conviction or that. Are not such statements a confession that their minds are closed; that they have shut themselves within walls over which they can not see, much less climb? Under such circumstances how can they participate in responsibility for a democratic society? How can they pass judgment upon ever new and pressing problems?

This is neither a promising nor a satisfactory outlook for democratic society. In more languages than one, men are writing books and papers to tell us that parliamentary government has failed; that Western civilization is upon the downward grade; that democracy is a futile hope and can not be made to work. In confirmation they point to those very characteristics of men and women that we would strive so vigorously to correct by means of adult education.

There is no way of keeping minds open save by keeping them in contact with ideas: ideas of yesterday, if these have shown by their survival that they are probably sound; but better still, ideas of today; and best of all, ideas of tomorrow.

It takes a long time for ideas to get started; it takes much longer for ideas to get hold of people, and still very much longer for people to get hold of ideas. If we can only devise ways and means to reach the human being who has passed out of the formal period of instruction and to keep his mind open and stimulated and guided, we shall build a society in which ideas will have a better chance to develop than they have at present, and one in which our people will be much better able to bear responsibility for public conduct, to shape public policy, and to choose public officials than they now are.

It is interesting to remember that adult education is one of the present-day problems that know no national limits, that speak no single language. Everywhere—in Italy, in Germany, in Poland, in Scandinavia, in Holland, in Great Britain, as well as in the United States—men are discussing this question of continuing instruction, training, and education of the adult.

The agencies of adult education in our country are many. We now carry on adult education by means of lectures; we do it by guided reading, by museums of art, by concerts and musical recitals, and by more formal instruction. We do it in any one of a hundred ways, but the object is always and everywhere the same: to keep the mind open and hospitable to what is new. This does not mean to dispense with convictions; quite the contrary. Convictions are the standards by which one judges, but their possession should not lessen one's readinesss and willingness to ask questions and to hearken to the unfamiliar and even to what might once have been distasteful.

The larger meaning of adult education takes us back to the fundamental problem of our democratic society. It has to do with our capacity as a people to understand, to be responsible for, and to conduct the affairs of the nation. There is no inherited short cut to political, economic, or social prosperity, permanence, and happiness. These have to be labored for by intelligent persons who have open minds and the courage to take up and to bear the responsibility for the great trust that democracy has placed in their hands.

To Meet the Challenge
of Free Choice

Dorothy Canfield Fisher (1879-1958)

IT IS NATURAL PERHAPS that, being a novelist, I should wish to introduce what I have to say by quoting poetry; authors are always doing that. And so, I shall start off with six lines from Keats:

> *Then felt I like some watcher of the skies*
> *When a new planet swims into his ken;*
> *Or like stout Cortez—when with eagle eyes*
> *He stared at the Pacific—and all his men*
> *Look'd at each other with a wild surmise—*
> *Silent, upon a peak in Darien.*

I have chosen these lines because I want them to prepare your minds for some of the wild surmising which it seems to me our present situation calls for, wilder than anything felt by Cortez-Balboa and his men upon that first glimpse of the unsuspected other half of our globe. For we who have set forth upon the quest of adult education are rather in the position in which Columbus would have found himself if he, instead of Balboa, had climbed to the top of that mountain to be struck speechless by the far blue vision of the unguessed-at.

We were quite sufficiently excited by discovering, only a few years ago, that education need not stop with Commencement Day. Incredible as it may seem now, most of us remember the period when the belief that a grown person can learn nothing was accepted, without question, as an axiom. And when, under Professor Thorndike's guidance, we went through the terrific intellectual effort of really looking at that hitherto unquestioned belief to see what grounds there were for considering it true, and when we saw that it was patently absurd, we experienced the sort of excitement that Columbus must have felt at the dramatic end of his first transatlantic voyage.

That was enough for any generation. One completely new idea—I mean this seriously—is about all that any human generation can stand without being shattered. But everything moves so rapidly nowadays. My generation of gray-haired people is called upon to enact the role not only of Columbus but of Balboa. We find that the huge new idea, under the impact of which we are still staggering, is only part of one even more stupendous.

What I mean is this: the movement for the continuance of intellectual life and growth in mature years is not a mere development of education, as we thought in the beginning. It is an inherent and necessary part of the problem that humanity must solve in order to adapt itself to what is perhaps the greatest change in the conditions of life since the emergence of our remote ancestors from water into air—our own emergence from the sustaining density of continuous effort enforced by material necessity into the thin new life-element, dangerous and difficult, of free choice as to what we shall do. What else do the free hours brought to mankind by mechanical invention mean but that in many of our waking hours we must stand up to the horrifying responsibility of deciding what we shall do with ourselves?

Of course, our nature being slow and conservative, a majority of the human beings suddenly flung up by the machine from the ocean of material necessity and stranded on the beach of free choice continue with nervous reflex movements to go on doing in useless forms what formerly was a condition of survival. The activities that used to take all of everybody's time but that now, with the aid of the machine, could be dispatched in a few hours—how desperately do we complicate them to make them fill as many hours as they were wont to take! Who of us has not known mothers who use their children as shields between themselves and the bright perilous face of leisure? Who of us has not seen the parent-child relation sagging under the unnatural weight put upon it by parents who now make an unfair demand that their children fill an undue share of the bottomless emptiness of lives from which the pressure of daily manual work has been removed?

In my opinion much of the frantic modern misery come from the panic-struck, "gone" feeling of people who snatch at emotion and excitement to stuff it into the gaping hole left empty in their lives, the hole that can really be filled only, as it always has been, by useful activity. But now much of that useful activity must be voluntary. And those who have not yet learned this new art of setting themselves to work are suffering intensely.

The leaders of the adult education movement, ploddingly cutting a path to what they thought was only a new corner of a continent well known to them under the name of education, have been brought to a lookout place from which they have caught their first glimpse of the endless tract that they are challenged to explore and exploit, and in a wild surmise have begun to understand that what they are facing is a totally new phase of human life, in which education must achieve in fact what has been its true purpose all along: individual *growth* in the thin new element of intellectual and artistic activities and of abstract thought.

The very tools that must be used in the exploration and settling of the new dimension of life into which we have emerged are strange and unfamiliar to us. Take the radio, for instance. Any one of us can see with half an eye that it is one of the most indispensable of the new tools for the enrichment of intellectual and spiritual life. But to people trained in the older ways of education the radio is as troublingly strange as a tool from Mars, because of the element of free choice embodied in the button which, twirled at the whim of the listener, can change or shut off the instruction that the well-meaning educator is conscientiously trying to broadcast.

Take another tool which it is evident that we must learn to use if we are to survive the hardships of life without hardships: the tool of systematic exploration of human personality to discover what sort of activity best suits any given human being. If, acting in his free time on his own accord, a man is to do anything worth while, it will be because he has found some worth-while activity that suits *him*. Therefore for the first time it becomes important to society to help a man find out what sort of creature he is, rather than to let him be crammed into a mold that crushes and breaks him.

I wish to stress the need for patient experimentation rather than for immediate attempts at definite constructive enterprise in adult education; and in this connection I should like to remind you that, in all experimentation, negative results are of great value because they narrow the field that future experimentation must cover. Attempts at establishing systems of self-education by lecture courses, or by specialized distribution of books, or museum visits, or discussion forums or guidance in the use of books and libraries, or art classes, or radio broadcasting, or parent-teacher conferences, or rural study clubs, or political study leagues, all provide authentic material for testing and analysis, and all are valuable, whether they succeed or fail, if the causes of success or failure can be determined.

Much may be learned, too, from the inevitable attempts to use the devices set up for self-education as channels for the spread of partisan propaganda. That is one of the very real dangers of the present and future for adult education, one that we must study in order that we may know how best to counteract it and hold it in check. But we must also study with energy means to counteract the opposite danger: that the essential conservatism of mankind will take advantage of whatever mechanism is invented for free self-education and will use it in the interests of unreasoning adherence to the *status quo*.

And finally, there is the greatest danger of all, the danger inherent by the nature of things in all attempts at teaching. Every one of us knows with what insinuating treachery complacency, dogmatism, and the love of authority creep into the hearts of teachers. It is an occupational risk as real as that of lead or radium poisoning. May I close as I began with a quotation, giving you what Ruskin has said so eloquently upon this very subject:

Take the desire of teaching—the entirely unselfish and noble instinct for telling to those who are ignorant the truth we know, and guarding them from the errors we see them in danger of—there is no nobler, no more constant instinct in honourable breasts; but let the Devil formalise it, and mix the pride of a profession with it—get foolish people entrusted with the business of instruction, and make their giddy heads giddier by putting them up in pulpits above a submissive crowd—and you have it instantly corrupted into its own reverse; you have an alliance against the light, . . . a company of the blind, beseeching those they lead to remain blind also.

I think the key phrase in that fine passage is the one about "pulpits above a submissive crowd." If I had my way, I would admit to the band of men and women dedicated to the cause of adult education only those who, with right hand held high, would vow themselves with all their hearts to the service of what seems to me the true purpose of adult education: to break up the dumb, submissive, defenseless crowd into active, thinking, unsubmissive individuals.

Creation and Education

Robert Redfield (1897-   )

EDUCATION IS OF COURSE learning something. More importantly, it is becoming something. Although knowledge is needed for education, an educated person is not the same as a man who has knowledge. An educated person is one who is at work on his enlargement. If we learn things that become parts of us, if we make efforts to develop our own particular understanding of life and of the order of life's goods, it is education we are doing. A person is something that it takes time to make; there is on everyone an invisible sign, "Work in progress"; and the considered effort to get along with the work is education.

Thought of in this way, education is not as common as one might suppose. The institutions that we call "educational" are engaged only now and then in the development, in children and young people, of understanding of the order of life's goods. Schools and universities provide care of the young, offer recreation and pleasant associations, teach many useful skills from reading and writing to surgery and the preparation of legal briefs, and occasionally, desirably, indispensably educate.

So much of life goes just to keep things running, to police action, to bolstering the dikes against catastrophe. In our national life we have small freedom to decide how to spend the income of our immense national wealth. Most of it is firmly committed to paying for past wars and to trying to protect ourselves from or in future wars. In the schools we have got ourselves into a situation where we have only limited freedom to educate. You will see a schoolroom with fifty children and one teacher; the teacher uses most of her energies in keeping some kind of order. In a high school or college, also, much that goes on is merely custodial. Part of the budget goes to keeping the young people out of trouble and reasonably happy. If parents feel sure that this much is being accomplished, they are thankful and content.

If an occasional adult turns to the task of making himself grow in understanding of the order of life's goods by way of books and reasonable discussion, he meets a world and often a neighborhood that are unfavorable to his effort. Time and the will for education are in short supply. There are the pressures of immediate circumstance; there are work, entertainment, and the enjoyment of life in other ways. There are the innumerable problems of personal and public life. Many people today are passive or pessimistic; the tone of much public life is harsh and threatening; the danger of war by indiscriminate slaughter continues.

Nor is there much encouragement for education by adults, of themselves, in the examples and expectations that we encounter in our communities. What appears in most current print or broadcasting is for the most part irrelevant or ignoble. And one's neighbors are not likely to expect one to start work on one's own development through the pursuit of learning. Education, being a growth of the self, is in nature endless and hardly begins in the schools, but there is a widespread mistaken idea that all that sort of thing is over in school and college. Thoughtful people, who read a good many books, are today sometimes looked upon as a little queer, possibly as dangerous. The pursuit of learning by grown men and women is not very popular.

I state these difficulties so that we may take them into account in judging the worth of what I say here about what education is and how it goes on in men and women. No doubt I have overemphasized them. To the peasant of India wanting to learn just to read and write, America is vastly fortunate. Compared with other peoples, we are blessed with unusual material provision for such education as we may want to undertake. Where else is the working day so short? Where else have people such means to enjoy books, travel, and time to think?

In the very general sense of becoming something, everybody gets educated; everybody becomes something in the course of his life. The questions are, How good or bad a something? And, who decides what I become?

To meet the necessity of becoming something or other as one grows up and grows old, there are at least four distinguishable possibilities. The first way is no longer open to us; it was the way in which, in primitive societies, education was brought about merely through living the expected life. Taught by the example and the simple instruction of those around him, the American Indian or the African tribesman arrived at such wisdom as he needed in his well-integrated and largely stable world.

The other three ways are open to us in these later and more difficult times. Each is called "education" by those who approve of that way of making people.

One can become what a dictatorial authority decides that one should become. This is education in a Nazi or Communist state; it has had its full demonstration in George Orwell's book, *Nineteen Eighty-Four*. In such a making of people, the choice of what to make is taken away from each individual, and the sense of freedom, so far as it exists, comes from identification with the nation, or the race, or some principle of history. Just now we are struggling both against the Communist way of making people and also against the rise of the same tendency among ourselves to take this way of becoming. We are submitting to this tendency when in response to a demand from some indignant faction we exclude favorable mention of the United Nations from a schoolbook, or when we become afraid to study the writings of Karl Marx. This struggle on two fronts is noise and bitterness rather than thought; it is one of the difficulties that today impede any effort to make one's self as one wants to be.

A second way of meeting the necessity to become something or other is to become whatever at that time the people living around one are, changing to something a little different as people around one change. This, on the whole, is what many of us in this country do. It is sometimes called "adjustment" or "adaptation" or "socialization." This method, like the preceding one, leaves most of the work to others with a result that one is moderately comfortable and fairly acceptable to those who made one what one is.

In this country we will not choose the first of these ways and will defend ourselves against both foreign and domestic antagonists from having it imposed upon us. The lesser danger and the harder to avoid is the second way of becoming something. It will take some little thought and effort to avoid becoming the chameleon of the world's peoples, the easy adjuster to the immediate expectations of the suburbs or the neighborhoods in which we live, creatures whose characters are in their skins, not in their selves.

The third available way of bringing about the making of one's self avoids both dangers. It is the path I imagine us to choose in so far as we turn our interests and energies to our own education, as grown men and women. It is to take charge of one's own education, to put work into it along lines of one's own choice, and so produce something of a self-built self. This is in fact occasionally accomplished. It is a way open to anyone who wishes to give himself a good deal of interesting trouble.

For one who takes this responsibility, the experience that is education comes to be recognized, as it occurs within one's self or as one sees it occur in another. Education is to be distinguished from such other experiences as excitement, pleasure and having an opinion. I have ventured to identify its characteristic, distinguishing cycle of development. It begins in a reaching out of the mind and spirit, an entertainment of possibilities of significance and value in things seen, heard about, imagined. If this exploration of a universe that thereby begins to expand for one is to become education, it requires, as Whitehead so well presents the matter in his book, *The Aims of Education,* the discipline of order and precision. Further facts must be considered. Ideas must be doubted and tested. In describing this phase of the cycle, one emphasizes the interaction of mind and mind, idea and idea, fact and fact, as forms of that conversation by which the cycle of the mind proceeds. And finally, there is an act of appropriation, a taking to one's self, on one's own terms, the piece of knowledge that has been offered. Although teachers are needed, education is always in part one's own act. As the child grows older, there comes to be more awareness of one's own effort to learn and to become, the third phase of which is an experience of growth by an act of affirmation. Something—an idea, a fact—is offered by book, teacher, or the experience of life. If it flows over and past one, there is no education. If it sticks to one, and becomes training or habit, nevertheless there may be little or no education. If one deals with it, thoughtfully and reasonably, in terms of what one already is and with a result that thereafter one is by some degree more than one was before, there is surely education.

It is this third aspect of the educational experience that concerns me now. For it, the word "participation" might be used to suggest the sharing of the act of learning by both teacher and student, or the part that is taken by the reader of a book in the ideas of the book. The word "incorporation" might emphasize the way in which something learned is built into one's self. And "application" points to that involvement of learning in the life of action with our fellows of which I shall speak later. But I choose the word "creation," because man is a maker, and the making of his better self, through learning, is the end of that activity which I am now examining. It is by trying to make something which we feel to be part of us and yet something which we can give to another, that we make ourselves.

Creation, not always connected closely with education, is an experience that all may have. Sara, age three, creates a song by changing one word of a song her mother sings her. Now she sings a song that is "her very own." The Pueblo Indian potter varies one line of a traditional volute and knows herself an artist. I read today of an American who devotes his life to improving the effectiveness of the handles we grasp on the tools we use. Such creations are narrow, but they provide the sense of being a creator.

Greater creations may be achieved not only by the professional artists or scholars but by other people who are carrying on some private study for the joy it gives them. That part of the Maya hieroglyphic writing known as the Supplementary Series was deciphered by an American chemical engineer in the course of the journeys by train that he took in connection with his business. The glyphs had been for years a puzzle to specialists. The ancient Mediterranean script known as Linear B, written by the Greeks of Crete and Asia Minor, was recently made readable by the efforts of a young English architect.

The great creations of art and science and scholarship no doubt contribute to the education of those who achieve them and also provide works and ideas which become materials for the education of others. The coming to understand something—to understand it in that degree and kind which makes the thing learned a part of one's mind and self—is a creation, too. In this case the thing made is more private and personal. It is never wholly so. Education is an exchange in which each learner helps build the other as he builds himself.

Learning that educates includes an element of invention. In anthropology we speak of a process called "stimulus diffusion." Peoples learn from other peoples not only by imitating one another but also by observing one another and then doing something in a different way that reaches the same end. After Chinese porcelain had been coming to Europe for almost two centuries, European potters, stimulated by the beauty of the Chinese product, set themselves the task of finding a way to make it and succeeded. In the early nineteenth century a Cherokee Indian, who was entirely without schooling or knowledge of English, was impressed by the white man's writing and was stimulated to invent, single-handed, a syllabary. He had not grasped the alphabetic principle, but the example of writing that he saw and only partly understood was enough to cause him to invent. It seems to me that my own experience as a teacher might provide examples of learning by stimulus diffusion. More than once I have been a little startled to hear some old student of mine thank me for the wonderful insight I gave him years ago: he then tells me I said something to him which I am sure I never said. I said something, and he was stimulated to think something else. I do not recommend this method of instruction; I mention it only to emphasize the element of originality in educative learning.

In the self-educating learner, the imagination, working on the infinite suggestiveness of the world around one, moves the mind to arrangements of ideas and value that are both new and old. An idea is not the same when it is learned by you as when it is learned by me, provided the learning be more than mechanical repetition. I am a different learner; the thing learned is thereby different; therefore there is creation. Montaigne made the point when he wrote to the Countess of Gurson advice as to how her son should be brought up. He wrote, "For if by his own discourses he embrace the opinions of Xenophon or Plato, they shall be no longer theirs, but his. He that merely followeth another, traceth nothing, and seeketh nothing." I accept Whitehead's assertion that "the appreciation of literature is really creation." He goes on to say that the words we read and the music we hear are not mere stimuli to evoke an equivalent response. Learning that is educational is more of an original production, a self-modifying act, than is suggested by the words "stimulus" and "response." "No one, no genius other than our own, can make our life live." Whitehead therefore deplored the deadening weight of what he called "inert ideas" in so much schooling. In contrast, to take a thought, a judgment of appreciation, or the significance of a fact into one's own thoughts and feelings, is to give it the place there which one's self feels to be just, is to perform an act of creation in the self. I think of this dinstinction between inert ideas and the self-modifying creative act when I read a bad textbook and elsewhere listen to a good teacher. The textbook offers me inert ideas. The good teacher—man or book—offers me something of which to make something of my own. I am led along a course of fact and thought with which I am compelled to struggle, which I am compelled myself to order and reform.

When we try to learn in company, or with one companion, this struggle with its creative result is thereby helped along. The efforts of one to understand and to appreciate are provoked and tested by the efforts of the other. This may happen among schoolmates, between husband and wife in an adult education class, and even between people of very different origins and natures. I count among my teachers a certain Maya Indian whom I knew in his remote village in Yucatán. He talked with me about common human problems out of his own very different experience. When Tolstoy was teaching in his school on his estate, he was one day stirred to excitement in recognizing literary ability in an eleven-year-old peasant boy. A creation akin to his own appeared when the boy insisted that the old peasant in the story he and his schoolmates were writing should be made to put on a *woman's* cloak on hurriedly leaving the hut. Tolstoy saw that the detail was right; Fedka's imagination suggested "the picture of a feeble, narrow-chested peasant . . . the late hour, the peasant undressed for the night . . . the women going and coming, getting water, feeding cattle, the external disorder of the peasant's life." Tolstoy found this revelation of creative power terrible and delightful. He learned something then about children and about art. And the boy Fedka learned as he created.

It follows that education is in opposition to imitation and conformity.

These have their place in learning: one conforms in order to learn rules of grammar; one imitates the teacher when he shows how the lathe is to be used or pronounces the French word that one is to repeat. But in education the learner, by his own efforts, by so much makes himself over: there comes about in him a rearrangement of the understood, the important, and the desirable. The rearrangement is not permanent; mind and feeling, with developed discriminations, are now a base from which the cycle begins again. With widened powers to understand and to appreciate, the work in progress is resumed.

Sometimes when we try to educate we only regiment. Consider the children who after viewing an educational television program on clay modeling all proceeded to make the clay rabbit exactly as the demonstrator had made it. We should have applauded this uniformity if the attempt had been to teach the combinations of the multiplication table. For the modeling of rabbits the standardized result was not what was wanted. I fear that many a school talk about freedom and experiment covers hidden pressures to do the thing as the formal method or immediate convenience suggests. Schools are such busy places; schoolteachers have too much to do.

In spite of the report as to the clay rabbits, I have the impression that on the whole children are more spontaneous, more easily original, than are adults. It would probably be better for adult education if in this respect grownups were more like children. I have some sympathy for that man who, after the lecturer had finished explaining some experiments with a white rat in a maze and had invited questions, arose to ask, "What, in later life, became of the rat?" To pursue, with real interest, even an irrelevance is a step toward education. To accept without question is not.

On the other hand grown people, if they choose, can find times and places for creative learning. They are freer to make their own arrangements for the effort in such a way as to meet their own needs and interests. They are not so busy with mere training, and they do not have so closely to obey the teacher. Indeed, they can well be teachers of each other, as they are in many an organized discussion group today.

As adults we bring to the educational effort something that children cannot bring: the experiences of adult life. Recently I joined in a series of educational discussions in which twenty men took part. Each of us had read the same texts, on one day pages from John Winthrop's history of the Plymouth Colony, on another, a short novel by Melville. But each man brought to the discussion something of his own: that which he had himself lived that bore upon what had been written. Was Captain Vere right in condemning Billy Budd, a youth he knew to be innocent of soul? A man sitting at our table had had comparable responsibility as an army officer. We read a debate as to Communism in the schools and asked the question: Is there anything that should never be taught to anybody? At once one said that theft and murder should never be taught to anybody. But then another spoke, saying that in Counter-Intelligence during the war *he* had been taught theft and murder. We read a paper by William Graham Sumner in praise of capitalism and an economic enterprise absolutely free. The members of this discussion group, executives in growing and successful corporations, brought to Sumner's view an experience that apparently confirmed what Sumner wrote; they adopted his words with no little enthusiasm. But then one pointed out that Sumner's position was strongly unfavorable to all legislation with regard to wages and hours, and, indeed, unfavorable to private charity. And some of the men present thought well of laws protecting some wage-earners, and many had worked hard at raising money for charities. It seemed that the position they had first adopted had to be reconsidered. The issues of life and the issues of books are united in adult education because the learner has met some of the hard questions in his own experience.

I am struck by Sir Richard Livingstone's statement that "the young, whether they know it or not, live on borrowed property." They borrow, with incomplete understanding, the experiences of older people. In a widened sense, the proposition is true of everybody, young and old. We all live on mental property borrowed from our predecessors. The accumulations of our forefathers' experience, as recorded in books, we only partly understand. We have not had their experiences. As we live our somewhat different lives, we learn again the truths they learned. But they are not quite the same truths. Or, you who find this form of words unacceptable may allow me to say that we come to know the same truths in the contexts of our different experiences.

The learning of the individual may be compared to the learning of each generation, each age. As the age creates out of the knowledge of the past its own new form of learning, so the individual takes from books and discussions parts of an accumulation and creates his own developed self therefrom. I think of how you and I learn, when I read Henry Osborn Taylor's account of how medieval Europeans took and made over classical and patristic learning. He stresses the long time that it took for the medieval thinkers really to assimilate, to make their own, what they read:

"With each succeeding generation, the subjects of medieval study were made more closely parts of the intelligence occupied with them, because the matter had been constantly restated and restudied in terms more nearly adapted to the comprehension of the men who were learning and restating it."

At length they made the ancient thought "dynamically their own . . . they could think for themselves in its terms, think almost originally and creatively, and could present as their own the matter of their thoughts in restatements, that is, in forms essentially new." This is, I think, the outcome that is education also in the individual. As life is so short, it is not often that one reaches, in more than a few matters, this complete assimilation into one's own mind and feeling, of that which is given one to learn. The period of schooling is surely too brief. As one continues education throughout life, this assimilation, this conversion of another's learning into one's own creation, is more nearly reached.

Taylor sees, in the literature of medieval times, three stages in the assimilation of the earlier learning. First, what he calls "conning": the ancient book was read, and hardly more than repeated. The theologian copied an early text and added only a simple commentary. Second, "its more vital appropriation." This stage Taylor finds expressed in medieval works in which, with little form, the writer set down an opinion he had read in one authority, then a contrasting opinion from some other authority, and finally offered his own attempt at adjustment of the two. I have seen the equivalent in many a good student's notebook. In this stage education is occurring. The third stage—still following Taylor— is represented by the few really great medieval writings, notably the *Summa of Aquinas,* in which a great body of learning, thoroughly considered, is restated with added elements of thought. This last stage of the assimilation of "borrowed property" is, in small degree, represented in our own separate educations in so far as we restate parts of others' learning with elements of thought drawn from our growing structure of judgments of the relevant, the important, and the good.

I would cling a moment longer to this comparison of education with the assimilation by a whole people of the learning of earlier times. Taylor emphasizes the important part of emotion in the development of medieval learning. He says that the transformation of classical and patristic culture was accomplished as much by artists as by scholars, and that the emotions, the passions, of the scholars were involved in their recasting of earlier thought. He reminds us of the cathedral of Chartres, of the devotional prose of St. Anselm, of the chivalric romances, and especially of the passionate feeling that imbued religious thought. I think that in its own minor form that learning by the individual which educates is also carried along in a current of feeling. Teach your pupil to think? Livingstone replies, "Teach your pupil to think and feel."

It seems to me that feeling is a part of thinking, that we learn easily when we care strongly about what it is that we are learning. The feeling is itself something to be enlarged and disciplined. The passion with which one approaches a topic is both a hindrance to learning and a great strength. It makes it difficult to think clearly but it provides an energy for thinking at all. I felt both the advantage and the disadvantage of strong feeling in intellectual exercise in the course of that series of discussions with business executives that I just mentioned. These men came to the discussions with strong and favorable feelings about the free enterprise system and the importance of increasing material production. They also had strong feelings about taxes. As these were two subjects in which my own feelings were somewhat less forcefully mixed, from my point of view the emotional involvements of these men were something of an obstacle to their clear and critical examination of productivity as an element in the good life. On the other hand, it was their very passion with regard to these questions that carried them into the subject, carried them into it with a fierce intensity. Then it was that I was reminded of the strong feelings of the medieval churchmen and thought for a moment that the disputation in which I was taking part was as much theological, in a broad sense, as it was economic. Someone indeed raised the question if there was not a religious quality about faith in free enterprise and material production. The discussion became a very good one.

In talking about the place of feeling in education, Livingstone's principal point is that the discipline and the cultivation of appreciation are essential objectives. The making of the better self is not only a training of the intellect. It includes also the improvement of those discriminations by which we see that a thing is beautiful and good and admit it not only to our understanding but to our delight. One attends to something in the world about us not always to act upon it, not always to analyze it, but sometimes with an attitude of simple openness to its goodness. This attitude is itself subject to development, to refinement. In it feeling is a strong component. In this aspect of education passion is controlled, and feeling enhanced and made sensitive to disciplined judgments. Livingstone refers to this part of educated men as the "other eye . . . the eye which enables them to contemplate, enjoy, and adore." And Whitehead puts it roundly when he says that beauty is the "aim of the universe."

In this lecture I have spoken of education as a making, through learning, of a better self. I have put forward a conception of education that identifies it with the growth of the individual. In the process whereby we try through study and discussion to effect that growth I have emphasized what is personal, original, creative. It would almost seem, from this emphasis, that education is something that any man should be able to do out of his own unaided experience, as if the attempt had not been made before.

Of course this it not true. Education is possible only because we have access to the learning achieved by those who lived before us, and the making of the self that is education finds its building materials in that older learning. The comparison of the education of the individual with the mastery of classical knowledge by the thinkers of the Middle Ages is not only a comparison. The education of the individual and the transmission of the common heritage are aspects of the same thing. The learning of each one of us is a part of that learning whereby our age takes over, and yet remakes, the learning of the peoples who lived before us. While we seek our own education, we also work at the transmission of knowledge through the generations.

Therefore becoming educated is a social obligation as well as a personal privilege. If all the books were burned and no one told us legends of the past, education and civilization would collapse together. Our studies make our times as well as ourselves.

If, then, I send my child to school, I am concerned not only with what the school helps to make of him but also with what the schools—and all other efforts to educate—make of all of us. I am involved in decisions as to what to study, and what kind of person is to be made by the studying, both for myself or my child and for all of us, everywhere.

As I think about what I have said here, it seems to me that I have evaded a question that lies behind the matters that I have talked about. I cannot answer the question, but I can point out the direction in which I think we can go in continuing to struggle with it.

I have said that education is an individual enterprise. And, in talking of the intercourse we have with one another in the course of education, in admitting that we borrow the intellectual and moral property of other people, living and dead, in our studies, I recognize that education is a social experience. How much is individual, and how much is in common with others? I have said that in education mind and feeling explore, converse, and then create. Of what material is this creation accomplished? I have replied: Of two experiences, my own, and that stock of experience which has been accumulated for me by millions of predecessors.

Then should I not be told: Define, then, this common stock. Tell us what books we are to read, to what learning we are to attend. Does it matter whether we all choose different books? Shall I study Sanskrit literature while another studies mining and metallurgy in America? I made a comparison between the assimilation of ancient learning by scholars of the Middle Ages and the education of the modern American.

But is not the comparison more than a little misleading? Modern Americans are not in the position of medieval scholars. Then the Western Europeans had but the Western heritage to consider, and hundreds of years in which social change went but slowly, as compared with the explosive changes of today. Today we have the world's traditions open to us; the people and the problems and the heritage of every people and nation impinge upon us; and the rapidity with which changing circumstances demand instant decisions makes it impossible to find an exclusive basis for an education of a hundred and sixty million people in the deliberate reconsideration, throughout a dozen generations, of a few related books. Your description of the educational experience is all very well, I hear it said, but what, today, shall we teach in the schools? And what shall be the content of adult education?

The question I have failed to put until just now may be expressed in terms of the problem of choice of the more ultimate values, the conceptions of goodness which education helps us to form. I spoke of education as the rearrangement of the important and the desirable. Is each to decide for himself what is important and desirable, and is each resulting program of education as good as any other? I said that education is the making of a better self. What is "better"? If my neighbor chooses to educate his children for better delinquency, or to revive Nazism, is his view of education to carry as much weight as my own?

What shall we study? For what moral end, if any, shall we study it? For a long time education was conceived as the inculcation of common values through the reading of the great books of the Western tradition. It is so conceived by many today, although the books are not widely read, and although many people are troubled by a lack of common values in America. In Livingstone's essay on "Character and Its Training" there is an eloquent statement of the view that common culture and common values are indispensable and that the source for these is still to be found in the exhibition of intellectual and moral excellence in the great men and the great works of the West. Others have expressed similar views, and Robert Hutchins and Mortimer Adler have more than stated this position: they have done something about it in effecting uniform publication of certain of these books and in getting thousands of Americans to read them.

I think that my own position is the same, with variations. I share the view that education requires reasonable discussion and that the best basis therefore is a good book that everybody in the discussion has read. I think, too, that many good books have been produced in the Western world. And I agree also with the men I have mentioned in supposing that it is part of the good life to share with one's wife or neighbor or fellow citizen strong convictions, born out of common experience or common learning, as to what is good and what is beautiful. I think that to live together without common values may be possible, but that it would be a life lonely and bare. That I think so I have been helped to see by David Riesman who in some pages of his stimulating writings has suggested a different position. (I do not think he has advocated it.) He tells us that people may live together in peace, may cooperate, without sharing common preconceptions. He reminds us of those social inventions, such as the market and skills of negotiation, that allow each man to get along with all the others by putting forward only some part of himself. To get along, he goes on to say, requires procedural consensus, "some shared values of a very general sort like due process, and among sufficient people in strategic locations, some less-than-fanatical attitude toward compromise and even corruption." Reading this, I tried to think of myself sitting somewhere reasonably secure from war and crime because of the market and procedural rules, like traffic regulations, and because other people somewhere were compromising skillfully with corruption. I tried to think of a nation and a world held together by these things and nothing else. And, passing the question whether in such an America I should in fact be safe, I felt pretty sure I should not like it. I should feel more than a little cold. A nation run only by traffic rules and the convenient compromising expediencies of other people is not the kind of nation I want, hardly more than it is the kind of family I want.

So I am for continuing the quest for values. I even see no harm in using the word and in sometimes talking about the subject. But I think we can promise each other only a quest. The alternative to more cooperation through the market and procedural rules is not a return to a real or imagined conditions of agreement as to values "based on choicelessness." Choice is the condition of man today and for the future, so long as man is free. The alternative to a life of expediency is not to turn back to some moral authority of the past but to press forward, each now seeking that part of the good which he finds he needs and which he finds he shares with others.

The books of the West will continue to help us. But we cannot expect them to do for us just what they did for those who read them in times when the meaning of life was found in an education and an experience more nearly the same for a few people in all Western Europe than it is today for many people in the whole world. We shall read those books against the questions and emphases of today: against the impact of our discovery of man's irrationality, against the involvement of all nations in a common fate, against the evil we have come to see that men can do, against the hydrogen bomb. The old books were written without knowledge of the profound alterations in man's condition. Yet the books of the West record a magnificent conversation. And now the conversation continues; things said before need to be said now in different ways to meet the questions of the changed condition of mankind. And to the conversation of the West come now to be joined the conversations that other peoples—Chinese, Indians, Muslims—have had, each within that tradition. Already a set of Great Books of the Western World appears just a trifle parochial. Many an Oriental has read some of them as well as great books of his own tradition, and soon we of the West shall find it quite natural to read his books as well as our own. For all traditions are becoming common property. The conversation becomes world-wide.

It seems to me that the state of education in our times and for any future which I should like my children to enjoy is one in which many choices are open to him who seeks to make himself grow. We shall continue to talk with many kinds of people who have different heritages from the past, and who take different positions with regard to the content and the source of moral authority. There will be some who find an ultimate authority in some chosen expression of ethical and religious rule. There will be others who are seeking certainty. There will be still others who do not carry on the search, finding that they can decide to do this and not do that, with satisfaction to themselves, but without certainty.

In one of the stories written by the Swedish poet, Pär Lagerkvist, mankind moving through eternity fail to find God when they all set out to seek certainty, and find him only when they go "to demand of him his boundlessness, his anguish and his space without end." And when God, an old man sawing wood, replies to their question as to why he did all this to them, that his only intention was that men should never be content with nothing, the woodsawer seems to grow tall, immense, and mankind move on in eternity having found a kind of peace.

This is where I suppose that we are now. Some of us will continue to search for certainty. I think that those who hope to find it and those who do not are together in so far as they ask questions about the ends of life. That has always been the human quest. Education is part of the pursuit. When we talk to each other in the course of the pursuit, we help each other in the common effort.

The Indian or the Chinese who reads his own book asks these more ultimate questions, and when he does so, he is closer to me, more helpful to my own education, than is my American neighbor who never asks them. It is a curious fact of modern life that one can sometimes find immediate understanding with someone born and brought up in a part of the world remote from one's own, and yet find a gulf of misunderstanding with an American neighbor close at hand. I think this is because the more ultimate questions, of happiness, virtue, and the nature of the good, are the same questions in every tradition, while the seekers and the accepters are more different from each other than are the seekers from one another. There is nowadays some talk about the lack of understanding between intellectuals and other people in America. Mr. Edward L. Bernays, in an address he gave this year, referred to the current glorification of the doers and the scorn for the thinkers. "Doers" are with us mostly businessmen, and thinkers, I suppose, are in many cases professors. Mr. Bernays' remedy for the bad relations between the two is to urge the doers to use the special knowledge of the thinkers in getting done the things the doers have to do, such as solving problems of distribution and of what is called "industrial relations." It seems to me that this solution ignores the real difficulty. I do not think the misunderstanding or lack of confidence is so much between thinkers and doers, as it is between the people who ask only, "How shall we get this done?" and the people who ask, "Why should we do it?" It is a separation between the questioners and the takers-for-granted. In our country it is mostly material productivity and individual initiative that are taken for granted; in Russia it is a narrow doctrine policed by the state. But when, anywhere in the world, one asks, against some background of experience, some tradition of questioning and answering, the same questions as to the ends of man and the nature of the good, one has joined a conversation and a quest in which all humanity can ultimately share.

The end of man's existence is not cooperation. It is not even safety. It is to live up to the fullest possibilities of humanity. And man is human only as he knows the good and shares that knowing with those to whom he is, in humanity, bound. It is not necessary that we begin with the same assumptions. It is not necessary that we read the same books, though it is very helpful to do so, especially when we meet to carry on education. What, I think, is most necessary for pursuing the conversation is that we ask the same ultimate questions. The question, "Can we all, on this earth, get along together?" is, of course, an immensely important question because it has to be answered successfully if we are to ask any other. But even more important is the question, "Why should we try to do so? What should we work for, live for? What is the good life?"

Lagerkvist's story, about the talk of mankind in eternity in the course of the search for God, seems to me to describe the historic stages of this conversation. Once men talked only each of his own experience, his own local life. But, as civilization took place, discontent seized us and we began the thoughtful search for meaning, truth, certainty. In the West we associate the beginning of this search with Socrates. Thereafter, for a time, Western mankind seemed to find certainty in some unity of thought. But the movement of man cannot be stayed. We go forward, even toward uncertainty and doubt. Indeed, as our minds grow, so does "the soul's longing"; we must be free to question, to seek, though it is anguish to do so. So we come to a stage in our journey when we are aware that we gather together the experience each has had. In this later stage, when we speak, the words are not about ourselves, "but about the meaning of life, as each sees some part of it, on behalf of everyone." Now, some of us, even in the bad state of the world, begin to ask question, not as its answer affects only me, or America, or the West, but as it affects all people.

If I should choose a few words to describe the endless act of creation that is education, I should choose these: Education is conversation about the meaning of life, as each sees some part of it, on behalf of everyone. The words are too large for your needs and mine when we prepare to discuss a reading or a topic in some class or discussion group. Though we have in fact joined the quest and entered the "dialogue of civilization," we do not have then to think of our small places in the great enterprise. It is enough if we find the effort a significant joy.

The Role of Creativity

Alex F. Osborn (1888-   )

THE HISTORY OF CIVILIZATION is essentially the record of man's creative ability. Imagination is the cornerstone of human endeavor; it is, without doubt, responsible for man's survival as an animal, and it has caused him, as a human being, to conquer the world. It may well lead him to subdue the universe. The harnessing of atomic energy is a recent spectacular triumph of the human imagination over almost insuperable odds. Modern society, with its emphasis upon the progressive synthesis of technological and pure science, is admittedly dependent upon imagination as its life-blood. It is axiomatic that to think intelligently is to think creatively.

Art as an Avocation

Frank L. McVey (1869-1953)

THERE IS A RESPONSE in every man's heart and mind to beauty. For centuries the traveler across the valley of the Tiber has seen the dome of St. Peter's glistening in the sun. The picture has not only filled him with enthusiasm for his religion; he has also been greatly impressed with the massive magnificence of the building. Poets have told and men have dreamed of St. Paul's in London. Whistler made an etching of it, as he saw it through the channel of the streets. The traveler from abroad as he comes up the harbor of New York is amazed with the beauty and impressiveness of the skyline of our greatest city. In his heart is a thrill, not alone because of its material greatness but because design and impressive form tell a story of creation. The men who have looked upon these great monuments and others elsewhere have without question been affected by them. They have caught a bit of the meaning expressed in harmony and design, and in an unconscious way they have translated these things into their living.

The ordinary concept of art is that it is something extraneous to ourselves, belonging in practice to the few and possessed in form by the rich. We say it is difficult to understand and a futile thing to know. But the artists tell a different story. A painter friend of mine once said to me, "There is too much *talk* about art. I can tell all I know in an hour." And he is an excellent painter. In a lecture the other day Rockwell Kent said, "Art is an intensification of all the things we all are." Just so! It is only through art that we come to a larger fruition of our powers, interest, and appreciation.

For many years I have had a desire to do something in the field of art. I have used a pencil in an amateurish fashion since boyhood days. When I expressed this desire to a friend of mine he urged me to try, and so a decade ago I began to paint. Looking back over that period I can see a considerable growth as the result of my reading and study of books and the work of artists. Because of the fear of ridicule, it was with some trepidation that I began. But after all, what did it matter what other people thought, if I enjoyed painting. And so the plunge was made. I bought Birge Harrison's *Landscape Painting* and East's *Landscape Painting* and read them many times. I attempted to understand how a flat surface can show form, distance, and tone. I wrestled with the variations of color and the meaning of values and I became so enthusiastic that I went to school each summer for three years. Out of that experience has come considerable self-development as well as some accomplishment.

The benefit I have derived from the study of the fine arts has given me a genuine interest in art as an avocation. When I turn to it I am confident that my mind will be relieved of worry as soon as I face a canvas with brush and color. My work in art has made me see things more clearly and has given me a larger conception of the meaning of life. Rather interestingly it has brought into our family life an understanding of art that we did not have before. It has given us an appreciation of artistic things and beautiful surroundings. It has led me to look forward to an increasingly interesting life.

I have referred to the effect that imposing buildings have upon the traveler. Too often he looks upon them as the work of a genius who is different in kind from the rest of us. The fact of the matter is that the art spirit is in every one of us and that we can all express it in everyday living and in practice by doing whatever we do as well as we can.

To leave the matter here would be to "leave it on the doorstep" of the average individual. There must be some agency that can bring the art spirit into the life of the adult, and it seems to me that that agency is the college. It is true that colleges ordinarily deal with young undergraduates. Nevertheless, here is a great group of adult persons who need direction and who have, I am sure, an interest in using the fine arts as a means of satisfaction. If the colleges throw open their doors to adults and teach them by unacademic methods the history of art, art appreciation, its theory and practice, these colleges will develop a wider interest in adult education. There are in the United States at the present time a great many groups that are painting for their own pleasure. But organization, direction, and a sympathetic attitude on the part of the colleges are necessary to bring out in every college community this spirit of art appreciation.

Making Pictures

D. H. Lawrence (1885-1930)

ONE HAS TO EAT one's own words. I remember I used to assert, perhaps I even wrote it: Everything that can possibly be painted has been painted, every brush-stroke that can possibly be laid on canvas has been laid on. The visual arts are at a dead end. Then suddenly, at the age of forty, I begin painting myself and am fascinated.

Still, going through the Paris picture shops this year of grace, and seeing the Dufys and Chiricos, etc., and the Japanese Ito with his wish-wash nudes with pearl-button eyes, the same weariness comes over me. They are all so would-be, they make such efforts. They at least have nothing to paint. In the midst of them a graceful Friesz flower-piece, or a blotting-paper Laurencin, seems a masterpiece. At least here is a bit of *natural* expression in paint. Trivial enough, when compared to the big painters, but still, as far as they go, real.

What about myself, then! What am I doing, bursting into paint? I am a writer, I ought to stick to ink. I have found my medium of expression; why, at the age of forty, should I suddenly want to try another?

Things happen, and we have no choice. If Maria Huxley hadn't come rolling up to our house near Florence with four rather large canvases, one of which she had busted, and presented them to me because they had been abandoned in her house, I might never have started in on a real picture in my life. But those nice stretched canvases were too tempting. We had been painting doors and window-frames in the house, so there was a little stock of oil, turps and colour in powder, such as one buys from an Italian drogheria. There were several brushes for house-painting. There was a canvas on which the unknown owner had made a start—mud-grey, with the beginnings of a red-haired man. It was a grimy and ugly beginning, and the young man who had made it had wisely gone no further. He certainly had had no inner compulsion: nothing in him, as far as paint was concerned, or if there was anything in him, it had stayed in, and only a bit of the mud-grey "group" had come out.

So for the sheer fun of covering a surface and obliterating that mud-grey, I sat on the floor with the canvas propped against a chair—and with my house-paint brushes and colours in little casseroles. I disappeared into that canvas. It is to me the most exciting moment—when you have a blank canvas and a big brush full of wet colour, and you plunge. It is just like diving into a pond—then you start frantically to swim. So far as I am concerned, it is like swimming in a baffling current and being rather frightened and very thrilled, gasping and striking out for all you're worth. The knowing eye watches sharp as a needle; but the picture comes clean out of instinct, intuition and sheer physical action. Once the instinct and intuition gets into the brush tip, the picture *happens*, if it is to be a picture at all.

At least, so my first picture happened—the one I have called "A Holy

Family." In a couple of hours there it all was, man, woman, child, blue shirt, red shawl, pale room—all in the rough, but, as far as I am concerned, a picture. The struggling comes later. But the picture itself comes in the first rush, or not at all. It is only when the picture has come into being that one can struggle and make it *grow* to completion. . . .

Myself, I have always loved pictures, the pictorial art. I never went to an art school, I have had only one real lesson in painting in all my life. But of course I was thoroughly drilled in "drawing," the solid-geometry sort, and the plaster-cast sort, and the pin-wire sort. I think the solid-geometry sort, with all the elementary laws of perspective, was valuable. But the pin-wire sort and the plaster-cast light-and-shade sort was harmful. Plaster-casts and pin-wire outlines were always so repulsive to me, I quite early decided I "could't draw." I couldn't draw, so I could never do anything on my own. When I did paint jugs of flowers or bread and potatoes, or cottages in a lane, copying from Nature, the result wasn't very thrilling. Nature was more or less of a plaster-cast to me—those plaster-cast heads of Minerva or figures of Dying Gladiators which so unnerved me as a youth. The "object," be it what it might, was always slightly repulsive to me once I sat down in front of it, to paint it. So, of course, I decided I couldn't really paint. Perhaps I can't. But I verily believe I can make pictures, which is to me all that matters in this respect. The art of painting consists in making pictures—and so many artists accomplish canvases without coming within miles of painting a picture.

I learnt to paint from copying other pictures—usually reproductions, sometimes even photographs. When I was a boy, how I concentrated over it! Copying some perfectly worthless scene reproduction in some magazine. I worked with almost dry water-colour, stroke by stroke, covering half a square-inch at a time, each square-inch perfect and completed, proceeding in a kind of mosaic advance, with no idea at all of laying on a broad wash. Hours and hours of intense concentration, inch by inch progress, in a method entirely wrong—and yet those copies of mine managed, when they were finished, to have a certain something that delighted me: a certain glow of life, which was beauty to me. A picture lives with the life you put into it. If you put no *life* into it—no thrill, no concentration of delight or exaltation of visual discovery—then the picture is dead, like so many canvases, no matter how much thorough and scientific work is put into it. Even if you only copy a purely banal reproduction of an old bridge, some sort of keen, delighted awareness of the old bridge or of its atmosphere, or the image it has kindled inside you, can go over on to the paper and give a certain touch of life to a banal conception.

It needs a certain purity of spirit to be an artist, of any sort. The motto which should be written over every School of Art is: "Blessed are the pure in spirit, for theirs is the kingdom of heaven." But by "pure in spirit" we mean pure in spirit. An artist may be a profligate and, from the social point of view, a scoundrel. But if he can paint a nude woman, or a couple of apples, so that they are a living image, then he was pure in spirit, for the time being, his was the kingdom of heaven. This is the beginning of all art, visual or literary or musical: be pure in spirit. It isn't the same as goodness. It is much more difficult and nearer the divine. The divine isn't only good, it is all things.

One may see the divine in natural objects; I saw it to-day, in the frail, lovely little camellia flowers on long stems, here on the bushy and splendid flower stalls of the Ramblas in Barcelona. They were different from the usual fat camellias, more like gardenias, poised delicately, and I saw them like a vision. So now, I could paint them. But if I had bought a handful, and started in to paint them "from nature," then I should have lost them. By staring at them I should have lost them. I have learnt by experience. It is personal experience only. Some men can only get at a vision by staring themselves blind, as it were: like Cézanne; but staring kills my vision. That's why I could never "draw" at school. One was supposed to draw what one stared at.

The only thing one can look into, stare into, and see only vision, is the vision itself: the visionary image. That is why I am glad I never had any training but the self-imposed training of copying other men's pictures. As I grew more ambitions, I copied Leader's landscapes, and Frank Brangwyn's cartoon-like pictures, then Peter de Wint and Girtin water colours. I can never be sufficiently grateful for the series of English water-colour painters, published by the *Studio* in eight parts, when I was a youth. I had only six of the eight parts, but they were invaluable to me. I copied them with the greatest joy, and found some of them extremely difficult. Surely I put as much labour into copying from those water colour reproductions as most modern art students put into all their years of study. And I had enormous profit from it. I not only acquired a considerable technical skill in handling water colour—let any man try copying the English water-colour artists, from Paul Sandby and Peter de Wint and Girtin, up to Frank Brangwyn and the impressionists like Brabazon, and he will see how much skill he requires— but also I developed my visionary awareness. And I believe one can only develop one's visionary awareness by close contact with the vision itself: that is, by knowing pictures, real vision pictures, and by dwelling on them, and really dwelling in them. It is a great delight, to dwell in a picture. But it needs a purity of spirit, a sloughing of vulgar sensation and vulgar interest, and above all, vulgar contact, that few people know how to perform. Oh, if art schools only taught that! If, instead of saying: This drawing is wrong, incorrect, badly drawn, etc., they would say: Isn't this in bad taste? isn't it insensitive? isn't that an insentient curve with none of the delicate awareness of life in it?—But art is treated all wrong. It is treated as if it were a science, which it is not. Art is a form of religion, minus the Ten Commandment business, which is sociological. Art is a form of supremely delicate awareness and atone-ment—meaning atoneness, the state of being at one with the object. But is the great atonement in delight?—for I can never look on art save as a form of delight.

All my life I have from time to time gone back to paint, because it gave me a form of delight that words can never give. Perhaps the joy in words goes deeper and is for that reason more unconscious. The *conscious* delight is certainly stronger in paint. I have gone back to paint for real pleasure—and by paint I mean copying, copying either in oils or waters. I think the greatest pleasure I ever got came from copying Fra Angelico's "Flight into Egypt" and Lorenzetti's big picture of the Thebaid, in each case working from photographs and putting in my own colour; or perhaps even more a Carpaccio picture in Venice. Then I *really* learned what life, what powerful life has been put into every curve, every motion of a great picture. Purity of spirit, sensitive awareness, intense eagerness to portray an inward vision, how it all comes. The English water colours are frail in comparison—and the French and the Flemings are shallow. The great Rembrandt I never tried to copy, though I loved him intensely, even more than I do now; and Rubens I never tried, though I always liked him so much, only he seemed to spread out. But I have copied Peter de Hooch, and Vandyck, and others that I forget. Yet none of them gave me the deep thrill of the Italians, Carpaccio, or the lovely "Death of Procris" in the National Gallery, or that "Wedding" with the scarlet legs, in the Uffizi, or a Giotto from Padua. I must have made many copies in my day, and got endless joy out of them.

Then suddenly, by having a blank canvas, I discovered I could make a picture myself. That is the point, to make a picture on a blank canvas. And I was forty before I had the real courage to try. Then it became an orgy, making pictures.

I have learnt now not to work from objects, not to have models, not to have a technique. Sometimes, for a water colour, I have worked direct from a model. But it always spoils the *picture.* I can only use a model when the picture is already made; then I can look at the model to get some detail which the vision failed me with, or to modify something which I *feel* is unsatisfactory and I don't know why. Then a model may give a suggestion. But at the beginning, a model only spoils the picture. The picture must all come out of the artist's inside, awareness of forms and figures. We can call it memory, but it is more than memory. It is the image as it lives in the consciousness, alive like a vision, but unknown. I believe many people have, in their consciousness, living images that would give them the greatest joy to bring out. But they don't know how to go about it. And teaching only hinders them.

To me, a picture has delight in it, or it isn't a picture. The saddest pictures of Piero della Francesca or Sodoma or Goya, have still that indescribable delight that goes with the real picture. Modern critics talk a lot about ugliness, but I never saw a real picture that seemed to me ugly. The theme may be ugly, there may be a terrifying, distressing, almost repulsive quality, as in El Greco. Yet it is all, in some strange way, swept up in the delight of a picture. No artist, even the gloomiest, ever painted a picture without the curious delight in image-making.

Music and Human Values

a. Ernest Lévy —
in a Letter to Barnett Byman

I BELIEVE THAT ART in general, and music in particular, is not a mere amusement, a mere ornament of life. The series of world catastrophes in which we are involved are the outcome of an evolution that has begun at the end of the Middle Ages with an ever increasing development of the intellectual side of our nature. To-day humanity, with its armies of specialists who, as Nicholas Murray Butler puts it, are people who "know more and more about less and less," resembles a huge ant-hill. Only, the ant state is held together by natural instinct. Humanity has no such instinct. She has to rely on her consciousness of spiritual principles, which alone can guarantee the awareness of *values* without which the intellect and its inventions will run amok. There is no need to explain what that means—we are unfortunately experiencing it. We are witnessing the terrible revenge of the *affective* side of our nature, whose integration into our daily life has hardly been attempted. Sentiment, feelings, ideals—all that has been relegated to small corners of our civilization, as a matter of concert-halls, museums, Sunday-religion. Our inner life has been thrown off balance, and let's not forget that it is our inner life that fashions the outer world.

To a humanity looking for elements of hope, music ought to be an important matter. We may even say that man will begin to recover the moment he takes art as seriously as physics, chemistry, or money. There is no other human activity that asks for such a harmonious cooperation of "intellect" and "soul" as artistic creation and, especially, music (I do not say this only because I am a musician! I have very good reasons to say so!). Music is human. Music is also extra-human inasmuch as it is a mirror of universal laws. To destructive analysis music opposes synthesis. To the uniformization of science, which reduces qualities to quantities, music opposes a hierarchy of values. *Our mechanized minds need to be musicalized.* We have developed only half of man's possibilities, or rather, have developed that half completely out of proportion to the other half. We have deified the intellect, we have separated it completely from the other side of human nature. We must seek a synthesis. Music as an art and as a science can do it. This is not a petty problem. It is *the* problem of our time.

b. *Felix Mendelssohn (1809-1847)* — *in a letter to Conrad Schleinitz*

What you write me about your increased business rejoices me much. You know how often we have talked the subject over, and I cannot share your sentiment that any one profession is preferable to another. I always think that whatever an intelligent man gives his heart to and firmly grasps must become a noble vocation; and personally I only dislike those in which there is nothing personal and in which all individuality disappears; as, for example, the military profession in peace, of which we have instances here. But with regard to the others, it is more or less untrue. When one profession is compared with another, the one is usually taken in its naked reality, and the other in the most beautiful ideality, and then the decision is quickly made.

And how easy it is for an artist to feel such reality in his sphere and then to esteem *practical* men happy who have studied and known the different relations of men toward each other, and who help others to live their own life and progress, and at once see the fruits of all that is tangible, useful, and benevolent instituted by them; and just on this account an upright man has the hardest stand to make, knowing that the public are more attracted by outward show than by truth. But individual failures and strife must not be allowed to have their growth in the heart; there must be something to occupy and to elevate it far above these isolated external things. This speaks strongly in favour of my opinion, for it is the best part of every calling, and common to all: to yours, to mine, and to every other.

Where is it that you find beauty when I am working at a quartet or a symphony? Merely in that portion of myself that I transfer to it or can succeed in expressing; and you can do this in as full measure as any man, in your defence of a culprit, or in a case of libel, or in any one thing that entirely engrosses you, and that is the great point. If you can only give utterance to your inmost thoughts, and if these inmost thoughts become more and more worthy of being expressed—all the rest is indifferent.

c. Piotr Tchaikovsky (1840-1893)

Kamenki, July 6, 1878

Your letter has come, dear N. F., and I hasten to reply. You want to know my methods of composing? That is a rather difficult question, my friend, because the circumstances under which compositions are born vary a great deal. But I shall try to describe to you in a general way how I work, and to explain the process of composition I must first divide my compositions into two categories:

1. Those written on my own initiative, through sudden inclination and urgent inner necessity.
2. Those inspired by eternal means such as the resquest of a friend, or publisher, or commissions; for example, my Cantata written for the Polytechnic Exposition, or the Slavic March, written for a Red Cross concert.

I hasten to explain that, as shown by experience, the value of a work does not depend upon which category it belongs to. Frequently a composition that was artifically engendered turns out quite successfully, while pieces invented wholly through my own inspiration are sometimes less successful for various incidental reasons. The circumstances surrounding the composer at the time of composition, upon which his state of mind depends, are very important. The artist must have tranquillity when he is creating. In this sense, creative activity is always objective, even musical creativity, and those who think that the artist can use his talent to relieve himself of specific feelings of the moment are mistaken. The sad or happy emotions he expresses are always and invariably retrospective. With no particular reason for rejoicing, I can experience a happy creative mood, and on the other hand, in the happiest circumstances I might write music filled with darkness and despair. In short, the artist lives a double life, an everyday, human one, and an artistic one, and these two lives do not always coincide. Anyway I repeat that to compose, the important thing is to rid oneself of the troubles of everyday existence and to surrender oneself unconditionally to the artistic life. But I am digressing and I must return to my classification.

For compositions belonging to the first or inspired-from-within category, not even the smallest effort of will is necessary. It is enough to submit to one's inner voice, and if the everyday life does not rise up to crush the artistic life, work proceeds with the most wonderful ease. One forgets everything, the spirit trembles with sweet excitement, and before one has time to follow the swift flight to its end, time has gone by unperceived. There is something somnambulistic in this state—"*on ne s'entend pas vivre.*" It is impossible to explain these moments. Whatever emerges from the pen at such times, or merely remains in the head, is always of value and, unless interrupted from without, will be the artist's best work. It is unfortunate that outside interruptions are absolutely unavoidable. One must go to work, one is summoned to dinner, a letter comes, and so on. That is why compositions in which musical beauty is evenly balanced throughout are rare. That explains why there are seams, ends hanging out, unevenness, irrelevance.

For commissioned work one sometimes has to create one's own inspiration. Very often one must first overcome laziness and lack of inclination. Then there are various impediments. Sometimes victory comes easily, sometimes inspiration entirely escapes me. But I believe it is the duty of an artist never to submit, for laziness is a strong human trait, and nothing is more harmful to an artist than to let laziness get the better of him. One cannot afford to sit and wait for insipration; she is a guest who does not visit the lazy but comes to those who call her. Perhaps there is good reason for the charge that Russia lacks creative activity and that the Russian is terribly lazy. He loves to procrastinate; he has natural talent, but also natural lack of self-discipline. One must acquire this; one must conquer oneself and not lapse into dilettantism, which affected even so powerful a talent as Glinka. Endowed with great original powers of creation, he lived to a ripe old age and yet wrote amazing little. Read his memoirs and you'll see that he composed like a dilettante, at his leisure, when the mood came. We are proud of Glinka, yet we must admit that he did not fulfil the task his genius set before him.

d. Robert Schumann (1810-1856) —
in a letter to Friedrich Wieck

I returned from my tour in Switzerland and Italy a fortnight ago, poorer by a few napoleons, but richer by my increased knowledge of the world and a store of precious memories. I declare you can have no notion of Italian music until you have heard it under the Italian skies which called it into being. How often did I think of you in the Scala Theatre at Milan! How charmed I was with Rossini, or rather with Pasta's interpretation! I leave her name unqualified to show my respect—I might say, my adoration. In the Leipzig concert-room I sometimes experienced a thrill of awe in the presence of the genius of music, but Italy has taught me to love it. Only once in my whole life have I had an impression of the actual presence of God, of gazing reverently and unrebuked into His face; this was at Milan as I listened to Pasta—and Rossini! Do not smile, dear master, for I speak seriously. But this was my sole musical treat in Italy. Their music is, in the ordinary way, hardly fit to listen to. You have no conception of the sort of slapdash facility with which they reel off everything. . . .

Schubert is still my one and only love, the more so as he has everything in common with my one and only Jean Paul. To play his compositions is with me like reading one of Jean Paul's novels. . . . There is no other music that presents so bewildering a psychological problem in its train of ideas, its apparently abrupt transitions. It is rare to find a composer who can stamp his individuality plainly on such a heterogeneous collection of tone-pictures, and still rarer are those who write, as Schubert did, as their hearts prompt them. Schubert unburdened his heart on a sheet of music-paper just as others leave the impression of passing moods in their journals. His soul was so steeped in music that he wrote notes where others use words—so, at least, I venture to think.

Creative Expression for All

Henry Schmidt, Jr.

JUST WHAT IS MEANT by creative expression? Most writers instinctively shy away from the word "creative." They think of it primarily in connection with the great painters, musicians, sculptors, architects, and writers who possess some inner urge or fountain of inspiration that is denied to other mortals. But creative expression is a matter of degree. It may show forth in all manner of ways: the choice and arrangement of furniture in the living room or the clothes selected and the manner of wearing them. For the most part, however, modern work life gives few opportunities for genuine self-expression. One of the charges made against the industrial age is that the machine has made useless the craft skills that were widely employed by earlier generations in the day-by-day business of living. The modern housewife, for instance, has the various labor-saving devices, the availability of prepared foods, and ready-made clothing to lighten many of her burdens. At the same time they have robbed her of certain satisfactions—opportunities for creative expression—that her grandmother and great-grandmother enjoyed.

Certainly, the American way of life up to the turn of the century afforded many channels for such expression. The farmer who made most of his own farm tools and equipment, fashioned much of the furniture that went into his house, built his own barns and made all the repairs and additions to his own home—such a man developed a variety of skills and capacities in which he could take pride. Similarly, his wife seemed to take more pride in her kitchen creations, the mouth-watering quality of the cakes and pies she baked, the fluffiness of her raised biscuits and her special recipe for shortbread. To outfit herself and children for church and Sunday School demanded no small amount of skill and versatility. The rag rugs and patchwork quilts she made in her "spare" time were often of a high order of handcraft quality.

The pre-industrial era cannot be recalled, but some of the aspects of life in that day are missed in modern industrial society, such as the opportunity to be more creative in jobs and in homes—the opportunity to use the hands in craftwork. The increasing preoccupation with hobbies of one sort or another by our generation is an evidence of the loss we have suffered. A virtual army of men have set up elaborately-equipped wood-working or metal-working benches in the basements of their homes and spend their evenings and weekends happily turning out all sorts of products that may or may not have an immediate use.

The current "Do-It-Yourself" vogue is another example. Some cynics contend that the movement has come to a head chiefly as a protest against the high cost of manufactured goods needed around the house. But the urge to paper a wall, build a terrace, or finish off an attic has more than economy behind it. The psychologist knows that, fundamentally, it is an effort on the part of machine-dominated job holders to recapture some of the submerged satisfactions of making a complete object by oneself. In this connection, however, it may be pointed out that in striving to compensate for this loss there is the advantage of the increased time afforded by the shift from a seventy or so hour week to one of forty hours. In other words, some thirty hours a week are freed in which to seek satisfactions in some form of creative activity of deliberate choice.

In addition to all these forms of creative activity there is the whole field of arts and crafts which offers an even broader opportunity for self-expression. As suggested above, the true creative artist's capacities and values are regarded as radically different from those of other persons. It is astonishing, however, to discover how many ordinary people possess talents they have never had a chance to develop—individuals in whom a genuine creative urge has been buried under the pressures of earning a living or raising a family. A lawyer doodling on a scratch-pad during a dull trial makes an amusing caricature of the judge and recalls wistfully how at one time he thought of becoming a cartoonist. An insurance salesman waiting to see a prospect remembers an early ambition to become a concert violinist. A housewife emptying the ashtrays in the living room is suddenly reminded of the happy and exciting class in ceramics she attended during her high school days.

There are thousands and thousands of middle-aged men and women in this country in whom the creative fire still smoulders and awaits only a determined effort to fan it into an effective flame. Nor is the opportunity limited only to those who "played around" with some incipient talent in their youth. Many a person, past his half century mark and handling a paint brush for the first time, or getting the feel of wet clay in his fingers, has sensed that he was tapping a creative urge he never knew existed, something that satisfied some great and unguessed need within himself.

In all this the word *need* has been stressed, for the creative urge is something that presses for expression and that, if too long dammed up, can often lead to serious frustration. Conversely, if it is given free rein, the individual can achieve a measure of self-realization that is more truly satisfying, perhaps, than anything previously experienced over his entire lifetime. Any form of creative activity, seriously pursued, is a method of self-discovery and self-expression for which there are no set limits. There is continuous growth as a person develops his skill or attains new insights into the essential nature of his chosen art or craft, a joy of accomplishment as one gains a greater and greater command over his medium.

The older individual can still look for a very considerable degree of pleasure and satisfaction in taking up some form of creative activity of this nature as a major occupation. In certain of the arts and crafts manual dexterity is just as pronounced in the later years as in youth. The reward is the fun of engaging in a new experience and acquiring a reasonable competency in a new field of effort. Then, too, the middle-aged man or woman has the advantage of years of experience and observation which provide a more mature approach to such a venture. Ability to perceive, interpret, and evaluate has been sharpened throughout the earlier years. And the actual practice of one of these arts and crafts helps develop a greater appreciation of the essential values of a wide range of other art forms.

Creative activity of any sort has a tremendous therapeutic value. It is a great "untier of inner knots," an unscrambler of confusions, a safety valve for blowing off emotional steam. It preserves the mental and physical well-being and can help one find inner peace and harmony. Through such activity one can give meaning and substance to the so-called empty years that stretch ahead after the children have left the home. It will help establish a new and heartwarming pattern of living that will endure through all the remaining span of life.

In recent years there has been a steady growth in many forms of creative expression in the arts, crafts, hobbies, gardening, music, and do-it-yourself activities. The signs of it are in evidence in communities throughout the nation. Most towns and cities have adult education curricula that include an increasing number of creative arts as well as the appreciation of arts. Local communal centers, such as the YM and YWCA's, the Woman's Clubs, the churches, and the Senior Centers are offering more and more courses that give free play to the creative urge. In many a community there are private teachers of the arts and crafts, some of whom have formed little groups for weaving, basketry, and wood and metal working. Some communities, like Silvermine, Connecticut, have developed separate centers for the arts and crafts, with special studios for each.

Regional societies and guilds often hold classes as well as periodic exhibits. In New Hampshire, the League of Arts and Crafts has established a network of centers throughout the State which engages the leisure time of nearly 2,000 members, 85 per cent or so of whom learned their skills after the age of fifty. These older men and women are creating all manner of hand-crafted products, sometimes at home, often in community groups. They get expert instruction and advice. Those who create quality products are rewarded by acceptance of their creation for sale in the shops run by the League throughout the State. In southeastern states the Southern Highlanders serve their people in a similar manner. Many other states and regions also foster the creative arts for their citizens.

Libraries and other public buildings are today being used for public displays of local talent. With indoor facilities bursting their seams, one small community recently set up a mammoth outdoor exhibit of all forms of painting, drawing, and photography spread out over 1500 feet of the main street in its business area. It proved to be a huge success.

Even business concerns are encouraging the creative arts. For many years many banks have been turning their lobbies into annual art galleries to display the work of their employees in all manner of arts, crafts, and hobbies. Some large corporations hold similar exhibits and award incentive prizes for excellence. Such companies also use their house organs to tell the stories of unusually creative employees, showing photographs of them at work in their homes. The industrial relations and personnel directors of these companies know that an outside creative interest is frequently the making of a better adjusted worker.

On many a Main Street can now be seen a little shop that specializes in supplies and equipment for the arts and crafts. One may carry only art supplies. Another may have all kinds of hand-tool supplies and equipment for leatherwork, ceramics, weaving, glass painting, and basketry. Down the street may be a store specializing in cameras and supplies for the photographic art, which has zoomed in popularity in the last ten years. On the same Main Street the average hardware store is devoting space to all manner of small machine tools, rotary saws, and wood turners. New synthetic materials, new paints, and putties, new solders and adhesive all provide new avenues of activity to a new breed of artisans—the do-it-yourselfers. What cannot be bought locally can certainly be purchased by mail—art courses galore, all manner of metal, wood, and leather working supplies and materials, ceramic supplies. Correspondence schools offer courses in most of the arts and crafts.

There is also a growing number of interesting magazines serving the creative arts, crafts, and hobbies. The general collector has his magazine, as does the specialist like the stamp collector. The photography fan has many to choose from. Some magazines, like *Craft Horizons,* cover a variety of fine arts, while others, like *Profitable Hobbies Magazine,* serve the craftsman who wants to turn his craft to a profit.

Gardening, too, has an increasing number of magazines and books to serve the nation's millions of backyard creators with dirt and hoe. The circulation of the magazines in the science and mechanics field reaches astronomical proportions. In them is page after page of suggestions for ways to make things yourself. Moreover, the creative soul who seeks to supplement his income can find plenty of ways and means. There are now thousands of outlets for quality hand-creations through gift shops, department stores, and special hobby shops. Some of these are on the highway, some in the community. Some, like the New York City handcraft shops of America House and the Southern Highlanders, sell only top quality creations. Many a handcrafter has an agent who sells his wares, while others are lucky enough, or good enough, to have customers who beat paths right to their own doors. Still others have established successful mail order businesses. Few get rich, but many find that their creative efforts bring a reasonably substantial and fairly steady flow of dollars to their bank account.

Certainly, a wide range of opportunities exists for everyone who has the energy and the imagination to take advantage of them, as in the case of Allen Holter. Mr. Holter worked for a publishing company and a natural intellectual curiosity led him to investigate the history of printing presses, type faces, paper, and bookbinding. An urge to experiment led to the purchase of an antique handpress, which he put into condition, and also to the acquisition of some exceptionally fine type faces and some of the best printing paper. Then, logically enough, after providing evidence of his skill, it led to a contract for hand printing some limited edition books. His zeal for printing spread throughout his family to his wife and daughters. Among them they developed the skills of type-setting, paper-selection, printing, and bookbinding. Working as a team in a fascinating home workship, they had found an interest that completely absorbed them, gave added meaning to their individual lives and to their living together as a family unit.

Then there is the experience of Carl Logan. It began innocently with some modest success with a new camera. This led to an award at a local photography show, then to a desire to become an expert and to avid study of all the literature on photography, then to attendance at a local course in photography, to purchase of better equipment and the desire to develop his own prints with his own effects, then to more achievements and further recognition, and finally to paid photographic assignments from industrial concerns. The excitement had spread to his wife, whose latent desire had always been to write. What a team it would make, she thought, if she could write and Carl could provide the photographic illustration. Both the Logans had taken canoe camping trips, so "why not write and produce books on canoeing?" The Logans now have several successful books to their credit. Life for them has always been a creative adventure. Mr. Logan has just been retired from his job but he disapproves of the word retirement. "A better word," he says, "is commencement." He talks about the "fulfillment years" ahead of him and looks forward to them as eagerly as a youth does to starting his career after graduation from college.

Another good example is Albert Townsend. When Mr. Townsend was retired as a teacher of history from a Massachusetts high school, he planned to turn into a serious pursuit a hobby in which he had only been "dabbling"—the creation of perfect miniature models of early American furniture. He had started to accumulate some knowledge and tools for this interest but had never found the time to develop his skill to any appreciable extent. Retirement gave him that opportunity. When he did develop the necessary degree of skill, he started to expose his miniature creations to the public. His little pieces of furniture promptly brought outbursts of enthusiastic appreciation whenever he showed them. People bought them eagerly and he found he could easily sell all he made. He intensified his study of the history and lore of furniture and soon was sought after to give talks on the subject before clubs and organizations. The local press wrote stories about him. People in his community identified him with his absorbing interest and openly admired and respected him. Al Townsend had not retired one whit. He merely switched the course of his life and is as busy, alert, and alive as ever.

Not everyone, of course, who turns to some form of creative activity in his later years can expect to achieve so great a measure of "success," as we ordinarily use the term, as these examples illustrate. Nor does it matter. The real touchstone of success is the sense of individual accomplishment and self-realization that such activities afford the middle-aged and older person.

Few things, indeed, give more substance and meaning to the later years, and few things will carry one more triumphantly through the arduous adjustments all must make to the advent of old age.

Suggestions for Further Reading

The Creative Process, a symposium edited by Brewster Chiselin. New York: A Mentor Book (paperback).

Thirty-eight personalities, from Einstein to Van Gogh, from Nietzsche to D. H. Lawrence, tell in their own words of the rhythm on which they ride. With an introduction by the editor, giving information on the lives and work habits of a multitude of creative artists.

General Education in A Free Society, report of the Harvard Committee. Cambridge: Harvard University Press, 1945.

A profound effort by a group of educators, scientists, and philosophers to state the objectives and the kind of education needed by people who wish to live in a free society.

Learning Comes of Age, by John Walker Powell. Association Press, New York, 1956.

A survey and interpretation of the aims, instruments, clientele, and leadership of adult education—as it is now and can be in the future.

Mass Leisure. Eric Larrabee and Rolf Meyersohn, editors. Glencoe, Ill., The Free Press, 1958.

A collection of more than forty articles and essays dealing with the origins of leisure, attitudes toward work and leisure, trends and satisfactions in uses of leisure, and forecasts of what's to come. Many conflicting opinions inviting the reader to take sides and to rethink his own position.

Reed Harris (born in 1909 in New York City), writer and business executive, is president of Publications Services, Inc. in Washington, D.C. He has been a free lance reporter, an editor, and an official of a number of governmental agencies including OWI and the Department of State. He is associated with a number of national organizations, largely in the field of management. His writings include authorship of two books, Travel's Windfall *(1939) and* How to Get a Better Job When You're Over 35. *He was also Executive Editor of the* American Guide Series *(1936-39) and founder of the National Society of Seniors.*

". . . The opportunities to grow old and to participate effectively in group life stem very largely from social rather than innate factors and from acquiring individual skill and initiative instead of, or in addition to, biological endowments. These same opportunities may be won or lost by pressures or changes in the social milieu, or by the apt or inept attempts at adaptation by the particular individual. It takes the two parts, neatly fitted, to make for wholesome and prolonged participation. The secret of success for anyone facing a long life, therefore, is to find for himself a suitable place in his society in which to age with grace and usefulness, and to participate tactfully and fully up to the very end, if at all possible."

—LEO W. SIMMONS

"Social Participation of the Aged in Different Cultures," *The Annals,* January 1952. Quoted by permission.

7

The Challenge of

Citizenship

REED HARRIS

THE JET AND ATOM AGE has brought with it problems in government
—local, national, and international—and in community life which,
added to the old recurring problems, require the wisdom of more
heads and the work of more hands than have ever before been applied to such matters. Yet hundreds of thousands of educated brains
and trained hands that could be turned to solving these public problems are being allowed instead to lie almost unused. The hands and
heads are, of course, those of the multitude of people who have
reached the second half of life, and consequently have an increasing
amount of leisure time.

Failure of the community at large to draw upon the advice and
skill of people in middle life and beyond, and failure of such mature
people to volunteer more often, are not the result of a conscious,
willful attempt by some controlling group to hold back this po-

tentially powerful force. The failure is the product of gradual and unfortunate developments that have pushed older people into the background.

Using Mature Advisers

The good habit of calling upon older citizens for advice or for government service—which long was a part of normal life in most parts of the world, as described by Professor Simmons—has fallen into disuse, partly because purely physical progress, in which young people play an important part, has been confused with true social progress, in which older persons must assume a major role, and partly because problems of government and civic affairs today are so complex that their solutions are increasingly left to the "experts," often young technicians. It is assumed that, because younger citizens are chiefly responsible for today's material developments, they are in a better position to advise and to lead than people past forty-five years of age. And to some degree this may be true where the problems are principally physical, as in the operation of complex machinery, the development of new electronic accounting methods, and the selection of new fire fighting equipment for an airport. But the assumption is tragically wrong when it is applied to problems of human relations, for here indeed the mature person can supply overwhelmingly superior wisdom and understanding.

The science—or art—of government or of conducting civic activities is basically concerned with human relations. A governmental unit, or a community chest, even if it could become 100 percent efficient in its physical operation, would fail miserably if it neglected human relations. Thus, there is a great need for mature understanding and the wisdom of age.

Advantages of Age

But what are the special qualities, the priceless bits of knowledge that the middle-aged person has that makes him so much better than his younger counterpart in dealing with human problems and adjustments? Adlai Stevenson, in a non-political speech, said it well when he explained that what a man knows at fifty that he did not know at twenty boils down to this: "The knowledge he has acquired with age is not a knowledge of formulas, or forms of words, but of people, places, actions—a knowledge not gained by words, but by touch, sight, sound, victories, failures, sleeplessness, devotion, love—the human experience and emotions of this earth and of one's self and other men. Perhaps, too, a little faith, a little reverence for things you cannot see."

In this advantage that the older man holds over the younger lies one of the important reasons for choosing constructive citizenship as a major field of activity and interest in later life. "The great use of life is to spend it for something that will outlast it," William James, the philosopher, once said. Creative, constructive citizenship supplies the ideal opportunity to attain that goal.

Active participation by thought and deed in improving government, political action, community cooperation—these are the elements in constructive citizenship. It calls for understanding, for judgment, for patience, often for long hours of work with little immediate reward, and sometimes for great courage; but the ultimate results are good for everyone, because they contribute to making the world a better place in which to live. The older man or woman is in an excellent position to engage in politics in this mature way—a way Dr. Harry Overstreet describes as "trying to match laws to ideals, tinkering the social mechanism back into running order when it has broken down, making one social invention after another, dedicating himself to causes larger than those of his own self-interest, bridging partisan gaps and working for the common good."

The middle-aged man and woman have the great advantage of time to study civic problems and the causes behind them. They can be more judicial, more altruistic in their approach than can persons tied to immediate economic gains or losses related to governmental and community affairs. Since judgment and reasoning ability reach their peak latest of all the abilities of men, it makes considerable sense, while younger people are producing and reproducing, for older people to govern for the welfare of all society. "Intelligence and reflection and judgment reside in old men, and if there had been none of them, no state could exist at all," said that great Roman, Cicero, some twenty centuries ago. "Old age, especially an honored old age, has so great authority that this is of more value than all the pleasures of youth."

Today's attitude toward older people in positions of governmental or civic importance is unfortunately too seldom one of honor and too often one of skepticism. In any discussion of the subject, there is almost always at least one person who will say, "But people past forty are fuddy-duddies, stick-in-the-muds. They are blindly conservative. They would push back the clock."

Blindly Conservative?

The facts do not support this gloomy verdict. The widely-held idea that older people are, just by the mere fact of aging, rigidly conservative, unwilling to consider the value of new ideas, is quite wrong and clearly does not form a valid reason for keeping older people out of active roles of citizenship. What is confused with "blind conservatism" is often simply the working of the healthy skepticism that comes with experience. A middle-aged man who learned in his youth that snake oil, whether medical or political, will not cure all the world's ills, will resist buying a familiar-looking liquid even though the bottle is now labeled "Vita-Rich Super-Strength Reptilian Oleagum." His refusal to buy does not necessarily mean that he is an old moss-back, unwilling to consider new remedies.

It is that basically sensible attitude of the snake-oil doubter which seems regularly to be confused with unreasoning conservatism, even by such careful and scholarly evaluators as Professor Stouffer in his book on *Communism, Conformity, and Civil Liberties.* As Dr. Edward J. Stieglitz has reported, character tends to become somewhat fixed in old age, but simply through intensification of the personality of youth. The generous youth may become an over-generous older man. The stingy may turn into obvious misers. But the tolerant will become increasingly tolerant and understanding. An older person, unless given a really convincing reason to behave otherwise, will resist changes that go counter to his beliefs or his preferences; but, since those attitudes will be liberal in one man and conservative in the next, this particular habit of applying the brakes is balanced off in any broad group of older people.

The views of an elderly Thomas Jefferson would hardly be called conservative, at least in the political thinking of 1956. A look at the Supreme Court of today, made of men past middle life, will show not a group of conservatives or liberals but of men of all shades of opinion. The late Associate Justice Oliver Wendell Holmes was liberal in his attitudes and judicial opinions when he was in his eighties;

but he had been like-minded, though apparently less intensely, when he was in his thirties. Henry Clay, the great American statesman, was a high-spirited progressive at seventy-five. And the late Senator George Norris was certainly a fighting liberal even in his last year of life. Good biographies of a number of men who lived long lives will not reveal a majority who turned extremely conservative in later life.

Social Courage

When the history of the current decade is written, it will be discovered that a great deal of the social courage that has pushed back forces of knownothingism and reaction has been shown by older men and women. They have sometimes worked quietly and behind the scenes, but without them the country might have been overrun by the same type of mentality that breeds communist or fascist dictatorship. For in a day of growing conformity, of fear of being "different," of easily-spread charges of subversion awaiting anyone who calls for social innovation, men and women in their high-earning years, their parental years, are hesitant to advance new ideas or to assert themselves about old and established ideas that may be temporarily out of favor. Even when his conscience says that a man should take the unpopular side in some civic dispute or on some national political question, he holds back—for fear of meeting with disfavor, of even losing his job, and perhaps being blacklisted.

The continuance of a vigorous, free nation, growing in social maturity, requires dissent and differences of opinion honestly advanced. There must be no surrender to the totalitarian habit of automatically considering any opposition to majority ideas as traitorous.

Reaffirming American Faith

What does this faith mean for the older citizen? It means a God-given opportunity to stand up and be counted, to help preserve sanity and the true Americanism that honors the rights and duties expressed in the Constitution and its Bill of Rights and in the Declaration of Independence. It means remembering and acting upon the wise words of men who started this nation on its great adventure. It recalls the words of Thomas Jefferson as he took over the Presidency in 1801: "All . . . will bear in mind the sacred principle that, though the will of the majority is in all cases to prevail, that will to be rightful must be reasonable; that the minority possess their equal rights, which equal law must protect, and to violate would be oppression. Let us then, fellow citizens, unite with one heart and one mind. Let us restore to social intercourse that harmony and affection without which liberty and even life itself are but dreary things. And let us reflect that, having banished from our land that religious intolerance under which mankind so long bled and suffered, we have yet gained little if we countenance a political intolerance as despotic, as wicked and capable of as bitter and bloody persecutions." He also reminded his hearers that "every difference of opinion is not a difference of principle" and that if there were citizens strongly opposed to the government, other Americans should "let them stand undisturbed as monuments of the safety with which error of opinion may be tolerated where reason is left free to combat it . . ."

As free men, opposed to all totalitarian doctrines, Americans today are as nearly unanimous as any national population could be in their absolute opposition to communism, and this is as it should be. But there are unscrupulus individuals, in politics and out, who have taken advantage of this fact and use the word "communist" to blight anything or anyone they may oppose. The man who thus loudly proclaims himself "anti-communist" while using near-communist methods to fight his opponents, and who maliciously applies the communist label to anyone he dislikes, should be stopped in his tracks and exposed for what he is: more anti-American than anti-communist.

How to Help

But what can the middle-aged citizen do to exercise his influence? Except through group action, to be discussed later herein, there may be very few opportunities for the older person to make his views felt on a national question; but there will almost always be ways to apply American principles to local situations. It can be done by arguing against the man or group that tries to keep all "controversial" discussions out of public halls; that tries to prevent students from reading books that present *both* sides of current public questions; that likes to apply a label of "subversive" or even "communist" to a

legal but unpopular minority group that wants to foster public housing or reroute an express highway, or talks against racial segrega-
tion. It can be done by speaking up for fair play, due process of law,
and the right to be heard, even for people and causes heartily dis-
liked. Sometimes the action may be nothing more than speaking
quietly to a friend on a committee controlling programs in some
auditorium; or writing a letter to a newspaper; or voting in a
group meeting. Much will depend on the strategy and tactics used
and the courage to carry out a plan.

It is highly improbable that, even with the great increase in the
number of old people that is anticipated, the United States will
ever become a gerontocracy—a society ruled exclusively by the old.
The tradition that this is a young man's country will die very hard
indeed. But the "generational dialectic"—the running conversation
or disputation between the young and the old that is basic to human
life—will in any case go forward. If the older citizens allow themselves to be crowded off the public stage, their contribution to the
conversation will be ineffective; and they will suffer frustration, a
crippling sense of defeat, and exhibit a tendency to impotent
acrimony about the way things are going. In no sense do they de-
serve such a fate, as is argued here; but it is very apt to come upon
them if they themselves do not take action to avoid it—not by organizing old folks' pressure groups but by deliberately seeking
effective roles as discussants and actors in the affairs of their communities and the nation.

Joining Civic Activity Groups

Individual action is often less effective than that of a group. Thus,
most persons who want to be active citizens will wish to join at
least one organization the principles of which seem most in accord
with their views. And if there is an important issue that needs public airing or citizen action, and no organization exists which has
such special interest, sometimes the citizen will wish to help form
a committee or association to carry on the necessary work.

"The pro-social voluntary association in America is our great un-
sung laboratory for the making of citizens," Dr. Overstreet has written. "It is the means—in many cases the only means—whereby the
average citizen is encouraged to feel other than helpless about the

affairs of his society. Whether the association is local, national, or international; and whether it works to promote child welfare, community recreation, aid to the needy, public health, adult education, inter-faith understanding, international understanding, or racial justice; it is made up of people of different party affiliations, different creeds, different nationalities, often different races and different economic classes.

"In such an association, a readiness for mutual understanding is encouraged and rewarded with approval; a carrying over of fixed partisanship and prejudice is discouraged. In it, therefore, men and women of good will have the blessed chance to care about something that relates to the common welfare; to do so in the company of people who have been permitted to take off their artificial labels of party and class; and to achieve actual results that both change society, in some measure, and build their citizenship-confidence, so that they can bring about further change when it is needed."

Clara Barton's Example

In case there are those who have the idea that work in a civic activity is for the young, or at least not for anyone past fifty or sixty, it is well to mention the story of Clara Barton, who founded the American Red Cross when she was sixty-one and served in that organization for twenty-two years before resigning, at eighty-three, over a difference of opinion. She went on to found another association of civic importance, and served as its president until she was ninety-one. Another remarkable woman, Lillien Martin, after enforced reirement from her teaching position, went out to found a child guidance clinic; and then, still later, at seventy established the Old Age Counseling Center in San Francisco, actively directing it until her death at ninety-seven. The late Richard Welling, well into his eighties, continued the active chairmanship of the National Self-Government Committee, concerned with stimulating better student self-government in schools. Lawyer Welling also was an active force in the progressive, non-partisan City Club of New York, which constantly promotes better government in the city and the state of New York.

The list is long, even in the prevailing atmosphere of over-reliance on youth. And the list will be much longer as more people discover the worthwhile possibilities of devoting the later years to constructive citizenship.

Breaking Down Loneliness

In their civic activity, older men and women can do much to revive in any community or neighborhood the characteristics that were so desirable in the old-time American small town: freedom, friendliness, fullness of human association. At the same time, they will be breaking down barriers of loneliness and the unmerited sense of uselessness so often felt by older members of the community.

The challenge of creative citizenship is a great one, and the senior citizen can approach it with a firm sense of his age-mellowed understanding of human relations, the essential ingredient in all governmental and civic activity. There is unlimited demand for constructive citizenship—from improving schools to getting better people elected to city and county offices; from supporting better roads to giving understanding support to the peace-making efforts of the United Nations. Above all, there is the deeply important daily battle to preserve the liberties that have kept these United States a beacon for free men throughout the world for more than one hundred fifty years.

Time Out for Reflection

You, perhaps, and certainly many of your friends and neighbors, are giving time to one or more community activities. What are

—the satisfactions in such activity?
—the problems arising from such activity?
—the channels for getting others into such activity?

Are there certain kinds of community problem—delinquency, schools, recreation, adult education, slum clearance, etc.—that older people can help with better than younger adults? Should some of them be left to the younger adult group? Why?

Stouffer's *Communism, Conformity, and Civil Liberties* (see suggested readings at the end of this chapter) gives evidence that older people are more conservative, more intolerant, than younger people. Do you think this is true among your own acquaintance? Is it true of you? What are the implications for the participation of older people in civic and community affairs?

The late Henry L. Mencken left these sentences among his notes: "The average man never really thinks, from end to end of his life. The mental activity of such people is only a mouthing of clichés. What they mistake for thought is simply repetition of what they have heard. My guess is that well over 80 percent of the human race goes through life without ever having a single original thought. Whenever a new one appears, the average man shows sign of dismay and resentment."*

How do you react to Mencken's statements? Do they annoy you? To what extent do you think Mencken exaggerated?

---

* Quoted from *Minority Report, The Notebooks of H. L. Mencken*, © 1956, by permission of the publisher, Alfred A. Knopf, Inc.

READINGS   CHAPTER 7

Ten Years of Leisure!
Edmund Quincy (1808-1877)

THE TEN YEARS of Mr. Quincy's life from 1813 to 1823 were years of comparative leisure. Though he was a member of the General Court for the chief of the time, his duties in that capacity were confined to a few months of the year, and were not of a very engrossing nature. In 1815, after the declaration of peace, he removed from Oliver Street, and took a lease of a house in Summer Street, one of the handsomest and most commodious in Boston, with ample stableroom and every convenience that was then thought essential to a gentleman's town residence. Here the winters were spent. The summers, which were always lengthened out at both ends as much as possible, were passed at Quincy. After leaving Congress, he took the management of the farm into his own hands. He was an enthusiast in whatever he undertook, and he entered into farming with all the zeal of his ardent temperament. His agricultural experience, like that of most gentleman farmers, was rather profitable to others than to himself. He was full of experiments, which, though not eminently successful as to the lucre of gain, were of great value to the farming interests of his neighborhood and of the State. He brought improved implements to the notice of the unbelieving farmers round about. He set an example in the matter of root culture, and of the succession of crops, which redounded to the general benefit, if not to his own personal advantage. And latterly he introduced the custom of soiling or stall-feeding of milch cows. . . .

One of his favorite schemes was the substitution of hawthorn hedges for the old-fashioned rail-fence of New England. They kept themselves in repair, he would say, and so saved the expense of renewing the fences of dead wood, which was a material item in the cost of farming. At one time his whole farm was fenced only with this verdurous wall, and the system worked exceeding well as long as the cattle were kept in the stalls. But when, in 1823, he was obliged to give up the supervision of his paternal acres for that of the city of Boston, and the tenant to whom he let them insisted on pasturing his cows, the hedges were found not to be equal to the occasion. A hedge might be sufficient to restrain the wanderings of the civilized cattle of England, which had been accustomed to be led into fat pastures for generations; but it was otherwise with the hardy kine of New Hampshire and Vermont, whence the herds of the lowland country were chiefly recruited, which, brought up to browse in the woods and on the mountains, made little account of any obstacle that offered itself in the shape of green leaves and twigs. The thorns they seemed to regard as an appetizing condiment,—a kind of *sauce piquante,*—thrown in to increase the pleasure of the meal. So, in the end, rail fences had to be provided to protect the hedges from the beasts. However, his experiment settled to the hedge question as far as New England was concerned. . . .

So it fell out with my father's farming as it is apt to do with that of gentlemen who are not able or willing to give themselves entirely to the minute economies of the business, and are obliged to leave to others the small details, on a strict attention to which the prosperity of farming, as of every other calling, depends. It gave him much amusement, but cost him much money,—more than it was at all convenient to him to lose. The only profitable manufacture connected with his farm was one of salt, for which he established works along the length of his property on the sea-shore, and which made remunerative returns as long as the duty on salt was retained. His salt was always in particular request with the Cape Ann fishermen for curing their fish. But it was a pleasant life that he and his family led during those summers. The house was always filled with company. He delighted in exercising hospitality, and there was scarcely a Saturday in the year, in town or country, that was not solemnized by a regular dinner-party. Every afternoon in summer a succession of visitors thronged the house. In those days the universal summer dispersion of the well-to-do inhabitants of the town had not set in. Very few of the Boston gentlemen had country-seats, and the custom of exchanging their roomy and comfortable town houses for the narrow hospitalities of Saratoga and Ballston, then almost the only places of summer resort, was far from general. Sea-bathing was an undiscovered luxury, and the mountains had not yet been invented. Tours were slow, tedious, and expensive, and a visit to Niagara was more of an event in life then than one to the second cataract of the Nile is now.

People stayed at home in their pleasant garden-houses, and gave summer parties to each other and to the visitors from the South and from Europe, who were always established in greater or less force in Boston during the hot months. The excursions which filled up the long afternoons left on their hands by the early dinner-hour of fifty years since often took the direction of Quincy. The neighborhood of Ex-President John Adams undoubtedly increased the number of these pleasant visitors, as no stranger of condition ever came to Boston without seeking an introduction to so celebrated a public man, and very few returned to town without taking my father's house by the way. His own personal celebrity, however, and the pleasantness of his home and domestic circle, were attractive enough in themselves, without that additional inducement, to secure a continual round of company. He had his books mainly at Quincy, and the exigencies of a growing family made it necessary to provide a small building apart from the main house, where he kept his library, and where he spent the chief of his time when at home, and not engaged in looking after his laborers or in the society of his visitors. His library was large for that day, and considerable even for this, and contained a very competent collection of the classics, and of the English and French authors. His journal, which he kept with tolerable regularity during portions of these years, bears testimony to the regularity of his literary industry and the variety of his reading. Law, ethics, Cicero, Lord Bacon, Madame de Staël, Colonial history, especially the part relating to the religious establishment, and the old English divines, made up a portion of his multifarious reading, often digested, analyzed, and commented upon. . . .

On the 1st of May, 1823, he was inaugurated as the second Mayor of Boston, in Faneuil Hall, and entered at once upon the discharge of his new duties with characteristic activity and zeal. During the mayoralty of his predecessor, the administration of the affairs of the city had not differed materially from that of the town it had superseded. Mr. Phillips was a man of excellent abilities, sound judgment, and sterling integrity. He retained his seat in the State Senate and his place as its President, and performed the duties of his civic office in the spirit and after the fashion of a faithful chairman of the Selectmen under the town government. Mr. Phillips was strictly my father's contemporary, and perhaps his most intimate and valued friend from boyhood. His death, which occurred very suddenly in June, 1823, was severely felt and deeply deplored by my father, as the heaviest loss he had met with since that of his mother. Mr. Phillips had been in the public service of Massachusetts, in one station or another, for almost the whole of his mature life, and the State had no more trusted and respected citizen. He will be known, however, to the present generation, and hereafter, chiefly as the father of his celebrated son, Mr. Wendell Phillips.

Mr. Quincy's first step towards the establishment of a more vigorous administration of affairs was to claim the privilege of doing the chief of the work himself. He made himself chairman of all the committees of the Board of Aldermen, and took the laboring oar into his own hand. The opposition of the Overseers of the Poor to the removal of the paupers from the almshouse in Boston, the condition of which had grown to be absolutely disgraceful to the city, prevented the completion of that favorite measure of his until 1825, when it was finally effected. The evils attendant on the promiscuous mingling of the honest poor with rogues and vagabonds were mitigated by the establishment of the first House of Correction, properly so called, in Boston, during the first year of his mayoralty. A building in the jailyard was used at first for this purpose, but the establishment was afterwards removed to South Boston, near the House of Industry. The separation, more important yet, of the young convicts from the old in places of penal restraint, led to the establishment of a House of Reformation for Juvenile Offenders, the results of which, both direct, in the large proportion of young persons who were saved to society by its means, and indirect, by the encouragement which its successful experiment has given to the system elsewhere, have been of the happiest nature. These institutions were long regarded as models in their several kinds, and Mr. Quincy always looked upon them with peculiar satisfaction as being largely creations of his own. The House of Reformation for Juvenile Offenders excited the particular admiration of Messrs. Beaumont and de Tocqueville, when they visited Boston in the course of the inquiries with which they were charged by the French government. They expressed an earnest wish that such an institution could be established in France; "but," M. de Tocqueville added, "it would be essential to its success that Boston should lend to it the first superintendent and organizer of her own institution,"—the Rev. Eleazar M. P. Wells, D.D., whose life has been one long service of the unfortunate and suffering classes.

The internal police of the city was another matter which called for the anxious attention of the new Mayor. The maintenance of order, the abatement of nuisances, the protection of the public health, the suppression of impudent vice, and the swift and sure overtaking of crime, devolved upon him, and with no sufficient force to fulfil these demands of his office. The policing of cities was very imperfectly understood in this country, or in England, until the reform initiated by Sir Robert Peel. Mr. Quincy had to work with such instruments as law and custom afforded him, and he used them to the best advantage. The entire police force then consisted of a constabulary twenty-four strong, and a body of eighty night-watchmen, of whom not more than eighteen were on duty at the same time! It seems hardly credible that a city of between fifty and sixty thousand inhabitants could have been kept in peace and safety by so small a force, and I apprehend that it was without a parallel in this country or in Europe. . . .

Still, quiet and well-ordered as Boston was, in general, there was one disgraceful district which had set at defiance for years the attempts of the town authorities to reduce it to order. Infamous houses were openly maintained, the resort of the worst part of the population. Murders had notoriously been committed there, and it was believed that by no means all had been brought to light. The head of the old town police told Mr. Quincy that this nuisance could not be abated without a military force. No man's life would be safe that should attempt it. Mr. Quincy asked him if vice and villainy were too strong for the police; to which he replied: "I think so. At least, it has long been so." "There shall be at least an attempt to execute the laws," said the Mayor; and he proceeded to make it. On examining the terms of the City Charter, he found that he had not the powers under it necessary for a summary suppression of this nest of vice and villainy, so he was obliged to act only in his capacity of a Justice of the Peace throughout the Commonwealth. His first step was to issue a warrant for the arrest of the fiddlers who inspired the orgies of the dance-houses, under an old Provincial statute never repealed, aimed at those troublers of the nightwatches; and his next, to take away the licenses of all the tippling-shops and bar-rooms in the region round about. Deprived at once of music and of drink, the enemy succumbed to the authority of law without resistance. . . .

Another department of urgent importance to the city, which it was Mr. Quincy's good fortune to put upon a better footing than ever before, was the Fire Department. This existed in a very primitive form when he came into office. Engines were provided by the town, manned by voluntary companies, and officered by fire-wards elected by the people. The engines were of small power and at a fire depended entirely for their supply of water upon fire-buckets passed along lines of volunteer spectators reaching to the nearest pump. . . .

It was not without difficulty that the necessary powers for a reorganization of the department were obtained from the Legislature, and, when obtained, the inhabitants, whose consent was to be first had, sanctioned the change by a majority of only about a hundred. The system thus introduced, though far enough from the admirable one which now exists, soon commended itself to the entire community by the greater sense of security which it inspired, of which the fact that the insurance companies at once, of their own accord, reduced their rates by twenty per cent, was a satisfactory proof.

The circumstance of the greatest local interest in Mr. Quincy's municipal administration was the building of the Faneuil Hall Market-house. The conveniences for the provisioning of the city were at that time of a very limited description, and one of the first considerations which occurred to him after entering on his office was, how these could be enlarged and improved without great expense to the city. From first to last he encountered opposition in every shape,—of the selfish interests of the property-holders whom it was necessary to buy out, of the parties whose vested interests in the old state of things were endangered, of demagogues who were ready to lay hold of any occasion of persuading the people that they were in danger of ruin, and of cautious citizens who dreaded the creation of an unmanageable city debt. I have not the space, nor would it be generally interesting at this day, to trace the whole progress of this remarkable transaction; and I cannot state the result better or more compactly than he has done it himself in his Municipal History of Boston. "A granite market-house, two stories high, five hundred and thirty-five feet long, fifty feet wide, covering twenty-seven thousand feet of land, was erected at the cost of one hundred and fifty thousand dollars. Six new streets were opened, and a seventh greatly enlarged, including one hundred and sixty-seven thousand feet of land; and flats, docks, and wharf-rights obtained of the extent of one hundred and forty-two thousand square feet. All this was accomplished in the centre of a populous city, not only without any tax, debt, or burden upon its pecuniary resources, but with large permanent additions to its real and productive property." The land made by filling up the dock on a part of which the Market-house stands sold for enough to pay the whole expense of the operation, while the taxable property of the city was increased by the value of the warehouses built upon it. . . .

It is hardly necessary to say that Mr. Quincy gave great attention to the condition and improvement of the public schools, and I believe they had never been in a better state than they were during his official term. The only innovation which was attempted in his time upon the old customs of the town was an experimental High School for girls, which had a brief trial of a year or two, and was then abandoned. . . .

The Middle-Aged Woman
in Contemporary Society

Agnes E. Meyer (1887-   )

SOCIAL PROBLEMS ARE my daily diet. But I confess that I who was a middle-aged woman many, many years ago, never realized at the time that I was a problem. We worry about delinquent youth and neglected old age. Must we now also worry about the middle-aged woman? Then the middle-aged man is the only person left in our society who isn't a problem, unless, of course, he is married to one of these problematical middle-aged women. . . .

Our society today is so complex that most women—and men, too, for that matter—do not know where their efforts for its simplification could be applied. The technological revolution with its rapid urbanization and other social dislocations has been hard enough upon men, but it has disrupted the lives of women far more drastically. Accelerated by wars both hot and cold, this revolution has shattered the old social structure, undermined the family, and weakened traditional moral standards. At the same time economic forces have drawn some twenty million women into the labor market and the professions. Most women work of necessity, many because they are especially talented. But the force of our economic maelstrom is such that few people can resist being drawn into it. It has now come to the point where many married women work and neglect their children because they feel they must have a paid job in order to hold the respect of the community. As a result, homemaking has become depreciated. It is one thing if women work because they must help support the family and other dependents or because they have a special contribution to make to society. It is quite another thing—it is socially undesirable—if society forces the mother to take a job in order that she may respect herself and gain the respect of others. No wonder that the average stay-at-home housewife is confused. She is no longer sure what society expects of her. Women have gained an unparalleled freedom in American only to sacrifice it to the rat race for success—and success in our country, alas, means financial success.

There are other bitter heritages with which the middle-aged woman has to contend. The feminist influence taught women to see themselves as rivals of men rather than as partners of a common endeavor, whether on the job or in the home. I concede that the early feminists had so many legal, political, and economic disadvantages to combat, and most males were so stupid in their opposition to progress in these areas, that hostility between the sexes was difficult to avoid. As a result, we have many worried, restless, immature females who complain bitterly that there are not enough women in the United Nations, the government, and diplomacy. Others actually rebel against the inescapable fact that they are women. Simone de Beauvoir's book *"The Second Sex"* is the most brilliant and sinister example of this pathological state of mind. Her whole position is summed up in her quotation from another sickly personality, the misogynist Kierkegaard, who said: "What a misfortune to be a woman! And yet the worst misfortune is not to understand what a misfortune it is."

Dangerous as this dissatisfaction with their own womanhood may be to women's psychology, it is not more insidious than the reaction now in full swing which tempts women to be nothing but females. The preoccupation with glamor so prevalent in America today is the pernicious result. No self-respecting woman—or man for that matter—should neglect outward appearances; but too great a preoccupation with it is a sign of a superficial attitude toward life. I shall never forget a luncheon I attended some years ago in Washington in honor of Gabrielle Mistral, the distinguished Chilean poetess, who won the Nobel Prize in 1946 and Lisa Meitner, the famous physicist, who made valuable contributions to the development of the atom bomb. The faces of these two great women, worn by the furrows of deep thought and powerful character, were a shocking contrast to the surface beauty but robotlike similarity of the American women. The two foreigners had individuality which had ripened through experience, whereas the Americans looked like mass-production jobs just off the assembly line. The contrast was unforgettable. It illustrated vividly the overemphasis among our women on what is called sex-appeal. I thought of George Meredith's line in "Modern Love": "We are betrayed by what is false within."

Yet our women have long had the greatest freedom to lead courageous, individualistic lives, for our institutions have been friendlier to them than those of any other nation. But many lack the self-discipline needed to ration that most precious of all things, time. "To affect the quality of the day," said Thoreau, "that is the highest of arts." Instead of cultivating this art, too many women fritter away their days by allowing every petty detail to distract them. Mrs. Lindbergh, in her charming prose poem *"Gift from the Sea"* rightly deplores what she calls the *Zerissenheit*, the dismemberment of the average housewife's life. Psychologists will tell you that many of them clutter up their lives with trivialities, that they actually welcome distraction because they lack clear-cut, worthwhile objectives and therefore do not develop the will-power to organize their time and use their leisure for more continuity of thought and action. Much of this lack of discipline results, I believe, from the attitude toward marriage entertained by many American women. When they get their man they feel the goal of life has been achieved and renounce further ambitions for self-development. As a result, the sheer ignorance of American women is appalling. In our country, where women have had the same opportunities for education as men, this is inexcusable. George Gallup has given me figures which prove that American men are not too well informed on current events, but the record of the women in every test is far lower. Here are the percentages of correct answers to simple questions:

	Correct	
	Men	Women
How many U. S. Senators are there from your state?	56%	41%
How many states will elect members of the U. S. House of Representatives this fall (1954)?	15%	8%
What is the population of the United States?	50%	23%
Will you tell me who Anthony Eden is?	50%	39%
Will you tell me where the Suez Canal is?	54%	32%
What do the letters NATO stand for?	27%	15%
Who is head of the Chinese Nationalists?	60%	42%

These are but a few of Dr. Gallup's surveys which indicate that too many women after leaving school let their minds go to sleep. Today ignorance of the elementary facts of political life, geography and international problems is a danger to our embattled nation. The young married women as well as their middle-aged sisters should be encouraged to look upon life as a perpetual opportunity for self-development. Let them take heart from another statement of Thoreau: "I know of no more encouraging fact than the unquestionable ability of man to elevate his life by a conscious endeavor." Assuredly one of the greatest crimes any human being can commit is not to develop his or her potentialities to the utmost.

Daily life, itself, could become the finest source of education for the middle-aged woman if she had a vision of the possibilities for constructive action that lie at her very doorstep. For the old American community with its intimacy and traditional loyalties, in which children grew up feeling themselves to be individuals, has been shattered and a new social order has not yet come into being. People of all ages now feel so lost that they long consciously and unconsciously for the close relationships of simpler days when it was still possible to enjoy an emotional sharing of ideas, and to live a life of warmth and close association with family, neighbors and friends.

Our prime need today is the restoration of smaller neighborhood groups in our vast urban congeries,—an integrated, orderly community in which the family and the individual can lead secure, disciplined, happy lives. We must apply our immense resources of social and scientific knowledge to create a social structure in which people can readily find assistance in times of trouble as well as avenues of service to the general welfare.

How do we create order? This is a vast topic, which occupies the minds of all thoughtful professional and lay leaders in our most progressive cities and counties. I have just come from Buffalo, where an exemplary beginning has been made to coordinate the work of the public schools, the public and private child welfare and family agencies, the juvenile court, the youth squad of the police department, the church groups, in fact, the city's whole plethora of social organizations, not merely to check delinquency but to prevent it. Buffalo is trying to create a city atmosphere in which children can grow up to become whole and wholesome personalities. This is the kind of over-all, intelligent planning needed, if we are going to catch up with social problems that now grow by leaps and bounds because we try to solve them in piecemeal fashion instead of keeping our attention on planned, coordinated methods of achieving the good life.

Now what can the average American housewife do to help in such a rather complicated endeavor? This question immediately suggests that there is no such thing as *the* middle-aged woman. They are as diverse in social, economic, and educational background as any other human category. But every woman, whatever her training and status, can make some contribution to the improvement of community living.

Yet we should be able to reach the hearts of most women if we appeal to their maternal instincts and ask them to extend the love they have for their own children to all children who are in need. Although there are women too egotistical to escape from the prison house of the self, most American women could be galvanized into action by this emotional approach, if they knew how to translate their motherly impulses into constructive outlets. We have just found this out in Washington. The *Washington Post and Times Herald* recently published an admirable series of articles on the disgraceful conditions in the city's Receiving Home. Immediately, this newspaper was flooded with letters and telephone messages from women asking: "What can we do to help?" So numerous were these requests, that the District Welfare Department and the United Community Services were obliged to appoint a trained social worker to screen the avalanche of volunteer offers in order to make the best possible use of them.

Guidance is so essential to the average woman who does not know how the wheels of local government go round, that a service center is needed in every big community as a link between the volunteer and the public or private welfare agencies. It would not only help the volunteer put her abilities to the most effective use; it would also save the person or family in need much distress by advising them without loss of time where to go amongst our enormous tangle of welfare agencies for the kind of help they need. After the war we had such community service centers for the veteran. Unfortunately, we dismantled them because we failed to realize that guidance in our complex social structure is just as necessary for the civilian. In Great Britain these agencies were continued. Called Citizens Advice Bureaus, they have become one of the most useful supplements to democratic government. Every such Advice Bureau has at least one professional woman worker. The rest are volunteers. The general inquiries they receive are about one million annually. For more detailed description of their use and organization I refer you to my book entitled *"Out of These Roots."*

One crying need in every community is for more foster homes for dependent children. If we are ever going to get enough of them, this service to children must be recognized as the important and merciful function it is in a democratic society. If a few middle-aged women with some means and empty rooms who have status in their communities would volunteer for this vital, humane service, foster care would soon be dignified and gain a prestige in every community that would tempt other women to compete for foster children as many of them now compete for the adoption of children.

Women who prefer executive work to personal service should take a good look at the frightful and usually overcrowded children's institutions, especially the public ones that are a shame to our American life. I was in one such home for dependent children in my own city of Washington recently from which these unfortunate youngsters, if nobody adopts them, are graduated to the Training School at twelve years of age and marked as criminals for life through no fault of their own. How can any sensitive woman sleep peacefully at night, while these crimes against helpless little children are a commonplace throughout our country?

Merely the lack of adequate recreation facilities for teen-agers who have outgrown the Boy or Girl Scouts and are too young to go to work is another major problem to which our middle-aged women should devote themselves in every American town or city. We have prolonged adolescence without creating a definite role and status in our society for these formative years. Unless these youngsters have an exceptionally stable home, they live in a social vacuum without responsibility commensurate with their growing capacities and their human need to be useful. So they naturally form gangs to fill the desire for close relationships, for belonging; and the gangs fight each other or engage in some other form of hell-raising because they have nothing else to do. . . .

Now I concede that voluntary work, whether in social work or education, has been made difficult because many professionals are impatient with the layman. But necessity is changing this psychology, especially among the educators who are confronted by the need for popular support to get the big appropriations they now need. The teachers are also learning to use lay helpers to take charge of study periods, to help with clerical work, and a dozen other chores that can just as well be done by any intelligent person. We should also urge any middle-aged woman who has been trained as a teacher, social worker or in any other profession to take refresher courses and get back on the job. Wayne University's College of Education has taken the lead in carrying an intensified course in training college-educated mothers to become provisional teachers by carrying their courses into local communities. This example has been followed up in San Diego, San Francisco, the University of Southern California, Claremont College, Ohio University and others. Social-work schools might well follow the same pattern. For there isn't a community in the country that does not suffer from a shortage of trained personnel.

We must break down the prejudice so prevalent in our country against the employment of older people. At the same time, the middle-aged woman must not yield to the powerful economic pressures of our industrial society, which lead many of them to think that only the paid job is respected. The greatest, the most lasting contributions to our civilization have been the result of voluntary effort of free men and women. Our nation was founded by the courageous voluntarism of its earliest settlers. The Declaration of Independence and the Constitution are among the greatest monuments in the history of mankind to the moral force that is engendered when enlightened men act together for the preservation of freedom and human rights. Since these heroic beginnings, voluntary action has remained the well-spring of the nation's political, economic, educational and social progress. It made possible democratic reforms which in many other nations came about only through violence. At a moment when this great force of voluntarism is needed as never before, it has been impoverished in our country by the so-called "experts" who are jealous of their status, by materialists who think that the size of a person's pay check is the measure of his human worth, and more recently by demagogues who fear the freedom of the mind and freedom of action.

I am convinced that unless the growing power of the state is balanced by the growing power of local initiative, freedom in the long run cannot be preserved in our country. We find fewer and fewer capable officials in the Federal government because the training ground of great political leaders has always been the grass-roots. Instead of complaining that we haven't enough women in high places, women must now get to work and perform the humdrum tasks of local politics, proving that they can get out the vote, that they know how the machinery of politics functions in the community, the country and the state, if they wish to develop the knowledge and the power essential to constructive political leadership.

The political inertia that was so marked in recent elections is shameful. Here is one of the greatest opportunities for the middle-aged women who have no jobs, for they have the leisure for active participation in local politics. Nor must they be discouraged by the fact that they are tied to the home and cannot accept State or Federal positions. If all our counties, cities and villages were efficiently and honestly governed, the Federal and State governments could not usurp the powers which do not properly belong to them. Thus local government is the most important field for political activity. If local leadership continues to abdicate its responsibilities, it is only natural that Federal leadership will try to fill the gap.

It is a hopeful sign that the women's organizations like the League of Women Voters, the Federation of Business and Professional Women, and the American Association of University Women are beginning to take a more active part in local and State politics.

Let me sum up why I think the middle-aged woman should look upon her environment with fresh eyes and a new vision of her opportunities and responsibilities. The family is the foundation upon which our whole social organization rests. Having brought up her own children, she must hold the three generations together no matter how far apart they may live. The grandchildren will never become delinquents if they feel that they must be a worthy part of the ongoing generations. The old people will not wander around like lost souls in a Dantesque hell, if they have the affection and respect of their descendants. But there are, alas, in every community, children and old people who have no families, for whom friendly human relationships must be created. The unoccupied middle-aged woman must therefore extend her sense of family and her instinct for good housekeeping to the whole community. But I cannot put too much emphasis on the fact that the women who wish to volunteer for public service must know where they can go for advice and guidance that will make their contributions count. When the *Washington Post and Times Herald* received its flood of requests for voluntary service, it published a long series of the many ways in which the volunteer can help. Every local newspaper could do this, provided it could also tell the volunteer exactly where to go for expert advice on the best use of her abilities. Only by such guidance, whether in a service center, the public school or existing welfare agencies, can we reawaken widespread interest in community reorganization and communitywide planning that will be emotionally, intellectually and continuously sustained. Then the community will come to life as a place that all Americans can regard, as we older people regarded the cities and villages in which we grew up, as their home town in the deepest sense of the word.

In conclusion, I should like to remind all women of the most penetrating advice given by that great statesman, Sir Winston Churchill, to an American government official: "Never allow democracy to appear impotent." In this period when a powerful wave of social reaction is sweeping the country, we are in danger of doing just that. Yet if we are to save civilization from destruction, the American people must prove to themselves and to the whole world that democracy is sincere in its demands for equal opportunity for all mankind. At no time, therefore, has it been more imperative that all women—but especially those with the most leisure—should devote themselves to eliminating the many injustices of our society. The wide gaps that still exist between our democratic ideals and the sordid realities need not be discouraging if we see our shortcomings as a spur to greater effort.

American women must now use adversity to sharpen their intelligence and clarify their vision of woman's responsibility for the preservation of the highest human values, for woman is the natural guardian of life's continuity, of its human relationships, its cultural quality, its moral content and social solidarity. We need not fear the power of the Communist appeal, if American women accept the task of reminding our country and the world that our republic is not devoted to mere creature comforts but strives with intelligent and unfaltering zeal toward an ever-higher concept of man's destiny. If it is difficult to carry out the high role of woman in our modern society, it is also a great honor to be a woman in this critical historical period. Now that destruction threatens us from within and without, woman must again recognize her responsibility to society as the fundamental conservative and vital one that it always has been. For woman as mother, not merely of her own children but of all childhood, represents the focal point of time and eternity, and the perpetual triumph of nurture over nature, of freedom over servitude, and of life over death.

Adequate Adult Education

(Excepts from recommendations for the President's Committee on Education Beyond the High School, prepared by a group of graduate students at the University of Chicago.)

IT IS IMPERATIVE in our growing, changing, democratic society that adults continue learning. Four persistent and widespread conditions make continuing education for all adults essential.

Adult education represents a necessary second chance for millions of men and women in our country who have had no opportunity to complete a minimal education.

Adult education provides an opportunity to acquire the many skills and understandings that cannot be learned in childhood.

Adult education can help develop new interests which are basic to self-fulfillment.

In our complex world adults need to learn the skills and develop understandings to cope with new social and economic problems.

We have not yet made adequate educational provisions for helping our adult population to make up these deficiencies, to meet the requirements of mature adulthood, to satisfy emergent interests, and fulfill the demands of continuous social change. As a consequence, today we are unable to deal adequately with crucial problems that threaten our well-being as individuals and as a nation.

Widespread lack of citizen participation in government and public affairs at every level—in the local community, in the state, and in national and world affairs—is a grave threat to our democratic process. This lack of participation involves more than mere apathy. It suggests a lack of understanding of issues, a lack of ability to make decisions and take appropriate action.

The acute need for an increasing supply of scientifically and technically trained personnel must be satisfied to meet the expanding demands of an age of automation and atomic energy for peace and war.

Increasing longevity is resulting in critical social and economic needs for a large part of our population. There are basic needs in housing, health, employment and recreation for the older adult. A revision of current attitudes and practices in relation to older adults is needed to remove restrictions which now limit the creative energies of this increasing portion of our population.

Growing problems of juvenile delinquency, mental illness, family tensions and divorce make the issue of adequate family and parent education imperative. These conditions are intensified by rapidly expanding urbanization.

Educational limitations that restrict the individual's intellectual, aesthetic, and spiritual growth deprive our society of resources in creativity that it urgently needs.

Through a broad variety of institutions, organizations, voluntary groups and individuals, adult education already is helping adults to manage many of these problems. If adult education is to meet the kinds of demands that are now pressing upon it, additional resources which can only be supplied on a national level are required.

Suggestions for Further Reading

Communism, Conformity, and Civil Liberties, by Samuel A. Stouffer. New York: Doubleday & Company, Inc., 1955.

> An intensive analysis, based on scientific sampling and interviewing, of the extent to which Americans tend to conform to certain patterns of thought and of their attitudes toward communism and toward preservation of democratic freedom. Compares people in different occupational, residential, and sex age groups.

The Heritage of America, Henry Steele Commager and Allan Nevins (eds.). Boston: Little, Brown & Company, Inc., 1951.

> A fresh view of American history, as seen through the eyes of people who were on the scene. The book brings past happenings close and shows where situations in the past were very much like some of those we face today. Gives the reader new perspective and practical ideas for dealing with human situations we all face as active citizens.

The Mature Mind, by Harry A. Overstreet. New York: W. W. Norton & Company, Inc., 1949.

> Many pages are devoted to discussion of the way a mature mind deals with modern social problems: community living, politics, government, the influence of press, radio, and advertising.

Ernest W. Burgess (born in 1886 at Tilbury, Ontario) has retired from the Chairmanship of the Department of Sociology at the University of Chicago, but from nothing else. His career has included the presidency of the Gerontological Society, Association for Family Living, American Sociological Association, National Conference on Family Relations, American Society on Social Issues, Social Science Research Association; chairmanship of the Social Science Research Council, and the editorship of several important journals including The American Journal of Sociology. Among his publications are The Family from Institution to Companionship *(with Harvey J. Locke (1953);* "The Growing Problem of Aging" *in* Living through the Older Years *(1949);* "Human Aspects of Social Policy for Older Persons" *in* Old Age in the Modern Society *(1954); and* Personal Adjustment in Old Age *(with R. Cavan, et al.) (1949).*

"The thing that is peculiar to America is the commonness of associations between people who have no other bond with their fellow citizens than their humanity, their citizenship, and their concern for the good of the community."
—LEWIS GALANTIERE

"The practice of democracy means that I, one person, one humble person, nevertheless feel some responsibility if the officials for whose election I was responsible go too far out of line."
—CLYDE K. M. KLUCKHOHN

"The really urgent reason for allowing the widest latitude to the expression of the individual mind is that only the societies which encourage freedom of expression survive, flourish, and prosper."
—HENRY S. COMMAGER

Quoted by permission from Arthur Goodfriend's WHAT IS AMERICA? Simon and Schuster, Inc., 1954.

8

Participation
Through Organization

ERNEST W. BURGESS

THERE EXISTS AT PRESENT this perplexing paradox: as persons age, their leisure time increases, but their social participation and membership in organizations decreases. The solution of this paradox lies first of all in proclaiming the significance for human welfare and happiness of two fundamental facts: First, man to be healthy at any age must keep physically and mentally active. Second, man as a social being in modern society finds the highest fulfillment of his potentialities in creative activities, in social participation, and in membership in organizations.

Once people recognize these facts, they will act upon them and consign this paradox to the limbo of antiquated contradictions, for man is a social being. He develops his personality and his interests in a series of social groups: the family, the play group, the school, the church, clubs, and other organizations.

In the rural neighborhood of a century ago our great-grandparents lived their social life almost entirely in the family, the school, and the church. Nearly all recreational activities were carried on in friendship groups without any formal organization. The development of industry and the growth of cities and the increasing specialization of individual interests and activities have completely changed all that. Today if a person is to participate in an activity, some degree of organization is usually necessary. It may be provided commercially, as by a bowling alley, a motion picture theatre, or a tavern; but more often it is promoted by membership in an organization—a social club, a fraternity, or some other voluntary association. Here we will discuss only non-commercial organizations which command the leisure time of their members.

Membership in a social group provides the individual with at least four significant satisfactions: *a sense of belonging, the pleasure of sociability, the satisfaction of activity,* and *a routine of attendance at events.* Let us examine each in turn, for they illustrate why participation is strongly to be recommended.

Belonging to a group establishes and maintains the identity of the individual member. Men and women tend to think of themselves in terms of the groups and organizations to which they belong. A person with no group affiliation is usually, is not always, lonesome and unhappy because isolated. The unaffiliated individual feels futile and unimportant. If he is to count for something and make his influence felt, it must be through some collective association. He needs a sense of belonging.

Groups and organizations always promote *sociability* among their members, even when that is not their ostensible primary purpose. The coffee-break in the office or factory is not merely a recess; it is an enjoyable get-together. The time set aside for refreshments and talk at formal meetings for serious purposes is similarly to be viewed. Luncheon clubs like the Rotary, Kiwanis, and the Lions emphasize friendliness and sociability, as if to illustrate the significance we insist here they have.

Both formal and informal organizations center around one or more definite *activities* which appeal to the members—are often the reason for membership—and which encourage self-expression, like sports, games, music, art, social-welfare services, politics, education, and religion. Either the organizations provide facilities and opportunities which the members taken singly could not possess or command, or they provide the stimulus to activity which only the rare self-starter could supply by himself, or both. Thus a golf club maintains a club house and a course and the stimulus to make use of them.

Groups, organizations, and institutions foster a regular schedule of events to bring their members together and accomplish their aims. The Ladies' Aid meets the third Thursday afternoon of each month, the Drama Reading Club has bi-monthly evening get togethers, the church holds Sunday morning and evening services, and prayer meetings on Wednesday evening. Such scheduled events give their members something to which to look forward and for which to plan. At minimum they "break up the monotony."

Now, while these *satisfactions* are to be derived from a wide variety of organizations, it is obvious that a particular individual cannot gain them simply by joining an organization at random. He must first assess his personal values and interests and then seek out an organization that matches them. Only then will the satisfactions mentioned be won. It is plain that a wise choice at one stage of life will not necessarily serve at another. It must be assumed that choices change with age.

Appraisal and Re-Orientation

The life cycle may be divided into four main periods: *childhood and youth, early maturity, middle maturity,* and *later maturity.* Each of the stages has its distinctive function in the life of the individual. *Childhood and youth* are the time of preparation for adult life and its responsibilities. *Early maturity* is the period of achievement in establishing the family, rearing children, and beginning an occupation. *Middle maturity* is concerned with the appraisal and re-orientation of life. *Later maturity* ideally affords the opportunity for a new freedom and a new fulfillment.

The periods with which this discussion is concerned are middle and later maturity. Middle maturity may be considered to begin at forty to fifty years and to continue to the time when persons usually retire, or to sixty-five or seventy. One event that marks the beginning of middle maturity for a married couple is the departure of the children for college or for their own homes after marriage. At that point the parents are ready to consider new interests and activities.

Among other points they can now decide is what organizations will best promote their interests and foster their creative powers. The choices can be lined up much as follows:

INTEREST	ORGANIZATION
Health and physical fitness	*Sports and games clubs*
Economic benefits	*Lodges and remunerative hobbies*
Intimate human associations	*Golf, bowling, and other social activity clubs*
Education	*Adult education courses, discussion groups, lectures, conferences*
Creative expression	*Painting, music, ceramics, writing classes, and clubs*
Service to the community	*Civic action and welfare societies*
Religion and ethics	*Church activities, YM and YWCA, and other character-building agencies*

The next step is to determine how far their interests are being met by the groups and organizations to which they already belong. Possibly they are completely taken care of, but it is rather more probable that there are gaps. In fact it is almost certain that they are not finding the *fullest* potential expression of their interests and talents at their new stage of life.

The third step, then, is to canvass the organizations available to the middle-maturity married couple, to discover which will best serve the interests, as newly defined.

In modern society the available organizations can be classified as *intimate social groups, voluntary associations,* and *institutions.* Let us consider each type in turn.

An *intimate social group* is one made up on the basis of friendship. The members get together on the invitation of one of them for a dinner, a party, or a card game. Conversation on matters of common interest is free and easy. Sociability and companionship are the reasons for the existence of these small social groups.

Voluntary associations are groups which are formally organized, like athletic clubs, luncheon groups, and fraternal societies. At minimum they maintain a membership record and a secretary, to take general charge of the machinery necessary to operations. At maximum they develop a constitution and by-laws, a board of directors, a full set of officers, and may even be incorporated as non-profit organizations under state laws. The purpose is to serve one interest —or perhaps more than one—of the members. The member enjoys certain rights and privileges, and accepts certain obligations, such as observation of the rules and the payment of dues.

Institutions are usually organized to promote social-welfare programs. They serve their members, to be sure, but they also perform a service to the community. Some, like the government and the churches, have a long history. Others—the public schools, for example—have existed for several generations. Many are comparatively new developments, like family-service societies, civic associations, and day-centers for older people. In larger cities there are printed directories of the local institutions.

Any person can belong to examples of all the broad types. In fact, he perhaps should.

Intimate Social Groups

Intimate social groups cannot be taken for granted, or neglected, in assessing the present, or thinking about the future. In fact, they should be cultivated as matters of fundamental importance. For instance the industrialization and urbanization of this country have greatly reduced unplanned communication and contact between parents and grown children, grandparents and grandchildren, and with remoter relatives. Many people "hardly know" their cousins. But within the family circle areas of common interest often exist that could be used as the basis for fruitful association.

Inter-generational association can be organized around family events like Thanksgiving, Christmas, New Year's, and the celebration of birthdays and other anniversaries. On such occasions inter-generational ties can properly be emphasized. Grandparents, if resourceful, can discover activities of three-generation interest. The women in the family may find a common bond in sewing, embroidery, and the preservation of family heirlooms. The men may find a pool of interests in occupational lore, talk about cars, fishing and hunting, or family traditions. Grandparents frequently find that an attractive summer home draws the children and grandchildren during vacation time. In "getting acquainted" members of a family create their own ties and satisfactions.

Outside the family, friendship groups often date back to acquaintance in childhood or youth, shared experience at high school or college, proximity of residence at some period, or association in work or play. The middle-aged couple is often a member of an "intimate social group" that meets weekly to play cards or for dinner and conversation. These things are such commonplaces that we think nothing of them, but they have surprising meaning for a full life. Such groups often originate also in associations at work and are sometimes exclusively the property of the husband, like poker-playing or bowling groups. Unfortunately these groups tend to break up when a man retires. He is then faced with the task of replacing a long-continued association, and often it is not easy.

Voluntary Associations

In this discussion voluntary associations may be classified into two main groups—the less and the more formally organized. Or into those not incorporated and those that are incorporated. Or into strictly local and autonomous groups and those which are affiliates of a national society.

Unaffiliated Local Community Associations

Every local community, rural or urban, has a few informal voluntary associations that have grown up, seemingly spontaneously, to meet definite social interests. Actually such associations never originate spontaneously. Rather at some time or other they were but an idea or a dream of some individual. Stirred to action, he or she told others of the idea, and, after considerable effort, an appropriate organization is born; and, with care and planning, it achieves maturity and stability.

In any given community there may be clubs for various sports and games, hobby clubs, special luncheon and dinner clubs to foster particular interests, and highly specialized clubs to promote foreign-language conversation, the collecting of first editions, or to study biological specimens—the range is overpoweringly enormous. Right now "discussion groups" are enjoying a nation-wide boom.

Nevertheless an individual or couple may fail to find a local group devoted to his or their particular interest. It is often feasible to set about organizing a new group. First it must be ascertained whether or not there are others in the community to whom this interest appeals. Then the logical person to promote it must be determined, and the best method of promotion selected.

Research at the Social Relations Laboratory of Harvard University by Robert F. Bales and his associates seems to indicate that small groups have two kinds of leaders: those who have the ideas, and those who are best-liked. To form a successful group, therefore, probably two leaders should join forces, thus assuring that the idea is clearly to the fore, and that the person who naturally gathers people around him can function successfully.

Some examples will show how this works. A music club was the brainchild of a middle-aged woman whose children were grown. As a young woman she had had musical training, but after marriage she found no time for practicing. It occurred to her that there must be other women in the community similarly situated; so she spoke to friends about establishing a club, and they spoke to other friends. A music club soon emerged, meeting monthly in homes. Light refreshments provided for sociability. In rotation, each of the members arranged and gave a program of vocal and instrumental music. As a closing event of the year, the husbands were invited to a full evening program followed by a party. This is an example of an old, persistent, but frustrated interest finally finding satisfying expression.

A dinner club was organized by a community leader around the idea of member-participation at each meeting. If there was an invited speaker, he had to keep his remarks brief. The members, seated around a large square of tables, were the focus of interest. After dinner each was called upon to read a poem, tell a story, sing a song, or otherwise make a personal contribution to the fun. A simple and gay way for everybody to put in his "two cents."

A group of congenial and thoughtful members of the Los Angeles Rotary Club hived off to become a discussion group on "World Affairs Are Your Affairs." A special interest group within a large group is entirely legitimate.

Before launching such a group yourself, you will find it profitable to analyze some existing groups, to find out what made them successful; and, if you can, take a look at the records of groups that failed, to ascertain the reasons for their failure.

Affiliated Locals of Nationwide Organizations

In contrast to the one-of-a-kind, or autonomous, organizations, many of the local clubs are affiliated with city-wide, state, or national organizations. The range of activities that are organized nationally is simply enormous, but some idea of it can be given here by citing more or less at random from the World Almanac [1] some organizations, total membership (when given), and national address.

Alcoholics Anonymous, 150,000. Box 459, Grand Central Annex, New York, N. Y.

Altrusa International, 13,500. 332 S. Michigan Ave., Chicago 7, Ill.

American Affiliation of Tall Clubs (for tall people), 2,000. 3954 West 10th St., Chicago 43, Ill.

American Camping Association, 5,384. 343 S. Dearborn St., Chicago 4, Ill.

American Feline Society, 41 Union Square, West, New York 3, N. Y.

American Home Economics Association, 22,500. 1600 20th St., N.W., Wash. 9, D.C.

Gerontological Society, 1,000. 660 S. Kingshighway Blvd., St. Louis 10, Mo.

Gideons International, 19,000. 212 E. Superior St., Chicago 11, Ill.

Institute of American Genealogy, 1,500. 407 S. Dearborn, Chicago 5, Ill.

International Associated Hobbies, 5,000. 2252 East 8th St., Tulsa 4, Okla.

International Association of Lions Clubs, 520,000. 209 N. Michigan Ave., Chicago 4, Ill.

Kiwanis International, 236,835. 520 No. Michigan Ave., Chicago 11, Ill.

League of Women Voters, 127,000. 1026 17th St., N.W., Washington 6, D.C.

---

[1] The majority of the organizations listed here are to be found, along with many others, under the heading "Associations and Societies in the United States" in the *World Almanac and Book of Facts* which is issued annually in a revised edition.

National Council of State Garden Clubs, 350,000. 160 Central Park South, New York 19, N. Y.

National Federation of Grandmothers' Clubs of America, 15,000. 203 No. Wabash Ave., Chicago 30, Ill.

National Horseshoe Pitchers Association of America. Crestline, Calif.

National Music Council. 117 East 79th St., New York 24, N. Y.

National Society of Colonial Dames of America. 2715 Q St., Washington 7, D.C.

Needlework Guild of America, 1,000,000. 124 So. 12th St., Philadelphia 7, Pa.

Rotary International, 411,000. 16000 Ridge Ave., Evanston, Ill.

Senior Citizens of America, 1129 Vermont Ave., N.W., Washington 5, D.C.

Women's International Bowling Congress, 700,000. 694 So. High St., Columbus 6, Ohio.

The majority of these national organizations are built upon local and state units; in fact, they live only as the local units thrive. They give a husband or wife as wide a range of choice as there are human interests. A selection among them is ordinarily determined, apart from personal interest, by the influence of friends, relative cost of membership, standing of the organization in the community, and the accessibility and frequency of meetings. Membership in a local affiliate has certain advantages over membership in a strictly local association. First, association with a nation-wide movement affords pleasure in one's field of interest; second, the national office usually offers the local units help with problems; third, the national conventions are attractive prospects, for Americans "love" conventions; and fourth, a national organization usually issues a publication that keeps one posted on developments and events, through articles and news items.

Institutions

The purpose of an institution is not only to be of service to its members but also to promote the welfare of society at large. Many institutions have a professional paid staff, but nearly every one also offers members special opportunities for participation in the work. The church ordinarily provides a wide program of activities other than religious work. There are opportunities to be an officer, to join a committee, take part in the choir or chorus, participate in membership canvasses, teach in Sunday School, join men's and women's Bible classes, or to participate in the Sunday evening forum.

The school, focused on the younger generation, nevertheless always welcomes parents and grandparents to programs and events: athletic contests, debates, and musical and dramatic occasions—especially good for three-generation attendance. An adult education program is specifically designed for the grown-ups of all ages.

General and mental hospitals recognize the value of services volunteers can perform for patients. Patients without relatives or friends greatly appreciate visitors prepared just to chat, to write letters, or read aloud. Entertainments by outside groups are welcomed into the recreational program.

Welfare agencies, public and private, increasingly recognize the worth of volunteers in supplementing the activities of the paid professionals. Applicants are interviewed by a specialist, given a short training course, and assigned to work, as helpers, in association with the professionals. Many people find this a most satisfying use of their time.

Moreover, facilities are often made available by welfare agencies, or like-minded institutions, which are especially designed for the aging. In Milwaukee, Minneapolis, St. Louis, and other cities Golden Age Clubs are actively promoted by such groups. In Atlanta, Cleveland, Detroit, New York, San Francisco, and other cities activity centers have been established for the aging, with recreational, educational, and general cultural activities. A motion picture has been made to portray the range of activities available, "Such A Busy Day Tomorrow." [2] Active aging people not only participate; they can and do take leadership.

Leisure Time and Personal Fulfillment

Can the value of the use of leisure time *in organizations* be appraised? In all probability, it can be, but as yet nobody has produced a comprehensive evaluation. There are, however, several findings of specialized studies which indicate some of the advantages of group-participation leisure. Here they are for consideration:

---

[2] This film can be obtained on loan from the Committee on Aging, U. S. Department of Health, Education, and Welfare, Washington 25, D. C.

A study of residents in two cottages in a home for older persons revealed that persons who participated in group activities such as card playing, shuffle-board, pool, pinball, and horsesohe, had on the average a much higher "happiness score" than individuals who engaged only in solitary activities like walking, reading, sewing, embroidery, and listening to radio and watching television. This clearly indicates that group activities assist in personal adjustment, and promote happiness.[3]

A study of groups of persons attending a day center for older people in New York indicates that visits to health clinics by the same persons were reduced by 50 to 70 per cent in the period after attending the center, as compared with a like period before joining. This would seem to show that participation in organizational activities moderates excessive concern about bodily ills, real and imaginary.[4]

Although these findings are but clues to the probable character of the values inherent in joining in organized activities, they do indicate that, in planning one's future, there is every warrant for making a place for group activities. As we began by saying, it is highly paradoxical that so many people fail to make such a place; and intensely so that older people should be lax about a point so vital to their own and the community's welfare.

---

[3] Burgess, Ernest W., "Social Relations, Activities, and Personal Adjustment," *American Journal of Sociology*, Vol. 59, 1954, pp. 352-60.

[4] Cavan, Ruth S., et. al., *Personal Adjustment in Old Age.* Table 47, p. 196. Chicago: Science Research Associates, Inc., 1949.

Time Out for Reflection

Professor Burgess suggests that middle life should be a period of appraisal, during which one examines his organizational affiliations to determine whether or not they are meeting his needs effectively. In which organizations do you have membership? What meaning does each organization have for you?

Looking ahead over the next ten or twenty years, you probably anticipate certain changes in your life—more free time, perhaps retirement from work, desire to learn a skill you do not now have, or to do something for your community. Do you anticipate that such changes may call for a change in your membership in organizations? Are there some you think you may wish to drop? Are there others in which you would like to have membership?

"Know yourself" was a favorite admonition of Socrates. He believed that an individual was not prepared to get the most out of life until he had thoroughly examined his own interests, capacities, and talents. Have you thought carefully about what you want most out of life? Have you ever experimented or taken aptitude tests to discover whether or not you have hidden talents—for creative arts, for organization, for working with other people? How would you go about it in your community, if you really decided to discover what untried skills or talents you may possess?

Is religion more important to older people? Is religious satisfaction best sought through active church membership? How active are you?

You Can Join Sections
of the Adult Education
Association of the U.S.A.*

Purpose

SECTIONS ARE ESTABLISHED within the Adult Education Association to serve the following purposes:

1. To develop and maintain communication and a sense of fellowship among members interested in specialized aspects of adult education.

2. To plan and conduct a meeting at each national conference of the Association for members with special interests to work together on common concerns.

3. To keep the total membership of the Association aware, through contributions to our publications, through resolutions to the Delegate Assembly, through special reports, conferences, and other activities, of (a) developments in their special interest areas that have implications for the general movement, and (b) the significance of their particular area in the picture of adult education.

4. To serve in a consultative capacity to the Association and its members on problems in their areas of competence.

5. To promote the advancement of theory, research, and practice within their special interest areas.

6. To develop such other activities and services as may be appropriate to the needs and interests of their members and the purpose of the Association.

---

*(Ask your Public Library about membership.)

Affiliation

Sections are self-directing and largely self-financing groupings of AEA members. Members may affiliate with them without additional fee, subject only to such assessments as each section itself may prescribe. Since the sections meet simultaneously at conferences, members are requested to limit their affiliation to a maximum of three sections.

Sections for the Year 1958-59

COMMUNITY DEVELOPMENT—For those members concerned with the use of adult educational processes and agencies in the development of communities.

EDUCATION FOR AGING—For those members concerned with the development of educational programs designed to help individuals live more fully and purposefully in their later years, especially after retirement.

EDUCATION AND INDUSTRY—A continuing forum for discussion between adult education specialists in industry and inter-related members of other adult education specializations in the adult education movement.

EDUCATION FOR NON-ENGLISH SPEAKING ADULTS—For those members concerned with the preparation of immigrants to live usefully and happily in America.

HOME AND FAMILY LIFE EDUCATION—For those members concerned with the extension and improvement of education in all aspects of family life, including marriage, parent-child relations, economic management, the use of leisure-time, and the like.

FUNDAMENTAL AND LITERACY EDUCATION—For those members concerned with the elimination of functional illiteracy in this country, and with the improvement of programs, methods, and materials for the teaching of illiterates.

INTERNATIONAL AFFAIRS—For those members concerned with educational programming in international affairs and with increasing knowledge about international relations among adult educators.

LABOR EDUCATION—For those members concerned with educational programming for labor union members and with developing closer relations between labor educators and other adult educators.

LIBERAL ADULT EDUCATION—For those members concerned with the special problems involved in extending and improving the liberal education value of all adult learning.

MUSIC IN ADULT EDUCATION—For those members concerned

with the advancement of musical education for adults and the improvement of musical instruction.

PUBLIC AFFAIRS EDUCATION—For those members concerned with the analysis of plans and practices in civic and citizenship education for adults, including the mass media.

RESIDENTIAL ADULT EDUCATION—For those members concerned with the promotion of educational opportunities in residential settings, both short-term and long-term, and the improvement of knowledge and practices in residential adult education.

RESEARCH AND EVALUATION—For those members concerned with the extension of research on adult education problems, and with the advancement of methods for evaluating adult educational activities.

RURAL ADULT EDUCATION—For those members concerned with the education of adults in rural settings, including extension activities, farm organizations, and other rural educational institutions.

YOUNG ADULT EDUCATION—For those members concerned with the development of educational programs for young adults (to age 30) and improving our knowledge of the special problems of this age group.

Religion and Religious
Observance in Old Age

Leroy Waterman (1875-   )

OUR RACE IN THIS atomic age has, without warning, suddenly found itself in an undreamed-of setting of what may be termed cosmic emergency, in which all human values, including religion and religious observance, have been thrown into an over-all new perspective, to which religious thinking has as yet scarcely awakened, to say nothing of having made inevitable adjustments.

No serious consideration of religion henceforth can avoid this problem. It will be necessary first, to try to see what the new perspective is, and then to consider both the adjustments that are called for and what our available resources are for making them. It may be needless to say that there are plenty of inherited as well as natural handicaps to the treatment of our topic.

All the other topics on this program deal with tangible data concerned with the problems of aging. Scientific facts are everywhere available for their discussion. But in the realm of religion we enter an area of the intangible, where there are no fixed data nor any unquestioned standards for evaluating the phenomena that come under consideration. Moreover, religion that in ages past has always been taken for granted, is today sharply challenged. It is repudiated by many as outmoded and a hindrance to human progress.

What makes the matter still more confusing is the fact that in the dominant religion of western civilization, the highest authorities cannot agree either as to what constitutes the content of religion or how it must be observed. Christianity has proved highly fissionable and has, so to speak, exploded into a growing multitude of disparate fragments. These entities manifest a double tendency: on the one hand some of them tend to coalesce again with other units; others manifest a contrary trend toward still further disintegration. These fragments constitute the religous bodies to which one belongs and professes allegiance. They make their appeal for support in a highly competitive field, on the basis of correct belief, authentic rites, authorized leadership, and a select society.

Such phenomena are the end results of highly complicated, age-old processes. The outcome is institutionalized religion, which consists of a partnership between an institution and that thing which we call religion, in which union the institution becomes not only a partner and often a major partner, but in such combination in the past history of religions, religion itself has, on numerous occasions, been eclipsed and totally excluded. Under these circumstances current forms and programs of religion can hardly be expected to furnish an adequate basis for the helpful discussion of our topic.

In view of these facts, therefore, an intelligent treatment of our subject would seem to call for the clarifying as far as possible of the ultimate nature and aim of religion itself. And at the outset it may be worth while to point out that all is not well with the conventional forms of religion as they appear officially today. This is not to overlook the fact that the number of their adherents is probably increasing, although statistics of their losses are not always available, nor is it to lose sight of the fact that they have conscientious, able, and devoted leaders. The serious fact is (and it should be possible to state it in the presence of the friends and adherents of religion) that current religion, particularly the Christian religion, has not and is not accomplishing what, on its own confession, humanity has had every right to expect. And there is no other force at hand to do the thing needed, without which at the present juncture our world is in the gravest danger in all its history.

Here is a thesis that should challenge old and young alike. Is religion that important to our present existence? And, if so, is it the religion that has proved inadequate, or does the fault lie with those who have failed to live up to its requirements? We shall try our best to see.

First then as to the universality of religion in human experience. The followers of Karl Marx have openly declared to the world that they have discarded religion as something outgrown and pernicious. It has been well said, however, of that philosophy that it nevertheless has its patron saints, its martyrs, its gospel, and an ardent devotion to a cause that professes to be concerned to a very high degree with the preservation of human values; and these phenomena are the accompaniments of religiosity. There are also numerous other people today who will assert they do not believe in religion or that they have no religion. In almost all cases where men thus deny or renounce religion, what they really mean is their repudiation of a particular form of religion, but that does not signify that they have repudiated their religious nature nor that they can do so and remain human.

It is the anthropologists, who cannot be charged with undue enthusiasm for religion, but whose special business it is to study the more primitive races, who have answered our question in the affirmative by asserting that there are no men found anywhere on the earth who do not have religion.

What then is this religious quality that appears universally in the human race and in no other living creatures, a phenomenon within every human being that alone makes possible religious institutions everywhere, in all ages? From what has already been said, it should be evident that the religious urge in man's nature is not to be regarded as something artificially thrust into it or superimposed upon it from without, or that was picked up as it were by chance, but rather as built into the very foundation stones of personality through the process of life unfoldment.

It is unnecessary for our purpose to trace the process, but only to call attention to certain phases that still have significance for man's life today. We may conveniently start with man's ability to conceive of himself as a spiritual being, that is, apart from his physical body. This ability is found among all races. It matters not how this was acquired. This achievement changed his entire outlook on existence and the whole meaning of the universe around him. When he perceived himself as distinct and separable from his body, it opened up before him an endless vista, which capitalized his inmost being as having unending worth and value. From that time forward and forever afterward the values of personality became increasingly more precious than all other goods. This is now summed up for us in the familiar words: "For what shall it profit a man if he gain the whole world but part with his own life?"

One of the greatest boons that has ever been conferred on human life is the growing sense of the sacredness of personality. An increasing lack of this trait is an ominous sign in our time. This quality is primarily due to religion, and without religion it could never have been. Everyone, therefore, who does anything to enhance it is performing a truly religious act of the first importance. Democratic personal rights, which are among our most valued possessions as a nation (or should be), are not founded upon or secured by the laws we have to conserve them, but upon the degree of the sacredness of personality in the minds of men that underlies and implements such laws. Let that factor once deteriorate and disappear and all the laws in the world will never be able to preserve democratic rights. The rule of dictatorships is a sufficient illustration.

The preservation and enhancement of this sacred quality should be a real part of religious observance, though very little of it can be performed in churches. It is limited to no age bracket, but should certainly characterize those of later years, who have lived long enough to appreciate its value, since the measure of its recognition and effectiveness depends on the rank and file of men who embody it. In other words the working level to which it rises in society depends on the level it reaches in the average individual. Lynching, for example, could hardly take place in a community where abhorrence of such acts represents the average sentiment. Too often in such case, while the majority of the community would never participate in lynching, it may well fail to disapprove the deed itself. Racial discrimination that places color above personality is a religious sin. In the face of that widespread evil today, insistence on recognizing personality on the basis of true merit only should be a very real part of religious observance both within and outside the churches. It is also capable of special application to the aging, who because of ill health, for example, may not be able to attend a communion service in a church. Communion depends on having sentiments in common between the parties concerned. The place is secondary. Any one to his dying day, whether in church or out, may continue to be a center that radiates an attitude against race prejudice, and this can be done with the full assurance that it is always highly pleasing to a God who is no respecter of persons. The limitations to religious communion are not so much physical as mental.

In view of all the diversity in religion today, is there such a thing as a constant aim in all religion? Is it a sound aim? What determines it? And how is it possible for men to be in such disagreement about religion if this is so? It is often assumed that the aim of religion is God, that the soul of man has an innate aspiration for the Infinite, that determines the aim. The history of religions does not bear this out. When man awakened to the abiding values of personality, the revelation, for it was also that, was so arresting, so alluring that his efforts to preserve those values constitute the most persistent, enduring, and consistent endeavor that still characterizes man as man. Therein the aim of religion stands revealed, as constant through the ages as the magnetic needle that always points to the pole. All religions from the beginning have embodied it, and in all of them somewhere it comes to focus in that word "salvation." The essential differences that separate all religions are differences in method to attain that end.

Herein the nature and aim of religion are seen to be sound. This is so because they furnish the only basis on which civilization can be held together and by which mankind can persist. But whether they will produce a civilization that can ultimately save mankind, depends largely on the concept of that salvation, for that will go far in determining how it is to be achieved.

In ancient Israel, during the period of the nation and later, the doctrine of immortality as yet played no part in connection with the worship of their national God, and accordingly salvation was conceived in terms of national prosperity; and the values of personality were regarded as sufficiently conserved in the on-going generations of the nation, under the national God. It was in this frame of reference that the great prophets of all time gave their message. For the first time in history able and devoted men, patriots, poets, thinkers, and prophets all rolled into one were able to devote themselves to the main problems of human living. They accepted the proposition that salvation could be expressed in terms of outward prosperity under God. But unlike those moderns who are satisfied to be able to show that prosperity can be found to exist at least for the few, these ancient thinkers were able to see that if the ideal was valid, it should be valid for all, unless it were the person's own fault. But they noted that this was not the case with the majority, and moreover the reason was not that the people lacked religious devotion according to existing standards. This led to the first sweeping critique of formal religion, to the effect that the offerings made to the deity and their formal worship were inadequate, misleading, and of no avail; and then on the basis of the requirements for securing outward well-being for the average man, they declared that economic justice and fair play between man and man were demanded, and if true it must be what God wanted, and since it had always been needed, it must have been what God had always wanted, and not their ritualistic worship. From this vantage point these men were able to see that these requirements must be based upon the wholly ethical character of God and the universe. This is the greatest single revelation in religion. Another poet-prophet went further and said that fair play between man and man requires more than economic justice. It demands the justice that operates in the give and take of personalities, that at its best is called love, and this too by the same kind of reasoning was shown to be a part of God's character. Having made these spiritual discoveries the great seers were able to draw another logical conclusion and declare that such a God could be no respecter of persons or of nations and hence there could be no such thing as a chosen people. He must on the contrary be equally concerned for all men as His creatures.

Here was a unique phase of revealed religion that is not yet fully grasped or appreciated. It furnished the first systematic diagnosis of the problem of human living that could bring salvation to mankind as a living organism, and this is our burning world problem today. It is the glory of the New Testament to clarify and to specify the requirements of prophetic religion in terms of personal relations. For Jesus insisted that the world is one neighborhood and that all men are God's children and are therefore brothers. He also took particular pains to point out that in all human relations the legitimate viewpoint of others should always be taken into consideration. On the basis of such teaching, he was able to say that the Kingdom of God (a very old phrase in his day, to which he gave the new meaning as the kind and quality of human society that God wants) is now in your midst, actually within your reach, already within your grasp, and therefore it is strictly a human responsibility.

The early Christians failed to grasp this thought, and after two thousand years it has still not registered itself in the Christian consciousness. Meantime it has become clear that the salvation or the destruction of our species hangs precariously in the balance. The best in our religious heritage has clearly laid down conditions for its salvation and these are demonstrably sound and adequate. But today, strange to say, they stir no new initiative in a humanity that is at its wit's end; they yield no confidence to a world that is desperately afraid. And the reason? The professedly religious people on the whole are not interested, primarily because the Christian churches from the beginning were not concerned with this life, which they regarded as hopelessly doomed. Thus the blueprint furnished by Jesus for the reign of God on earth missed them entirely and they gave themselves up to Jewish apocalyptic ideas of the hereafter and a salvation based on the principle of the Jewish ritualistic law.

What hope has this type of religion to offer to a desperate humanity today? What way out does it point to the distraught youth of the world? What solace is it to the aged to be told that the destruction promised ages ago is now about to happen? Actually, the cataclysm that now threatens us is wholly in men's hands and therefore a purely human responsibility, in which Christians bear a very heavy share, because of their religious inheritance, and therefore those who rely on the atoning work of Christ for their soul's salvation have no grounds for assuming that this covers delinquency for not being mightily concerned and in the very forefront of all those who are manfully striving to avert a final world catastrophe.

What then can the churches as at present constituted offer to the aged? Is it a sacred asylum in which to end their days? But that asylum can afford no more safety today than any other spot on the earth. There are two main questions now facing Christendom. First, not as commonly assumed, "Can Christianity save individual souls?" but, "Can Christianity itself be salvaged?" This is recognized as improbable unless men can find a sound basis for world peace. This latter also is a purely human problem for which every one of us, regardless of age, must take a full measure of personal responsibility. The second question is not, as usually implied, "Is the Kingdom of God on earth anything more than a utopian dream?" but, "Will the churches be able to see in time that the program of that Kingdom as stated by Jesus offers the one hope of their own salvation?" Religion, at its best, may be stated as citizenship in the Kingdom of God, in which every personal relationship is fraught with religious significance, a potency to bring all men nearer together at the feet of God.

The aging need a feeling of security, not just an easy chair by the fireside, but the assurance that comes from participation in activities that are heart-warming and recognized to be supremely worth while. Today more of such activities can often be found outside than inside the churches, and they are all optional and a matter of personal preference. Only religion can say what is supremely worth while. As long as the churches assume that their supreme task is to save individual souls out of a perishing world, only preachers and evangelists can do the superlative tasks. But if and when the churches accept the ideal of Jesus, that they must save human society or admit that they have forfeited the main reason for their existence (Jesus said that a bit of leaven must leaven the whole lump if it has any virtue), all activities must then take on a new evaluation. Neither conversion, profession of faith, nor formal worship will be the superlative. On the contrary, the most important things will be those that make for the solidarity of society, for mutual understanding and human brotherhood, by pressing for economic justice among all classes, by promoting kindness, sympathy, and co-operation among all peoples, nations, and races. These will be the superlatives. The churches need to

be able to say that these things are now superlatively important, because all that is desirable and valuable in human life is dependent on putting these things across. The whole lump must be leavened or all will
perish, including the chance for the Kingdom of God on earth, and the
human experiment will have failed.

We know today that when war comes it involves the whole population.
All must serve and suffer. Religiously this is a world emergency situation.
There are no safe dugouts. There is not sand enough in which to bury
our heads. The churches need to be centers that radiate contagious good
will, first within their own borders, second among themselves as churches
of the community, third into all surrounding society. Wherever there are
hot spots they should be there, in support of every effort being made to increase good will and understanding among the nations, looking toward
their ultimate organic unification. With such an outlook, the churches
should be able to utilize the efforts of all in these matters of supreme importance to our continued existence.

Suitable activity should thus be found for the aging and the aged.
Every struggle for civil rights and social justice, every stand for moral
principle, every rebuke of vice and moral delinquency, every effort to
alleviate suffering and distress and to show kindness and sympathy to
those in need should be much more thoroughly organized within the
churches and emphasized as supremely worth while. It is a great thing
for the aged to feel that they still have a part in all such things. Sometimes just to be counted, which everyone can do, is an important service
in all causes that depend on an enlightened public opinion. The churches
cannot expect to accomplish their world mission without the enthusiastic
backing and support of this ever-increasing group of elderly people. This
resource has as yet been scarcely touched. Within this group, as of old,
are the wise men and the wise women of every age. Their experience and
their best wisdom combined and integrated with the newest insights into
the meaning of our existence in this fearsome world situation provide the
surest hope for the future of man.

Suggestions for Further Reading

Helping Older People Enjoy Life, by James H. Woods. New York: Harper & Bros., 1953.

A highly readable description of the organization and activities of leisure-time social groups for older adults. Written by one of the pioneers with extensive, first-hand experience.

Recreation for the Aging, by Arthur Williams. New York: Association Press, 1953.

An imaginative discussion of varied ways in which older people can spend time healthfully and pleasantly and maintain stimulating human contacts. Written by the head of the National Recreation Association.

Democracy Is You, by Richard W. Poston. New York: Harper & Brothers, 1953.

After several years of service as a consultant to groups bent upon improving their communities, Mr. Poston prepared this guide to citizens eager for action. Affords ample evidence of effective participation of the "average citizen."

For biographical data, see Chapter 1.

"Educators will compile different lists of the qualities which characterize an educated man, but the lists will be neither as long nor as conflicting as one might suppose. Most of us agree that we would wish the educated man to be marked by intellectual curiosity, the capacity to think critically, and the capacity to weigh evidence dispassionately. We would wish him to be tolerant, temperate, balanced in judgment; and we would wish him to possess certain general qualities such as maturity, magnanimity, and so forth. We would not wish him to be intellectually lazy or slovenly, and we would not wish his rational processes to be at the mercy of his fears and prejudices."

—from LIBERAL EDUCATION

A summary of a discussion by the Trustees of the Carnegie Foundation for the Advancement of Teaching, printed in the 1955-1956 Annual Report. Quoted by permission of Carnegie Foundation for the Advancement of Teaching.

9

Creating a Climate
for the Middle Years

CLARK TIBBITTS

THIS SERIES OF ESSAYS on *Aging in the Modern World* has had the underlying theme that all of us, particularly those of us in the middle and later years, are challenged to adapt ourselves and our ways of living to a culture that has been changing more completely and more rapidly during the past two or three generations than in all the preceding years of man's existence.

In this period we have achieved longer and healthier life. The production of material wealth has markedly increased, its distribution is more equitable, and we have won simultaneously unprecedented leisure. We spend as many of our waking hours away from work as on the job. But are we successfully meeting our non-material individual needs with equal success?

We are all conscious of many new satisfactions, but there are nevertheless clear signs of restlessness and anxiety. That this is "the age of anxiety" is often asserted. Mental illness has become a national problem. Under a surface of complacency there appears to be widespread discontent, disorientation, and spiritual restlessness.

Hence the questions: Can our new culture meet our basic personal needs? Can we be sure that the new phase of life upon which we have put so much emphasis in these discussions will really be a period of regeneration? Are we certain that all will find new interests and new roles that will give a sense of personal fulfillment and spiritual satisfaction?

We cannot hope to answer these questions dogmatically, but we can undertake to discuss matters that appear to be closely related to the answers. The answers themselves must come from each individual involved in the task outlined. When the individual answers are "added up" at some time in the future, we may be able to formulate conclusions of the widest relevance and applicability.

OUR BASIC PERSONAL NEEDS

What precisely are the needs, apart from the drives man shares with the lower animals, that an individual seeks to satisfy? Many psychologists, sociologists, biologists, and philosophically-minded people generally have wrestled with this question, seeking to identify the instincts, wishes, or desires common to all men and which motivate their conduct throughout their lives. A standard thesis is that there are such drives, that each culture has peculiar ways of giving them expression, and that it is likely that the ways of satisfying them must change as the conditions of living change.[1]

But the specialists have not yet succeeded in agreeing on what the inborn drives are. The following formulation is, however, widely accepted and, at minimum, forms a satisfactory basis for reflection.

1. The Need for Relatedness, or Association with Others

One obvious characteristics of man is his need to live, work, and play in association with other human beings. The need for relatedness finds expression in love and in the desire to do for one's fellow

---

[1] Two useful elaborations on this search for a satisfactory statement of basic needs: Erich Fromm's *The Sane Society,* New York: Rinehart & Co., 1955 and W. I. Thomas' *The Unadjusted Girl,* 1923.

men. It finds satisfaction in family life, in associations at work, and in participation in organizations of one kind or another. New opportunities for association, or relatedness, must be found as some of the old ones taper off or disappear in middle age and the older years. Professor Burgess has emphasized this in his essay.

2. The Need for Creativity

Man's whole existence, says Fromm, has been characterized by a built-in desire to master his environment, to improve his way of life, to fulfill his need to bring about something new. It is this urge that appears to be at the bottom of the phenomenal discoveries and inventions which have changed our culture. It accounts in part also for all forms of creative and artistic expression. It accounts for our efforts to improve the organization of community life.

Traditionally, the growing child, the worker, the parent has found ample opportunity for expression of his creative impulses. But what about those who are reaching the middle years today? Are there enough opportunities for creativity—in a society in which much of the work is planned by a few and routinized for the many?—in a society becoming increasingly complex and in which there is a marked tendency toward centralized decision-making and control? —in a society which is just beginning to face up to the problems of the middle aged and old? Mr. Grattan has touched upon these and similar questions.

3. The Need for Security

Man's universal need for security is met, during his early years, by the protection afforded by his mother and the family group. All stabilized societies have developed forms of behavior and institutions designed to protect members against harm, deprivation, loneliness, unattended illness, and other conditions which might threaten comfort or survival.

An outstanding characteristic of our present-day society is that the responsibility for security is shared between the individual and the institutions designed to support him. Many of the earlier arrangements have lost their force or disappeared: Few of us have access to a plot of land from which to draw sustenance by our own efforts, the extended kinship group offering security to all its members has practically disappeared, the availability of remunerative employment has passed beyond the individual's control, and so on. Therefore man's search for security under modern conditions has led to the invention of a variety of social institutions designed to serve this end, like those we know by the name of "social security" and also annuities, pensions, and so on.

4. The Need for Individuality, or Recognition

All societies have afforded some recognition to the individual for his prowess or contribution to group welfare. Equally the individual was nevertheless often subordinated to the goals of the group or even to the aspirations of a small ruling clique.

History has been marked by a continual struggle for greater individual freedom. Democracy is thought to afford maximum opportunity for individual development and satisfaction. It is the form of society that has as its reason for existence the fullest development of the potentialities of every individual member.

Professor Havighurst, in his essay, pointed out that an individual's sense of status and recognition may be threatened in middle life and suggested the importance of finding new roles in which to seek new status and recognition.

5. The Need for Orientation, or An Intellectual Frame of Reference

Beyond the four needs just discussed, men must feel, it appears, that there is purpose to their lives and to the society in which they live. It has been suggested [2] that as we grow older we become increasingly aware of the need to find a rational explanation of the objectives, customs, and values developed in the course of human history, and to define a personal relationship to them. We appear to want to be assured that there is order and purpose in our society and to share in them, particularly as they express themselves in terms of the individual.

Primitive societies found useful roles for those who had completed their parental and work roles, as Professor Simmons showed.

---

[2] "The Human Life Cycle and Its Interruptions—A Psychologic Hypothesis," by M. E. Linden and Douglas Courtney, in *Mental Health and Mental Disorder,* Arnold Rose, editor, New York: W. W. Norton and Company, 1955.

How are middle-aged and older people to be oriented in a society which makes few formal demands upon them and has yet to define useful roles at all clearly?

These are perhaps the fundamental drives each individual seeks to satisfy in the culture in which he lives. Whether or not he succeeds is determined, in large part, by the extent to which the culture affords him opportunities. The drives can be satisfied in a variety of ways, but conditions must be favorable if any way is to succeed.

WHAT KIND OF SOCIETY

Within our lifetimes we have seen an unparalleled development of our material culture, followed by an extension of educational facilities, health services, recreational facilities, religious organization, mass communications, and mass entertainment. For the most part these new institutions and services have been directed to satisfying the needs of children and young adults. Social inventions designed to satisfy the needs of middle-aged and older people have been slow in coming. What is required to speed up the process?

1. Need for Understanding

This series of essays has been based upon the assumption that it is necessary to understand the nature of the changes taking place in our society and their implications. It has been pointed out that, throughout history, man has mostly centered his efforts on production, on gaining a living. Now this single-minded concentration is no longer sufficient. Increasing attention must be given to man-as-consumer—consumer of things, services, and time-as-leisure. We know that, thus far, we have not hit upon a finally satisfactory definition of man in the latter role. In fact, it is only lately that the meaning of it has begun to be explored. A writer like Edward Bellamy touched upon it years ago, but he was writing a utopian romance. Those dealing with the question in the context of current reality include writers like David Riesman, George Soule, the researchers of the Twentieth Century Fund and the National Planning Association. All agree that our current achievements in production and leisure are not merely to be related to an economic boom but rather reflect a trend upward that promises to continue for a long time. We need better to understand what this means. The explorations of it are the frontier of sociology.

2. Recognition of Middle-Aged Drives and Potentials

There is no evidence that with the attainment of middle age there is any diminution of the desires for human companionship, creativity, security, individuality, or sense of orientation. On the contrary. Completion of youth and the parental role represents but one stage in life's cycle. Middle age, the period in which forms of satisfaction relevant to the earlier stages of life tend to become outworn, appears to bring increased consciousness of the force of the basic drives we examined earlier.

Recognition of the potentials of the middle-aged is increasing, but there remains, however, much room for *community* recognition of the fact that middle-aged and older persons require opportunities to satisfy their aspirations.

3. Maintenance of Health and Energy

Good health and high energy reserves are as essential as any other conditions to continued performance. Dr. Donahue and Professor Havighurst have stated that physical, physiological, and some mental capacities begin to show measurable declines during or even before the middle years. Nevertheless the declines are gradual and slow and—particularly in the mental realm—go on for many years before they seriously interfere with well-rounded living.

Much remains to be learned about the natural aging process and about the diseases that hasten decline. For more than two decades the Congress, the great foundations, and private individuals have been contributing to the support of research along these lines.

However, health knowledge is useless unless it reaches the individual and is applied by him. Only so can it become effective. It is only recently that physicians and other workers in the field of health have recognized the possibility of maintaining vigorous and disease-free bodies into the middle and later years. Annual physical checkups are strongly urged, not simply to offer a chance to detect and check disease but to offer the individual the opportunity to gain even better average health. New nutritional knowledge is a notable assist to that end.

Yet only a beginning has been made so far. Much remains to be done before a truly up-to-date health service is available to all and, indeed, before all of us are wise enough to make use of what is now commonly available.

4. Income Security

The *sine qua non* of continued activity and social participation is an income sufficient to meet the requirements of well-rounded living. For most people in the middle years income is not the most serious problem they confront. Earnings are likely to be at a peak at this time. Educational and other expenses of the children are beginning to taper off. Wives may just now be returning to paid work after years away from it.

On the other side of the ledger, the wish to save more may be strong, for retirement is in sight; there may be an increase in medical expenses; and there may be pressure to spend more on cultural interests and travel.

The financial problem comes to a head on retirement. For most people income normally drops off to half what it was during the working years. To live within one's retirement income may be a major task. It takes a lot of careful planning.

Wider recognition that retirement is an integral part of the life cycle may lead to some thought about increasing normal retirement income. It would be logical to increase it as our national productivity rises. It is also likely that more and more people will do an improved job of preplanning retirement. They will take care of many items before they actually stop work, like the insurance of medical expenses. And society may decide to take a hand by making some services, like education and recreation, more widely available out of tax funds.

5. Education for Living

A condition of a satisfactory life is the possession of information, understanding, and the capacity to make decisions. Education can make a big contribution at this point.

In a rapidly changing society it is obvious that education must be a continuing and lifelong process. This is increasingly attaining popular acceptance; and opportunities for such education are multiplying.

A design for education for maturity and long life is beginning to appear. To be sure, there are many questions to be settled before it takes anything like final shape. And not only questions about what to teach. Who should pay for it, the client or the supplier, the individual or a tax-supported government agency? And how will you get the people who need it most to show up for instruction? Adult education is voluntary, not compulsory.

6. Opportunity for Expression and Participation

Implicit in all that has been said thus far is the thesis that the individual will try to satisfy his needs through continuing association and self-expression in family and community life. It can be assumed that the personal motivation is present. But will society provide the necessary opportunities?

As things stand today, the community sometimes places a premium on the experience of some of the middle-aged and retains them in positions of leadership. For others, perhaps equally gifted, it does little or nothing; and they gradually withdraw into inactive roles, deterioration, and helplessness.

The problems at issue are (1) defining and providing roles that exact from the individual the output of thought and energy of which he is capable and (2) attaching to these roles so provided, the recognition and status granted to them in earlier societies and, in our society, largely granted only to the roles of early adulthood.

Let us take a look at some of the roles so far devised for the middle aged and older people and ask if they really exhaust the possibilities in our culture.

Widely common are enlistment in such important community tasks as fund soliciting, political office, membership on governing boards, visiting and teaching shut-ins, transporting disabled and infirm persons to clinics, manning activity centers, religious counseling in association with churches, assisting classroom teachers, and helping to feed hospital patients and to teach craft skills to those ready for them.

Older people themselves are seizing the initative. The Old Guard in New Jersey, the Sunset Clubs in New Hampshire, and the Senior

Citizens Associations of Los Angeles and San Francisco are self-initiated groups set up by older people to provide educational and recreational opportunities for themselves and to promote housing and other programs to meet their specific needs.

An outstanding example of a new community institution focused on the basic needs and desires of people in the middle and older age groups is Little House, in Menlo Park, California. Little House was conceived and created by an organization of women who wanted to satisfy their own needs for creative activity, individuality, and community service. What they created is a community center with a rich and varied program of liberal education, art and craft work, lectures on health and nutrition, social events, personal counseling, and opportunities for voluntary services. From an uncertain beginning. Little House has grown to a membership of twelve hundred persons, who are being literally regenerated in the second half of their lives. Perhaps the most satisfactory feature of all has been the eagerness of Little House members themselves, as their self-confidence revives, to contribute to the happiness of others and to make their community a better place in which to live.

Great strides forward have been taken by man at various points in his history. The taming of fire, the discovery that grains could be cultivated, the invention of tools, made it possible for man to build permanent communities and take care of such aged as survived. The invention of writing facilitated communication and made it possible to make the records which are indispensable in giving culture continuity. The multiplication of the units of power at the disposal of each working individual provided the basis for a constantly rising standard of living. The regard for the individuality of each human being that is inherent in democracy has made each person more important to himself and his group. Perhaps the next great forward step will be the discovery of more satisfactory ways of living from birth to death, not only in material terms but in terms of cultural and spiritual values.

Time Out for Reflection

Instead of questions, we present here for the reader's considera-
tion a check-list, in outline form, presented to the 1959 Confer-
ence of the American Library Association by John Walker Powell.
As you consider each item, ask yourself whether you agree, dis-
agree, or need more data. Most of the items have been covered
in this book, and additional sources suggested.

The Issues and Problems of Aging

are *primarily* the result of American attitudes and expectations; *second-*
arily, of our changing economy. The latter are secondary because they
could be handled if the former were changed. It is to the former that
education is addressed. It must take place mostly at middle age; for the
adjustment that is made then will presage that to aging, and is the threshold to it; and it is only at middle age that the new and realistic vision
of the older years is emotionally possible.

The *reality-problems* are familiar:

> vocational obsolescence, which has set in even before retirement
> and is hopeless after, because of high-tension technical opera-
> tions, fast control-reaction time, rapidity of innovation, etc.
>
> splitting of family into separate small families
>
> geographical mobility; anonymous, inappropriate housing.

The *results* are:

> impersonal dependency (social security, insurance, etc.)
>
> loss of identity; alienation from continuing social groups
>
> social segregation of older people
>
> loss of familiar domestic, local, and national horizons.

Attitudes and expectations are mainly *negative*:

> toward age and the aging (cf. emphasis on youth in entertainment, advertising, magazine fiction)
> toward retirement (fear of poverty, idleness, uselessness, illness, death)
>
> lack of *knowledge* about the *norms of change* in body, mind
>
> lack of *understanding* of *stage-development* in life roles
>
> lack of *belief* in *increased powers at maturity* (learning, judgment, comprehension, perspective); in the *creative* power of maturity; in *leadership* potential
>
> lack of *confidence* in neededness and wantedness
> > in the ability to *count* for something
> > in the will to *stand* for something
>
> lack of *communication*: with; among; about.

The *result* is:

> lack of *self*-confidence, of the ego-strength requisite to either *service* or *solitude*.

In short: The American *image of man*

> —as producer and provider rather than artist or sage (cf. the Puritan preoccupation with productivity; and the American ego-ideal of self-reliance)
> —and as a biological organism seeking satisfaction through adjustments measured by values of tension and release

places the ultimate accolade on *survival* rather than *significance;* on *contribution* more than *the achievement of a person;* on *making things go,* more than on the *stillness at the vortex.*

Thus the very highest achievements that old age can bring are denied reality and value, in the very society that achieved man's first breakthrough into mass longevity.

How can we set about converting these negations into affirmations, these difficulties into opportunities? What part can you play?

327

READINGS   CHAPTER 9

The Development of

Mature Individuals

John C. Whitehorn

PERHAPS MATURITY IS in human life an aspiration rather than an achievement, something toward which we human beings may struggle but never
quite reach. At any rate, maturity is never a gift which comes to one, like
a trust fund, upon reaching a specified birthday. Whatever approximation to maturity one may attain is attained through action, not by mere
waiting.

Four Stages of Immaturity

For clinical use I find it convenient to distinguish four stages of *immaturity*, designated for fairly obvious reasons as the infantile stage,
the childish stage, the early adolescent stage and the late adolescent stage.
I shall briefly describe these levels, with some comments on the means
of recognizing them:

Infantile Level

At the infantile level one expects from others a limitless amount of
service and consideration—without any automatic feeling of reciprocal
obligation. This attitude was most clearly, though paradoxically, expressed by one of my patients when she said, "I'm no baby. I know what
I want, and I want what I want when I want it." The outstanding emotional need at this level is for affection or attention.

Childish Level

At the childish level, there has developed some sense of responsibility, but it is a delegated responsibility of the kind that is completely erased by a good excuse. The alibi habit is the characteristic expression of this stage. Great circumstantiality in speech is a useful clinical clue. Persons at the childish level of immaturity expect reliability in others, but only formal effort, up to the "excused" level, in themselves. They may expend much more effort in framing acceptable excuses than might be required to get a job done. Obsessive scrupulosity is a substitutive way of establishing merit, rather characteristic of this level. Praise or blame is the focus of attention. The great emotional need of the childish level is for security, characteristically sought in attachment to others—older or more powerful persons who may appear reliable and interested.

Early Adolescent Level

At the early adolescent level, exhibitionism and prestige-seeking are the outstanding manifestations of a strong push to gain personal significance, and to sustain it by repetitive demonstration. The striving for self-sufficiency requires extrafamilial supports, and those are characteristically found in idealistic hero worship and its gangs.

Badges and trophies have high value as demonstrable symbols of prestige. The sense of group responsibility develops at this level, limited in range to the gang or even more limited to one's buddy, but rather fanatical in its intensity. The great emotional need at this stage is for assurance as to personal significance, rather than simply affection or security.

Now personal significance can show off only in a social setting. It can never be wholly individualistic. There is therefore at this level a correlated growth of social sense expressed in personal loyalty or small group loyalty.

Late Adolescent Level

The late adolescent level is the stage of -isms—romanticism, idealism, or cynicism, for example. The sense of social responsibility has become more generalized in the form of loyalty to a cause, as well as to a person or group. The tendency to excess is still present as in earlier adolescence, but it is doctrinaire excess rather than physically strenuous excess. The pseudosophisticated "line" of talk, the "wisecrack," and the sophomoric savant are easily recognizable manifestations. Sexual interests are expressed in pairing off and in courtship behavior, but success in that field, or the anticipation of success, has the emotional quality of a conquest rather than of mutual devotion.

Three Emotional Needs

In connection with the presentation of this outline of levels of immaturity I have found it helpful to relate them to three emotional needs. They are (1) the need for affection, (2) the need for personal security, and (3) the need for personal significance. I have characterized them as needs because it appears to me that a person has to have some satisfaction in these three items in order to develop and maintain the social assurance required for effective participation with others. The three form a series having relatively different degrees of importance at different stages of personality development. In a rough way, the motivational patterns pertinent to these needs can be used to evaluate levels of maturity.

The Need for Affection

The predominant emotional need in infancy is the need for affection. Affection assures protection, care, and nourishment. But affection means more. It fosters enthusiastic responsiveness and attitudes of eager expectation in the most elementary social situation of parent and child.

Affection provides some assurances of favoritism at a time of great dependency when some special favoritism is greatly needed. In some persons, the infantile pattern of dependency upon affectionate favoritism persists and persists and persists. One may say that the person has clung to infantile values, or has been fixated at such levels through extreme attachments, but it is my impression that the principal reasons for such an extreme block in maturation lie in the failure of the home to provide the security needed to negotiate the next steps in emotional development.

The Need for Personal Security

In order to participate with comfort in the competitive life among other children, or even to endure without extreme distress the uncertainty of parental absence, little children need to gain from their experiences a reasonable expectation that the universe is dependable. If mother has to leave, mother does come back. Food is forthcoming at suitable intervals, and so is affectionate attention.

Later, the custom of sharing goodies and the custom of taking turns inculcate a faith that fair play characterizes the operations of the youngster's universe. This faith is supported and strengthened by the interventions of parental figures supporting principles of fair play and justice.

Without the faith built on such experience, one feels very much alone and in danger, not only from aggressive attacks, but from one's own tendencies to aggression, which might elicit overwhelming retaliation.

Lack of support or lack of firmness in parental figures endangers this security; frequent and unpredictable conflicts between parents wreck it; favoritism and overprotectiveness from parents inhibit its development. The reasonable expectation of fair play is a condition necessary for a person's eager exploration and adventure in the give-and-take of social living. The practical advantages so gained are great and the emotional rewards are very large. The bargain is a good one and most youngsters appear to perceive, in time, that it involves obligations to adhere to fair practices oneself.

The psychiatrist not infrequently encounters patients whose faith in fair play or whose sense of security has gained so little validation from experience that they have had to rely throughout life upon favoritism, in the infantile pattern. Lacking the sense of security that comes from a faith in fairness, some infantile personalities live life timidly and with great circumspection.

Other infantile personalities, with careless abandon, dare foolish risks and impulsive adventures, apparently as means to gain repeated manifestations of the protector's favoritism and power. I have seen such examples in which it appeared to me that the protector took a childish or infantile delight in the extreme expression of favoritism and indulgence, and I have been tempted to label this partnership *infantilisme à deux*.

These more timorous and circumspect infantile personalities are close neighbors in the classificatory sense to childish characters who made, so to speak, too tight a contract in their security-bargain, committing themselves to extremely meticulous codes of conduct. One suspects, and the suspicion is sometimes confirmed by adequate histories, that such youngsters have earlier suffered a fairly severe deficiency in regard to their affectional needs.

The Need for Personal Significance

The childhood phase of personality growth, with the emphasis upon the development of personal security, covers a good many years and a good deal of experimental role enactment whereby the boundaries of social tolerance may be fairly widely explored.

But the widest extravagances in testing the limits are likely to appear in adolescence. In the usual course of events in our culture, one feels in adolescence an increased need to achieve and assert some sense of individual personal significance—sometimes very assertively against authority figures such as parents, sometimes in exhibitionistic physical exploits, and often, during later adolescence, in a rather exaggerated radicalism or excessive reactive conservatism.

We are also familiar in our culture (probably more so than in other cultures) with the grown-up, middle-aged adolescent, grasping at opportunities for self-display, insatiable in the pursuit of badges of distinction, chasing after sexual exploits or other types of mastery, dramatizing attitudes of impudence or contempt of propriety.

In psychiatric case material one can find abundant evidence that difficulties of adjustment and psychopathological states often involve motivations based on extreme needs for asserting personal significance. As a clinician and a therapist, I do wish, however, to put in some good words for these adolescent motivations, even in the older age groups. Behavior thereby motivated may be exasperating, but the patients who manifest it do get well, pretty regularly. Such motivations may prove very useful at certain stages of psychotherapeutic strategy.

Toward a Mature Personality

Complete maturity, then, is an ideal, only approximated in reality. Speaking approximately, therefore: in the mature personality a flexibility of social attitudes has been achieved. This is expressible in a variety of roles developed through life experiences which have served to fulfill emotional needs reasonably well.

The mature individual has not graduated to a stage in which he no longer has these needs; rather, he has attained flexibility in accepting and acting out the roles which satisfy these emotional needs. In developing his personal accommodation to the basic human condition of life—*inter-dependence*—he has had gratifying experiences of leadership and of loyalty, of domination and of submission.

To get along well with people in varying stages of maturity, the mature person needs to maintain the capacity for playful good humor. He can, on appropriate occasions, quit being so soberly "grown-up," and enter into adolescent and childish activities with spontaneity and gusto. He can share with lively sympathy in the emotional values pertaining to those less mature levels of social development.

He can not only enter into immature emotional contexts, but can come out of them again, as occasion requires, and resume more responsible roles, also with good humor and some measure of playful enthusiasm. Indeed, it might be said that the mature person—in order to maintain the emotional attitudes required by the fact of persisting interdependence, and to handle the friction generated by such interdependence—has to retain, and exercise, some propensities for childishly playful curiosity and amusement.

The particular emotional needs which have been given special emphasis in this formulation are (1) the need for affection, which is paramount in infancy, (2) the need for personal security and trust, gratified by the culture's provisions during childhood for inculcating fair play and the basic decencies of mutual respect and tolerance; and (3) the need for personal significance, which in our culture becomes particularly prominent in adolescence.

At maturity one does not graduate from these needs but attains an advanced stage of competence in social roles well suited to satisfy such needs in varied ways, and to behave toward others in ways that satisfy their emotional needs. Failure of life experience to fulfill these emotional needs may seriously distort personality development in a manner somewhat analogous to the enduring chronic effects of temporary nutritional deficiencies.

Without some appreciation of these emotional needs and the levels of immaturity which seem to characterize persons who have endured extreme deprivation of these needs, I would find myself much handicapped in my professional work, for I would be made extremely anxious or would feel intensely frustrated by situations which, in an adult, common-sense view, would not seem to call for such reactions.

How Much Free Choice?

Having spoken now at some length about the environmental factors, and about the deficiencies in social environment which may seriously limit the development of mature attitudes through the deprivation of emotional needs, I should try to balance the discussion by some reference to a person's role in his own development. It happens that I am not one of those who believe in complete 100 per cent determinism. To a small extent, but to a significant extent, human beings, as I see them, seem able to exercise some degree of choice in their behavior.

According to Ludwig Bolk's "foetal theory" of the origin of the human species through genetic repressive mutations which made man enduringly infantile, and which prevented his developing the fully specialized repertoire of his simian cousins, we may be handicapped by such deficiencies, but we have gained a degree of freedom in modifying our behavior.

We have gained some chance of escape from the coercive force of instinctive patterns of life. We have developed processes of domestication and socialization which permit a certain degree of freedom of personal preference or choice.

It is indeed one of the significant achievements of civilization to have gained for so many an enlargement of their individual freedom of choice of behavior. The rules required by the social nature of human living are not too rigidly restrictive. Some leeway exists so that individuals may give acceptable expression to their temperamental differences, and so participate with gratification and enthusiasm within the broad patterns required by their mutual interdependence.

Unfortunately many people feel, unnecessarily, that they are oppressed and deprived, and fail therefore to develop their opportunities and capacities. The educative process, as distinguished from mere instruction, consists essentially in awakening people to the more enthusiastic and spontaneous exploration of their available freedoms. The potentialities for growth and development, for greater maturity and achievement, thus evoked provide for the educator a sort of vicarious enlargement of life, a gratification shared also by the psychiatrist when he is able to evoke in an immature patient the faith and enthusiasm by which he achieves a more advanced level of personal growth.

The Mature Attitude

Edgar Z. Friedenberg

I SHOULD LIKE TO BEGIN this analysis by re-making three points about which there is considerable agreement among most persons who have considered the attributes of maturity. The first of these is that the mature individual can certainly *not* be recognized by any *particular* set of beliefs or convictions which one may expect to find in all such persons. There are no ideological tests for maturity; there is not and cannot be any series of questions through which those entitled to call themselves mature might be identified by their common answers.

The second is that there is, nevertheless, a relationship between personal maturity and a fundamental style of life which may be called virtuous, and has been called this since the time of the Greeks. We do recognize the mature individual through the net attitude toward the experience of living which that life-style expresses. It is in general a humane and responsible attitude, even though it may lack specific components of any particular prevailing moral ideology.

The third point is that maturity means, not the end of growth, but the condition in which growth is most fruitful. Before an individual—of whatever species—achieves a degree of maturity, most resources must be spent on development of a stable apparatus for living. When this has been realized, resources then become available for his prime functions and purposes. But stability in maturity is never static. It is completely dynamic; the mature individual is one whose energies are most fully absorbed in being himself and fulfilling his purpose, which is a very active state indeed.

It seems evident, then, that attitudes characteristic of maturity must be attitudes toward life itself, rather than toward any given issue. Persons, to the degree that they are mature, do hold in common a characteristic orientation toward life, although there may be no area of agreement among them on particular ideas. This orientation is observable, not as the background of their activities, but as a part of the pattern which they create for themselves in the process of living. As they grow, and grow more experienced, the pattern becomes richer and more subtle. It also becomes more clearly defined in their every act of being.

This pattern of living, itself, constitutes the attitude of maturity. In order to discuss it, we must use the word "attitude" in its sense of a customary posture or position, as in "receptive attitude" or "a defiant attitude," or even, "I just don't like his whole attitude." It is not sufficient, and would lead to confusion, to limit the concept of "attitude" in this context to that of a belief or emotional response.

When we speak of a person's attitude toward Negroes, we should not refer merely to whether he is prejudiced against them and how much. We mean rather the condition assumed by his entire self when a question concerning "the race issue" arises and he has to do something about it. I think that personal maturity is indeed revealed by certain common characteristics of attitude in this sense, regardless of the particular issue which may be involved or the way the person decides to vote on it. In this paper, I shall examine these characteristics, and the dynamics which seem to underlie their operation.

Four Facets of Maturity

There are many ways in which these characteristics might be defined. I think it will be fruitful to discuss four of them, which I shall call *awareness, objectivity, emotional responsiveness,* and *civility.* I am using these terms very much in their usual sense; but I am concerned with certain of their implications which are not always stressed, so I had better explain what I mean by them and how I think they are operative in the mature attitude.

Awareness

By *awareness*, I mean simply the power a person has to know what is going on around and within him, and to take conscious account of it. There are two rather clearly distinguishable aspects of this. Awareness is, on the one hand, a matter of education and intelligence. One cannot be aware if one is simply too dull or ignorant to read the signs.

On the other hand, awareness is equally a function of ego-dominance and emotional well-being. It is not enough to see the signs, and be intellectually qualified to interpret them. One must also be willing and able to allow them to penetrate and to *accept their implications.* So much of our energy seems to be taken up from day to day in trying to communicate with people who show quite clearly by their defensiveness that what is going on has got through to them, but who are totally absorbed in the crucial task of remaining unaware of it. Most responsible people, I believe, by the time they are middle-aged, cannot help recalling several disagreeable occasions on which they have been injured or betrayed by persons who were resolutely unimpeded by insight as they carried out their destructive purpose as steadfastly as a wasp building a nest. Some of us have even known individuals so twisted in their perception of reality as to believe we were acting that way ourselves.

In calling *awareness* an aspect of maturity I am asserting that a mature individual approaches life with the capacity to perceive, and to permit himself to understand, the complexities of his involvement in it. I do not, however, wish to imply that one achieves this condition simply by hanging around on the surface of the earth for a quarter of a century or more. Nor, certainly, do I wish to imply that stupidity, ignorance, or malice may be the more easily condoned by relating to them flaws in the process of growth.

One of the few really unpleasant consequences of the influence of psychoanalysis has been the tendency to evade moral judgments by taking refuge in neurosis. The bad guys of history, from Heliogabalus to Hitler, were doubtless all, in my terms, immature; but this is not the slightest reason why anyone should have put up with them. It does follow, however, that it is the capacity of the human being for growth which spares most men their character and their destiny. This, I think becomes increasingly clear as we examine the other three aspects I have attributed to the mature attitude.

Objectivity

The second of these is *objectivity*. This is a conception closely related to the psychodynamic aspects of awareness just discussed; but it goes much further. By *objectivity,* I mean the capacity of the individual to break through the skin-barrier without confusion; to discern the properties of external reality without attributing to it the properties he would wish it to have, or believing himself to be responding to it when he is actually responding to his own needs and feelings. All aspects of maturity have moral significance; the objective person does not bear false witness, which is not the easiest of the Commandments to observe.

This conception of objectivity implies nothing whatever about detachment or impartiality. An objective person, if he sees a man beating a dog, will not confuse the dog's feelings with his own feelings about the dog. He will not confuse his objection to the beating with his delight in seeing himself as the kind of man who *does* object to it. But he may also be too forthright to permit such considerations to sickly over the native hue of his resolution; and it will reflect nothing on his objectivity if he goes right ahead and slugs the man—so long as he does it because he saw something real which really made him angry.

In the world in which we live, it is probably impossible and surely undesirable for an objective individual to be dispassionate. There are only two ways in which he can remain so, and each involves a serious failure in objectivity. He can stay dispassionate if he does not see what the external world is like; if he does not really believe in Suez or nuclear fission. This is a common form of detachment, reaching peak perfection in waxy catatonia.

Or—and this is even more common and more serious—he can stay dispassionate through a kind of reverse solipsism, attributing to himself the feelings and moral attitudes which he detects in the external world, making use of adaptive anxiety to achieve ethical neutrality. This is the garden variety of conformity, on which the modern state seems largely to depend for cohesion. It is good-humored and makes life easier; why should Big Brother waste effort watching us, when we are so cautiously watching ourselves for him? It leads to the tolerant and well-rounded view—the patience to give equal TV time to the murderer and to any confused liberal who still wants to step out of line and speak for the victim. This may be tolerance, but it is not objectivity; and it is not maturity.

Reality being what it is, objectivity should lead *to* passion, not away from it. This is not a particularly novel point of view: ". . . a true knowledge of good and evil," Spinoza wrote, "cannot restrain any emotion insofar as the knowledge is true, but only insofar as it is considered as an emotion."

Modern life, however, treats knowledge of good and evil precisely as if it *were* an emotion; and rejects the emotion as a subjective state having no valid relation to reality. We distrust people who "get too involved." We use the word *disturbed* as a synonym for *sick*, and mean by both *unbalanced*. By treating genuine and deeply felt devotion or indignation as if it were neurotic *per se*, we alienate people from the most important meanings of their life and forestall their growth.

Emotional Responsiveness

It is in the strongest possible agreement with Spinoza's view that I have designated *emotional responsiveness* as a fundamental aspect of the mature attitude. Real men and women love and hate. They may not be easy to get along with, but you can count on them. They love and hate with awareness and objectivity; they understand their world, and they respond to it according to their own values.

What is involved in this emotional responsiveness? It is difficult to analyze, but at the root of it are clearly two traits: self-respect and empathy. The kind of self-respect which is needed is remote indeed from the categories of clean-living which one learns in scout camp; it is equally distinct from the grandeur of minor princes. It is effective to the degree that it is unconscious.

This is true not merely because unconscious processes tend to influence us more powerfully than conscious decisions. Nor is it true merely because conscious self-respect so easily turns priggish and alienates us from real experience of other persons and of the world.

It is true because what people have in common as human beings is largely the stuff of presymbolic experience. What we respect in ourselves, if we are to be capable of genuine response to other persons and life around us, must be a humanity which existed before it was molded and embossed by our particular lives, in our particular series of social roles, in our particular branch of Western culture. Our particular branch of Western culture is very often cheap and nasty. While it gave us the tools with which to communicate with one another, and the terms in which to do so, it has often weakened us in our use of them.

If we have retained a respect for our personal share in common humanity, no matter what shape we are now in, we have the basis for emotional response to any man. Not, to be sure, with love. The day is late, and there are shadows which were not cast by lovable persons. But we have the basis on which to respond to some men with love, and to all with authenticity. The instrument of this response is empathy.

Empathy is the capacity, also unconscious in origin, to feel with other persons; to sense their emotional condition. Unlike awareness and objectivity, it probably does not increase with age. A small child does not know enough to interpret reality accurately, and cannot distinguish

reliably between himself and the outer world. But infants, perhaps unfortunately, are connoisseurs of emotional climate; they have a lot of
sensitivity to lose before they are fit for adult life. Those who lose least
of it in the course of development are able as adults to fuse understanding and feelings into a degree of perception which is "miraculous."
Saints are recruited from their numbers, which tends to keep the quality
of miracles from descending to the merely magical.

Empathy, to be sure, is the source of compassion in human affairs;
and as such is highly prized. More attention should be given, I think,
to its function as the source of precision as well. Our common humanity
knows quite well that mankind can be tricky as well as noble—is most
human when it is being both at once, with a complexity which may defy
analysis but not detection.

If the capacity for empathy has been retained as awareness and objectivity have developed—then we know, and we are no less compassionate
for knowing. We know exactly. As we comfort the widow in her bereave-
ment, we can accept the unexpressed release along with the very real
grief. We can spank our children when we must without expecting them
ever to quite forgive us. We can watch the candidates for public office
assert their fellowship on television, and know that the cold clutching
at our hearts is functional rather than organic; we need not send for
Dr. White quite yet.

Through self-respect and empathy, then, we respond with feeling to
other persons and to the common situation which binds us together. We
view this situation with full awareness of its meaning; and we can distinguish our role in it from that of other persons and other factors. We
can act; and when we act, we know what we are doing and why, from
the bottom of our hearts.

Is there more to the mature attitude than the habit of approaching
life in this spirit? Although this would make a very good average, I
think there is one more necessary attribute. I have called this final
essential characteristic of the mature attitude *civility*.

Civility

Civility, like emotional responsiveness, involves and is derived from
self-respect and empathy. But it contributes to maturity something
distinct, which is the complement—even, in a measure, the antithesis—
of emotional responsiveness. Civility is the virtue which makes civic
life endurable. It functions to preserve the integrity of individuals who
must pass their lives in a changing succession of ambiguous groups;
and it does so in part by keeping a distance between people. Its purpose
is not isolation, but privacy; and it works through understanding—not

concealment. In a private home or a good Continental hotel, one does not lock one's door. People don't come barging in. But if they do, there must be locks; and if they break the locks, there must be guns.

Among civil persons, one needn't lock one's mind or one's heart. One's neighbors know when they are welcome there. Some may become lovers; the others, knowing themselves no less welcome than before, quietly note that the hours for unexpected visits have been altered. This gives them more time to cultivate their own gardens. What they grow they may send to the fair if they wish to compete for a blue ribbon or an honorable mention. But if there is no honorable mention for this class of event, they may still enjoy it among themselves. They are aware; they know what is going on; they are responsive, and responsible. They trust one another, even though they have been acquainted for years. There are no spies.

These are the sort of persons whose attitude I call mature. I need hardly say that they do not dominate modern society. Modern society makes enormous demands on the maturity of those who would live full lives in it; but it does not encourage any aspect of maturity.

The conditions of contemporary life make it very difficult to become aware. This is usually attributed to the complexity of our society; but it is by no means self-evident that our society *is* more complex than that of the renaissance or antiquity. It is certainly more intricate and has more moving parts. Our difficulty in becoming aware seems more nearly due to a built-in obscurantism.

The administrators of our communications, being themselves among the most rapidly moving parts, are neither willing nor able to pause and give account of the total apparatus. The mass media have come to function rather like the specially designed industrial lighting developed during World War II, which concealed installations more effectively than detailed camouflage ever could.

Only certain specialized organs, such as *Fortune* or the *New York Times*, which circulate chiefly among individuals wholly established in our culture and its *ethos*, yield genuine insights. They are good enough, and honest to boot—there are very few issues of general policy about which any citizen need understand more than can be learned from them. But they do not fall into the hands of children or servants; and no comic book or TV show would permit itself to be so wise. Those accustomed to be comforted by monsters, supermen, and Desi and Lucy would find that the *Times* scared the pants off them.

Objectivity is opposed by the dominant processes of cooptation and interlocking veto-groups which characterize American society. Every individual, that is to say, who tries to do anything or get anywhere is reminded frequently and forcibly that what other people think of him is more important a determinant than his own goals and values. Under these conditions, it takes the soul of a saint in the hide of an elephant even to remain certain that one has a separate identity of one's own, and that the distinction between subject and object is meaningful.

To be fair, one must note that our culture has in some degree taken account of its disastrous tendency toward alienation by institutionalizing powerful therapeutic forces, like psychoanalysis, to countervail against it. But they are not sufficient to redress the balance. The great threat to our objectivity remains that which caught up with the college president in Randall Jarrell's delightful *Picture from an Institution,* whom Jarrell describes as so well adjusted to his environment that it was difficult to tell which was the environment and which was the president.

Emotional responsiveness suffers from the decay of the Kantian imperative. In a society in which individual advancement is more highly prized than love, in which people compete for status, and home is a good place to be from, the Kantian imperative doesn't stand a chance. We use other men as a means, and seldom as an end withal. How dare we love or hate, when we never know who may be useful? We seek rather to understand one another, not in the fullness of our hearts but as one might a 1950 car, which will still give pretty good service if we know its quirks and don't try to push it too hard. Ultimately, if we are doing well, we may not even trade it in. People are sometimes sentimental about cars.

But it is civility which seems to encounter the most formidable checks, and to be most continually breached. There is in modern life a truly Panic quality, malicious and goatish. We are appalled by the hostility in which we dwell together—but so much so that we sometimes fail to notice that it is rancid as well as bitter. There is no dignity in it. The gossip at dusk trills over his Martini, and sages and statesmen are stoned through the streets like yellow dogs. On every enduring monument one finds, as Holden Caulfield noted, an ugly word crudely chalked.

We do not despair

It is noted in the *Times.* A few months ago there was an exemplary issue. It had in it ugliness and terror enough; British boys had been hanged in reprisal for the hanging of Greek boys; Algeria was in a state of civil insurrection; Prime Minister Eden was being pilloried because a British Naval officer had lost his life while engaged in an act of inexplicable espionage on behalf of what must have been, in terms of British traditions of decency toward guests, a peculiarly foreign power. But the story most symbolic of our times contained no element of tragedy. It was, in fact, about the only really funny thing in the paper that day.

An unknown transport plane, wandering over the Gaza strip, was intercepted by the Israeli air force and forced down at Lydda airport. There it proved to be British. The plane, that is, and the crew were British. The passengers were Rhesus monkeys which had undertaken the journey to London to permit their livers to be used in the preparation of Salk vaccine. They were recognized as unusually public-spirited monkeys and no more anti-Semitic than most, and were dispatched again toward London and Destiny without let or hindrance when it was found that their papers, such as they were, were in order.

Well, the monkeys made it; so perhaps, one ought not to give up. Though immature—the livers of elderly monkeys are not suitable for Salk vaccine—their behavior throughout the incident was composed and detached; they did not permit themselves to become involved, and the cloud of suspicion soon passed.

The role of man is harder to play. The casting is often poor, and the direction—if there is any—rather inept. The whole drama has too much spectacle and too little characterization and development. The same situations are repeated in every act.

But it must be noted that the monkeys did not invent the vaccine. We did. I don't think we have very sound grounds for pride in our superior technical proficiency, which is an ambiguous virtue. What is important is that we were able to see some reason for inventing it in the first place. We do object to children's being paralyzed. We do try to change what we object to. We do perform miracles—not only of technology, but of organization and intellectual continuity—in the effort. Even when, having spent our lives scaling apparently insurmountable technical obstacles with final success, we find ourselves bemired in the ponderous procedures of Government itself, we do not despair.

Despair is not a component of the mature attitude.

Suggestions for Further Reading

The Education of Henry Adams. New York: Houghton, Mifflin Co., 1918.
> All of 19th century Europe and America enter into the education of a New England boy. One of the truly great reflective writings on 20th century America. Those who find his thesis of "20th century multiplicity versus medieval unity" attractive should certainly read also his *Mont St. Michel and Chartres,* now available in paperback book.

Adventures of Ideas, by Alfred North Whitehead. Mentor Books edition, 1955.
> A superb essay on human values, by one of the 20th century's foremost philosophers.

part III

SOME ASPECTS OF
RETIREMENT

While this is a book about *aging rather than for the already retired, still its purpose is to focus thinking on the* approach *of such problems. Therefore a sort of Appendix seems to be appropriate, in which some aspects of the retirement question are presented to stimulate further inquiry.*

Dr. John Walker Powell (born in 1904 in Duluth, Minnesota) is a writer and consultant in adult education. Besides experience in community services administration, and in community and psychiatric research, he has devised and directed several significant experiments in adult group study. He has been lecturer in education at the George Washington University and at Teachers College, Columbia University, and program consultant to The Fund for Adult Education, among other institutions. His principal books include Education for Maturity *(1949) and* Learning Comes of Age *(1956), cited in this volume.*

"There is another kind of interest that is not an interest in knowledge for its own sake . . . but . . . an interest in rationality. . . . I refer to the adult's desire to talk things over. This desire has been misrepresented as a desire to learn something in the ordinary sense of learning. It is not that. The adults want to clarify their thoughts, . . . to talk out their worries and untangle their deliberations.

. . . Adults need to become objective, but this is not the scientist's objectivity of disinterestedness. It is objectivity in the sense of a control over passions that have been aroused by strenuous interpersonal conflicts. It is objectivity in the sense of a remembrance of important considerations forgotten in the heat of battle. It is objectivity in the sense of the mobilizing of all relevant knowledge that one has previously acquired and bringing it to bear upon the immediate problem. It is seeing all of the angles. It is a focused study.

. . . I should like to call it civic religion. . . . Our republic . . . requires meditation as well as prayer. . . . The functions of civic religion are vital to the well-being and sanity of society."

—WAYNE A. R. LEYS
"The Two Roles of the University in Adult Education."
Journal of Higher Education,
January 1955.

10

This Question
of Retirement

JOHN WALKER POWELL

ANTHROPOLOGISTS LONG AGO recognized that in many primitive cultures there were fixed points at which individuals passed from one age-status to another: the child passes into puberty, the adolescent into manhood or womanhood, the active adult into the elder. Each of these transitions was marked by tribal ceremonies, pleasant or painful, that marked the tribe's acceptance of the individual in his new status. These ceremonies were, long ago, given the name "rites of passage."

In our country, there have been at various times and in various classes similar rites: the boy's first long trousers; his first razor; college graduation; the debutante's "coming-out"; the celebration of marriage itself.

"Retirement" has become, in our accelerated machine culture, a "rite of passage," and, like those in other cultures, it is looked forward to with both happy anticipation and anxious dread: anticipation of the new freedom it promises; dread of the new worries it creates.

One famous recipe for retirement, for example, is that offered by a President of the United States: "You put a rocking chair on the porch, and sit in it. Then, after about six months, you—very slowly—begin to rock." Other models have been exemplified by other Presidents; and many enticing pictures of the life of retirement have been drawn by insurance and investment advertisers.

But certain sobering facts remain. In the words of a recent author, "We think old people should be glad to lay down the burden of work. Turns out that retirement is our number one man killer in the mid-sixties. Medical miracles can prolong life threatened by illness; but no one has yet found the cure for retirement." [1]

The very values our society teaches us to cherish most highly—self-reliance, work and achievement, contribution to family and to society—are the ones retirement threatens. Our very identity may seem to be lost as we step off the merry-go-round of gainful employment, and face the threat of dependent idleness.

Yet the wisdom, the experience, the judgment, the skill of our older persons constitute one of our greatest national reservoirs of human resource. It will not, however, be tapped by any social miracle. Its value must be realized through (1) community and company planning, and (2) individual and group initiative.

In the last decade or two, enormous amounts of study, discussion, and experiment have been devoted to the economic, social, and personal gains and losses of retirement. Labor and management alike have debated the compulsory age limit, the possibilities of job transfer, the questions of educational planning and economic cushioning. The U. S. Department of Health, Education, and Welfare has staffed a permanent committee on the matter of aging; and most large communities have committees studying its implications for them.

But much—indeed most—of the job remains to be done by the individual: You. And the two most important things to recognize are these:

(1) Gradually, just as "aging" has moved from the status of a "problem" to that of a promising achievement, so our thinking is moving from the painful prospect of "retirement *from*" to the more

---

[1] But see the contradicting data in *The Journal of Social Issues,* listed in Suggested Readings for this chapter.

optimistic—and more important—question of "retirement *to*." The affirmative meaning of leisure, and the opportunities for creative personal fulfillment and service, alone or in company with others, are vital to one's planning for the later years.

(2) The time to prepare for retirement is *before* the event. We begin "aging" the day we are born; and all of life is, in one sense, a training for its later years. Increasing recognition of this fact is leading to courses or units on aging and retirement in college, and even in high school, when the personal aspects of the problem pertain mostly to one's parents. Adult education, including radio and television, is putting increased attention upon the *prior* study of our later years.

Remarkable in our society also is the increasing gift of leisure it is making to all of us in our working years: leisure which we can, and should, use to *develop, test, and practice* the kinds of things we will do, and the kinds of persons we will be, after retirement comes.

The book thus far has therefore been addressed primarily to men and women in the pre-retirement years. But the wealth of literature on retirement itself, its circumstances and effects, if not its cause and cure, is growing steadily. It is the aim of this final section to call attention to some of the approaches that have been developed, or are being tried, and that have suggestive value for the thoughtful reader who wants to consider actions which he can take by himself, or which he can initiate by enlisting the help of others.

READINGS

CHAPTER 10

The Role of Leisure

Reuel Denney (1913-   ) and David Riesman,
(1909-   ) rapporteurs

WE THINK THAT THIS record will have meaning for all who are interested in the changing role of leisure in modern life. Is leisure leisureful if it becomes a problem? Do we need training for competence in leisure? Are the mass media of communication and entertainment that fill the leisure hours of so many people doing a proper job? All these themes and many others were touched upon by this roundtable in a discussion that was deliberately unsystematic and exploratory.

William C. DeVane, dean of Yale College and director of the Division of Liberal Arts at Yale University, tried to pin down the subject of discussion. He observed that there was leisure at various times in life. The leisure of the child is a different thing from the spare time that modern industry provides for the active worker, and that again is a different thing from the enforced leisure of the retired worker. John W. Dodds, professor of English and director of Special Programs in Humanities at Stanford University, thought Mr. DeVane's point an important one; leisure for his 15-year-old son is something quite different from leisure for him. He added that leisure could be considered as an attitude of mind rather than merely spare time. David Sarnoff, chairman of the board of the Radio Corporation of America and director of the National Broadcasting Company, agreed that leisure is a state of mind. He went on to emphasize that we ought to distinguish also between leisure in a normal world and leisure in an abnormal world full of tensions and war clouds:

Mr. Sarnoff. If we are discussing the problem of leisure at the present time, we are discussing merely the problem of how to escape from the things that are troubling us all day, how we can forget the problems of the day when we are through struggling with them in the office and elsewhere. But if we are discussing leisure in a normal atmosphere, where we have done the day's work and it has no more than the usual problems, then the question is how best to utilize that leisure, how to advance happy living, how to advance education and culture and better understanding.

Mark Starr, educational director of the International Ladies' Garment Workers' Union, AFL, distinguished between leisure for an elite and leisure for all, pointing up the modern problem of leisure.

Mr. Starr. Our problem today is leisure for the mass. There has always been an elite in every civilization which has enjoyed leisure. Sometimes they have used it to make people put up the Pyramids; sometimes they have used it like Plato, whose leisure depended on the slave class. Someone was doing the dirty work of the world. Our problem now is that we don't need a slave class any more; we have so harnessed our technical resources that leisure is now within the reach of a greater number of people than ever before. . . .

Running through the whole discussion was something that the chairman, Lynn T. White, Jr., president of Mills College, called "an ambivalence of attitude" toward leisure. In a conversation with another roundtable member the night before, he said, a mutual sense of guilt at taking part in a roundtable on leisure had come out.

Chairman White. We said, "Ha, ha, I have no leisure; why am I involved in this?" It was a sense of guilt and, at the same time, a sense of pride. In other words, we feel leisure is a cultural value. Theoretically we would rather like to participate in it, but we are sort of proud that we are such responsible members of society that we really have no time for leisure.

This ambivalence was related to a deep division of opinion that gradually appeared among members of the group. One idea was, as Chairman White put it, "that leisure is leisure, and that it is perfectly all right to do nothing either to improve yourself or to justify your existence to society." Another view was that leisure is to be used constructively for some purpose, not for mere idleness. Miss Santha Rama Rau of India, author, and student of both Asian and Western cultures, first put the issue acutely:

> Miss Rama Rau. I am wondering why leisure is a problem at all. Surely, nowhere else in the world do people fuss about what to do with their spare time. I think it is rather sad that some kind of guilt has been built up in this particular society so that people feel that they should be productive in their spare time. Production rolls with such a speed that now you feel you are useless unless you are making a bookcase or turning out a car or whatever you do. I think it is unfortunate that respect is gone for the man who simply sits in his rocking chair and thinks, if he happens to feel like it, or does nothing if he happens to feel like it. I think that is really the sickness underneath all of this. . . . So long as leisure is considered as a problem, it is certainly never going to be solved. What is wrong with lying on the beach and relaxing?

Charles B. Fahs, director for the Humanities, The Rockefeller Foundation, agreed with Miss Rama Rau and thought that we tended to overemphasize the distinction between leisure and work or between leisure and good forms of activity. Partly because of a linguistic difficulty, we have a problem and start worrying about what should be done during leisure time. Mr. Dodds and the chairman agreed that Americans evidently have a Puritan conscience on the subject of leisure—the very existence of a roundtable on the topic suggested that.

When Mr. Sarnoff confessed that "of all the problems which trouble me in the world at the present time, leisure is the least of those," Walter P. Paepcke, chairman of the board and chief executive officer, Container Corporation of America, spoke up for "exactly the opposite point of view."

> Mr. Paepcke. I think our fault today is that we are so busy with the urgent that we do not have time for the important; that we are always telephoning and seeing people and thinking and doing this and that, and when we come home in the evening we are dead tired.

Mr. Paepcke felt that our civilization will probably go down as similar to that of the Romans, not the Greeks. We will be known for our aqueducts, our roads, our laws, and for other concrete developments, but not for our philosophical, cultural, or artistic achievements. We have a somewhat distorted picture of success, not honoring the humanities or philosophers sufficiently.

CHAIRMAN WHITE. Mr. Paepcke is identifying leisure with the entirety of cultural activity.

MR. PAEPCKE. If I were a painter, I would say anything I do after I finish my painting is my leisure time. If I happen to be in the paper mill business and I go home from that, anything I do after that is my leisure time. I think we are confusing leisure with idleness.

MISS RAMA RAU. As I said before, what is wrong with doing nothing?

MR. PAEPCKE. I think there is something wrong with that. I think if we do a little thinking, or if we are being of some good to ourselves or to our neighbors, that is one thing. . . .

MISS RAMA RAU. You cannot be good to yourselves or to your neighbors if you do it under any kind of compulsion. If you happen to feel that you want to do nothing but lie on the beach and get a sunburn. . . .

MR. PAEPCKE. Then you might as well say that if one likes to get drunk, then it is all right to drink until ten or eleven.

MR. SARNOFF. Suppose you have done a useful day's work and you are engaged in creative work, and you have used your creative faculties for eight hours a day on your job, what is the matter with doing nothing after that? Why do you have to create any more that is useful or anything else?

Mr. Paepcke then stressed the importance of continuing one's education through life, and Reuel Denney, assistant professor of social sciences, University of Chicago, picked up one of Mr. Paepcke's earlier points.

MR. DENNEY. I agree with Mr. Paepcke's idea that leisure after work may come by looking at the works of man, his artistic achievements. After a day's work, leisure does not come easily, and one of the ways to get it is to be involved in an appreciation of someone else's work. This taking a look at how other people do things is a way of moving oneself toward the do-nothing state. It is like a kid who watches the garage mechanic; he can stand and watch fascinated for a long time because somebody else is working very well.

Mr. Denney's defense of the passive watcher seems to have escaped Mr. Sarnoff or not to have satisfied him, for, being worried by the implications of Mr. Paepcke's remarks, he took off by asking the chairman whether he would mind a "little frank discussion." Once assured on that, he defended the business career from Mr. Paepcke's observation that it was not a total way of life. Mr. Sarnoff felt that if a businessman did a good job at work he did not need to apologize either for that or for what he did afterwards. If he wanted to read a book or listen to a symphony, that was fine too. Mr. Sarnoff thought that there was no need to feel that he *had* to. If he uses his leisure in such a way that he has a happy state of mind, brings a happy atmosphere into his home and to his friends, and doesn't make trouble for his wife and his children and his community, that is the most useful thing he can do with his leisure.

MR. DODDS. You wouldn't argue that leisure should not be spent in mental and challenging pursuits, would you? The charge is brought against educators that they are always wanting to improve somebody's mind. There is nothing against it, I suppose?

MR. SARNOFF. Certainly not, but I would not want to impose an obligation to do it.

MR. DODDS. We are never going to legislate it. Obviously, nobody is going to do the same thing all the time as a leisure pursuit. I am a little surprised to discover a person in your profession saying leisure doesn't make any difference; it doesn't need to be discussed.

MR. SARNOFF. I stand by that position; I would still sell radios whether you define the issue or not.

Mark Benney, author and social scientist, London School of Economics, observed in this connection that the British, through taxation policy, were enforcing a self-improving attitude toward leisure. They were, in effect "nationalizing" leisure, with no entertainment tax levied on what the government thinks are good plays, whereas, of course, gambling is taxed, saloons are taxed, the music halls are taxed. [Note that on the day the Conference opened it was reported that the House of Representatives in the American Congress had voted to exempt the Metropolitan Opera, symphony orchestras, and ballet from the admissions tax.] Mr. Benney then turned to the issue of the Puritan conscience, asking why some people at the table seemed to define leisure as leisure and others as work which has to be done in order that one may get on better with his neighbors.

Charles H. Sawyer, director of the Division of the Arts and dean of the School of Fine Arts at Yale University, identified himself—and this took a fair amount of courage—with the Calvinist position. "Leisure for what?" was his question. He suggested that most of us need leisure as pauses for reflection. Some need it as a relief from monotony, and possibly looking at one of Mr. Sarnoff's television shows helps in that respect. Other people want leisure for the enrichment and the enhancement of the individual, and Mr. Paepcke had suggested leisure for contributions to the community itself. Mr. Sawyer regarded all these uses as important.

The chairman turned next to Howard Mumford Jones, professor of English at Harvard University. Like a few others, Mr. Jones had come prepared not only with a viewpoint but with facts and figures. The viewpoint was that business civilization had substituted happiness for satisfaction—the latter being better. The figures to back up Mr. Jones' position were drawn from his content analysis of the ads in the *Saturday Evening Post*. Of 167 faces he found 114 that were smiling or laughing; eight blissfully asleep and obviously happy; six men blowing smoke rings—well known, he said, to be happiness. It was plain that Mr. Jones was against this smiling, fatuous happiness. He found, indeed, the whole system of advertising to be one great vacuity that induced its readers not to look for anything else in leisure but this vague happiness.

Mr. Starr, who qualified, in the chairman's words, as "another spokesman for the Puritan conscience," felt that one could possibly get happiness by Miss Rama Rau's method of loafing in the sun but not for long by the fake happiness depicted in the ads which Mr. Jones had counted up.

> MR. STARR. We are spoiling our kids to a certain extent unless we show them that the only real satisfaction is something they do for themselves. One evil that is spoiling our leisure is "spectatoritis." We go and watch the other guys do things. The only real satisfaction comes through putting something of yourself into something and expressing yourself. That means self-discipline, and that is the real enjoyment which leisure can give.

Leo Lionni, art director of *Fortune* magazine, took up the cudgels for the view previously expressed by Miss Rama Rau. Describing himself as "a man with partly Calvinistic, partly Jewish, and partly Catholic background, who was raised for fourteen years in a country where *dolce far niente* is considered one of the most wonderful things in life," he observed that Americans feel sinful about sometimes doing nothing, and at the same time they admire the "poor, underprivileged, and yet happy Italians" for being able to do nothing.

> MR. LIONNI. I think the thing that should be explored is whether the incapacity for doing nothing has not caused many bad things in our society. For instance, heavy drinking, I think, is to a great extent due to the incapacity for doing nothing. . . .

Repeatedly the roundtable came up to the problem of the elderly in our society and that special kind of leisure known as retirement. But each time it backed away, partly out of a feeling that the subject of "geriatrics" has been receiving so much attention lately and is such a large topic in itself that a general group like this one could do little with it in a brief session. However, the importance of the problem was recognized, and it was one of the subjects on which the roundtable definitely urged the need for further study.

Mr. Starr referred to the situation in the coat and suit industry where, thanks to enlightened management and progressive unions, a man can retire at sixty-five. "It is not made compulsory. If it were made compulsory, we would kill a lot of the old men, because they know how to do nothing but work." Mr. Starr regarded this as a great indictment of our educational system and of the narrow life to which these men have been confined hitherto. . . .

To Mr. Higgins, the problem of retirement seemed the most acute problem of leisure that we have today, and in his view it is becoming more and more acute. Mr. White was inclined to agree.

> CHAIRMAN WHITE. This is perhaps the most critical area of the whole problem of leisure. In the very first half hour of our roundtable, there were several members who felt it was so complex that the word "geriatrics" should no longer be mentioned at the table. I have rather regretted that. I don't quite know what we could do in a short time, but we might be able to define the areas of our ignorance.

As examples of our ignorance, Chairman White suggested that "we simply do not know what can be done to make retiring people feel they are still significant in our society. I think we do not know how we can build attitudes during the more active working periods in people's lives which will sustain them in the period of retirement. Perhaps we have to glamorize leisure as we have not."

Both Mr. DeVane and Miss Rama Rau pointed out that preparation should begin at an early stage for the late and important stage of retirement. Miss Rama Rau spoke in this connection of competence in the use of leisure, which requires specific attitudes and a specific training of the mind.

Millard O. Sheets, artist, and professor of art at Scripps College, had early alluded to a division of the American people into those who participate actively in their recreation and leisure activities and those who simply want to be entertained. He thought that there was a tendency for less personal participation all the time, and that this has something to do with a sense of frustration and lack of satisfaction. In turn, he traced some of the difficulty to "a lack of fundamental experience early enough to enjoy many of the cultural and real activities of leisure."

Miss Rama Rau felt that there is a problem in American culture in the lack of capacity for enjoyment on the part of adults. No child, she said, is without capacity for enjoyment and for spending its time amusing itself over things which leave grownups standing with astonishment. The children certainly do not lose that capacity even through their early school days. "From my experience in American colleges, they don't even lose it at college." But at some point in an American's life, in her view, his capacity for enjoyment seems to go.

> Miss Rama Rau. Where does this thing happen? At what point in the life of Americans do they suddenly become incapable of feeling cozy in their leisure time, of enjoying themselves in whatever it is, whether it is constructive or nonconstructive? Somewhere it happens, because if it did not happen somewhere, why, then, would there be this terrible feeling when retirement comes that suddenly life is over?

These questions of competence in the use of leisure and the ability to play kept coming up in the roundtable in application to all ages and many different types of leisure situations but most acutely, perhaps, in connection with the retirement problem. Mr. Higgins believed that a tremendous educational effort should be made with people before they reach the age of fifty. He felt that few people could acquire new ideas for the use of leisure after that age. Perhaps at thirty or thirty-five one ought to develop an interest in some activity which he could enjoy when he reaches retirement age.

> Mr. Higgins. I have known many, many people who have gone to seed when they have retired, simply because of the absence of ideas about the employment of their time. My own company leans over backward to keep men as long as we can, because we have had too many like that. They have not committed suicide, but they have died quickly.

MR. LIONNI. In Italy people don't commit suicide when they stop working.

MR. STARR. A conference the other day came to the conclusion that one should begin to prepare for old age in the prenatal period.

Mr. Benney traced part of the difficulty to the fact that our environment has changed as a result of modern industrialism and the rise of cities, while our ideals of leisure activity have tended to persist. This analysis belongs to what might be called, he said, "the ecology of leisure."

MR. BENNEY. Most middle-class professional people inherit a set of values which includes an attitude toward leisure based on a survival of rural, upper-class attitudes. The old aristocratic sports—hunting, shooting, fishing—were good things to do, and living in town was something to be avoided. But the majority of people have to live in towns. And towns have been built by the Puritan conscience: they are meant for business and not pleasure.

The result is that there are only limited kinds of leisure which can be undertaken in towns. There is the leisure Mr. Sarnoff provides in the home, and other leisure activities in the home. There are the mass entertainments that go on in large buildings.

We have to remember that the town planning background, tied to our Puritanical value system, has encased us in our peculiarly urban limitation of leisure activity. At the same time we institute a whole set of conflicts in how to find pleasure in the city, because we say to the poor worker how happy we would be if he would go swimming, fishing, or hunting and all that sort of thing which comes down from the rural and aristocratic past. Meanwhile, the town worker is listening to soap opera. And to attain a sense of participation he increasingly becomes interested in entertainment about entertainment; he wants to know more and more about the people who entertain him.

CHAIRMAN WHITE. He reads the movie magazines.

Mr. Starr, Mr. Sheets, and others had deplored "spectatoritis" and all alleged trends toward forms of leisure that involve less personal participation. But not all members were convinced that this trend is a reality.

MR. LARRABEE. The specter has already stalked the table of the moronic American who is entirely a watcher and never participates. I know of no evidence whatever that this is actually a true statement of the country today. It may not be a nation of Sunday painters, but it is well on the way to becoming one. . . .

There is an argument—quite a reasonable one—by a psychologist who has examined reading habits that a number of widely circulated publications in this country deliberately adopt policies contrary to those of their readers in order to establish an active relationship. A man can say "I certainly disagree with that"—and when he has done it he has had a satisfying experience.

Mr. Riesman, as noted earlier, also contended that we tend to underestimate the activity of the spectator (e.g., the manually skilled watchers of a wrestling match). Also, we tend to have "vested interests in other people's leisure."

MR. RIESMAN. We must speak of active and creative leisure, not only with reference to the Sunday painters and so on, but also with respect to the increase in the capable and competent critics of the media. . . .

MR. DENNEY. Speaking of spectator skill, one of the problems of leisure arises because people may be trained early in their lives to work and to use their leisure in ways which are not necessarily useful to them later in their lives. . . .

Mr. Sawyer, speaking as a museum director, returned to the question of "vested interests in other people's leisure" and pleaded guilty to a concern for the way in which people spend their leisure.

MR. SAWYER. It is a definite problem of values. Admittedly all of us who are concerned with this are trying to impose a conviction of values on other people. We think we are doing it for good and legitimate reasons. We may not be.

Mr. Dodds took the view that anybody who is concerned about our civilization will be concerned to see that "each individual, to the extent of his intellect and capacity and condition, is able to arrive at as great a degree of self-fulfillment as he could in that civilization—the highest degree of spiritual well-being, personal poise." The use a man or woman makes of his leisure time would contribute to or detract from that self-fulfillment. A humanist surely has some responsibility to aid the individual to arrive at a maximum of his inner resources; and, if this is so, the use of leisure time becomes quite important. There are kinds of satisfactions, inner ones, "which it seems to me it is our job to stimulate and encourage, if not to impose."

On Being Retired

T. V. Smith (1890-   )

SINCE THE TIME when the memory of man runneth not to the contrary, our Western civilization has been dominated by two images: the travel and the fight eidola, both of which are hostile auspices for the respectability of age. Both are refulgent with light for the paths of youth and middle age. Migrating from different tribal centers, men have historically met one another in various parts of the globe. To travel far was always to meet; and to meet was sooner or later to fight; for those who are met at the boundary are barbarians, each to the other. The only thing to do to barbarians is to fight them, and if possible to annihilate them. To annihilate them we have not been able; but in fighting them we have all done our share. Children of migratory ancestors, we sophisticated simians dream of traveling even when there is no further place to go; and children of warriors, we dream of fighting even when our arms have been thrown away. Our poetry is warlike—Homer, Milton, Shakespeare—and our fiction—Tolstoy, Hugo, Hemingway—goes forward in the haze of battle. Because of the sheer hardships of travel and the harsher incidence of war upon vital statistics, as well as the backwardness of science, men have not historically lived to be old. When by chance they did, they supported themselves on errands in a self-supporting family group. Poorhouses were few, and were for the uprooted and the piteous. A worn-out pedagogue could not respectably go to the poorhouse; not even yesteryear.

So much so has our past been of traveling and fighting that if the news were suddenly broken to our subconscious that the migratory days of humanity are over, that indeed there isn't anywhere else to go, few of us would know what to do with ourselves—until we happened to bethink ourselves, with our television children, of the moon or Mars. The mind can keep up an occupation which the body has long since discontinued. We can and we do make life itself a "pilgrimage" and the competition of virtue we transform into a metaphysical fight. "Onward, Christian soldiers, marching as to war." This is what I mean in saying that we are a journeying troupe, dominated by these two ancient eidola.

Symbolic of our culture, to the point of utter neatness, was the couple who met Orson Welles's cosmic scare by rushing out of the house with their suitcases hastily packed! Whether our fighting days are as passé as our migratory days remains to be seen. Certainly, the travel image remains lustrous long after it ceases to be functional. But if we continue to fight, we'll hardly continue to travel; for there won't be many of us left—and we'll be busy picking berries outside our mountain caves. Either way, it is the dominance of images which today we still have mightily to contend with.

Now these concrete images—of travel and fight—achieve abstract form in our philosophies of life. I have spoken already of our career-line itself conceived as a pilgrimage from this to a better (or worse) world. The political emphasis of modern times (both of democracy and of communism) upon equality envisages a leveling-up, never a final downgrading. I hesitate to think what our loyalty to equality might prove to be if through misfortune the only transformation possible should come to be a leveling-down.

Diverse though our individual philosophies of life be, our Western philosophy of history has concentered upon the notion of progress. That apostle of modernism, John Dewey, has gone so far as to say that if there be a single moral end, that end is "growth." Justice Holmes writes to Sir Frederick Pollock—one octogenarian to another—that the death of the aged does not grieve him. They've had their day, he says. But the death of the young is grievous: it is tragic, he adds, to die before you have had a chance "to try out your powers." The emphasis upon growth is clearly the ideal which befits youth and those still rising to a climax of their capacities.

This leaves anomalous those of us who are on the decline. Growth reached, what then? Well, then the call would seem to be for one to *surcease*. Why worry about a falling star in a rising world? But the doctors won't let us older people die, short of suicide; and the theologians won't let us commit suicide with dignity and proper peace of mind. How to be old and still to be respectable becomes a question for all who are well past their prime.

At the mercy, as we are, of both medical men and the medicine men of the race, we aged must keep on being, and being for a longer and longer time. But we are anomalous even as we grow more numerous. From our situation arise many problems. There is a sociological problem, but that we leave in a specialized age to the sociologists. There is an economic problem but we don't want the economists to be without a job. There is a political problem, especially in Florida and California; but why should we do the politician's work? He's paid, or pays himself, to do it. None of these problems represent, I suspect, what we as "retiring" individuals are most interested in. We're not interested in merely existing; we want to go on living as people who matter. The problem-mongers would turn us into "cases" long before we have ceased to be persons.

Shall we, then, like another ancient of days, live to preside at the funeral of our own reputation? We are quite willing to retire. Certainly I am. And all the more because I find myself of late, in the heat of lecturing, forgetting what the lecture is about and even forgetting what the subject of the sentence is to which I am vainly and publicly trying to hitch a predicate. I can see that for me to get out would solve problems for those anxiously awaiting signs of my dotage; but to solve their problems does not properly dispose of me.

It is quite a situation we are in, and it deserves a large-minded survey. It is not merely that our culture is, as I have said, dominated by the images under which we aged can play little constructive part. It is not merely that we lived in a period which glorifies beauty and prematurely casts able-bodied men, and even more so women, upon the heap. It is that we lack a philosophy which makes old age respectable and which would prevent the normal process of decay and death from appearing as a surd in the life of reason.

To call it a day, however, does not automatically ring down the night. There is still work to be done and light, albeit failing light, in which to do it. Certain vital juices still course through the gnarled trunks of many of us, albeit they course more gently than before. Or, to change the figure, when the old fire horse hears the bell, he may still involuntarily flex his muscles and even try to trot alongside the steaming steeds. . . .

What do we retire *to?*

Our answer to this question begins where we are and it extends to the time—forewarned by our retirement—when we shall not be at all. Let us reverently survey our remaining life and let us serenely contemplate our death. We have earned the right to be candid with ourselves, and we perhaps owe it as a duty to tell one another the truth. The larger truth is that retirement is prelude to what Crowfoot, leader of the Blackfoot Confederacy, described in these quiet but moving words:

> A little while and I will be gone from among you, whither I cannot tell. From nowhere we come, into nowhere we go. What is life? It is a flash of a firefly in the night. It is the breath of a buffalo in the winter time. It is as the little shadow that runs across the grass and loses itself in the sunset.

That truth we had better assume than unduly to presume upon increasing longevity. Certainly we will not live forever. And yet, mortality has given me no commission from either God or man to preach about it. But even a retiring teacher may think out loud about human destiny, letting his slips of speech fall where they may. I see that you are not only retiring but are also getting old; and I know what that eventually means. I can see it in you better than you can see it in yourselves. It is pervasive in men and women of our generation. I have never gone to but one of my college class reunions, and I'll never go to another. I was utterly embarrassed by the way classmates flaunted every sign of decay from arthritis to garrulity. I could not tell them without cruelty, but I can now say for truth's sake, that I was literally the only one of them whom the years had passed over and left young. But let us to the answer of our question, moralizing only in proper places as we go along. Whither our retirement?

1. Memory of the honorable estate *from* which we retire is the first treasure-trove *to* which we retire; for memories will go with us to the end of our days and will often, "in vacant or in pensive mood," as Wordsworth says,

> . . . *flash upon that inward eye*
> *Which is the bliss of solitude.*

More of solitude, and then more and more of it, we will have from here out. A dear friend, who is eighty-six, tells me that this is what has touched him closest about age: that he has outlived those who had a community of memories, and that communication becomes more and more difficult and thin. We shall all be further and further reduced to our own thoughts. Our legacy will probably grow richer for us in recall than it was in transaction.

Recall is, then, the first of our beads which we shall tell in retirement. With warm memories we have meat to eat that mere worldlings know not of; for, as Emily Dickinson says:

> *It may be wilderness without,*
> *Far feet of failing men,*
> *But holiday excludes the night*
> *And it is bells within.*

2. The next of our beads is a larger leisure in our second childhood than we have known since our first childhood. Little leisure have we known in fact, despite our limited hours of teaching. We have grown tired and yet worked on through passing days and well into many a

night. And this has happened to us so continuously that on romantic rebound we have made a heaven of leisure, a heaven nobody could stand for a week once he got rested up. Mark Twain found this out through Captain Eli Stormfield's experience in the Hereafter, found out, I mean, that sittin' on a cloud-bank with a halo that got heavy, with wings he could not maneuver, and with a harp which he could not coax beyond a single tiresome tune—that such a heaven was no fit place for a grown man, who requires oscillation between the opposites which in his character he houses.

Next to forgetting the first law of imagination, that in the realm of fancy *anything may mean anything*, is a forgetting more fatal still to our happiness: namely, that satisfaction expands only into satiety—or back again to lack and want. It is clear to any thoughful man that leisure must be informed with appropriate endeavor. It itself is not enough to fill retirement to the full.

It is not enough, but it *is* something; and we shall now get our first full-sized dose of it for many a busy year. I, for one, mean to make the most of whatever leisure I actually find lurking around my trailer door. It will be good to loll at breakfast after having turned over for another snooze. It will be good to play a little at last, even to indulge in scrabble, for instance. I have never had time for it. An older friend has accused me, because of this lack, of what he calls "the great Un-American Inactivity." It will indeed be good to slow the pace and do a little plain and fancy sauntering, whatever form it take. Justice Holmes says, with his eye upon senescence, that "the riders in a race do not stop short when they reach the goal. There is a little finishing canter before coming to a standstill." This our new-found leisure will afford for each of us, "a little finishing canter" as the day dies away.

3. But what, after all, is leisure save unpressured work? Clearly idleness for such as we is odious. So I court as my third bead self-rewarding work that is freely chosen to fill the leisure hours. We will, of course, keep on doing what we have been doing, but not so much of it. And let us not kid ourselves, as we cannot kid each other, that the quality of our output will be proportioned to the quantity of leisure now at our disposal. If you have long spent more time dreading to write or grade papers or mend the leaking faucets at home than you have in doing the job; if you have made excuses all your life for not doing proudly what you were paid to do; if you have chronically waited to do your best until there was nothing else to do—then you will hardly bloom out now as editors' models, registrars' pets, or other Beau Brummels of senescent virtue.

That masterpiece of research you've put off to retirement you'll likely now in further easy stages put off to eternity. I'll not bet even on your stopping smoking now that you have nothing else to do, when you couldn't stop before this because you had everything else to do. Walter Mittys will be Walter Mittys.

Every year our accumulated character gets more and more the best of our resolutions, and surrender to habits of inefficiency or of self-exculpation becomes the visible stigmata of our fate. "There," said the sot from the gutter, as he watched the successful man whirl by in a Cadillac, "there but for me go I." This dominance of habit holds hardly less of virtue than of vice. When the normal lethargy of age has had its way with our dwindling resolution, we shall in our new-found leisure be mostly doing less and less of the more and more we have promised ourselves to do. This continuity of character is a small enough boon for retirement; but it is something to know that we can, and probably will keep on doing the same we have been doing, in diminishing degree. In that way we won't be slipping up on ourselves. Let us put it down, then, as a law of our nature and the arbiter of our fate, that we shall not do much which we have not been doing, and shall do less and less of what we have been doing. This reliance upon character I count as my third authentic bead.

4. Let it, however, be the fourth bead of our rosary for old age that we can and probably will do something, a little, of the different. Surely we have all promised ourselves that come retirement and leisure, we would do something "worthwhile"—and little doubt each has dreamed therewith of innovation. Seldom is the labor of our livelihood wholly self-rewarding, and retirement is a chance to even accounts with ourselves before we die. . . .

That is the fourth of my beads: our ability to do something of the different to bemuse our new-found leisure.

5. The fifth of my beads comes so close to branding me a "do-gooder" that at the expense of arousing suspicion I wish to forfend myself of the accusation. To be a do-gooder is, as you must know, something semi-heinous in our generation. But to do more good than we have done is still a general aspiration, and one quite honorable. But do you know the difference here involved? The doer of good does something *with* people; the do-gooder does something *to* people. The do-gooder makes "easy simplicity of lives not his own." No do-gooder does so little good as an old do-gooder. When you have not saved the world in sixty-five years, you will hardly save it in the remaining years, not even if you redouble your effort to make up for bedimming goals.

Against that background of clarification, let us develop our foreground of aspiration. We all want to do some good. If we had more time, if we were less hurried, if we were more sympathetically available to those around us—how useful we might be! We sigh at the thought. But, behold, these conditions are measurably fulfilled by our retirement! At any rate, we'll have more time for others than we have had, and we'll be under less tension than heretofore. All around us is good that cries to be done. . . .

No, I am not ashamed to add to my rosary a bead I shall often tell— the gentle notation to do some good. This bead is the fifth on my string.

6. Passing now from action to understanding, retirement will give me a chance to comprehend more things more fully. This is a bead acquired particularly under the aegis of war. As action gets maximized, understanding gets minimized in the life of man. The day after I returned to my university from three years in the army, I said to a group of graduate students: "The trouble with us veterans is that we know so much more than we understand." They showed an exposed nerve by breaking into applause, as graduates are not wont to do. After the war I was lunching with two majors of my staff in Italy and said to them in utter confidence, for they were both wise guys who, I thought, understood what we were about:—I said, "I don't mind confessing to you men that as your superior officer I never knew what it was all about!" They replied in unison, as if rehearsed: "Did *anybody?*" I want now to read the war books to see what it was all about.

Nor is incomprehension confined to war. Peace has its own vast unirrigated tracts. I've got a lifetime worth of wonder, for instance, as to my own participation in American politics. And politics and war apart, there are vague motivations to be talked over with friends, and quarrels to be cleared up, and complexes to be irradiated with clearer light of fuller understanding. No doubt, "it is well," as Justice Holmes says, "that some of us don't know that we know anything." This same Holmes, eighty years old, "blushed," as he put it, to admit that he had never read John Locke's *Treatise on Government,* and then proceeded to read for the first time Aristotle's *Ethics.* "I was amazed," he adds, "to see how much later thinking and even English law had been affected by him—or rather had found their seed in him."

There are indeed books to be read, old books as well as new, and there are experiences to be threshed out to distill what meaning they have while there still is light to read by and intuitions to guide attention.

7. If my sixth bead be, as indicated, a better understanding of action, my seventh bead—a sacred number on which to end!—is a substitution for action in the fallow years at hand. Our previous acceptance of action

as man's lot clearly answers to the prime prejudice of a race whose tribal eidola have always been traveling and fighting. But it is this parent-predisposition to action which has left age with decreasing claims to respectability. I make, therefore, as the seventh bead to beguile my retirement the "unguiltiness of inactivity," if I may so broach what I now wish to explain. . . .

I think that of all the goods to which we are privileged to retire, the most precious one to me personally is this riddance of the animal, the irrational, impulse to act upon every possible occasion. "For God's sake do something!" That there is such an impulse is certain and no less certain is it that resistance to the impulse leaves a sediment of guilt. But it is a part of virtue to resist this pressure of primal conscience, as one resists other temptations. There is a heroism of omission no less profound, but much more difficult to exemplify, than the heroism that comes from the all too easy commitment to action. The "true believer" is committed to falsity—or worse.

I, for one, will welcome the right of old age to withstand all easy commitment. All my life I have been abashed at having to decide things in the name of reason for which there were no adequate reasons. I know there were not, because equally reasonable men are always deciding such things differently. And the more important the issues, the more differently they get decided. I do not complain at what was necessary in the days of my prime—and this commitment to action is a necessary adjunct of our animal life—but I do now rejoice that those days are gone.

No longer will I have to claim that I know how to raise grandchildren when I didn't know how to raise the children that begot them. I can love the grandchildren and share know-how with them, without having to preach to their parents. No longer will I have to rationalize my party preference, when I never could keep the parties dependably apart anyhow. I can now love my country as much as ever, and can be as stout as any partisan, without straining myself to give reasons which show the other partisan to be unreasonable. No longer will I have to stand up and be counted when I much prefer to sit down and think; or to think hard and consecutively when what I want to do is to enjoy the unassessable ramblings of reverie. Yes, it's quite a treasure-trove to which this seventh bead tells me the way.

I think I have earned the right to make up my mind constantly and that right I mean to avail myself of to the full. . . .

The Retirement Myth

Julius Hochman (1892-   )

. . . IN THE NEW YORK Dressmakers Union of the I.L.G.W.U., where a retirement fund was recently inaugurated, a record was kept by an inter-
viewer of some of the reactions of workers who applied for retirement but
finally decided to continue working. Here is a typical case. A worker
of 69 sat for half an hour pondering the question and finally said: "If I
don't go on working, tell me, what will I do with all my time?" Another
worker declared: "If I work, I'll stay healthy longer mentally and
physically."

It is obvious that instinctively the worker has deep inner resistance
to withdrawal from work. The evidence accumulated by geriatricians
ad psychiatrists amply indicates that retirement is frequently followed
by crisis and severe emotional disturbance, sometimes even by death.

Why this resistance, why this inner conflict? Why the reluctance to
accept benefits offered? Unfortunately, modern psychology has not
given adequate attention to this question. Perhaps some suggestions of
the answer can be found in a footnote in Sigmund Freud's *Civilization
and Its Discontents*. Freud writes:

When there is no special disposition in a man imperatively prescribing the
direction of his life-interest, the ordinary work all can do for a livelihood can
play the part which Voltaire wisely advocated it should do in our lives. It is
not possible to discuss the significance of work for the economics of the libido
adequately within the limits of a short survey. Laying stress upon importance
of work has a greater effect than any other technique of living in the direction
of binding the individual more closely to reality; in his work he is at least
securely attached to a part of reality, the human community. Work is no less
valuable for the opportunity it and the human relations connected with it provide for a very considerable discharge of libidinal component impulses, nar-
cissistic, aggressive and even erotic, than because it is indispensable for subsistence and justifies existence in a society. . . . And yet, as a path to happiness, work is not valued very highly by men. They do not run after it as they
do after other opportunities for gratification.

Let us first consider Freud's remark in the earlier part of this passage:
"Laying stress upon the importance of work has a greater effect than
any other technique of living in the direction of binding the individual
more closely to reality; in his work, he is at least securely attached to
a part of reality, to the human community." To the economist, work
may be only a way of earning a living, but to Freud it is more, much
more. It is also a way of life. For the average man, it is the bond with

reality, the means of communal contact and participation. It serves to identify the individual with society, past, present, and future. It functions as a high form of sublimation, helping to make out of man a social, a civilized being. That is why forced retirement usually precipitates such a severe emotional crisis: it is nothing less than the rupture of the pattern that has hitherto given meaning and value to life.

With the rise of trade unionism, millions of workers have been able to achieve a wider sense of belonging than even their work has succeeded in conferring upon them. The union gives the worker added stature in the community. Through his union he asserts himself as a person. Through collective bargaining, he becomes a partner in industry. From time to time, he demonstrates his power by using his collective strength to improve his lot in life. As a union member, he becomes a major contributor to philanthropy at home and abroad. He exercises influence in his community. He becomes an important factor in politics. The newspapers note his actions and make him part of history. Forced retirement means isolation from the labor collectivity and a collapse into individual insignificance. No wonder it is felt to be so dreadful by most workers threatened with it.

It will be noted that in the passage I have cited, Freud observes that "as a path to happiness work is not valued very highly by men. They do not run after it as they do after other opportunities for gratification." This conclusion is of course based on European experiences and does not altogether represent the attitude towards work in our culture. I have, however, found a distinct difference in attitude towards work between the older and the young worker. In my own rather amateurish survey of the attitude of workers to forced retirement, I have found two quite contradictory reactions: older people want to continue working and shy away from retirement; but strangely enough it is the young to whom retirement appeals. Why this curious difference in attitude? I venture the following as a possible explanation. Every young person starts life with illusions about himself. He believes he can, and hopes he will, do something great. Usually, he does not admit to himself the illusory element in these dreams, but as he gets on in life, he necessarily adapts himself to reality and goes about earning his living as best he can. Yet he does not give up the hope of attaining his secret aims. Some day, he keeps telling himself, he will get the chance, and when anyone comes to him with a scheme by which he will some day be able to retire and do the things he has always wanted to do, he welcomes it. As he grows older, however, and begins to approach his retirement age, he begins to realize that what he hadn't been able to accomplish at 25 or 30, he is not likely to do at 65; and the very hope that once led him to look forward to it now makes the prospect of retirement quite distressing—because he knows that once he retires he will have to admit to himself that his great expectations were always largely illusory. Thus, the paradoxical attitude of the young man, if examined a little more closely, really confirms the analysis I have been trying to develop.

It is generally recognized that the happiest people are those fortunate few, who, through a combination of special faculties and inner drives, become the great creative artists, scientists, philosophers, and statesmen of their time. These men do not retire; their work is their life. They frequently live to a ripe old age and remain active to their very last breath. The great mass of people are not quite so fortunate. Most of them are forced to accept work not to their liking, but, even so, work becomes the bond between them and the community, between them and social reality. It constitutes their main social function and creates that sense of belonging without which life is hardly livable.

This is especially true of our American culture. Our entire educational and social pattern emphasizes a man's place in the working community. It is dinned into us from the start that we must be useful citizens, that we must do our share of the work, that we must make our contribution to society. The conventions of our civilization demand that a man either make money or earn money. He does not truly "belong" unless he is usefully employed, in the broad sense in which our civilization views usefulness. The playboy is looked upon with contempt because he is a stranger to man's normal activities. Yet the forced retirement idea is based on the conception that a man who has been taught all his life that he must be socially useful through work can make a sudden transition to idleness and still retain his self-respect. This notion is dangerously false. His very youthful hopes, as we have seen, now operate to intensify the fear of forced retirement. The realization that the things one had always dreamed of doing to establish oneself in the eyes of society are nothing but illusions tends suddenly to deflate one's self-esteem and to precipitate a serious emotional crisis.

To Retire or Not
Harold Hall (1898-   )

. . . THE MAJORITY OF YOUNGER executives said that they would want to leave their companies at normal retirement age. Most of them expressed the feeling, "I'll welcome retirement; just give me the chance to get away from this business pressure." Only a small proportion of these men added the cautionary proviso, "If I have enough money." The fact that twice as many said they would prefer less rigorous company assignments as said they would want to remain on a full-time basis is also an indication of an expressed desire to lessen business pressures. The "similar" or "different" work they said they wanted for post-retirement activity was usually described in no more than general terms. On the other hand, hobbies and recreational-cultural activities were mentional enthusiastically and definitely as occupations. This enthusiasm was somewhat less pronounced among those who looked forward to public-service assignments.

In contrast, the majority of older executives wanted to continue with their companies because the alternative of retirement simply did not seem so attractive to them. Realization of the personal satisfactions they obtained in business was impressed on this group as they contemplated leaving their companies; the disadvantages of pressure all but disappeared from their minds. They placed new importance on the business and social recognition provided by their jobs. There was anticipation of a loss of prestige and standing inherent in a change. This feeling was especially true among those executives who had achieved their job ambitions relatively late in their business lives. It seemed more prevalent, also, among men who had no more than a vague idea of their post-retirement programs. Over-all, the executives who said they wanted to continue with their companies looked with disfavor on "retirement from" and lacked a concept of "retirement to."

Can Retirement Satisfy?

Eugene A. Friedman and Robert J. Havighurst (1900-   )

AS OUR TECHNOLOGY HAS BECOME more efficient, fewer workers have been needed to do the work of the country, even though standards of living were rising and people were consuming more goods and services. When the depression of the thirties brought unemployment, the older workers were discharged first, and the Social Security Act was passed to give these people an income. Then World War II brought full employment and kept older workers on the job but did not modify the expectation that had been built up especially in big business and industry and in government and civil service—the expectation of compulsory retirement at a fixed age, usually 65.

Retirement is a new way of life. The elderly man who has filled his day
...ith eight or ten hours of work must find new ways of living these eight
or ten hours daily. His wife must also learn new living patterns, with her
husband at home much more of the time. The person at retirement must
learn to do without the things that his work has brought him; and his
work has brought him more than his weekly or monthly pay.

For some people retirement is a goal toward which they have been
working. It is the culmination of years of hope, sacrifice, and planning.
For others it is a trap, a piece of bad luck for which they are unprepared.
What retirement means to a person depends partly on what his work
has meant to him. If he can get the satisfactions out of retirement that
he formerly got out of work, or if he can get new and greater satisfactions in retirement than he got in his work, then retirement is a boon
to him.

What does retirement mean in the life-cycle? Is it merely a narrow
band of years coming at the end of a full life and ending in death, or is
it a broad stretch of opportunity to enjoy one's self, to do things one
always wanted to do?

In either case retirement is a new way of life and carries some problems with it. There are problems of leaving work—of finishing things off,
of breaking off sharply or tapering off slowly, of deciding whether to
look for another job or a part-time job. Then there are the greater problems of entering the new life. These problems consist of learning how
to manage on a reduced income, how to use more leisure time, and how
to get new satisfactions to replace the ones that went with work.

Today about one person in four over the age of 65 is employed. Very
few of the women are employed. Less than half of the men are at work.
But a number of retired people could be effective workers. Estimates of
the number of retired people who are capable of doing productive work
under present-day working conditions vary from about one and a half
million to three million, from 12 to 25 per cent of the age group. All thirteen million persons over 65 are consumers. By 1975 there will be eighteen
million people in this age bracket—all living on goods and services produced by the members of society who are at work. Our tremendous productivity makes this possible. But the cost is a real one. If more older
people were productive, several advantages might be gained—older people themselves might live more comfortably, young people could be given
more education before they commence work, people in the 20-65 age
bracket might reduce their hours of work, or the whole society might
have more goods and services to consume.

The economic cost of retirement to the nation will grow as the proportion of older people grows, unless we revise our retirement policies.

For the individual there is sure to be some cost to retirement, if only the loss of the income which he has been earning. In addition, most people get other satisfactions from their work, and retirement means the loss of these satisfactions unless they can find other ways of gaining similar satisfactions.

As the time comes when work is not a necessity for the whole of adult life, older people are most affected by the change in significance of work. The primary function of work as the means of securing income is beginning to lose its significance for older people. Less frequently does the veteran of forty years of work say, "I have to work to eat. How can a workingman retire?" A pension can answer that question for him. He has earned the opportunity to retire and to live for ten or fifteen years of comparatively good health free from work if he wants to.

If work had only the function of earning a living and this function was discharged for life by the age of 65, everyone should welcome retirement at that age. But other essential functions of life are included in work. If these functions and the satisfactions they bring are lost by retirement, then retirement is an undiluted tragedy for a man.

The problem of retirement is to secure the extra-economic values that work brings and to secure them through play or leisure-time activity. Can this problem be solved? Can play have the same functions as work? Can play provide the satisfactions to older people that they formerly got out of work?

In Western society, work is by cultural definition sharply set off as the enemy of pleasure, love, consumption of goods, and almost every sort of freedom. Work is a task defined and required of one by other people. This historical cultural definition of work is not valid for many of the workers. They have found other and more pleasurable meanings in their work.

Let us consider the extra-economic meanings of work and inquire whether leisure-time activity, play, or recreation also have similar meanings, and, if so, how the meanings of work can be realized in leisure.

Being with other people, making friends and having friendly relations with people, is one of the principal meanings of work to people in all the occupations we have studied. This function is also served by clubs, churches, recreation agencies, and a variety of formal and informal associations in the person's nonwork life. The pattern already exists; the problem is to fill the void created by loss of work associations in nonwork life.

Work is not intrinsically more satisfying than play as a source of meaningful experience. On the contrary, recreation offers more variety and more flexible opportunity for creative self-expression and interesting experience than work does. The person who makes a hobby of woodwork-

g or pottery-making, or plays golf or bridge, "just for the fun of it," or
avels or goes hunting or fishing, is getting the same values from his
play as though he were doing work for the sheer enjoyment of the work
itself.

Our studies of the significance of work in the lives of people underline
for us the importance of an activity that fills the day, gives people something to do, and makes the time pass. Sheer passing of time seems to be
an important value of work. Work is admirably designed to provide this
value, since it usually requires orderly routines. Even the people who dislike their work as dangerous, unpleasant, or monotonous often recognize
the value of the work routine to them and cannot imagine how they
would fill the day if they were to retire.

Retired people work out a routine for themselves, reading the newspaper regularly, visiting the library every morning or at definite times,
attending church, sitting in the park on pleasant days, working around
the house in the morning, taking a walk downtown in the afternoon, going
to a club or a tavern at regular hours. But many people have grown so
accustomed to having their days organized about a job that they are
ill prepared to create a new routine upon retirement.

Nevertheless, leisure-time activities can be organized and scheduled so
as to fill the day and make the time pass happily. Play can be made to
serve this function fully as well as work.

In a work-centered society such as ours has been in the past, work is
certainly more effective than play in providing self-respect and gaining
the respect of others. It seems unlikely that the present generation of older
people reared with work-centered attitudes can get much self-respect
out of leisure-time activities. Most of them, if they are forced to retire,
will maintain their own self-respect and the respect of others by their
reputation as successful workers and their feeling that retirement is a
reward for a well-spent lifetime of work.

Women, however, have mostly gained their self-respect and the respect
of others through being good mothers and housekeepers and neighbors.
Women who have not been employed will usually be able to draw on
the sense of worth and social prestige as they grow older that they discovered in their middle years.

Thus we see that leisure activities can conceivably offer the extra-economic meanings and values which work has supplied to people. This is
fortunate, because leisure is on the increase at all adult years. A good
many people now work forty hours or less a week, which is only a little
more than half of the average work week a hundred years ago.

A person born into the "economy of abundance" which arrived about
1920 is growing up in a period when the use of leisure time and the con-

sumption of goods constitute the major problems of domestic society. A person born in the work-centered pre-1920 society is a kind of antediluvian. The older people of today have the ambiguous luck to have outlived the period when their work ideology was dominant, and so they must adjust, somehow, to comparatively early retirement with more leisure than they ever expected to have.

Meanwhile the meanings of play and of work have developed in our culture to the point where the old dichotomy of work and play has become meaningless. Formerly, play was a rest from the burden of work, but, as work became less burdensome, the dividing line between work and play tended to disappear. Formerly, play was a privilege and work was a duty, but, as work became less necessary, play took on some of the aspects of duty, and again the dividing line tended to disappear.

A new problem of design for living now confronts modern man. How can he fit work and leisure-time activity together into a satisfying scheme of life, with the relative proportions of work and leisure varying as he passes from adolescence to adulthood to old age?

The task set for modern man by the shift from a work-centered society to an economy of abundance with increasing leisure is that of *learning the arts of leisure*. By learning these arts well, people can enjoy retirement more than they enjoyed work.

The extra-economic meanings of work can nearly all be discovered and realized more fully in leisure activities. Hence we may state a principle of *equivalence of work and play*. In our economy of abundance, where work is reduced in quantity and burdensomeness to a level where it is not physically unpleasant, many of the values of play can be achieved through work and of work through play.

In addition, play has the unique value of activity free from outer compulsion—something only rarely found in work. The promise of leisure, then, is to combine freedom from compulsion with the satisfactions formerly found in work.

If this secret is discovered by people, the problem of retirement will be solved, provided economic security is also generally achieved. That is, retirement from work will simply be the signal to increase and adapt one's play or leisure-time activity so as to get the satisfactions from play that were formerly obtained from work.

But it is hardly to be expected that many people who grew up in a work-centered society will be able to apply in their own lives the principle of equivalence of work and play. That they do not do so is demonstrated in a study we have recently made of older people in a small midwestern city. This community, which we have called Prairie City, contains about seven hundred people past the age of 65. A cross-sectional sample of one hundred of these people was studied intensively. Forty-one of the people were either employed or had been employed and were now retired and were in fairly good health. (Another thirteen were at work or had retired and had such poor health that their physical activity was considerably impaired.)

The forty-one people were divided into two groups, those who were still employed and those who were retired. If they were applying the principle of equivalence of work and play, the retired group should have more leisure-time activities and a higher rating on a scale of intensity and scope of leisure-time activity. Results of a systematic comparison of these two groups indicate that those who were still at work had a small but systematic superiority over the retired group in the intensity and scope of their leisure-time activity and also that the employed group had a high rating on personal adjustment. Thus it is clear that the retired group is not compensating for retirement by spending more time and energy at play.

Further light is shed on the problem of substituting play for work by studying several men in this sample who had retired for reasons other than health. This group of men had average adjustment scores and ratings much below the men who were still at work. However, the best-adjusted man of the group has a very active program of leisure-time occupations. He has remodeled his home and added a section to it. He builds radios. He and his wife travel to Florida in the winter. They are active in a social clique that does a great deal of mutual entertaining.

In contrast to this man is another of the same economic status who says, "I farmed for forty-five years, and I wish I were still doing it." He putters around with tools in a shop in his garage but complains, "I just don't have much to do any more at my age." He never goes to the movies, has dropped out of clubs and organizations, and says, "I just don't go many places any more."

The first man is substituting play for work quite satisfactorily. The second man has not done so. Studying the lives of seven of the men leads to the conclusion that only two of the seven have been able to find satisfaction in leisure activity which compensates for the satisfactions they lost when they retired from work.

This small and inadequate investigation suggests a conclusion that is borne out by our experience in questioning people about the meaning of retirement to them. Most Americans are not ready to apply the principle of equivalence of work and play in their lives. Most of them are not accomplished in the leisure arts.

Possibly the generation now passing through adulthood will know better how to replace their work with play when they come to retire. They will have given more of their adult life to the practice of the leisure arts and so will be more experienced and possibly more resourceful in making use of greater amounts of leisure when they retire.

The personal problem of retirement for the average person will be made easier if our society provides more facilities and greater assistance for older people to learn to enjoy the leisure arts. This may be done through adult education programs, through public and private recreation agencies, and through churches and clubs.

In general, the trend seems inexorably toward more leisure time during adulthood and more leisure time during old age. We shall have to adjust ourselves to this trend, as we have to other changes wrought by technology. It should be possible for us to make something really profitable for us all out of increased leisure, but the task is yet to be achieved.

Mr. Chips and the New Schooling

James Hilton (1900-1954)

HEADMASTER RALSTON *undertakes to convince Schoolmaster Chipping that he should retire in favor of a modern teacher,—without success.*

"I don't want—to retire. I don't—umph—need to consider it."

"Nevertheless, I suggest that you do."

"But—umph—I don't see—why—I should!"

"In that case, things are going to be a little difficult."

"Difficult? Why—difficult?"

And then they set to, Ralston getting cooler and harder, Chips getting warmer and more passionate, till at last Ralston said icily: "Since you force me to use plain words, Mr. Chipping, you shall have them. For some time past, you haven't been pulling your weight here. Your methods of teaching are slack and old-fashioned; your personal habits are slovenly; and you ignore my instructions in a way which, in a younger man, I should regard as rank insubordination. It won't do, Mr. Chipping, and you must ascribe it to my forbearance that I have put up with it so long."

"But—" Chips began, in sheer bewilderment; and then he took up isolated words out of that extraordinary indictment. "*Slovenly*—umph—you said—?"

"Yes, look at the gown you're wearing. I happen to know that that gown of yours is a subject of continual amusement throughout the School."

Chips knew it, too, but it had never seemed to him a very regrettable matter.

He went on: "And—you also said—umph—something about—*insubordination—?*"

"No, I didn't. I said that in a younger man I should have regarded it as that. In your case it's probably a mixture of slackness and obstinacy. This question of Latin pronunciation, for instance—I think I told you years ago that I wanted the new style used throughout the School. The other masters obeyed me; you prefer to stick to your old methods, and the result is simply chaos and inefficiency."

At last Chips had something tangible that he could tackle. "Oh, *that!*" he answered, scornfully. "Well, I—umph—I admit that I don't agree with the new pronunciation. I never did. Umph—a lot of nonsense, in my opinion. Making boys say 'Kickero' at school when—umph—for the rest of their lives they'll say 'Cicero'—if they ever—umph—say it at all. And instead of 'vicissim'—God bless my soul—you'd make them say, 'We kiss 'im'! Umph—umph!" And he chuckled momentarily, forgetting that he was in Ralston's study and not in his own friendly form room.

"Well, there you are, Mr. Chipping—that's just an example of what I complain of. You hold one opinion and I hold another, and, since you decline to give way, there can't very well be any alternative. I aim to make Brookfield a thoroughly up-to-date school. I'm a science man myself, but for all that I have no objection to the classics—provided that they are taught efficiently. Because they are dead languages is no reason why they should be dealt with in a dead educational technique. I understand, Mr. Chipping, that your Latin and Greek lessons are exactly the same as they were when I began here ten years ago?"

Chips answered, slowly and with pride: "For that matter—umph—they are the same as when your predecessor—Mr. Meldrum—came here, and that—umph—was thirty-eight years ago. We began here, Mr. Meldrum and I—in—umph—in 1870. And it was—um—Mr. Meldrum's predecessor, Mr. Wetherby—who first approved my syllabus. 'You take the Cicero for the fourth,' he said to me. Cicero, too—not Kickero!"

"Very interesting, Mr. Chipping, but once again it proves my point—you live too much in the past, and not enough in the present and future. Times are changing, whether you realize it or not. . . ."

A Group-Study Approach:
Grand Rapids Learns
About the Aging

Wilma Donahue

THE COMMUNITY OF GRAND RAPIDS, Michigan, has a population of 175,000, of which more than average are 65 years and over. These older people have helped build the community; they have worked in its furniture factories which have brought fame to their city; they have built its churches and its schools, and have helped establish its local traditions; they have raised their families who have, in turn, continued to reside in the community.

The older people of Grand Rapids do not want to leave their city. Yet they, like other people in almost every other community, have a number of serious unmet needs. They need jobs but find it hard to get employment because of their age; they need housing better suited in size and design to their changing family size and diminishing energies; they need companionship because they have lost spouses and friends and have met social rejections; they need special health and house-keeping services but find that the community has little awareness of the importance of these services to their well-being; but most of all, they need to have their community and fellow-citizens know, appreciate, and use their skills.

In 1952, a group who had been meeting together in a University-sponsored adult education class on Education for Maturity decided that they were ready to do something to create more opportunities for older people like themselves to meet their own needs and show the community that its older people were still an asset. They asked for a course in which they could learn the techniques needed for developing programs to serve the needs of the older people in the community. Accordingly, an eight-week course entitled "Learning for Longer Living: Practice in Community Service for the Aging" was scheduled.

In consultation with a group of the prospective students, the staff and Advisory Committee developed the meeting plan which follows. The class convened at 5:30 p.m. At this time the students and staff had a box supper. The boxes were supplied by one of the churches at fifty cents each. The University provided free coffee. Following the meal there were a few minutes' recreation under the supervision of a weekly student committee. At 6:30 a fifteen-minute general session of the class gave time for a discussion of matters of concern to all project groups. Individual groups then met to plan their work for the ensuing week. Shortly before the close of the class period at 8:00 p.m., the entire group reconvened to hear progress reports and future plans.

Most of the 25 men and women who enrolled had been members of previous courses dealing with adjustment to later maturity, and thus had already acquired considerable knowledge about the problems of the aging. Although the average age of the student group was slightly more than 60 years, the range extended from the late 30's through the 70's.

At the first session the class reviewed census data for Grand Rapids, and a study of available community programs and facilities for older people.

For example, the Council of Social Agencies had established a Committee on Aging more than two years before to make studies of the needs of old people and make recommendations to the Council. The Recreation Department had sponsored several community parties for older people and had established a number of "Over-Sixty Clubs" to provide social outlets.

General concern about living arrangements and shelter had led to the building of a generous number of old-age homes under the auspices of churches and other private groups. Many nursing homes were established to fill the need for sheltered care of the chronically ill. The museum and public libraries were offering programs suitable to the interests of older people, such as special exhibits, hobby classes, and Great Books courses. The public schools had a rich program in which adults could learn new skills and could keep mentally alert through participation in discussion. The University of Michigan Extension Service had for a number of years offered preparation for retirement through its courses in Living in the Later Years.

Although it appeared from the listing of programs and services that much had already been done for the older people in Grand Rapids, the students declared there was too little being done in the areas which had already received attention, there were other important problems which had been overlooked altogether, and there had been too little education of the community about the existing programs and about the unmet needs of older people.

The students selected three projects which they felt would make a definite contribution to the community and be within the range of their abilities to execute. The three projects were: (1) employment opportunities for older people; (2) friendly visiting for older people; and (3) education of the community about the values of older citizens.

How did the working groups set about obtaining their goals and what did they accomplish? Let us illustrate by describing in some detail the Education Project.

Seven people selected the Education Project. At the first meeting they elected a student as chairman and decided that the faculty supervisor should serve in the role of advisor and resource person. They also defined four goals for their project: (1) to inform the community about the problems arising from the aging of the population; (2) to call attention to older citizens as assets to the community; (3) to demonstrate the contribution which older people make to the work and culture of the community; and (4) to illustrate the persistence of skills and abilities of older people and to show the relationship to health and happiness of the use of such skills in purposeful activity.

With these goals established, the students considered ways of attaining them. They decided to issue a weekly bulletin describing the work of all three project groups. Because they considered it imperative to use the regular channels of mass communication, the students planned as part of their first assignment to interview representatives of the press, radio, television, library, museum, and advertising agencies to invite them to serve on their Consultant Committee.

Each student assumed responsibility for at least one project and agreed to serve also as a member of the planning committee for one or more of the other activities undertaken by the Education Group. Some of the projects were to be carried out during the eight-week period in which the class was meeting; others were to be planned during this time but were to be carried out in the several months following the official close of the course.

At subsequent class meetings the students reported their progress, and developed plans for the next week's activities. The Consultant Committee met with the group upon several occasions; and the group also kept a liaison with the other project groups in order to represent their work adequately in the programs and news presented to the community.

Here is what this project group of seven people did:

Publications

Two local newspapers ran a total of ten stories about various phases of the class projects. A full page spread of pictures appeared of older people at work in community service. The University of Michigan Extension News, reaching thousands of people throughout the country, carried a detailed report of the course.

One of the most important efforts of the group was the publication of the Weekly Bulletin, which was distributed to all members of the class, to all Consultant Committees, and to other people who requested it. The circulation reached a peak of 150 copies per week. The Bulletin contained weekly progress reports and pertinent items of information about problems of the aging.

A "Directory of Recreation Opportunities for Older People in Grand Rapids" was published with the following sections: social recreation; arts, crafts, music, literature; museums, art galleries, and zoo; education; radio and television; local tours. The Grand Rapids Recreation Department, City Library, and other community agencies distributed copies of the directory widely.

Radio

The class arranged with the local radio station for a series of six fifteen-minute broadcasts. The students selected the topics, developed the content of the programs, and took part in the broadcasts. The following topics were discussed: friendly visiting; occupational opportunities for older people; homes for old people; what churches can do to serve the aging; recreation for older people; cultural interests as a source of enjoyment for older people. The students managed to secure the dinner hour for these broadcasts, although to give them this time, the station had to cancel the time of a popular radio news commentator.

Television

The students used the theme of "The Persistence of Skills Learned in Early Life" for a thirty-minute telecast. Two older people demonstrated skills which they had learned early in life, and three members of the class held a discussion about the importance of engaging in constructive activities through life.

Exhibits and Demonstrations

A Hobby-A-Week library program was carried out after the close of the class. A committee from the library worked with the Education Project committee in the planning and presentation of this activity. The class members assumed responsibility for identifying the craft to be exhibited, for collecting the items to be shown, and for a live demonstration by an older craftsman at least twice during each week. The library displayed books describing the craft on exhibit and served punch during the afternoons on which the demonstrations were held. Some of the students served as hostesses. The project lasted for 16 weeks.

Another project which was planned during the class but which was carried out several months later was the Grand Rapids Senior Skill Show. Working with the local museum, the class held a two-week exhibit, displaying the work of over 100 senior citizens. The students planned the show, collected the items to be exhibited, and made arrangements for all types of publicity. The museum staff arranged the exhibit, which over 8000 people viewed during the two-week period. The Senior Skill Show has since become an annual event in the community.

Community Conference on Aging

As a final effort, the Education Group decided to hold a one-day Grand Rapids Conference on Aging, at which each of the three project groups would report its findings and make suggestions for further community action.

For the first time during the work of the class, the faculty advisors became somewhat anxious and suggested that the group might want to invite some of the so-called experts in fields of employment, friendly visiting, and education to take part in the conference program along with the students. This suggestion was a mistake because the students quite stole the show from the experts.

At this conference, the community learned that the social agencies had reported at least 829 older people in need of friendly visitors. The students recommended, and the Council of Social Agencies subsequently established, a friendly visiting service through the Volunteer Service Bureau of the Council.

The group surveying occupational opportunities for older people reported that 50 per cent of the large Grand Rapids industrial companies surveyed would not employ workers 65 and over under any circumstances. The survey also revealed, however, that the older workers currently employed were considered by their employers to have better attendance records and to show less job turn-over than younger workers; and in no single work characteristic were the older workers generally inferior.

The students recommended that special counselors be appointed in private and public employment agencies whose duty it would be to advise older job applicants and to develop job opportunities for them.

There can be little doubt that the older people who participated in this course *felt* needed, not because they were made to feel needed, but because they found that they *were* needed. They had discovered that there were important tasks to be done which they, more appropriately than any other group, could undertake and carry through successfully. They had pointed out needs; they had initiated community action; and they had acquired the cooperation of important organizations and individuals in carrying forward their plans. And most importantly, they had played a role familiar to them in the past, one in which they had responsibility and opportunity for exercising personal initiative and individual choice.

A Public School Approach:
Pre-Retirement Education

Weldon R. Oliver

A SIGNIFICANT EXPERIMENT in adult education has recently been completed in Niagara Falls, New York. It is an original project in pre-retirement education with groups of employees from three of the city's major industries.

The unique character of the experiment is to be found not in the subject matter of the program, but rather in the cooperative approach to pre-retirement education with the public school, the university, and industry joining hands in an educational venture for which all three have long been conscious of an ever growing need.

It is only natural that these three groups should have combined their efforts in meeting the challenge of this problem. Thoughtful industrial leaders have sensed for some time that much more could and should be done to prepare faithful employees for one of the most important periods of their lives—that of retirement. The testimonial dinner, the gold watch, and the parting handshake contribute little, if anything, to the future well-being of departing workers, many of whom still have 10, 15, or 20 more years ahead of them, years for which meaningful substitutes must be found for the satisfactions which formerly came from earning a living and doing one's job well.

Origins of the Program

The Adult Education Division of the Board of Education through its community contacts had become aware of the rather serious need for retirement counseling for the many industrial employees who annually were separated from their jobs at age 65. From conversations with personnel directors in the city's principal industries, it was discovered that local practices in the area of preparation for retirement were practically uniform—a very minimum of retirement counseling was available to retiring workers. But almost without exception these same industrial representatives revealed a genuine concern over their failure to provide such counseling and expressed a keen interest in developing some project which might better equip them to offer a more practical retirement planning service.

On November 19 and 20, 1954, the Adult Education Division, together with a committee of community leaders, sponsored a two-day conference on "Community Problems and Leadership." Preparation for Retirement was one of the three problem areas explored.

Cooperation with Industry

One immediate outcome of the conference was an expressed desire by some industrial personnel directors to determine the steps necessary to bring pre-retirement programs into their respective plants. A small committee consisting of seven employee relations men and the director of adult education was formed, and a number of meetings were held during the next several weeks. This group decided to sponsor a one-day conference on problems of retirement, with attendance limited to personnel representatives from local industrial plants. The director of adult education was authorized to provide for this meeting the best leadership available.

In seeking leadership for the one-day conference, it seemed wise to approach a great university which had pioneered successfully in the problems of the aging. The services of Mr. Woodrow W. Hunter, a research associate on the staff of the University of Michigan, were made available for leadership.

The report on the one-day meeting can be disposed of with the statement that it was stimulating and successful, with some 30 invited industrial representatives participating. At a later evaluation meeting of the sponsoring committee, it was agreed that the director of adult education should attempt to arrange a working agreement with the University of Michigan whereby the same leader would be available for another period to lead a pilot course in pre-retirement education.

Financing the Project

Subsequently, an agreement was executed between the University and the Adult Education Division of the Niagara Falls Board of Education providing that Mr. Hunter, as program director, spend two days per week in the city for a nine weeks' period to give active leadership to the development of programs with employee groups in three of the city's largest industries.

Costs of the program were shared by the three companies and the Board of Education.

Program Objectives

The specific aims of the programs were outlined as follows:

1. To promote a better understanding of the situations which arise as a result of aging and retirement from work.

2. To equip each individual with knowledge of what he can do to prepare himself ahead of time.

3. To assist each member to develop a personal plan for retirement.

4. To encourage positive attitudes toward retirement based on a recognition of the opportunities for healthy and useful living and of resources for realizing personal goals.

A major concern of the associated sponsors was the continuation of the program, if it proved successful, after the initial courses were completed and the experts had left. Three local program coordinators, all recently retired (two former plant managers and a chemical engineer), accepted active roles in the group meetings. While becoming completely familiar with the course content, they made valuable contributions to the discussions by drawing most interestingly and dramatically from their personal retirement experiences. Each assumed definite responsibilities for one of the three groups of older employees and succeeded in working effectively with participants and program director.

Training Local Program Leaders

As a result of this coordinator training program, there are available today three able and dedicated leaders who, working with the Adult Education Division, are prepared to offer an on-going pre-retirement program for groups throughout the community. Moreover, this local leadership training program demonstrated the old principle that older people are an important resource not to be overlooked in any attempt to develop a pre-retirement conditioning program as part of a total community adult education program.

To achieve the major objectives of the program, the course was organized around the following topics which were discussed in the order listed:

1. What is Retirement Going To Be Like?
2. How Can I Balance the Budget on My Retirement Income?
3. How Can I Earn Some Money After I Retire?
4. How Can I Keep My Health and Get Needed Medical Services?
5. What Can I Do with My Time After I Retire?

6. What Difference Does Retirement Make to Family Life?
7. How Do I Make the Best Decision of Where To Live After I Retire?
8. What Does My Total Plan for Retirement Look Like?

Group members were provided at each session with study materials prepared in booklet form. These materials also served as a guide to everyone involved in any phase of the program. At the opening and closing sessions a simple questionnaire, "What Do You Think About Retirement?", aimed at determining attitudes and the amount of thought and action that had gone into retirement planning, was submitted to all participants. These data will also serve in the evaluation of final results. Also, each was requested to itemize on a prepared form all living expenditures for a one-month period and then compare this with an estimated month's income at the retirement rate.

Resource Experts

An impressive array of resource persons supplemented the discussions and supplied valuable factual information. These included representatives from the Social Security Administration, the New York State Employment Office, the Public Library, the Department of Internal Revenue, The City Health Bureau, and the local Golden Age Clubs, as well as the plant doctor and a member of the plant personnel staff who answered questions on the company pension plan.

Many diverse organizational features within the three groups offered extremely interesting experimental possibilities. One group was made up of skilled printing tradesmen. A second was a mixed group composed of both hourly and salaried employees while the third consisted almost entirely of hourly laborers. The members of one group were accompanied by their wives (or husbands) at all meetings. In a second group a few wives attended, while at the sessions of the remaining group, no wives were present at any time.

Two groups met on company time, one in the morning, the other in the afternoon. The third group (husbands and wives) met in the evening. The first two groups met within the plant, the third at the adult education center.

Desirable Age Bracket

Each of the three groups was limited to membership of 25 to facilitate a friendly and permissive atmosphere in which participants could freely take part in the discussions, ask questions of personal concern and interact with the leaders and other group members.

There was a general feeling that pre-retirement courses should be provided for individuals at not later than age 55, and this belief was strengthened by our experience. For the purposes of the experiment, however, the three groups were recruited for the most part from persons 64 years of age in order to give those scheduled to be retired during the year the benefit of the group discussions.

This is not an effort at evaluation. But if I were to venture a guess, based on an intimate relationship with all facets of the experiment and with all persons concerned, I would say that we have fashioned in Niagara Falls a pattern for pre-retirement education which will be followed energetically for some time to come. Other industrial plants have indicated their intention to organize similar courses for their employees; and one of the three industries involved in the initial experiment already has taken steps to provide all its employees over the age of 55 (now numbering some 160) with the opportunity to join a group on pre-retirement education during the coming year.

This has proved an unique educational experiment at the community level aimed at meeting an adult need of long standing. The public school through adult education has advantageously used its resources and, as a catalyst, has joined the resources of the university and of industry in an educational undertaking which appears to have broad implications and lasting values.

A Labor Union Approach:
A New Life – Retirement
AFL-CIO Education News

RETIREMENT IS A NEW WAY of life for people. To many it is as sudden a shock as jumping from a warm to a cold bath. Though many groups are now becoming interested in the problems of retired people, society does not provide any means for people to prepare themselves for retirement. A person learns in an informal way or through the school system how to get a job, what kinds of work are open to him, how to adjust in marriage and other things. But as a rule there is little preparation for retirement. This is why unions are increasingly becoming interested in the retirement problems of their members; to make life as pleasant and rewarding as possible for the members.

"Just talking to the grocery clerk and the man who sells newspapers is not really social contact, at least not the kind retired people need," insisted United Steel Workers member William Taylor of Local 65 in Chicago. He and 22 other steelworkers and their wives were discussing "Personal and Social Relations or Mental Health in Later Years," a part of a unique education program sponsored by District 31 of the Union and the University of Chicago's Union Research and Education Project.

The Program "Your Pension and Retirement Days" consists of 12 to 14 weekly three-hour meetings designed to help steelworkers and their wives prepare for retirement. They are encouraged to begin to think about retirement and the problems they may face and to do something about these problems long before they retire.

Program Developing

The Program, now in its second year, is still being developed. It is built around a series of ten discussion topics, each of which covers a major retirement problem. When finally developed, it is hoped that skilled discussion leaders within the union can conduct programs using the materials.

The Program starts off with each person filling in an anonymous questionnaire asking questions about retirement as each participant sees it. At the completion of the program, the same questionnaire is again completed. A comparison of the two sets gives a check on the participants' progress and attitude changes during the course.

What do people think about retirement? Considering the reactions in a class of 25 rank-and-file union members and their wives, few have any realistic notion about the size of the pension or social security benefits they expect to receive. Twenty percent of the current class thinks both husband and wife would receive more than $170.00 a month from social security (maximum payment both husband and wife could receive today is $162.80). Forty percent do not have any idea what they will receive from the company pension.

Only 39% think retirement will be a "pleasant experience"; most are not too sure. In the same direction, better than 75% think retirement is a "problem to be concerned about."

Other questions reveal some of the problems anticipated by the people: slightly less than half—48% think that a person can be as happy "when retired as when working." And the most serious problems are thought to be finding living accommodations, money and health.

The questionnaire generally covers the same areas as the course.

A General Introduction to the Program: Session I: How and why retirement could be a problem; why the union is interested in the program.

"Why Do People Work?": Session II: Discussed here are the social and psychological meanings that work has for people—the reasons other than monetary that people work. This includes the ways retired workers can find substitutes for the companionship, feeling of accomplishment, use of time—and other non-financial outlets one gets from the job.

"What About Money?": Session III: This session reviews budgeting problems, both the kinds the participants are now facing and what they have to contend with when retired.

"Making Money after Retirement": Session IV: Most steelworkers will have to get a job of some kind when they retire—not only because they will need the money, but because of the social and psychological satisfactions people receive from their work. This session discusses the ways and means of getting a job and how to prepare for another line of work.

"Good Eating—Good Health": Session V: This is a review of the relationship between health and food—the kind of food people should eat and the problems of overweight and underweight.

"Your Body Grows Older": Session VI: Discussed here is the medical and physical side of aging, the physical activities older people can engage in and the problems of selecting and utilizing doctors.

"Personal and Social Relations—Mental Health": Session VII: The retired person assumes an entirely different social role than previously. Often this new position in life—the increased leisure from not having a job, the loss of a mate, the decrease in skill, and other problems—raises serious mental health problems for retired people.

"Family, Friends and Living Arrangements in Later Years": Session VIII: Being retired often means that one moves to a different locality, loses old friends, has different relationships with his family and has different living arrangements.

"Where to Live on Pension": Session IX: Many workers plan to move when they retire; others haven't even thought about it. This session raises the wide range of possibilities that are open to a retired person and discusses the reasons why a person should or should not move.

"The Union, Older Worker and Retired Members": This session dis-

cusses the role that the union has played in the members' lives and the obligations of the union and the retired member to each other.

Session X winds up the program after about 14 weekly three-hour meetings.

What can be said about the program? Is it worthwhile? The students who complete the classes all say they learned a great deal. To some, just knowing how to compute their pension and social security benefits makes the program worthwhile. Others say never before in their lives have they thought about retirement in the way it is discussed in the class. In a few cases, one can witness participants actually acquiring insights into their problems. But the real test of a program of this kind is what happens to these people in years to come. Will they be able to make a better life for themselves when retired as a result of the program? There is no easy answer for this: a considerable amount of research would have to be completed before this question could be solved.

An obvious benefit is this: most people who attend the classes are rank-and-file union members accompanied by their wives. For these people, in most cases, this is the first contact—except for strikes—that either the husband or the wife has had with the union. It comes as quite a surprise, especially for the wives (and for many husbands as well), that the union is interested in programs of this kind. This suggests that if rank-and-file members are going to be involved in union education, this will have to be accomplished by conducting those kinds of programs that are of most concern to these people. And perhaps retirement education is one of these.

Showing an interest in retired members is not a new thing for American unions. Many have had homes for retired people; others have recently started "drop-in" centers where retired members can gather. But pre-retirement education is for the most part new; if current population trends continue, it promises to be a major area of union education in years to come.

Albany – A Community
In Process

Raymond Harris, M. D.

LIKE ANY SOCIAL GROUP whose members live in a specific locality, share a common government, and have a cultural and historical heritage, your community has its own problems and its own difficulties with aging. These can best be resolved by knowing and using the principles of community dynamics which underlie every successful program. I speak as a medical man and community leader interested in the subject of aging. If I am qualified to discuss this subject, it is because I find aging personally intriguing, medically important, and hopefully inevitable. What I say today is based on my experience, ideas and research. I talk about things I was taught not in medical school, but in the school of life.

All of us like stories. You will understand better the community dynamics of aging if I tell you the Albany Story—how a tradition-bound, conservative community more than 300 years old recognized the significance of aging and developed a successful program of prevention and help for its citizens.

Let us begin with a simple chronological account and then analyze what really happened. In 1949 some older people met weekly for cards, talk and piano playing at the Odd Fellows Hall. Out of this grew a Committee on Recreation for the Aging which was set up by the Council of Community Services. The Committee encouraged the Council of Jewish Women and the Junior League to donate $1500 each to organize a Day Care Center for older people at the Y.W.C.A. A program director with educational and social work background was appointed. The Albany Board of Education accepted responsibility for the education activities. Art, crafts, films, and lectures were featured in this program. Spurred by increasing membership, the Center then transferred to larger quarters in the Albany Boys' Club. The Center operated from 9 a.m. to 3 p.m. while the Club was otherwise unused. A more formal Board of Directors was formed in 1952.

To encourage new members to join, we urged local newspapers, television and radio stations to publicize our facilities, and sent flyers to men and women on Old Age Assistance and to many organizations. Gradually, more and more older men and women came knocking on the Center Door. Meanwhile, classes in crafts and hobbies were underway. Retired businessmen signed up for courses in woodworking . . . grandmothers took up oil painting, weaving and etching aluminum trays. Every month there was a party with music, dancing and refreshments.

Later the Senior Citizens Center moved to larger quarters in Albany Bleeker Stadium Field House, where it became an agency of the Community Chest. In 1954 it won a Necchi award for the outstanding community project in New York State. A Committee on Aging was later set up in the Council of Community Services, which promoted an active, successful program for aging.

Now let us dissect the program and examine the elements to see why it worked. The Greater Albany Program for Aging is based on (1) services to older people, (2) education of the community, and (3) research. We can represent these three important components by a triangle whose base is services for older people and whose two other sides are education and research. The Community of Albany can be represented as a circle. Thus, we can depict our program as a triangle within a circle. From the community must come leadership, funds and diversified resources to support the program for aging. The larger the circle (Community), and the greater the resources, the greater can be the triangle (Program). *No program for aging can be any greater than the resources and interest of the community,* but a good program for aging can *expand the community resources* as Albany has done.

The leadership in any community is important. Initially the Committee on Recreation of the Council of Community Services, headed by the assistant superintendent of schools, provided competent leadership. This Committee has broad representation with members from the Silver Club, Golden Age Club, Council of Jewish Women, Junior League, City Club, American Women's Volunteer Corps, Salvation Army, and other civic groups.

Later, leadership was assumed by the Board of Directors of the Senior Citizens Center with Dr. Harris as the first president. A heart specialist in private practice, Dr. Harris was also assistant medical director at the Ann Lee Home, the county welfare home for older people, and Chief of Cardiology at St. Peter's Hospital. During his presidency, he stressed integration and coordination of programs for aging with existing community agencies.

The full range of community resources for the aging were not obvious at the outset, and the local know-how in aging was unorganized. To remedy this situation, Dr. Harris proposed a conference on aging to the County officials. After the conference was approved, consultants in aging from New York State Departments of Education and Social Welfare were called in for help in planning.

In 1952 the first Capital District Conference on Aging was sponsored at the Ann Lee Home. The Council of Community Services was a co-sponsor. Since the Welfare Department could supply no funds, authorities whose agencies would pay their way or whose interest in aging was great enough for them to pay their own way were invited. The main speaker at our first conference was Clark Tibbitts, who spoke on the National Significance of Aging. Two smaller workshops of specific interest to certain segments of the community followed the main session. The first conference attracted over 400 community leaders, agency representatives, and other people from all walks of life. The resulting publicity in the press, radio and television stimulated community awareness of the problems of older people. The talks were later published as a symposium in the New York State Journal of Medicine. The resulting public relations pleased the officials of the Ann Lee Home and the Albany County Welfare Department so much that these conferences became an annual event. Each year the program takes up some specific problem such as recreation, rehabilitation, volunteer activities, etc., which is first presented broadly on a national level in the main session and then specifically developed on a local level in the two workshops which follow. This Fall we will hold our Eighth Capital District Conference on Aging. We have succeeded so well that we can even pay speakers with a grant from the New York State Health Department.

These conferences are fundamental in the success of the Greater Albany Plan for Aging. Through them the Ann Lee Home has become a second center for work in aging. The enchanced local and national reputation of the Ann Lee Home reflects favorably on the city and county officials. At the Ann Lee Home they hear the ideas and examples provided by reputable national authorities at the Ann Lee conferences and are more apt to discuss them. Later they cooperate when their approval is essential. The ideas introduced at these conferences often become reality several years later. Two such achievements include the employment of a dietician and the establishment of rehabilitation facilities at the Ann Lee Home.

Other benefits accrued from these conferences. They brought experts to Albany, where they were available for local consultation and advice. They established rapport between local leaders and the national organizations with local chapters, such as Red Cross, Junior League, and the Council of Jewish Women. State officials became better acquainted with Albany leaders, thus laying a basis for the establishment of demonstration projects later. Within the community, these conferences brought together community leaders of various faiths, backgrounds, and organizations in a common cause to improve the lot of older people in the

Capital District Area. They provided close cooperation in joint aging projects with the Senior Citizen Center, the Council of Community Services, the Red Cross, the Visiting Nurses Association and other local organizations. Through discussion and example, surrounding communities were stimulated to improve facilities for senior citizens.

With these conferences the Ann Lee Home acquired a more important leadership role in the community. Favorable articles about the Home increased and the old "poorhouse" reputation was erased. The morale of the Ann Lee Home staff and patients rose perceptibly. Older people became happier about going to the Home, and requests for admission increased manyfold. The community became better acquainted with the progress of the Ann Lee Home and took more seriously the problems of older people which cause them to seek institutionalization.

By enlisting the support and interest of the county and city officials in aging, these conferences benefited the Senior Citizens Center. Through them the Senior Citizens Center obtained new rent-free housing in the Bleeker Stadium Field House and other help. Furniture of deceased or institutionalized welfare patients were loaned to the Center. Repairs by senior craftsmen were made in a workshop donated and furnished by the Council of Jewish Women and others. Patients from the Ann Lee Home were sent to the Senior Citizens Center for recreational and social activity on Thursday afternoons. At the Center they were welcomed and treated as regular members. Although reluctant to go at first, with time they became eager to go. Not all went for the same reason. For the majority, the opportunity to paint, work and socialize was the incentive; for some, the opportunity to visit a nearby tavern or to pick up their Social Security check was the incentive. These were soon weeded out and now only those Ann Lee Home patients go who benefit from the excursion. A similar arrangement was made with the V. A. Hospital to see how their psychiatric patients reacted among people.

Later it became obvious that a better program for aging requires a more flexible committee with broader representation. The Council of Community Services always cooperated with the Ann Lee Home and the Senior Citizens Center, but did not see its way clear to set up such a committee. Indirect pressure was exerted on the responsible leaders of the Council. Speakers at the Ann Lee Conferences from the Syracuse Council of Community Services and New York City pointed out the need (the newspapers reporting the conferences were asked to headline the recommendations for the committee), and the Senior Citizens Board passed a resolution urging the formation of such a committee. Finally, we gently hinted the next Ann Lee Program would list a meeting for people interested in a Committee on Aging. The Council could either be in charge or a committee or agency would be organized outside the Council. These pressures finally produced a Committee on Aging, as part of the Council of Community Services.

Demonstrated here is the beneficial interaction between the propelling forces of new ideas and the restraints of conservative community organization which harnessed these ideas for use in a traditional community. When the community is not ready, these ideas will fail; when the community is ready, they will succeed. This *cultural lag between ideas and action* can only be shortened, never completely eliminated. The technique for overcoming this cultural lag is part of the community dynamics of aging.

Any substantial program in aging must be guided by a philosophy. Ours contains six points:

1. Aging is a personal and local phenomenon.
2. The seeds of a happy old age are best planted early.
3. Oldsters must feel wanted.
4. Physical and mental activity is a biological necessity.
5. Flexible programs for aging within the traditional framework of a community are best equipped to solve the diversity of local problems of aging.
6. A scientific attitude and design enhance the value of a community program.

Let me show you how these points were put into action. In 1953 the Junior Chamber of Commerce came to us with a problem. Yearly, toys are collected and then distributed to children before Christmas by civic groups such as the Jaycees. Many damaged toys must be discarded. The Jaycees wondered if the senior citizens could repair them. From this request arose the Albany Hospital for Ruptured and Crippled Dolls located in the Workshop of the Senior Citizens Center. The Junior Chamber of Commerce, the Jaycees, the Junior Red Cross and other organizations provided money for expenses and volunteers. The Council of Jewish Women contributed the necessary surgical instruments, such as hacksaws, tin shears and Stilson wrenches. We awarded our senior citizen craftsmen honorary degrees of D.D.—Doll Doctor—which licensed them not only to operate on dolls, but also to repair all other toys, regardless of paints, origin, or material. Soon our Doll Hospital had sufficient artificial heads, arms, legs, and a sawdust transfusion bank for any emergency. The U. S. Marine Corps rushed the emergency cases to the Hospital where they underwent reconstructive surgery. Before Christmas the dolls and toys were discharged for convalescence and tender loving care to children in St. Margaret's Home and other places.

They remain there today as far as I know. In such projects Albany's senior citizens showed their worth to the community.

Another example is the local chapter of the American Red Cross, which became one of our most valuable agencies for aging. Volunteer Gray Ladies at the Ann Lee Home distributed liquids, combed patients' hair, operated a library and acted as hostesses at the Capital District Conference on Aging. They also ran errands and taught Ann Lee residents occupational therapy. The motor corps transported handicapped members of the Senior Citizens Center. Recently the Red Cross pioneered other important work in aging which I will discuss shortly.

To accelerate the steady but slow progress of the Committee on Aging we sought money from many sources, but in vain. All we received was gratuitous advice which, as you know, is the commonest commodity of agencies in aging, including our own. Nevertheless, we perservered and finally were able to persuade the Social Welfare Department to allot us $6,000 for a year's demonstration project. Cogent arguments in our behalf included an established Committee on Aging in a Council of Community Services setting, a community interested in aging, and the Ann Lee Conferences which had acquainted state officials with our competency. Not many communities have established agencies able to sponsor a demonstration; in many, the existing agencies are suspicious about the possibility of services being controlled by the state rather than the locality, and so are unwilling to become involved. In one city, where at first there appeared to be enthusiasm, a proffered grant for demonstration was turned down because local agencies feared any new project would compete with existing services.

Under the grant from the State Social Welfare Department, we hired a full-time consultant. With him we rejuvenated projects which had lain dormant, and started new projects which interested the counselor.

Counselling and referral services for older persons were established. This exposed the need for an inventory of organizations and community resources. The Exchange Club was encouraged to compile and publish a 24 page Senior Citizens Guide to services in Albany, a complete directory of all agencies offering assistance, services, facilities and activities related to aging.

Next came employment. The special older worker counselor in the Albany office of the State Employment Service reported unfilled positions for baby sitters and senior companions to elderly and sick persons. The Committee on Aging, the Albany Board of Education, and the Visiting Nurses Association arranged an intensive eight weeks training course for 50 older women. This course has now become part of the regular adult education program.

An on-going program of training friendly visitors to call on shut-ins in their own homes was developed and established by the Albany Chapter of the Red Cross in cooperation with representatives of the major religious faiths. The course trains volunteers who then teach the friendly visitors in their own groups. Red Cross consultants remain available for help and advice when the friendly visitors encounter special problems.

A cost-of-living committee obtained a reduction in Albany theatre rates for retired persons carrying special identification cards issued by the Senior Citizens Center. Similar reductions were obtained from the ball-park and for some musical programs.

Along with these diversified services for the aging, education, the second leg of the triangle, was promoted. The Ann Lee conferences annually educated the community and stimulated community awareness and interest in problems of older people. The Albany Public Library conducted adult discussion seminars based on *Aging in the Modern World,* developed by the University of Michigan. Although it was successful and received excellent newspaper and magazine coverage, it reached only a limited number of people.

So we turned to a medium with a larger audience—TV. Through the facilities of the Mohawk-Hudson Council on Educational Television, a six week series of live panel discussions was presented and later extended to 13 weeks. Material from *Aging in the Modern World* was adapted by the Committee, the Center for the Study of Aging, and the Public Library.

The press also helped to stimulate community awareness. Aided by the Committee on Aging, the local papers devoted many articles to aging, ranging from reports of local activities to syndicated columns. One newspaper devoted its annual Christmas appeal to a Fund for Needy Old People. Previously it had raised money for needy children. The 1958 appeal for the aged brought in nearly $12,000. This was about four times as much as had ever been raised before and indicated the extent of public concern for the needs of the aged. Fortunately the newspaper's approach was simple, dignified and sincere rather than maudlin, stereotyped and depressive. It emphasized the small things needed by older people to make them happy, such as a radio, a season ticket to a concert series, or a foreign language newspaper for a person who could not read English.

Housing is one of the most basic needs of older people. The subcommittee on housing of our Committee has been laying the groundwork for future activity in housing for senior citizens in Albany. Through our work the local administration has promised to set aside a specified number of units for older people in the public housing projects. Another newspaper has become keenly interested in the problem of housing. It continues to stress the need for public and low-cost housing for senior citizens in Albany and now plans a newspaper forum on housing, bringing in experts at its own expense.

Pre-retirement courses were conducted by the evening adult education division. The Cornell School of Labor and Industrial Relations sponsored a two day seminar for labor and industry in pre-retirement planning.

Research is the third leg of the triangle. Any community is a fertile source of research. Application of the scientific method in aging results in useful information which helps to define the problems and leads to more effective solutions. Small research groups of competent people should be encouraged to perform community studies in health, disease and other problems of aging. When necessary, experts can be brought in to supplement the resources of the community and to insure that the investigation has an adequate research design.

Our medical and community research in aging disclosed the need for a multi-disciplinary approach to aging and led to a novel, but important concept of medicine which integrates all the resources, people, agencies and services concerned with health and disease of people and communities. "Holiatry" or the medical treatment of the whole, is the term we coined for this phase of medicine. In Albany social scientists helped to plan our program and to direct the activities of our volunteers. In line with holiatric principles, we have also set up a Center for the study of aging, whose Board of Directors includes a cardiologist, a sociologist, two cultural anthropologists, a general practitioner, an economist, and a physicist. The Center has served as a research arm for our Committee. It is completing a survey of 1200 households in Albany County, enumerating the members of the household and securing additional information about those aged 50 and over. In a second project persons 60 and over, selected from the first survey, will be intensively interviewed on health, income, employment, leisure-time activities, housing needs and use of community resources. A third project is being designed to investigate the genesis of senility. The conclusions of these research studies will become the basis for future planning of committee programs.

Meanwhile, medical research in aging and cardiovascular diseases was going on at the Ann Lee Home and St. Peter's Hospital. Here the first studies in this country on the use of reserpine with older people were done. Arrangments were made with Dr. Luisada, Director of Cardiology at the Chicago Medical College, for doctors to study the cardiovascular systems of normal and diseased older people at the

Ann Lee Home. Several original medical reports resulted, including observations on heart sounds and blood pressure. Funds for these studies came from the Heart Association and drug companies.

You have heard what a community like Albany has done in aging. It hasn't solved all the problems of its older residents, but it does have a good, rounded thriving program. Its secret is not the presence of more facilities, of more public or private agencies, or any special abundance of funds. Rather, its success rests on organization, coordination and co-operation of the community and the enterprise, imagination and initiative of leadership. As chance favors the prepared mind, so progress favors the prepared community.

As I mentioned at the beginning, each community has its own culture and heritage. Our success has undoubtedly come because our program for aging was established within the traditional framework of our community. Within this framework we obtained the support of our community leaders, our politicians and organizations. Our program enabled them to participate, plan and promote with us. Observe that this traditional approach did not prevent us from uplifting a conservative community such as Albany to one of the most progressive cities in the field of aging with national recognition.

Our community, and yours, are in the process of becoming. What they become depends upon us. Your community has some type of leadership, some funds and some resources. Add to these the catalysts of ideas, imagination and necessity. These are also in your community. Do you want to find them? Just look about you—here and now!

There is nothing so potent as an idea whose time has come. The time for good community programs in aging is at hand. Make your own community a better place for people in the twilight of life; brighten your own future and your community's future by turning up the lamp of life so that your own may burn brighter.

Suggestions for Further Reading

Free Time—Challenge to Later Maturity. Wilma Donahue, Woodrow W. Hunter, Dorothy H. Coons, and Helen K. Maurice, editors. Ann Arbor: University of Michigan Press, 1958.

> The middle years are seen as the time for personal reassessment and establishment of new goals consistent with extended life expectancy and twenty-two added years of free time. Social and psychological factors involved in the transition to a leisure-centered society and speculations as to wise uses of free time.

Positive Experience in Retirement; A Field Study, by Otto Pollak. Homewood, Ill. Richard D. Irwin, Inc., 1957.

> Case studies of successful retirement carefully analyzed to illuminate the factors which made for success. There's more to it than meets the eye.

Retirement: A New Outlook for the Individual, by Gifford R. Hart. New York: Harcourt, Brace and Co., 1957.

> A retiree, on medical advice, decides that it was the best thing to do after all. Rewards are found, he says, in free choice of activity, relief from the strain of competition, and improved health, the last being consistent with growing evidence from research.

Retrospect and Prospect on the Retirement of T.V. Smith. Theodore C. Denise and Milton H. Williams, editors. Syracuse: Syracuse University Press, 1956.

> T.V. Smith contributes reflections, wisdom, and advice to colleagues and to do-good social planners in his essay "On Being Retired." Outlines his own retirement plan and tells why.

Adjustment in Retirement, The Journal of Social Issues, volume xiv, number 2, 1958.

> The entire issue is devoted to articles on health, family, and occupational adjustments in retirement.

A List of Useful Books and Articles

THIS LIST HAS BEEN compiled to assist the interested reader in several ways. First, it refers to books and articles which amplify the ideas already examined, often from somewhat different points of view. Second, it includes a variety of books, several of which are picture-books, which deal with the arts and also present man in his myriad guises. These illustrate the various capacities of human beings and suggest that no single pattern of life is so compelling as to *command* conformity to it, a point made in several of the essays. And third, there are references to books that describe plans and programs for older people, all useful to those who would like to "do something" for their fellows that is constructive and practical. The books mentioned in the reading lists at the ends of the essays, and those from which selections have been reprinted, should also be regarded as part of the list.

—WILMA DONAHUE, *Compiler*

Adult Leadership, published by the Adult Education Association of the U.S.A., 743 N. Wabash Ave., Chicago 11, Illinois.

> A magazine devoted to helping people who wish to be more effective leaders or members of groups—particularly of groups that have an educational focus or bent.

Age and Achievement, by H. C. Lehman. Princeton: Princeton University Press, 1953.

> Compares the age of greatest achievement among men of science, arts, letters, politics, military, and judiciary pursuits.

"The Aged in Rural Society," by T. Lynn Smith. *The Aged and Society.* Champaign, Illinois: Industrial Relations Research Association, 1950.

> Three aspects of the general problem are touched upon in this article: 1) the relative importance of the aged in rural populations; 2) the status of aged persons in rural society; and 3) the variations from time to time and place to place in the position of the aged in country districts.

"Aging and Retirement." *American Journal of Sociology,* Vol. 59, January 1954, entire issue.

> Includes Retirement Problems in American Society, Flexibility and the Social Roles of the Retired, Social Relations, Activities, and Personal Adjustment, and The Migration of Older People.

"Aging Creatively," by George Lawton. *Living Through the Older Years,* Clark Tibbitts and Wilma Donahue (eds.), pp. 113-29. Ann Arbor: University of Michigan Press, 1949.

> Outlines how people over forty may discover abilities and talents and be free to make unique contributions to society.

The Arts, written and illustrated by Hendrik Willem Van Loon. New York: Simon & Schuster, Inc., 1937.

> An engaging book about the arts, from prehistoric times to the present, giving definition and reciting history, all the way from painting and music to acting and violin-making. Dedicated to the idea that the art of living is the greatest of all. With illustrations strong, poignant, or piquant.

Authority and the Individual, by Bertrand Russell. New York: Simon & Schuster, Inc., 1949.

> A brilliant series of talks by a famous modern philosopher given originally over the British (BBC) radio. Theme: How can we combine that degree of initiative necessary for progress with the degree of social cohesion necessary for survival?

The Best Is Yet to Be, by Paul B. Maves. Philadelphia: Westminister Press, 1951.

> Emphasizes the utilization of some of the new assets of the middle and later years.

The Best Years of Your Life, by Marie Beynon Ray. Boston: Little, Brown & Company, Inc., 1952.

> Exciting accounts of middle-aged people who are using their new free time in creating with their own imaginations and hands.

The Complete Nonsense Book, by Edward Lear. Edited by Lady Strachey. New York: Dodd, Mead and Company, Inc., 1942.

> Hundreds of nonsense verses, rhymes, limericks, parodies, and stories. Written, mostly for the pleasure of his children, by Edward Lear, 13th Earl of Derby, and first published in 1862. Unfeigned pleasure and a positive way with the incongruities of language, and providing very good cranial pastime.

"The Creative Urge in Older People," by E. T. Hall in *New Goals for Old Age.* George Lawton, ed. New York: Columbia University Press, 1943.

> Discusses the reactivation of the desire to be creative after middle age and in later life.

"Drawing of This Hemisphere," by Selden Rodman. *New World Writing,* 4th Mentor Selection. New York: New American Library, 1953.

> An eminent anthologist, poet, translator, art critic writes that although New York City is the world's most important art market, the American climate is not yet economically benignant to the artist. With reproductions of choice drawings, one each of thirteen contemporary recognized painters, and short biographical notes.

The Dynamics of Aging, by Ethel Sabin Smith. New York: W. W. Norton & Co., 1956.

> This book helps people of all ages gain insights into the meaning of sustained happiness and zest for living.

Earning Opportunities for Older Workers. Wilma Donahue, editor. Ann Arbor: University of Michigan Press, 1955.

> Considers the present-day barriers to continued employment of middle-aged and older men and women and discusses methods for adapting jobs to fit abilities of aging workers and for creating earning opportunities for older people.

"Economic Aspects of Aging and Retirement," by Robert K. Burns, *American Journal of Sociology,* Vol. 59, January 1954, pp. 384-390.

> The nature and significance of compulsory retirement and the problems of adequate support for the aged pose new problems which may result in raising of the normal retirement age.

The Educational Experience, by Robert Redfield. White Plains, New York: Fund for Adult Education, 1955.

> The author explores the nature of experiences which are truly educational, reflects on the characteristics of profitable conversation, and offers an hypothesis that education is a continuous growth in understanding and that educated people are those who are always at work on their own enlargement.

Education for Later Maturity: A Handbook, compiled by Wilma Donahue under the auspices of the Committee on Education for the Aging, Adult Education Association of the U.S.A. New York: Whiteside, Inc., 1955.

Includes papers on education for aging, aging in the contemporary scene, capacities of older adults, educational programming in educational institutions, community agencies, and occupational groups, and training for work with older people.

The Education of Henry Adams, An Autobiography. Boston: Houghton Mifflin Company, 1918. (In The Modern Library.)

A highly intelligent and sensitive scholar and historian evaluates his long life in terms of the shifting scientific and political trends of the 19th and early 20th century.

The Face of the Saints, by Wilhelm Schamoni. New York: Pantheon Books, Inc., 1947.

An assembly of deeply moving likenesses of 100 saints, together with brief biographical notes. Likenesses exceptional in their grasp of underlying reality, and culled from such diverse sources as old coins, church mosaics, frescoes, miniatures, stained glass windows, tombs, death masks. Great visual lessons in the art of portraiture.

"Facing the Implications of an Aging Population," by Philip M. Hauser. *Social Service Review,* Vol. 27, June 1953, pp. 162-176.

The major factors affecting the problems of aging, and the need for personal, social, and economic adjustment to old age.

"Factors in Aging," by E. V. Cowdry. *Scientific Monthly,* Vol. 56, 1943, pp. 37-74.

Sketches some of the factors underlying the extensive changes the human body undergoes in the process of aging.

"Family Continuity: Selective Factors which Affect Relationships between Families at Generational Levels," by Marvin Sussman. *Marriage and Family Living,* Vol. XVI, No. 2, May 1954.

Study in which an attempt is made to establish the importance of selective factors which affect relationships between families at two generational levels. Factors investigated are socio-cultural background, type of courtship and marriage ceremony, residential locations, etc.

The Family of Man, by Edward Steichen. New York: Museum of Modern Art, 1955.

A photographic representation of man's life, pleasures, and problems, from birth to death. Described by its creator as "the most ambitious and challenging project photography has ever attempted."

Five Hundred Self-Portraits, chosen and introduced by Ludwig Goldscheider. Vienna: Phaidon Press, 1937.

Five hundred portraits by artists of all periods, in many media and countless moods. An inspiring, intrinsically dramatic presentation of human emotion, capacity, and technical skill.

"Flexibility and the Social Roles of the Retired," by Robert Havighurst. *American Journal of Sociology*, Vol. LIX, No. 4, January 1954, pp. 309-11.

> The author shows that conditions making for flexible adaptation to new roles are successful experience in a variety of roles during the middle years and deliberate cultivation of flexibility after the age of fifty.

Freedom Agenda Series, by various persons. New York: Carrie Chapman Catt Memorial Fund, 1953, '54, '55.

> Each pamphlet in the series provides background for worthwhile citizen discussions on current problems, including their historical origins. The publishing group is affiliated with the League of Women Voters, and the pamphlets attempt to maintain that non-partisan balance which is a characteristic of the League.

From Generation to Generation, by S. N. Eisenstadt. Glencoe, Illinois: The Free Press, 1956.

> This book analyzes how different societies assure their own continuity from generation to generation and discusses the contributions of each age group. Primitive and historical societies are compared with those of modern societies.

Gods, Graves, and Scholars, by C. W. Ceram. New York: Alfred A. Knopf, Inc., 1954.

> An enchanting and beautifully illustrated account of adventures in archeology, bringing yesterday into today's parlor with a diffuse, but peculiarly innocent touch. Makes all the past a "happy hunting ground" for the imaginative reader.

"Group Development and the Education of Older People," by Roger W. Heyns. *Growing in the Older Years,* Wilma Donahue and Clark Tibbitts (eds.). Ann Arbor: University of Michigan Press, 1951.

> Deals with the factors entering into group cohesiveness, group belongingness, and functional roles in the group, and considers the value of the group organizing to perform a useful community service.

Growing Up in New Guinea, by Margaret Mead. New York: William Morrow and Company, Inc., 1930. (In New American Library, paperbound.)

> A noted anthropologist explores the family life of a primitive island people—their attitude towards sex, marriage, and the raising of children —and finds intriguing parallels with problems of modern life.

Handcrafts of New England, by Allen H. Eaton. New York: Harper & Brothers, 1949.

> A fascinating story of the backgrounds and present-day practice of the creative hand skills in perhaps the richest craft region of the United States.

Holiday, The Magazine of Leisure for Richer Living. Philadelphia: The Curtis Publishing Company, Vol. 18, No. 3. March 1956.

> The March 1956 issue contains a collection of essays by practiced

users of leisure on the rewards they find in music, photography, collecting, gardening, travel, and other pursuits that call for intensive participation by the individual.

In-Laws: Pro and Con, by Evelyn Duvall. New York: Association Press, 1954.

This popularly presented, provocative report tells how to be a better relative by marriage no matter whether you are a father-, mother-, brother-, sister-, son-, or daughter-in-law.

In Quest of Knowledge, by C. Hartley Grattan. New York: Association Press, 1955.

A most readable discussion of men's attempts to continue learning throughout adulthood beginning with preliterate cultures and finishing with a prediction for the future of contemporary society.

John Dewey: The Reconstruction of the Democratic Life, by Jerome Nathanson. New York: Charles Scribner's Sons, 1951.

Sets forth in highly readable fashion the principal ideas of one of America's foremost philosophers whose thinking has touched a wide range of intellectual activities.

"The Later Years of Married Life" in *The American Family,* by Ruth Cavan. New York: Thomas Y. Crowell Company, 1953.

This chapter shows that the family situation of middle-aged people is a time of reappraisal and redirection for husband and wife, and that the need for adjusting continues to death itself which closes the family cycle.

Learning Comes of Age, by John Walker Powell. New York: Association Press, 1956.

The author discusses the kinds of learning that grown men and women want to help them understand their changing roles of worker, citizen, parent, and individual in the changing world.

Leonardo DaVinci's Note-Books, arranged and rendered into English with introductions by Edward McCurdy. New York: Empire State Book Company, 1935.

The inspirational intimate record of Leonardo's intellectual life and extraordinary versatility, with multitudinous observations from his notebook on matters literary, physical, philosophical, aesthetic, and cosmic.

"The Life Cycle of the Family," by Paul C. Glick. *Marriage and Family Living,* Vol. XVII, No. 1, February 1955.

Consideration is given to the different generations of the family.

Literary America, by David E. Scherman and Rosemarie Redlich. New York: Dodd, Mead and Company, Inc., 1952.

Thumbnail sketches and samples of their writing of ninety American authors who have provided good reading for leisure hours.

Live Better After Fifty, by Ray Giles. New York: McGraw-Hill Book Company, Inc., 1953.

Word sketches of scores of men and women who, around age fifty, are intensifying the pleasure of living through interests in the arts, crafts, and other self-expressive activities.

Living Crafts, by G. Bernard Hughes. New York: Philosophical Library, Inc., 1954.

Describes the origin, evolution, and present status of twenty crafts that have contributed greatly to our living and enjoyment.

Lust for Life, by Irving Stone. New York: Longmans, Green & Company, Inc., 1934.

The biography of the painter Van Gogh who painted so desperately and who tried so desperately to understand life, but who worked and died without society's help or blessing. On the whole true to fact, with the author completely dedicated to the genius of his subject.

Magic, Science and Religion, by Bronislaw Malinowski. New York: Doubleday & Company, Inc., 1954. (In Anchor Books, paperbound.)

A noted anthropologist explains the significance and interrelationship of these factors in the lives of a primitive people.

Man For Himself, by Erich Fromm. New York: Rinehart & Company, 1947.

Inquires into and interrelates psychology and ethics "leading to the realization of man's self and his potentialities." Concludes that man must determine his own humanistic standards rather than follow the authoritarian.

Man in the Modern World, by Julian Huxley. London: Chatto and Windus, 1947.

A provocative book by a noted biologist built around the theme that "the most vital task of the present age is to formulate a social basis for civilization to dethrone economic ideals and replace them by human ones."

Man the Maker. A History of Technology and Engineering, by R. J. Forbes. New York: Henry Schuman, Inc., 1950.

Describes accomplishments in the field of discovery, invention, and engineering from prehistoric times to this day. Written in a matter-of-fact, friendly, narrative style, and leaning strongly on the thesis that achievements are part and parcel of the cultures in which they occur.

The Mature Mind, by Harry A. Overstreet. New York: W. W. Norton & Company, Inc., 1949.

Many pages are devoted to discussion of the way a mature mind deals with modern social problems—community living, politics, government, the influence of press, radio and advertising.

Modern Science and Modern Man, by James B. Conant. New York: Columbia University Press, 1952.

A penetrating analysis of the revolution that modern science has provoked in the life of modern man by the former president of Harvard.

Music Through the Ages, by Marion Bauer and Ethel Peyser. New York: G. P. Putnam's Sons, 1932.

> A richly packed treatise designed to give the layman or student an understanding of the world of sound. Beginning with cultural origins, it covers the wide area from philosophy, rhythms, and schools, to nationalities and the now popular South American dances.

The New Frontiers of Aging, Wilma Donahue and Clark Tibbitts, editors. Ann Arbor: University of Michigan Press, 1957.

> Reviews recent research to make it available as a basis for community action and to dispel certain current myths regarding the older population.

Number: The Language of Science, by Tobias Dantzig. New York: The Macmillan Company, 1930. (In Anchor Books, paperbound.)

> Written for the "cultured nonmathematician," and describing the evolution of the concept of number from its beginnings among primitive people to its contemporary development. Albert Einstein called it "beyond doubt, the most interesting book on the evolution of mathematics which has ever fallen into my hands."

"Old Age," by I. M. Rubinow. *Encyclopedia of the Social Sciences,* Vol. XI, 1933.

> Describes the somewhat belated development of comprehensive social insurance in the United States.

"Old Age's Gain," by Martin Gumpert. In *Harper's Magazine,* Vol. 204, pp. 72-73, 1952.

> Based on a study of persons whose average calendar age is 80. All are still active in their fields and significant members of society.

Older Adults in the Church, by Virginia Stafford. New York: The Methodist Publishing House, 1953.

> A manual designed to help the church build a creative program for older people.

Older People, by R. J. Havighurst and Ruth Albrecht. New York: Longmans, Green & Company, Inc., 1953.

> Analyzes the activities of older adults in terms of their social roles.

Older People and the Church, by Paul B. Maves and J. Lennart Cedarleaf. Nashville: Abingdon-Cokesbury Press, 1949.

> A nontechnical study of the relationship of the Protestant churches to people over sixty years of age.

Out of My Life and Thought, by Albert Schweitzer. New York: Henry Holt and Company, Inc., 1949.

> A great doctor, philosopher, musicologist, and humanitarian tells an inspiring story of how he built hospitals in the African jungle. An amazing exposition of how endless and exhausting work produced food for his soul.

"Parenthood: Launching State," by Reuben Hill. *The Family*, revised edition, Willard Waller (ed.). New York: The Dryden Press, Inc., 1951.

A dynamic interpretation of what parenthood means.

"Parent-Adolescent Relationships," by Ruth Connor, Theodore Johannis, and James Walters. *Journal of Home Economics*, Vol. 46, No. 3, March 1954.

Changing relationships between parents and children as both grow older.

Planning the Older Years, edited by Wilma Donahue and Clark Tibbitts. Ann Arbor, Michigan: University of Michigan Press, 1950.

This is the second book of the "Older Years" Trilogy, a series of three volumes on Learning for Longer Living. It is devoted to the subjects of living arrangements, recreation, and employment for older people.

Personal Adjustment in Old Age, by Ruth S. Cavan, et al. Chicago: Science Research Associates, 1949.

Chapters on "Culture Patterns of Age Groups" and "Characteristics of Later Maturity" show the increase in leisure time with aging, and the decline with age in activities and group participation.

Profitable Country Living for Retired People, by Haydn S. Pearson. New York: Doubleday, 1953.

Selection of the right place, specialty crops, and soil care are among the many subjects covered. Based on the author's practical experience in New Hampshire.

"Public Oration," by M. Fry. *Old Age in the Modern World*, Report of the Third Congress of the International Association of Gerontology, pp. 4-14. London: E. & S. Livingstone, Ltd., 1955.

Offers the exquisite philosophy of a great woman who has attained later maturity while her mind is still at its pinnacle of creative thought and understanding.

Reason and Discontent, by Lyman Bryson. Pasadena: The Fund for Adult Education, 1954.

Three lectures on the role of adult education in helping men to achieve their fullest potential development and to shape a society which guarantees this opportunity to every one of its members.

"Responsibility of Education to the Older Adults," by Thomas A. Van Sant. *Growing in the Older Years*, edited by Wilma Donahue and Clark Tibbitts. Ann Arbor: University of Michigan Press, 1951, pp. 115-126.

Educators, along with other community groups and agencies, can plan specific programs for older adults which will give them information, knowledge, skill, and even attitudes that will help them live richer, fuller, and happier lives.

The Retirement Handbook. A Complete Planning Guide to Your Future, by Joseph C. Buckley. New York: Harper & Brothers, 1953.

Information on basic neds of retirees—financial security, health, living arrangements, recreation, and the best places to live in retirement.

The Room Upstairs, by Nora Stirling. An American Theatre Wing Community Play with a discussion guide by Nina Ridenour. New York: Human Relations Aids, 1953.

> A play about old and young people living together, designed to stimulate discussion of the problems involved.

The Role of the Aged in Primitive Society, by Leo W. Simmons. New Haven: Yale University Press, 1945.

> Cites original references to the roles of older people in many primitive cultures.

R.v.R. The Life and Times of Rembrandt van Rijn, by Hendrik Willem Van Loon. New York: The Literary Guild, 1930.

> The author chooses to be a contemporary of Rembrandt and gives a talkative account of the painter's life, times, family, friends. Written with deep savour of the period and an especially gentle salute to an artist buffeted by a commercial world.

The Sane Society, by Erich Fromm. New York: Rinehart & Company, Inc., 1955.

> Without endorsing Dr. Fromm's special thesis, we include the book in the list because it is highly provocative and intelligent and will stimulate the reader to take a new look at modern society and his part in it.

The Sea Around Us, by Rachel L. Carson. New York: Oxford University Press, 1951. (In New American Library, paperbound.)

> An enthralling, informative, and beautifully written story of how earth acquired its oceans, how life began in the primeval sea, etc.

Social Policies for Old Age. A Review of Social Provision for Old Age in Great Britain, by Barbara Shenfield. Glencoe, Ill.: The Free Press, 1957.

> Tells how the British, who got into the old age business before we did, are providing income security, health services, housing and community facilities for the older population and discusses steps yet to be taken.

A Social Program for Older People, by Jerome Kaplan. Minneapolis: University of Minnesota Press, 1953.

> A discussion of methods for the development of a program for older people, and the role and functions of the group-work consultant.

"Social-Psychological Factors in Aging," by J. T. Landis. *Social Forces,* Vol. 20, 1942.

> This study attempted to ascertain how dependent aged people differ from nondependent aged people and what the criteria are which make for happiness in old age.

"Some Clinical and Cultural Aspects of Aging," by David Riesman. *American Journal of Sociology,* Vol. 59, 1954, pp. 379-83. (Also in his *Individualism Reconsidered* [1954]).

> A penetrating analysis of the autonomous, adjustive, and anomic reactions to aging.

The Tapestry Book, by Helen Churchill Candee. New York: Tudor Publishing Company, 1935.

The history of tapestry-making from classical times to the present. Figures and foliage out of Beauvais, Gobelins, Aubusson, Savonnerie come gently into life. Done with a sweet and delicate air, with fine illustrations, with much useful material on looms, repairs, designs, for the delight of the weaving enthusiast.

Technology and the Changing Family, by William Ogburn and Meyer Nimkoff. New York: Houghton Mifflin Company, 1955.

This is not just another book on the family but one with a unique point of view—that of analyzing change in family life and tracing its causation.

Anderson, Sherwood	*Winesburg, Ohio* and *The Triumph of the Egg*
Buck, Pearl	*The Pavilion of Women*
Butler, Samuel	*The Way of All Flesh*
Cather, Willa	*My Antonia*
Corbett, Elizabeth F.	*Excuse Me, Mrs. Meigs*
Dickens, Charles	*Bleak House* and many other novels
Dos Passos, John	*U.S.A.*
Dreiser, Theodore	*An American Tragedy*
Eliot, George	*The Mill on the Floss*
Farrell, William	*A World I Never Made*
Ferber, Enda	*Giant*
Galsworthy, John	*The Forsyte Saga*
Hemingway, Ernest	*The Old Man and The Sea*
Hilton, James	*Good-Bye, Mr. Chips*
Lawrence, D. H.	*Sons and Lovers*
	The White Peacock
Lewis, Sinclair	*Babbitt*
Mann, Thomas	*Buddenbrooks*
	Stories of Three Decades
Marquand, John P.	*The Late George Apley*
Meredith, George	*Richard Feverel*
	Diana of the Crossways
Sackville-West, Victoria	*All Passion Spent*
Spring, Howard	*The Houses in Between*
Steinbeck, John	*Grapes of Wrath*
Tarkington, Booth	*Alice Adams*
Walker, Mildred	*Southwest Corner*
Wells, H. G.	*Tono-Bungay*
Wilder, Thornton	*The Women of Andros*

Index

Also by CLARK TIBBITTS and WILMA DONAHUE

Living Through the Older Years, 1949
Planning the Older Years, 1950
Growing in the Older Years, 1951

(Ann Arbor: University of Michigan Press)